Sally in Three Worlds

Sally in Three Worlds

AN INDIAN CAPTIVE IN THE HOUSE
OF BRIGHAM YOUNG

VIRGINIA KERNS

THE UNIVERSITY OF UTAH PRESS
Salt Lake City

The Defiance House Man colophon is a registered trademark of
The University of Utah Press. It is based on a four-foot-tall Ancient
Puebloan pictograph (late PIII) near Glen Canyon, Utah.

Library of Congress Cataloging-in-Publication Data

Names: Kerns, Virginia, 1948– author.
Title: Sally in three worlds : an Indian captive in the house of Brigham Young / Virginia
     Kerns.
Description: Salt Lake City : University of Utah Press, [2020] | Includes
     bibliographical references and index.
Identifiers: LCCN 2020017956 (print) | LCCN 2020017957 (ebook) |
     ISBN 9781647690151 (paperback) | ISBN 9781647690168 (ebook)
Subjects: LCSH: Kanosh, Sally. | Young, Brigham, 1801–1877—Family. | Indian
     women—Utah—Biography. | Kidnapping victims—Utah—Biography. | Indians
     of North America—Utah—Biography. | Indians of North America—Cultural
     assimilation—Utah. | Utah—Race relations—History—19th century.
Classification: LCC E98.W8 K47 2020 (print) | LCC E98.W8 (ebook) |
     DDC 979.2/01—dc23
LC record available at https://lccn.loc.gov/2020017956
LC ebook record available at https://lccn.loc.gov/2020017957

Errata and further information on this and other titles available online at
UofUpress.com

Printed and bound in the United States of America.

In memory of Ann

Contents

Introduction
Finding the Words

A SINGLE LIFE can illuminate an entire cultural and social world, or reveal an unremarked but vital part of the human story.

How can that life be told? The task is daunting when it centers on an Indian captive, stolen away from her people and homeland, sold, and cast alone into a new world, with no means to record what happened. She labored there quietly as a servant, in the shadow of a famous American family who for decades occupied the national spotlight. Most of the stories later told about her—a so-called wild woman made tame—drew on a familiar binary opposition of wild and tame. The structure made the stories, leaving almost no space for the realities of her experience. That structure, which represented her, also silenced her, and eliminated her past.

As an anthropologist, I wanted to frame the story of the captive's life in the language and culture of her upbringing, and also in the language and culture she later learned. Although few details were recorded about her, I found that the lens of culture brought her slowly into focus. It countered a common understanding of her time: that she was a nearly empty vessel filled, transformed, and improved by a civilizing process—the wild, tamed.

In this book, I tell the story of her life as an evidence-based narrative that does not impose abstract or essentialist oppositions. The following chapters are written in what I call ethno-narrative style, which centers on the enculturated lives of named individuals. That style makes the human beings—the "characters" of the story—accessible, whatever their distance across time and culture. As a form of writing, it can reveal the complexity

of individuals' lived experience: the links between their inner and outer
lives, and the cultural perceptions and interpretations that influenced
their emotions and actions.

Naming and humanizing individuals, especially those of differing
origin, also disrupts a strong cultural drift in discourse and narratives
toward binary constructions of moral character (good or evil, kind or
cruel, and so on). It highlights instead the reality of a human spectrum and
a shared humanity. In some cases, the ethno-narrative style may have the
power to disrupt and reshape compelling but distorted, even damaging,
essentialist narratives.[1]

I have invented nothing: not the names or words of particular people,
or the events of their lives, or the look of the places where they lived and
died. Instead, I listened to the voices of a hundred men and women from
another time. I pieced together splinters of the daily lives and memories
they recorded; certain words I encountered again and again in old books
and documents and diaries; factual evidence, from dates to names to numbers; and dozens of narratives, stories spoken and written. I tried, with
cautious inference and without invention, to fill the silent spaces in a life
cut in two by captivity.

That life holds meaning in itself, but also serves here as synecdoche, the
particular case that stands for a general process. In this instance, it stands
for the ancient and ongoing process of colonizing the wild: settling and
transforming wild lands, in part by rooting out or shooting out the native
wildlife. Colonizing the wild also includes efforts to transform and control, to assimilate or otherwise eliminate, the native people who call such
lands their home. That process of "taming" and "civilizing" the wild has
been going on for thousands of years in the world, and for some four
hundred years in North America.

This tale of one woman's life illuminates, more specifically, how people
living in American civilization have represented and treated what they
regard as wild. For the most part, and in brief, not well. A whole litany
of terms and phrases commonly written and spoken by Americans in the
nineteenth century, and into the twentieth and twenty-first, runs through
this telling. These paired, opposing words carry a negative or positive
charge respectively. They include *wild*—or *tame, civilized; the waste, the
wasteland, the howling wilderness*—or *a garden*, even *a garden that buds
and blossoms like the rose; wild Indians*—or *tame Indians; roaming, wandering, rambling*—or *settling*; and finally, the most arresting phrase of all,
sitting in the dirt. A contrasting phrase for the last one is *living in a house*.

At first I read some of those words as quaintly metaphorical, and as evidence of old prejudice and misrepresentation. Then I began to find *wild* and *tame* or *wild* and *civilized* used in nineteenth-century ways in standard works of the twentieth and twenty-first centuries. I wondered why they had proved so long lasting and compelling. The more I read, going farther and farther back in time, the more I saw that they express an enduring binary opposition: that is, a contrast between perceived opposites, two mutually exclusive concepts or terms.

The contrast between wild and tame, or wild and civilized, suggests a cultural model, perhaps one of great age. This contrast has no doubt long appeared highly salient to people who depend on domesticated plants and animals for their sustenance and survival, and who, as their populations grow, search for arable wild lands to colonize and farm. Such people, including the colonizing settlers I write about in this book, are especially vulnerable to wild forces. Speaking of wild in opposition to tame or civilized seems to make sense, cultural sense, in those circumstances.[2]

People who long lived on wild lands see the world differently. They do not necessarily have a concept of wild, marking off most of the world as separate from humans and their fabrications, or marking just one way of life as fully human. They do not necessarily separate the world sharply into two divisions, assigning opposing qualities to each. Concepts of wilderness and wildness appear to be largely absent, or present only as foreign constructs, among peoples who do not depend on domesticated plants and animals for subsistence.[3]

These categories, then, are not universal, but they do provide a master narrative structure that is common to American and other Western civilizations. This binary narrative structure is so accepted, so tacit, as to pass notice. I use terms such as *wild/civilized narratives*, or *narratives of wild and civilized* or *wild and tame*, for stories based on this structure. The oppositional categories of (negative) wild and (positive) civilized, the primary structural elements, are often embodied in actual opponents, typically men. In the simplest and perhaps most common narrative form, the central conflict takes the form of a violent attack or pitched battle or outright war. The antagonists are construed as subhuman or nonhuman wild forces; the protagonists, as fully human forces of civilization.

Opposing moral qualities and other features are often attributed to the adversaries, the wild versus the civilized or tame. These qualities include, respectively, evil or goodness, fault or innocence, ignorance or knowledge, deceit or honesty, cruelty or kindness, cowardice or courage, dirtiness or cleanliness, ugliness or beauty, danger or safety, chaos or order—and more. Such opposing qualities constitute, in a larger sense, perceived absence or presence: the absence or presence of what is good and valued.

The usual outcome of the win/lose conflict is the triumph of civilization, which brings about the defeat and destruction, or so-called taming, of the wild. That is to say, victory ushers in the impending disappearance, the absence, of the wild. This is the requisite happy ending for many people of civilization, the audience of readers or listeners or observers. Some narratives form just an episode in the larger, ongoing battle of wild against civilized; but whether an episode ends badly or well, the battle is finally won.

These tales of wild and civilized, as I came to see, have deep roots. Ancient Greeks and Hebrews, among others, recorded stories, discourse, and imagery of wild and civilized. A binary structure of wild versus civilized shapes some tales still told about the American frontier and the Wild West. And wild/civilized performances extend at least from the time of ancient Roman civilization and spectacle entertainments such as the wild beast hunts in amphitheaters; to the Wild West shows of Buffalo Bill in the late nineteenth and early twentieth centuries; to films and staged spectacles in our own times. The same structure, in other words, unites much discourse and performance as well as many stories—including those long told about the captive woman.[4]

As I saw again and again in writing this book, the particular words that we choose to represent people and places, and the way we use those words, help to shape how we understand their story. While the term *wild* has a negative valence in most of the works I read from the nineteenth century, my use of that word here differs. Unlike nearly all of the Americans and Europeans I write about in the following chapters, I do not see wild and tame as absolutes or an essentialist binary opposition—although one of my primary aims as narrator-ethnographer of this book is to convey their point of view as best I can.

Analytically, wildness is better regarded as the state of most of the world: of things and forces that are not human fabrications or otherwise under effective human control. Tameness is derivative, transitory, and a matter of degree: points on a continuum achieved temporarily, laboriously, by human effort to transform something wild and to control it. What we call tame is wild both by origin and by destiny. Dust to dust.

And therein lies the anxiety, which hovers silently in the background or stands squarely in the foreground in so many narratives of wild and tame. It can take great labor to transform something completely wild, and vigilance to keep it in that condition; but it can easily *revert*, to use a term familiar to nineteenth-century Americans. A tamed and trained horse, heir to generations of selective breeding, escapes and turns wild— or rather *re*-turns to wild. A farm field—cleared, plowed, planted, and guarded—turns to dust from drought or pestilence.

Many of the colonizing settlers I write about in this book witnessed just that, and later told stories of their struggles and suffering. People try with great effort to tame the wild; and then they witness wild forces reclaiming, in an instant or a day or a season or more, what took months or years of drudging labor to make. Or they chance upon old ruins of settlement, and see the effects of wild forces over time. Or they set out on a long journey or voyage, intruding into unfamiliar and perilous wild lands or waters, and they suffer. They cannot help but see the power of the wild world, and the odds against human control. No wonder they claim triumph and victory for favorable outcomes, however small and brief. No wonder some imagine utopian futures in which humans hold absolute control over the wild, having colonized and tamed all of wild nature.[5]

The Indian people I write about here—including the captive woman, born to and raised by an Indian family—understood that humans contended with, but did not control, the life forms and unpredictable, powerful forces of their world. They told stories expressing that insight: stories of unexpected danger, of life-and-death struggles that did not always end well. These were rooted in their experience of living by hunting and gathering, with the attendant hazards, and of fighting hostile strangers who intruded into their hunting grounds. This understanding of the human situation—of life in a world, a universe, existentially out of human control—no doubt qualifies as ancient knowledge, and as wisdom: the wisdom of hunter-gatherers.[6]

I use the term *wild land* for any place shaped primarily by wild forces such as wind, sun, and rain; and home primarily to self-propagating wild plants and free-living wild animals. Wild lands are the human ancestral homeland, the place of human origin. Until rather recently, as anthropologists measure prehistory, all humans lived by hunting and gathering on wild lands.[7]

The archaeological record shows that hunter-gatherers, living in small groups, usually moved seasonally, or more often, in a territory. The evidence of archaeology—and the historical record, including accounts of the captive woman's people—affirms that this way of life endured long after the first appearance of agriculture and settled life thousands of years ago. But slowly at first, and more rapidly over time, generations of colonizing settlers entered and transformed what had always been wild country. Their populations grew. They needed more food, and more arable land to produce it. Hunter-gatherers faced more and more incursions by foreign colonizers who wanted new land for their domesticated plants and livestock, and for extracting wood and rare minerals and metals. This happened throughout the world, often slowly. In North America, it sometimes happened in the space of one generation: just half of a lifetime in the case of the captive woman.

The settlement of Indian homelands in the American West by colonizing farmers, ranchers, and miners is a late chapter in that long story. Some of the places mentioned in this book were among the last of those western homelands seized and settled, and offered new settings for wild/civilized narratives. Again and again, colonizing settlers invaded unfamiliar wild lands, the homelands of native people, which led to conflict and violence. That gave rise to more tales of their battles against the wild.

Anthropologists, including archaeologists, often speak metaphorically of the earliest farming and herding as a revolution because it brought profound changes in human life. But the term is apt as well because the shift from foraging for food in the wild to producing food has always entailed physical violence on a large scale, much of it directed against native ecosystems. Native wildlife inhabiting wild lands has inevitably been assaulted, rooted out, killed. Native people have experienced the violence as well unless they vacate their homelands.[8]

Knowledge of our ancient human past is so recent that it was not available to the people I write about in this book. Those who were colonizing settlers shared very different cultural understandings of that past, while Indian peoples held still others. Many of the colonizers believed that some animals had been created tame ("cattle" or "livestock," in the language of the Bible), and others wild ("beast of the earth" or "wild animals"). Archaeologists had not yet recovered evidence that people domesticated plants and animals from wild progenitors thousands of years ago in various parts of the world. In that pre-Darwinian time, the colonizing settlers did not know that tame derived from wild. The captive woman and her people, in contrast, did not speak of wild and tame. They told of ancient animal-people such as Wolf and Coyote, and settlers did not grasp their meaning.[9]

I use the term *tame* here for what humans purposefully transform to some degree, changing the form, structure, or type in order to increase the usefulness to them. It refers to what they try to hold captive and keep under control: seeds of wheat and corn; a fenced and planted field; dairy cows; river water in a reservoir or irrigation canal. It alludes to the submission of animals who labor for people or otherwise do their bidding. A so-called tame animal follows orders, with or without the whip.

To many of the colonizing settlers I write about, like other Americans of their time, the meaning of tame—as a verb, in relation to wild land— was more expansive and extreme. To tame the land meant to remove, to displace and dispossess, as many inhabitants of wild lands as possible: native plants and animals, and native people. It meant to fill, transform, and improve what was seen as waste, or wild country of no value: to fill that empty territory with colonies of foreign settlers and their houses, livestock, and fields. They would thereby transform a so-called waste place into a place of value, improving it by means of their labor, and the labor of their livestock and any servants.

So too for the captive woman whose story I tell, whose life began on wild lands but was later spent as a servant in a city. As the colonizing settlers saw it, her wild, worthless habits had to be eliminated, removed and replaced. She would be filled with useful knowledge and skills—which is to say, taught to do useful labor for their benefit. To their way of thinking, taming would improve her.

In other places and times, people in positions of dominance have commonly used the word taming in relation to certain human beings: those they enslave or otherwise force to labor in useful ways. Famously, or infamously, the word also appears in the title of a classic narrative in the Western literary canon. Shakespeare's *The Taming of the Shrew* centers on a woman who resists her new husband's control, but finally becomes an obedient wife.

The hunter-gatherers whom colonizers of the American West called wild Indians or, later, tame Indians, were not, of course, either wild or tame as I use those terms. The captive woman and members of her tribe were fully enculturated people who had each undergone a long process of enculturation, or socialization, by their families and communities. The teaching and learning went on for years, often with the use of stories. Humans everywhere teach by telling stories.

Much of their teaching and learning centered on hunting native wild animals and gathering native wild plants on wild lands. The captive and her community of origin were people of the wild, so to speak. It later took years of fieldwork by several generations of cultural anthropologists to record a small portion of their deep knowledge, and to document some of their many skills.

Unlike the hunter-gatherers, who lived sustainably *on* wild land as predators of wild animals and plants, the colonizing settlers acted as predators *of* wild land. They needed to procure more and more wild arable land for farming as their populations grew. Call them people of the tame, or people of the plow and cow, who killed out wildlife on large swaths of land in order to create places of safety for their crops and livestock. In their understanding, this was their right, even their duty, and divinely ordained: the waste should blossom like the rose. They also saw it as sacred duty to tame and control, or civilize, the so-called wild people of the waste.

In truth, the process of transforming and trying to exert control can cause deep suffering. Consider the so-called taming of the *wild* West, which remains far less known than the fabled taming of the lawless Wild West. The true toll taken on wild lands—on the wild plants and animals as well as the native people who lived on those lands—has not yet been fully calculated.

Two other central concepts in this book, termed *civilization* and *settler colonization*, are closely linked to the histories of arable wild lands and their transformations. Civilization refers to what some anthropologists prefer to call complex society, a newer and neutral term that lacks the celebratory, triumphal tone of the words civilization and civilized. Complex society, or civilization, is a particular kind of social and political formation that first appeared at least five thousand years ago. Its defining features include the state, inequality, and large populations and cities sustained by intensive agriculture. Another common, if often overlooked, feature of complex society is an expansionist tendency: most notably here, the predation of wild arable lands.[10]

In English, complex society as a noun has no paired words equivalent to civilized or civilizing. That, as well as the greater familiarity of the word civilization, led me to retain the old term. Unlike many of the people I write about—who lived in civilization and had learned to believe devoutly in its virtue—I use the word in a neutral way, simply to identify a type of social and political structure. Like many other anthropologists, I do not count myself as an advocate—or as one who romanticizes other ways of life, a common charge that betrays anxiety. We who live in civilization are apt to feel uneasy when we learn that those who lived outside of it, in other kinds of social and political formations, detected its hardships. They generally preferred their way of life to the constraints, inequities, and discontents of civilization, whatever physical comforts and other benefits it offered.[11]

I use the term *settler colonization* for the invasion of native lands by foreign settlers, people of civilization, who try to replace indigenous populations and re-create settler-colonial society in a new place. Settler colonialism, as both an event and a structure, is now recognized as a distinct, ancient, and widespread form of colonialism. It characterizes the history of North America.[12]

The term *settler* denotes anyone who dwells, or intends to dwell, year after year in one place. *Colonizing settlers* or *settler-colonists* are, more specifically, those who enter alien territory with the aims of claiming, occupying, and remaining on that land. In most cases, they plan to transform the land by removing native wildlife, and replacing it with their imported crops and livestock. The elimination of the native, a well-known phrase in settler-colonial studies, is commonly used in reference to people. I want to emphasize here that the elimination of the native also extends to native plants and animals that have sustained indigenous people.[13]

Other aspects of identity, such as ancestry and ethnicity, also figure in the story told in this book. Most of the colonizing settlers I write about were Anglo-American or British by ancestry and cultural origin. Nearly all were former Protestant Christians who had embraced a new faith with distinctive doctrines and practices that set them apart from Protestants. I identify them here primarily as colonizing settlers who left the eastern part of America to live together in western wild country, and to tame that land. They also planned to tame the Indians, people of the wild who claimed and occupied the land as their ancestral home.[14]

The early settler-colonists later recalled their struggles, both their suffering and their success in taming the wild: memories that they recorded and that their descendants often retold as stories or reenacted and celebrated in performance. These wild/civilized narratives, set in the western territory they colonized, helped to create and define their ethnic identity.[15]

It is not my aim to deprecate or to celebrate the settler-colonists. The traditional stance of anthropology refuses such aims. Still, an attempt at understanding—at drawing a realistic cultural, or ethnographic, portrait—never requires denying harm done, or disregarding human strengths and resilience. The same is true even when the aim is advocacy, now a more common stance in anthropology. Knowledge of ancestry may affect perspective and position in complicated ways, as indicated in the last paragraphs of the Acknowledgments.

Most of the native peoples dispossessed and displaced by settler colonization of western wild lands had long lived there as hunter-gatherers. I use the general term *Indian* for them throughout the book because that term was standard in the nineteenth century and still has currency. But whenever possible, I use names of specific groups that were known to Americans of the time, and that English speakers still use: Utahs or Yutas or Utes, Paiutes, Shoshones, and Gosiutes. The term *Numic* refers to their linguistic identity as speakers of languages that belong to the Numic branch of the Uto-Aztecan language family. My use of the term *Americans*, in the context of the nineteenth century, does not encompass American Indians. They were excluded from full citizenship until the twentieth century.

I refer to most individuals by their first names, rather than by surnames, and invite readers to consult the Appendix and chapter endnotes for full names and biographical details. The reasons for choosing first names are largely practical. Indians did not have surnames. I use their spoken names as recorded in English texts, but without assuming that the renderings are correct. The captive woman, too, had no surname for most of her life. She was known for many years only by her first name, a common English one that she was given as soon as she entered the settler-colonists' world. I identify nearly all of the settlers she knew best by first names because they claimed a single surname, Young. They were members of Brigham Young's expansive family.

Except for a few instances, I avoid using the name of this famous man in the chapters that follow. He casts such a long shadow in historical and collective memory that it obscures other, lesser-known lives of individuals who share narrative space in this book. To prevent his taking too much of that space, he is herein called simply the Leader. That was, and remains, the central feature of his identity. Even fifty years after his death, one of his daughters still referred to him proudly in print by his sobriquet, the Leader.[16]

As leader, he became the preeminent colonizer of the wild American West. He led an immense number of his people, both his own relatives and his spiritual kinsmen, into the sprawling territory known as the Great Basin that stretches from the Rocky Mountains across high desert toward the Sierra Nevada Mountains. The territory that they colonized became, metaphorically, the house of Brigham Young. Hunter-gatherers who had long occupied that wild country as their homeland were soon confined to small, unwanted corners of the house. He and his followers, like the federal authorities and most Americans, saw such confinement, or captivity, on reservations as inevitable.[17]

The woman whose story I tell lived and labored in the literal house of Brigham Young. The first highly memorable moment in my search for traces of her life came when I saw her name and age listed in an early census of his household. I had previously made passing mention of her in a book, but without knowing of that record. I saw at once that I had misidentified her, in common with nearly everyone else who had ever referred to her in print—none of us with the guidance of that census entry or later ones. Those records made it clear that she was not a young child, as later said, but nearly adult when she entered the Leader's domain. Census entries and family records also contradicted the later claim that she was Brigham Young's foster child.[18]

When she was taken captive, she was fully competent in an Indian language and culture of origin, and no doubt always retained memories of her own family and her past. That knowledge led me to continue a long search for clues about her earlier life. A second memorable moment in that search came when I finally realized who she was by ancestry and upbringing. I identified her people by name, language, and place. This helped me begin to understand how she lived and what she learned before her jarring entry into a strange new world. It offered insights about how such a person saw the first settler-colonists and the new city they built in a high desert valley. It encouraged me to keep looking for evidence, elusive and meager though it was, and to keep sorting through a mass of conflicting details.

She entered that new world speaking no English. I use words from her native language as a means of giving her voice. These come from word lists provided by native speakers of her dialect and closely related dialects. They were elicited with care, recorded by hand, and translated into English in the nineteenth century. I think of these as her first words. Finding the words from her own language, along with ethnographic notes— all recorded during her lifetime by John Wesley Powell, the American explorer and scientist who came to identify as an anthropologist—shed light on her life before captivity.[19]

This evidence also offered a means of understanding something about her inner life, both before and after she was taken captive. She left no written record of her thoughts and feelings and perceptions. Reconstructing the shape of her cultural knowledge helped me to interpret, or gave me reason to question, what settler-colonists said about her expressed feelings and actions. Learning what she saw and heard in her new life among them, and how it contrasted with her old life, also proved illuminating. It made clear that many of the stories later told in print misrepresented her.

Only fifteen words in English have been attributed to the captive although she came to speak English with unusual fluency and skill. The remembered words were a direct question, a rhetorical question, and a teasing command, all uttered when she was in her late forties. Her station in life had shifted upward, and she was no longer seen then as a servant. Some people listened to her more respectfully, and remembered what she said.

To hear her ghostly voice and others', I read the early settlers' journals and memoirs, travelers' letters and chronicles, one woman's poems, and transcripts of the Leader's public addresses and court testimony. In some of them I found trace recollections of the captive woman, along with a few vivid accounts of Indian warriors and the lands they tried to defend from colonization. In one instance I found crucial words about her hidden in plain sight, in the pages of an old book whose author met her but chose not to name her. Reading texts that the settler-colonists read helped me understand some of their perceptions about wild land and so-called wild people, including the captive. I also located old maps, and searched old censuses, newspapers, and records of settlement, along with other official documents.

At first I listened to inherited memories, given by descendants of the men and women who inhabited that world. But I soon came to listen most carefully to the words of early settler-colonists who kept journals and diaries. Their reports convey emotional and experiential complexity—in contrast to the simplified, flattened contours of inherited memories passed down for generations, often as cherished stories about pioneer ancestors who tamed the wild. As a cultural anthropologist, I wanted to see the settler-colonists' everyday world through their eyes, to learn what they saw and how they saw it. I also listened to American and European visitors who, in letters and lengthy books, recorded their observations. All of this helped to fill some of the silences and spaces in the life of the captive woman.

Because she left no written account, I turned to captivity narratives written by Americans of her time. I read them cautiously, seeking reliable cultural guides, or ethnographic informants. First-person testimony by some former captives offered clues about her experience, which differed from theirs in a crucial respect: she *entered* American civilization as a captive, instead of being *taken* from it. Some of the American captives, especially those abducted as adults, escaped and returned joyfully to their first families. Others, captured as young children or as adolescents, wished to stay with their adopted Indian families, having come to identify completely with them and their way of life. They turned away from life in civilization, and chose to remain with people of the wild.[20]

The captive who entered the house of Brigham Young had a more complex experience of wanting to leave and wanting to stay. Most Indians taken captive ran away, fleeing at the first chance. She did not. Solving the mystery of why she stayed took years of looking for, and looking at, evidence of her earlier and later life.[21]

The scope of her narrative knowledge—what she learned from the stories she heard—grew and changed in ways that affected her deeply. She heard countless "Indian stories," as settler-colonists and other Americans called them. To judge from their content and context, these were anti-Indian narratives that non-Indians told to other non-Indians. Typically, they included negative judgments about the moral character and cultural practices of Indians, who were usually treated as a unitary category, rarely as named individuals. Indian stories, a specific genre of wild/civilized narratives, belittled, disparaged, and even vilified most native people. Representations of Indians as wild, living almost as wild beasts in wild nature, formed a staple feature.[22]

Finding those Indian stories that she heard again and again—and the stories later told about her, rife with contradictions and flights of fancy and factual errors—helped me to recognize other types of wild/civilized narratives as well. I recognized this narrative form in published and unpublished reminiscences, histories, and works of fiction; the discourse, in diary entries, newspaper reports, letters, and homilies; and the performance, in accounts of parades and plays. This structure gave meaning to remembered events, and thus shaped the telling and retellings of the captive's story, as I show in the last chapter.

During the seven years I spent writing this book, I lived for the greater part of each year in a canyon near the big valley where one of the earliest colonizing settlers bought the young captive. The two mansions where she worked for many years stand just fifteen miles away. The canyon road follows a trail that tens of thousands traveled to reach that territory in the high desert, or to go on to California: a torrent of people such as she had never seen in her earlier life.

I also located other places where she lived before arriving in the valley, and after she left. Some of those places remain sparsely populated, and wear the effects of settlement more lightly than the wild valley that was transformed and replaced by a city. Cultural anthropologists learn most by observing as well as by listening. What I saw of mountains and desert and sky during those seven years, and in those places, informs nearly every page of this book.[23]

PART I

Mountains and Sky

CHAPTER 1

The Trade

LATER, NO ONE REMEMBERED that snow had fallen. No one remembered how the mountains and sky looked on that cold day.

One man never forgot how the captive girl looked—her black hair singed and hacked short, her body thin, inscribed with burns and cuts and streaks of dried blood and ashes. All exposed.

Think of the scene, and her despair.

A small crowd of men, and one boy, stares at the girl offered for sale—or rather, for trade. No money will change hands. Then one of the captors pushes her forward, threatening to kill her unless there is a trade. She understands his words. He speaks her language. Do the strangers understand? Is she going to die now?

The captor grips her and repeats the threat. In that moment a young man steps forward from the crowd, and offers his rifle for the girl.

The deal is made. She will live. Now she belongs to him.

Years later, some of the settler-colonists remembered what they had heard about the trade. There were two captives, they insisted, but one had already been killed. No one had believed the first threats. No one had agreed to buy that captive. Some thought that the one who died was also a girl. Others said that a boy, a brother, had died. Still others said the boy was not her brother. They could not agree about who captured the two. Some said Wanship and his men, or his son, or Little Wolf. Others spoke of Wákara, whose very name inspired vaulting fear. A few blamed Baptiste, one of Wákara's allies.

Who the girl was, and where she came from, also remained unclear—
or if known, was soon forgotten. The settler-colonists did recall that they
saved the girl from certain death, from murder by wild people. They gave
her food and shelter, gave her a new home. They treated her with kindness,
and civilized her. That was a story of wild and civilized they told again
and again.

Among the people who were there that day, who saw the trade, one
recorded his memories. He wrote what he remembered nearly sixty years
later, as an old man recalling the events of a crowded lifetime, a life spent
trying to subdue and tame what he and others saw as raw wilderness. John
Young was only ten years old when he witnessed the trade, but a strong
image of the girl dug deep into memory and held fast for the rest of his
life. He remembered the cuts and burns on her bare skin, the mangled
thatch of hair. "She was gaunt with hunger," he said, "and smeared from
head to foot with blood and ashes." She stood before him in the snow,
nearly unclothed. The little boy had never seen such a sight.[1]

John had arrived in the big valley just two months earlier after making a
hard and lonely journey across plains and mountains in a wagon train, but
without his parents. He felt almost like an orphan on the long trip west.
His father, Lorenzo, had gone ahead with another wagon train. Lorenzo
traveled with Harriet, his second wife, Harriet's daughter Clara who was
eighteen and married, and her husband.[2]

Everything in this wild desert valley was new to John except for some
of the people. The high desert looked nothing like their old home in a
river valley, land anchored by green fields and trees, barns and houses.
The broad, swift-flowing rivers that John recalled—the Mississippi, the
Missouri—had no counterpart in this place of peculiar waters. He saw
snow-spawned creeks here, and hot sulfurous springs, and a short river
that carried a bounty of water north from a freshwater lake to a big lake
that was saltier than the sea. For newcomers who arrived from the East,
from tended lands divided by fenced fields and woodlots and roads, the
grand dimensions and sheer space of the big valley could feel dizzying.
Long shafts of light sometimes reached down from the clouds, illuminating mountains and sky.

On the day of the trade, John was with his father, Lorenzo, at their
new log house. Lorenzo was the first colonist to build a house outside
the walls of the settlers' fort, a mile away and next to a creek that spilled
down through a thickly forested canyon. Harriet sometimes suffered from

shortness of breath, which left her wheezing and gasping, and she had not improved after first reaching the valley in late July, the time of great heat and dust. She thought that moving to higher ground would help her. By the time Lorenzo finished building their small house in November, autumn had already stripped bare the canyon's oaks and maples.[3]

Just a few weeks later, a day after snow had fallen, Lorenzo heard shouts and piercing cries. They came from a nearby spot where unwelcome visitors had camped. The log house was isolated, and Lorenzo sent John hurrying to the fort to get help. He returned with Charley, Barney, and some other men. Charley was Harriet's twenty-three-year-old son. He had arrived in the valley two months earlier, at the same time as John. Barney had joined the colonizing settlers as their Indian interpreter. He was married to a Shoshone woman.

The reason for the shouts soon became clear. Some Indian warriors had returned from a skirmish with another band—or so John later heard. They had gained two young captives, someone claimed, pawns in the Indian slave trade who were being held by the chief of the other band. "One of these they killed," John recalled hearing, because no one had agreed to buy that boy—or girl. The captors, it was later said, had thrown the boy, or girl, into the boiling sulfurous water of a hot spring. John thought they were torturing the other captive. But the blur of events, the strangeness and the danger, made it hard to know much about the girl and her captors. Whether the shouts he heard were her cries of pain, or theirs of threat or triumph, remained unclear.[4]

"She was the saddest looking piece of humanity I have ever seen," John said long years after witnessing the trade. "They had shingled her hair with butcher knives and fire brands. All the fleshy parts of her body, legs and arms had been hacked with knives, then fire brands had been stuck into the wounds."

After Charley bought her, he took her to Lorenzo and Harriet's house. Harriet washed the smeared ashes and dirt from the girl's thin body, cleaned her wounds, and clothed her. Then Charley took the girl to the fort, through the gate, and into a walled world of settler-colonists. He gave her to his sister Clara.[5]

The captive knew nothing about these strangers. She knew little about the forces, other than her captors, that had delivered her into the strangers' hands, left her trapped inside high walls. Centuries of European invasion and settlement, the pursuit of prosperity and wealth, and the need for labor had led to a lucrative slave trade in Mexican territory and beyond.

She was one of many Indian women captured and sold. Some of them escaped.

Soon after they arrived in the valley, Lorenzo and Harriet, Charley and Clara, and the other settlers at the fort had begun to learn firsthand about the local slave trade, the trafficking in Indian women and children captured and sold by men. Barney already knew about the trade. For years he had made trips with a partner, a trapper like himself, to the next valley south, by the large freshwater lake at the foot of commanding mountains. It was home to people called Yutas or Eutaws or Utahs. Some Utahs captured children to sell to Mexican traders who came north looking for slaves. One of the most notorious traffickers was a chief named Wákara.[6]

The new settlers had taken wild land on the northern edge of Mexico to colonize. It was Indian country long before Spain, and then Mexico, claimed it. It remained Indian country despite those other claims. People who lived by hunting and gathering inhabited the very valley that the colonizing settlers had recently entered, a place they imagined as empty land that no one else wanted. Mexico largely neglected the wild hinterlands where traders bought Indian captives to take to slave markets.

The southwestern trade in Indian slaves had been foreign to Barney when he went west, but he did know about the southeastern slave trade. In his birthplace of Virginia, enslaved Africans and their descendants had been bought and sold for generations. They replaced the Indians once taken captive and used as slaves. Thomas Jefferson, himself a slave owner, condemned the earlier trade, which had remained legal until his grandfather's lifetime. "An inhuman practice once prevailed in this country of making slaves of the Indians," he said. Making slaves of Africans seemed to trouble him less.[7]

Far to the west, Indian slavery still prevailed after centuries of Spanish rule. Early Spanish colonists had found wild land for the taking, as they saw it, and they wanted good laborers at low cost. Wild Indians, enslaved, would suffice, they thought. They had got some by raiding Apaches, Navajos, and others who resisted their rule. They also bought captives from Comanches and Utahs, expert horsemen and raiders who traded slaves for the firearms they used for defense and for raiding.

Those raiders—*los indios bárbaros*, the Spanish called them—had little use themselves for the labor of so many captives. They lived by hunting and gathering, as well as raiding and trading, and needed to travel lightly and quickly across wild lands. But they did respond to the Spanish market for enslaved women and children, a market that threatened the freedom of their own people. Trading captives for firearms helped to insure their liberty and survival, even if it meant depriving other people of theirs.[8]

The captors sold their human wares to itinerant Mexican traders, or took them to slave markets at Taos and Santa Fe. As the fur trade declined, and the annual trade fairs known as rendezvous lapsed, Barney's partner began going south to Santa Fe to trade for goods. By then Barney had a new wife, a Shoshone woman who was a former captive, a new stepdaughter, and headquarters in the north at a new trading post named Fort Bridger.[9]

Barney's Shoshone wife knew more about American slavery than Mexican. She was born in freedom in Shoshone country, in the northern reaches of Spanish territory, which became Mexican territory, and north of the land where Fort Bridger later stood.

When she was a young child, just six or seven years old, her family went with a hunting party to the Black Hills, hundreds of miles to the east. As her daughter Adelaide later heard the story, Sioux warriors attacked them. During the fight, the little Shoshone girl was shot in the back. Whether her parents thought she was dead or dying, or too badly wounded to travel, they left her behind. Adelaide said simply that she recovered. When the young captive was about twelve years old a man who was remembered only as "a wealthy merchant" took her to St. Louis, more than a thousand miles by river or by land from her birthplace in the Green River country.[10]

Here the reported details dwindle to the vanishing point. Why the man wanted the girl, what he offered for her, whether he treated her as a slave, how she lived and worked in St. Louis during the next four years, and what she thought of her new life—all of that went unreported.

From the time of its founding, St. Louis, a commercial and settler-colonial site, had stood at the center of a thriving national and international fur trade. Indians brought furs of wild animals there to trade. Non-Indian trappers and traders left St. Louis for the western plains and mountains, in search of valuable furs, especially beaver. Some of the traders grew rich. The man who took the Shoshone girl south to St. Louis was said to be wealthy, but she could not have known if the measure was city standards or hardscrabble frontier standards. She had never had reason to make such close judgments about wealth. Among her people, there was more honor in giving than in keeping.

As Adelaide later told the story of her Shoshone mother, she resolved to leave St. Louis when she was sixteen. Like most Indians taken captive, she wanted to regain her freedom and return to her homeland and her family. She did not say good-bye. Instead, she made careful plans to elude anyone who searched for her, to vanish from St. Louis without leaving tracks.

One day during the warm season, she walked into the waters of the Mississippi River and swam out to an island where she hid for days—as enslaved workers often did, in a bid to escape captivity in Missouri. Many of those runaways were headed east, across the river and toward freedom in the northern states. The Shoshone girl headed west, to freedom in her people's country around the Green River.[11]

She finally left her hideout on the island, swam to shore, and followed the river north, where other rivers from the west flowed into it. Somewhere on her journey she stopped at a house where she met a trapper, French by origin, known as Exervier, or Xavier. He became her husband, and they struck out together for the western plains and mountains.[12]

The trapper and his young wife finally settled at a trading-post fort built at the confluence of two rivers, more than nine hundred miles from St. Louis. Their daughter Adelaide was born there. A fur company owned the fort, which two traders had built a few years earlier. Their trading-post fort, later called Fort Laramie, prospered. It was one of many set up in the wake of Lewis and Clark's exploring trip, which they launched from St. Louis, crossing western wild lands to reach the Pacific Ocean.[13]

Shoshone country stretched west of the fort. Shoshones had met Lewis and Clark some thirty years earlier, and remembered the two leaders and their men. They told amusing stories to their children and grandchildren about the two strangers, Lewis and Clark, who had made bad trades, giving valuable goods for used-up horses with sore backs. They also recalled the lone woman with the expedition, one of their own. Enemies had taken Sacagawea captive, and a French-speaking man had bought her.[14]

As it turned out, the young Shoshone girl who had fled from St. Louis remained in the orbit of its powerful commercial interests. The fur company that owned the fort had headquarters in the city. She and her trapper husband had not left civilization entirely. They had just arrived at one of its most remote outposts, built to serve commerce in St. Louis and beyond.

The new trading-post fort bordered a vast stretch of wild country. This frontier, as it was called, formed the leading edge of civilization and commerce intruding into wild lands, territory not yet taken by settler-colonists. At the fort, manufactured goods made in, and imported from, distant metropolitan workshops and factories were sold or traded for goods extracted from the wild, mostly furs and tanned skins supplied by native and non-native trappers. On the plains and in the mountains, the so-called wild Indians or wild tribes prevailed. They lived at liberty on wild lands, in bands that each claimed a territory in common.

When Adelaide was just four or five years old, her father died, a victim of violence. Another trapper shot him in the back, Adelaide said, but he did not die at once. She thought that he lingered for about ten days. Some people later claimed that he asked a fellow trapper named Barney Ward to look after his wife and daughter. Barney became her husband and Adelaide's stepfather.[15]

By the time Barney and his new family moved to a trading-post fort built by a former trapper named Jim Bridger, twenty years of the frenzied fur trade had ravaged beaver and other wildlife. Five hundred trappers at a time, Americans and others, had crisscrossed the mountains, killing wild animals for fur and for food. A devouring eastern and international market sought all sorts of pelts. The demand for beaver, to make fashionable felt top hats for men, seemed insatiable. Besides beaver, the wild West's most wanted list featured mink, weasel, otter, muskrat, deer, bear, fox, wolf, bison, and more.[16]

Legions of trappers killed many of the wild animals that grazed and browsed—from bison and antelope to deer, elk, and moose. They thereby eliminated native competitors of domesticated grazing livestock, the horses, mules, cattle, oxen, and sheep. That slaughter would enable the success of American settler-colonists who planned to raise crops and livestock they imported to the American West. Hunting by trappers also reduced the number of predators, including wolves. But the decline of wild prey meant that wolves would pose a greater and greater threat to the imported livestock.

Many trappers left the mountains just before colonizing settlers began to arrive. "Beaver and game had nearly disappeared," explained one American trapper who finally went to live near the Pacific coast. The near-extermination of beavers brought other changes as well. The slow collapse of their dams from disrepair meant death for the ponds and bordering wetlands. As those wild oases waned, green meadows turned sere, and valleys grew drier. Sagebrush and greasewood replaced lush grasses, rushes, and sedges. With the loss of good nesting and spawning places, birds and fish vanished. Other wildlife, from the surviving muskrats to the moose, also left.[17]

Despite these killing effects of the fur trade, and the dim prospects for much more profit from furs, some trappers, including Jim Bridger and Barney, chose to stay. Jim decided to enter the general trade, the trade in provisions, which had grown so lucrative at Fort Laramie. He built a trading-post fort nearly four hundred miles west, in Shoshone country where he had strong allies. It stood near a tributary of the Green River.[18]

Jim and his business partner from St. Louis, Louis Vásquez, still traded with Indian and non-Indian trappers, but over time they sold more and more goods to a swelling stream of overland travelers, mostly colonizers on the way west. A few years after Jim and Louis set up the business, the Donner party, a wagon train from Illinois, stopped for supplies before continuing on a hard journey to California. They carved out trails through the mountains, crossed waterless desert, and spent a winter trapped near a high mountain pass in California. Facing wild forces, from searing heat and wind to deep snow and cold, they fell into starving hunger, and then worse. To many Americans, the ordeal looked like a battle of wild against civilized.[19]

About a year after the Donner party paused at his fort, Jim and two companions were riding east across the Red Desert in the high heat of late June 1847, when they met a long wagon train. Some seventy wagons, with colonizing settlers at the reins, were headed west across the flat and open plain. As Jim soon learned, this party of travelers planned to turn south, and to stop where mountains met desert—instead of continuing west, as most did, to the fertile lands of California and the Oregon country. He noticed that they were mostly Yankees by origin, but the travelers did include a few fellow Southerners and three African-American men who were enslaved.[20]

Jim had spent time in the very valley of interest to the travelers, and held a claim as one of the first Americans to reach that place and to see the great saltwater lake. His keen memory for landscape made him a renowned explorer and guide. A friend later said, "He could make a map of any country he had ever traveled over, mark out its streams and mountains and the obstacles in it correctly, so that there was no trouble in following it and fully understanding it." Jim's friend, a U.S. Army general, added that "the whole West was mapped out in his mind." That knowledge would enable thousands of colonizing settlers, including those he had just met by the river, to reach their destinations.[21]

In middle age Jim was a tall and wiry man, rawboned and strong, with light eyes and a steady gaze. He had the fixed squint of a hunter and trapper, the result of many years spent outdoors in the hard glare of bright sun on rock face and snow. His colorful tales of exploration matched his seasoned look and his buckskin clothing. By then, he had lived in the mountains for twenty-five years, a near record for endurance. High risk and hard luck steadily culled the trappers' numbers even before the fur trade declined. A few returned to Missouri as wealthy men, but others had little to show for years of effort. Many never made it back.[22]

The leader of the wagon train, a man named Brigham Young, questioned Jim closely about the valley with the saltwater lake as two scribes took notes. Jim gave detailed answers about the mountains and valleys. He praised the fertile valley farther south, and its large freshwater lake, and land beyond. "Said if we wanted any of his services to let him know," one man recorded. Jim pointedly told the travelers how much the American Fur Company paid him, a sizable sum.

Despite his deep knowledge, he could not say much about the prospects for growing grain in the valley of interest. He had no direct knowledge about farming there because he lived as a trapper, trader, and explorer among people who hunted and gathered on wild lands. He did warn about frost in late spring or late summer, which could ruin a crop. Other trappers and explorers, who had passed through that valley in its lush season—in the first warm weeks of spring, when snowmelt rushed down greening slopes—thought of it as a blessed place. One called it a "beautiful and fertile valley," and another called it his home in the wilderness. But they did not live by farming.[23]

The leader of the wagon train decided to continue according to plan, and without Jim's services. He and his party of travelers—Lorenzo, Harriet, Clara, and the others—turned south, toward Jim's trading-post fort. They planned to stop there briefly before heading toward the valley with the big saltwater lake.

The vagaries of life had tested Jim even before he set out for the wild green yonder of the Rocky Mountains. Born to a westering family who left Virginia to settle far away in southern Illinois, across the river from St. Louis, he was an orphan by the age of thirteen. Five years later, he headed west again. William Ashley, also a Virginian by birth, had placed a notice in a St. Louis newspaper, hoping to hire a hundred young men as trappers and hunters for the fur trade. Jim, a poor boy without many prospects, signed on with Ashley's Hundred. That was just sixteen years after two well-born Virginians, Meriwether Lewis and William Clark, returned from their exploring trip across half a continent where fur-bearing wild animals still flourished. By the time Jim traded city life for the trapping life, Lewis was long dead, a young casualty of melancholia and a gun.[24]

Jefferson, who as president had put his protégé Lewis in charge of the ambitious exploring expedition, had nearly reached the great age of eighty when Ashley's Hundred left St. Louis. He still lived in the grand style of a rich Virginia planter on his estate in the foothills of the Blue Ridge Mountains, still as mired in debt as ever. For years he had spent lavishly to make improvements to the house and grounds. His fine mansion paid tribute, architecturally, to ancient Greek civilization as a progenitor of Western civilization. A French nobleman who visited Monticello noticed that the entrance hall was built in the Ionic style, the drawing room in the Corinthian, and the dining room and exterior of the mansion in the Doric.

In this most civilized place, Jefferson had mounted a display of the wild, his own natural history museum in miniature. A display of specimens from wild lands to the west—everything from the heads of native elk and bison to Indian weapons and other artifacts—greeted visitors in the mansion's spacious entrance hall, which they entered from a columned portico. An entire wall, one man reported, was "covered with curiosities which Lewis and Clark found in their wild and perilous expedition."[25]

The objects seemed incongruous in that setting, but artfully so. In Jefferson's entrance hall, his guests gazed at specimens from the native wild West—from faraway places soon to be colonized by settlers, wild riches reaped, wild lands tamed, and native people civilized or otherwise eliminated. Lewis and Clark had brought back the first trove of trophies. Visitors enacted the looming change from native wild to civilized when they walked from the mansion's entrance hall into a fully civilized interior—where they saw the fine furniture, the art, the slaves.

William Ashley's enterprise, with the workers known as Ashley's Hundred, eventually became the Rocky Mountain Fur Company. Jim was a partner. He stayed on for years in Indian country where he acquired Indian allies, married the daughter of one, and mastered Indian sign language. He could entertain his Indian hosts with preposterous and amusing stories that took an hour to tell, without saying a word if he did not speak their language.[26]

Later, people told many stories about the master storyteller. They said that he liked to regale American visitors with a thrilling tale of pursuit by wild Indians—sometimes twenty, sometimes a hundred, dressed for war and riding fast horses. In this tale of wild against civilized, the warriors chased him into a canyon, a box canyon as he realized too late. Trapped! "And what happened then?" his listeners demanded. "Why, they killed me," Jim drawled.[27]

Barney had much in common with Jim. The two men shared Richmond, Virginia, as their birthplace, and both came from families that had left Richmond to try their luck in other places. The Ward and Bridger families had also left behind the chance for their sons to have formal schooling. Neither man could sign his name, a skill not much needed in the mountains. Like Jim, who was about ten years older, Barney arrived in the Rocky Mountains at a young age. Once established there, he too married an Indian woman. Jim's first wife, known as Cora Insala, had died by the time he met the wagon train near the river. She was Salish, the daughter of Chief Insala, and the mother of three children with Jim.[28]

Most travelers did not know that the marriages of Indian women to fur trappers were working partnerships. The women brought many assets to those partnerships, including their knowledge and survival skills and their labor. Their families and other kin served as valued allies. The women traveled with their trapper husbands, shared the hardships, and did most of the work other than hunting and trapping. They served as interpreters and guides when needed. Jim's first wife, Cora, lived that life. So did Barney's wife. A woman could make the difference between comfort and hardship, success and failure, even life and death for her trapper husband.[29]

Unlike Jim and Barney, some trappers did not find their skillful, hardworking wives in the usual way. As an American traveler learned when he stopped at a rendezvous by the Green River, "Indian women are a lawful commerce among the men that resort to these mountains from the States and elsewhere." Four veterans of the fur trade told him about the slave trade in women, "a common occurrence" at that rendezvous, they claimed. They identified some of the trappers and traders who bought women from each other or won them by gambling. Call those captive women, sold and bought by men, Sacagawea's Daughters.[30]

Jim and Barney lived with their wives at Fort Bridger. When some of the earliest travelers passed by, Jim's partner, Louis, was absent. He had made the long journey back to St. Louis. He finally returned with a new wife who was Anglo-American, something nearly unknown among trappers and traders in the mountains. Narcissa was suited to be a trader's wife at a fort. American travelers found her friendly and sociable. But she did not have the skills and stamina of a trapper's wife, who moved from camp to camp in wild country, and worked all day, and slept in a buffalo robe on hard ground at night.[31]

Narcissa had chairs in her new home—a novelty in that frontier place. Chairs added another touch of civilization to the fort that became her home. Civilized women, as she knew, did not sit on the ground in the dirt. They sat on chairs, and ate meals at a table. By then, Jim had married again. His second wife was Utah, but she died shortly after giving birth to a daughter he named Virginia.[32]

Fort Bridger looked like a modest venture, and not very well fortified at that. A tall but flimsy stockade surrounded double log houses, each about forty feet long. The stockade protected livestock from wild predators and from capture, but did not serve as a true fortification. Sturdy swinging gates at the front of the fort opened to allow teams of oxen and cattle to enter a large enclosed space of an acre or two.

Along with horses, Jim and Louis kept mules, oxen, and cattle on hand for overland travelers in need of new animals. Their supply of provisions included sugar, coffee, tea, flour, and other necessities, from buffalo robes and pig iron to clay pipes, tobacco, and whiskey. By stocking and selling such wares to travelers they enabled thousands of colonizing settlers to continue on their long westward journeys. Jim and Louis had a reputation for dealing fairly with their customers.[33]

A visitor reported seeing Shoshone lodges outside the gates of Fort Bridger. The Utahs, he learned, lived "beyond the mountains." Some fifty to sixty people lived around the fort. Trappers, including Barney, occupied many of the lodges along with their Indian wives and children. A traveler saw women sewing buckskin into clothing and moccasins, some intended for sale.[34]

Arresting views of the High Uinta Mountains, which came suddenly into sight, startled travelers who had just spent long dragging days crossing a dry, flat plain. Jagged white peaks of distant mountains cut into the sky. Clusters of clouds loitered by the crests until the wind broke them up, roughly, and chased them out of sight. Some travelers found Fort Bridger's environs cold and forbidding even in July.[35]

This land of mountains and sky gave welcome to Barney's Shoshone wife. At the trading-post fort in the Green River country, she lived in the southern part of her homeland, near her people. They spoke words she had once known and then had not heard for long years. Her exile had ended, at least for a time.[36]

When the wagon train of travelers stopped briefly for rest and repairs at Fort Bridger, Clara was recuperating from a case of "the mountain fever," her mother Harriet recorded. Others had fallen ill as well, but the travelers soon resumed their journey. An Indian guide from the fort rode along with them for a day, and camped with them the first night.

They spent the next long days crossing a rugged landscape where range after range of mountains met the eye in every direction. The manifest scale of that scene, unbroken by human settlement, disturbed some travelers. One called it "truly wild and melancholy," although a brilliant summer sun lighted up land and sky.[37]

On this last leg of the journey, they had use of the new wagon trail broken by the Donner party a year earlier. The men had widened the trail by hand, mile by exhausting mile, so that their wagons could pass through thickets of bent, shattered oaks and brush. It had taken the Donner party a full two weeks of crushing labor to clear and cross forty miles of rough trail, but their successors covered the distance in just a few days. With each wagon train that followed, the trail widened more, enabling a faster, safer passage for colonizing settlers.[38]

On the last days of their journey, the travelers crossed a pass near the summit of a mountain, and then descended into a wild green canyon. The steep slopes bristled with quaking aspens and dark spruces near the top, then junipers and pines, then weathered oaks and green-leafed maples. Silvery sagebrush and yellowing grass and native wildflowers covered the lower slopes of the last mountain they crossed. They followed and forded a creek that flowed west, shaded by tall cottonwood and box elder trees. A tangle of bushes laden with wild berries grew near the banks.

When the travelers finally left the green shelter of the last narrow canyon, they glimpsed their destination. They saw a desert valley framed by snow-lit mountain peaks, an immensity of nearly level land veined with snow-fed creeks born high above. Harriet paused, and looked down in silence at what struck her as a treeless, sunburnt place. The luminous colors of spring had long since faded to the neutral tones of high summer. Water from snowmelt rushed down canyon creeks in spring, but by late July had slowed to a lazy flow.[39]

Harriet knew nothing of the seasons in this land—she who had always seen summer crowned by a fullness of green. Here she only saw barren wilderness stretching west to a hazy horizon. The naked grandeur of the land in that dry time escaped her notice. She could not foresee the coming season, the autumn rains, and a valley that would look, at first glimpse from a distance, like a rich river bottom.[40]

To other settler-colonists, the wild valley seemed to offer fine prospects for grazing livestock and for farming, even at the height of dry summer. One praised the "vast rich fertile valley" that lay before him, with the best springs, creeks, and rivers that he had yet seen on his long journey. Another remarked on green patches in the distance, stands of lush wild grass four to ten feet tall, food for their hungry livestock. A faint green line marked a river where willows leaned thirstily toward water, and narrow-leafed cottonwood trees shimmered in strong sunlight. In this open land, the men would be spared the hard labor of removing native trees before planting crops.[41]

That same land, scant of spreading trees, disappointed Harriet. She saw only the absence of shady orchards, left behind when she went west. But like nearly all settler-colonists, she planned to re-create her old way of life in a new place. She had brought the seeds of domesticated fruit trees and locust trees from her last home, and those seeds could be planted in spring.

Her daughter Clara, who made a habit of good cheer, recalled feeling satisfied by what she saw in the valley. She called it "a pleasant land."[42]

After the wagon train left Fort Bridger, and a week before it reached the valley with the saltwater lake, Barney's Shoshone wife gave birth to a daughter. He named her Mary, and called her Polly. Soon after that, Barney and his wife left the fort with their baby Polly and nine-year-old Adelaide, and followed the same trail to the same desert valley. They arrived by early fall, before snow fell in the mountains and stopped most travel for a season.[43]

With trapping and the fur trade in such steep decline, Barney had cast about for other opportunities. The Yankee travelers had not hired Jim, whose celebrity and expertise brought him high wages, but they might hire Barney at a lower rate. He offered his services to them as an interpreter with Shoshone and Utah Indians. Drawing on his fifteen years of experience as a trapper and explorer, he could also assist them as a guide, helping in the search for more wild arable land to colonize and farm. That included the prized land directly south, known to trappers and traders as the Valley of the Utahs. Their leader had learned about it from Jim, and also from a recent report by a famous explorer who recommended that very valley for raising livestock and crops. Such reports whetted appetites and also enabled quests for western wild lands. The reports, along with maps drawn by explorers, guided hundreds of thousands of colonizing settlers west.[44]

Promising words about the Valley of the Utahs tantalized the settler-colonists who had just reached the valley with the saltwater lake, but the fierce Utahs had long defended their bountiful homeland from intruders. Their fertile valley offered a wealth of good water from springs, from creeks that ran down from the mountains, and from the large freshwater lake. Trout and other fish filled the waters, and waterfowl thronged the surface in some seasons. Grass and trees were plentiful there. Although the soil looked good for farming, the Utahs grew nothing. They took their food from the wild abundance. Barney knew this directly from his past trading trips to the Valley of the Utahs. So did Jim, who had warned the wagon train of colonizing settlers to stay away from that well-guarded place. He told them, "in the Utes Land you must not stick a Stake."[45]

For the time being, most of the new settlers waited in the big valley. They kept at their consuming work of taming the wild land, as they saw it, by removing and replacing the native plants and animals. The men cut down trees in nearby canyons, and sawed the wood into usable pieces. They dug out wild sage, as they called sagebrush and other ragged, hardy shrubs. They turned the soil and planted familiar food crops, potatoes and turnips and cabbage, in hope of a late fall harvest that would supply seed for spring. They dug ditches to take water from creeks to their new fields of the imported plants. They killed wolves, coyotes, and other wildlife that might pose a threat to the tame animals they had brought west.[46]

There was no need to kill wild bison to insure grass for grazing livestock. The herds of native bison seen twenty-five years earlier by explorers had already vanished from the valley. Other wild game seemed abundant. Soon after arriving, one man counted "about 75 or 100 mountain goats, sheep, Antilope &c. in flocks and playing about the Hills & valley."[47]

The settler-colonists had been present in the valley for just days when the first trade took place. No captive changed hands. That came later. One man recorded, "Two Utah Indians came to camp, & trade[d] away two ponies for a rifle & musket."[48]

The newcomers' arrival, as intruders and strangers in a valley that they
supposed empty, had not gone undetected. The big valley and the nearby
canyons, despite how they looked to the settler-colonists, qualified as
claimed and occupied land. The eastern edge of the valley bounded Utah
country. In the hot, dry months, Utahs often hunted and gathered in the
coolness of the mountains and canyons, where narrow creeks carried life-
giving water down through the canyons and into the valley. They called
the spacious open land where the wagon train had stopped Tav'-o-kun,
Place of Sun.[49]

The two Utahs who entered the strangers' camp, which counted a hundred and forty armed men, showed courage that day—and a strong wish
to trade. One of the settler-colonists described their appearance, noting
that they were "of moderate size, pleasing countenances and dressed in
skins." As it happened, the Utahs had good horses to trade for guns, and
the newcomers needed more horses. "The Indians remained about the
Camp all night & appear very peaceable & are desirous to barter," another
man recorded.[50]

When the two Utah men left the next day with firearms in hand, they
could not have known that the strangers were not simply stopping to rest,
in the manner of most overland travelers or traders. They could not have
known that these strangers intended to stay, to settle and farm. The two
Utahs only wanted to make a trade. Their people had a long history of
trading with travelers, especially trappers and Mexican traders who passed
through their lands. So did the Shoshone-speaking people who lived in
the western part of the valley, near the saltwater lake. They too knew of
the strangers' presence.[51]

A few years earlier, an American trapper and trader—an old acquaintance
of Barney and Jim's—had traveled through the big valley. It was a "fertile Valley," he recorded in his journal, "intersected by large numbers of
fine springs." He was on his way south, skirting the lake to trade with a
chief he called by the name Want-a-Sheep. The settler-colonists later knew
him as Wanship, or One-ship.

On a day in late winter, the trapper reached a village near the lake, and
asked where he could find Want-a-Sheep. But Chief Wanship appeared
before anyone could answer. The trapper thought he was Utah, but the
chief spoke in Shoshone, inviting this guest to follow him to his lodge.
He was a tall, lean man with a thin face and piercing dark eyes. On that

day in late winter, he wore a buffalo robe thrown over one shoulder and gathered in folds around his waist.

The trapper dismounted from his horse and entered the chief's large lodge. After he and some of his men had smoked a pipe of tobacco with their guest, they exchanged news. The trapper spoke in Shoshone, a language that the others in the lodge, men and women alike, also spoke. Then they ate together, and finally the women left. The men smoked again until midnight, when most returned to their own lodges, and the women of Chief Wanship's family returned to theirs.

The trapper stayed for weeks with his friendly host, and "passed the time as pleasantly as ever I did among Indians," he said. He spent his days hunting waterfowl. They crowded the sky and lake and marshland, filling the air with loud honks and cries in that season. By then he had lived in the mountains for seven years, trapping and trading, but the era of the Rocky Mountains fur trade was drawing to a close. When he finally left, he headed north with furs he had got from the hospitable Chief Wanship and his people: "a nation of people contented and happy," he remarked.[52]

A few days after the settler-colonists had made the first trade with the two Utah men, fifteen or twenty Shoshones, including women, visited their camp. The presence of women signaled the Shoshones' peaceful intent. They found some Utahs at the strangers' camp that morning, to their annoyance. "They appear displeased because we have traded with the Utahs," one man recorded, "and say they own this land, that the Utahs have come over the line &c. They signified that they wanted to sell us the land for powder and lead." The same man noted that these visitors were not so well dressed as the Utahs, but they were about the same height, and he saw "many pleasing countenances among them." During that week, small parties of Utahs and Shoshones arrived at the camp almost daily to trade, offering horses and tanned skins in exchange for guns and clothing.[53]

As the settler-colonists soon learned, Chief Wanship and hundreds of Shoshone-speaking people occupied the very place that they had chosen as a new home. The newcomers heard the inhabitants' name as Cu-mum-buh, but Utahs called them Kumumpa. That name meant Others, or Strangers—and water, *pa*. They were Others, Shoshones, who lived near the big saltwater lake and smaller bodies of water.

Their homeland embraced lakeside marshes, rich in wildlife, and a stretch of river that flowed north from the freshwater lake. Another river flowed west from the mountains, and creeks and springs provided still more fresh water. Warm mineral springs offered healing. Kumumpa territory included much of the big valley as well as lands along the river that flowed from the mountains. They were not going to leave their homeland, even if the strangers gave them precious ammunition in trade for temporary use of the land.[54]

The visitors could keep their wagons there for a time. They could take pure water from the rivers, creeks, and springs, and gather dry wood for fires. They could hunt and fish. Their animals could graze on the plentiful grass. Surely they would move on soon. There were so few women and children with the strangers. More must be waiting somewhere else. In any case, the land could not support this number of people for more than a season, even when seeds were ripe and fish and game plentiful. There were too many grazing animals. They ate not only the grass but also the seeds that women gathered, storing some for winter food.[55]

Still, there might be advantage in helping these well-armed strangers. Their wagons held many trade goods, and they had already traded guns for horses. Relations with neighboring Utahs followed such an uneven course that the temporary presence of these unexpected guests could prove helpful. They might make good allies, and discourage the Utahs from making hostile intrusions into the big valley for a time. At any rate, it would be too costly to drive away so many armed travelers before they chose to leave.

Chief Wanship and his people had no way to know, or even to imagine, that ten times as many colonizing settlers were on the way to their valley at that very moment, rolling on day after day across the plains. The little boy named John—Lorenzo's son and Clara's stepbrother—was with those many men, women, and children who had waited until May and June to start west. The travelers were bringing thousands more grazing livestock. By one count, the animals included 2,213 oxen, 887 cows, 358 sheep, and some number of horses and mules—to say nothing of chickens, hogs, dogs, and cats. They covered twelve miles on some days, fewer on others, but kept rolling on, rolling on. Unstoppable.[56]

Within a week of the first trade with the two Utah men, the settlers received advice and a stern warning from their leader. He planned to leave on a journey east, to meet the arriving settlers on the trail, and then to return to the valley the next summer with still more people, thousands who had not yet departed. In the meantime, he strongly advised against trading away guns and ammunition to Utahs and Shoshones, lest they shoot cattle. He had been away from camp, exploring the valley, when the men made what he regarded as unwise trades.

He did not intend to pay any Shoshones for land that the settler-colonists occupied. "I understand they offered to sell the land," he said, "and if we were to buy it from them the Utahs would want pay for it too." Besides, there was land "enough for both them & us," he told his followers. He did not understand that Shoshones expected compensation only for the temporary use of their land. They had not offered to sell, surrender, and vacate it.[57]

Shoshone-speaking people held a strong claim to much of the big valley that they called home. They lived in a territory of known, named landmarks and waters. They spent long seasons near the big saltwater lake, and sometimes hunted pronghorn antelope on a large nearby island. A few years earlier, the American trapper and trader who visited Chief Wanship and his band had found them living in the valley in winter, as spring approached. The big lake was called Tit'-so-pi in Shoshone. Mountains south of the lake were known as O'-kar. The river that trappers called the Utah Outlet had the Shoshone name Pi'-o-wip. It ran fifty miles north from the freshwater lake to the saltwater lake. The river that brought water west from the mountains to the saltwater lake had two names, Sho-go'-gwun and U'-og.[58]

The settler-colonists' leader had told the men before he left that they should not trade anywhere near camp because it encouraged unwelcome visitors. That could only bring trouble. He urged them to choose a distant location as the official place for trading. Despite his advice, trading continued on what they had immediately claimed as their home ground. And it did bring trouble, just as predicted.[59]

Their leader had already been away for months when Charley gave his rifle for the captive girl. To judge from the first trade, with the two Utah men, she had the same value as a horse. She was worth one rifle. Some people later said that Charley parted with his firearm reluctantly, and only to save a human life, not because he wanted the girl. They implied that he had made a moral choice and paid a ransom, not bought a slave.

The trouble was, they now had one less rifle in their hands and the wild Indians had one more. Their trading partners of today might return as well-armed enemies tomorrow. And the trouble was, a good rifle was hard to replace so far from the workshops and markets of civilization. And for all this trouble, they now had a wild girl on their hands. A good Indian pony seemed more useful, a far better trade. The three enslaved

men at the fort, brought from the South with the first settlers, had much
more value than this new captive. They knew how to work, although one
of them was regarded as "hard to manage."[60]

For the present, the captive girl appeared nearly useless. Charley's wife,
who was due to give birth in just a month, wanted help with washing and
cooking—but the girl knew nothing about clothing or the settlers' food.
Charley decided to give the girl to his younger sister, who was not yet
twenty. Clara could take charge of teaching the captive to work. She was
the wife of their absent leader. Unlike the other married women, she had
no children, and no husband at hand who needed care.

Barney and his wife learned something about the captive by speaking
to her. Barney knew some of the words she spoke, but they could not
take him far. Whatever he and his wife learned about her the new settler-
colonists in the valley soon forgot. Her origins and identity remained
obscure to most of them. People referred to her simply as Clara's "Indian
girl" or "the Indian girl whom they called Sally."

As one of the first steps in civilizing the girl—the goal from the
moment she was forced into their world—she had been given an English
name. She became the namesake of a former captive, Barney's wife, who
was known as Sally Ward. They promptly forgot that, just as they nearly
forgot Sally Ward herself, the Indian woman at the fort who knew how
to turn their stiff deer hides into supple, washable buckskin for clothing.
She might have vanished forever from their memory but for the story
Adelaide told many years later about her mother's early life.[61]

Clara and most of the other settler-colonists at the fort had only secondhand knowledge of Indians and wild lands when they moved west. It came
from stories that they heard from each other, sometimes as family lore.
It also came from newspapers, books, and magazines. Narratives of wild
and civilized abounded.

Eastern newspapers carried harrowing accounts of abductions and
murder, of wild Indians taking colonizing settlers captive, or killing them.
Book-length captivity narratives also sold well, and many had become best
sellers. They were signature stories of settler-colonization, a product of the
ongoing intrusions by Americans and Europeans into native homelands.
Novelists and magazine editors took note of their popularity. James Fenimore Cooper had made captivity in wilderness part of the plot in some
of his most popular novels. Nathaniel Hawthorne wrote stories about
characters who had survived captivity.[62]

Magazines published both fact and fiction about recent abductions. That the fiction *was* fiction, and not fact, sometimes escaped the readers of these magazines. Readers of the novels sometimes also forgot that the stories, even if based on fact, were not strictly factual. The terrifying tales formed part of the settlers' narrative knowledge about Indians—what they learned from stories told and heard and read again and again. The stories tutored them about the bloody battle between wild and civilized.[63]

A man by the name of Henry R. Schoolcraft, who grew up in New York State due east of the place where Clara was later born, knew about those Indian stories, as Americans called them. In childhood, long before he became a well-known explorer and ethnologist, he had heard long sagas of attack, abduction, and slaughter, battles of wild against civilized. He recalled the macabre tales his father told at night by the hearth, in the light of a flickering fire, about serving as a soldier in the American Revolution. "In these recitals, the Indian was depicted as the very impersonation of evil—a sort of wild demon," the son recalled, "who delighted in nothing so much as blood and murder." What his father recounted was "inseparably connected," he explained, "with the fearful ideas of the Indian yell, the tomahawk, the scalping knife, and the firebrand."

Printed captivity narratives also reached the boy's hand from time to time. He read them closely. Even before the age of ten, horrifying images and ideas filled his imagination about the people known to him as "the bow and arrow race." They were murderers, wild demons all. So he heard from his father, and so he read.[64]

As colonizing settlers edged farther and farther west into wild lands, the sites of abductions and the settings of captivity tales moved as well. Years before Clara's family crossed the western plains and mountains, the Parker family—a large extended family, Virginians by origin—had left the United States for Mexican territory. They sold land that they had settled a few years earlier in Illinois, and moved nine hundred miles southwest to colonize wild country in a place known as Texas. The land where the Parkers made their new home was not only claimed by Mexico, but also happened to lie within Comanchería, the Comanche homeland.

A few years after the Parkers arrived and built a large fortified homestead that they called Fort Parker, Comanches and their allies attacked the intruders. They killed five of the Parker men and carried off captives, including two daughters of the family. The older one, Rachel, remained a captive until some Americans ransomed her. Rachel's book about her life with Comanches soon reached print under the title *Rachel Plummer's*

Narrative of Twenty One Months Servitude as a Prisoner among the Comanchee Indians. Written by Herself.[65]

Her young cousin, Cynthia Ann, was still missing when the book appeared in print. At the age of nine she had disappeared with her native captors into the vastness of the Texas plains. Her father was dead, killed in the raid on Fort Parker, but his brother took up the search for Cynthia Ann. After eight long years he finally gave up the hunt for the blonde and blue-eyed captive.[66]

Newspapers covered current events, and Cynthia Ann's story quickly faded from the American press. Gripping news of recent abductions crowded out speculation about long-missing captives, often assumed dead as years passed. Newspapers did not report at all on Indians taken captive, and sold in the slave markets of Santa Fe and other settler-colonial sites. Their identities and fates remained unknown, of no interest to the American reading public.

In the tenth year of her captivity, two years after her uncle finally stopped searching for her, there was at last an undisputed sighting of Cynthia Ann at a Comanche camp. By then Texas had seceded from Mexico and had given up its brief status as an independent republic to join the United States. According to a newspaper account, the American government agent who saw Cynthia Ann offered to trade twelve mules and two mule loads of merchandise for her, but the Comanches turned down the large ransom, saying that they would "die rather than give her up." They called her Naudah.

She wept silently during the negotiations, but not because she wanted to leave with the Americans. Naudah wanted to stay with her captors. They had become her family, and the Comanche way of life had become her way of life. She tried to hide herself from the visitors. Although she no longer spoke their language, she understood some of their words and their intent. Finally they gave up and left, but with a promise from the Comanche chief that he would ask his people to surrender her. She was nearly twenty years old.[67]

In the eyes of Americans, Cynthia Ann had degenerated, fallen away from civilization, gone wild. But perhaps she could still be recovered and redeemed. Perhaps this tale of wild and civilized would end well—as Americans saw it.

Fourteen years after the Parker family left Illinois for Texas, and eleven years after Cynthia Ann disappeared into the Texas wilds, Clara's family

TRAGEDIES
OF THE WILDERNESS;

OR,

TRUE AND AUTHENTIC NARRATIVES OF CAPTIVES,

WHO HAVE BEEN CARRIED AWAY BY THE INDIANS FROM THE VARI-
OUS FRONTIER SETTLEMENTS OF THE UNITED STATES,
FROM THE EARLIEST TO THE PRESENT TIME.

ILLUSTRATING

THE MANNERS AND CUSTOMS, BARBAROUS RITES AND CERE-
MONIES, OF THE NORTH AMERICAN INDIANS, AND THEIR
VARIOUS METHODS OF TORTURE PRACTISED UPON
SUCH AS HAVE, FROM TIME TO TIME, FALLEN
INTO THEIR HANDS.

BY SAMUEL G. DRAKE.

Happy the natives of this distant clime,
Ere Europe's sons were known or Europe's crimes.
CHURCHILL.

'T is theirs to triumph, ours to die!
But mark me, Christian, ere I go,
Thou, too, shalt have thy share of woe!
FRENEAU.

BOSTON:

ANTIQUARIAN BOOKSTORE AND INSTITUTE,

56 Cornhill.

1841.

A collection of captivity narratives published in 1841. Reproduction from the original,
Sabin Americana.

had also left Illinois. They had headed due west instead of southwest, stopping for a winter near the Missouri River, and setting out again in spring. They planned to colonize a different part of Mexican territory—in the north, in Indian country around the Rocky Mountains.

The murder of Joseph Smith, the leader of their church, by a mob, had led them to seek land to settle in a foreign place. Like their dissenting Puritan ancestors from England who had reached North America as colonists two centuries earlier, these Yankee settler-colonists were carrying their religion west. They too planned to create Zion in the wilderness. They left behind mob violence in settled lands, but not their anxiety about Indian attack as they crossed wild country.

The prospect of abduction or murder was never far from the minds of American travelers, even children, who entered wild places. A young member of the Donner party had listened on long winter nights to her grandmother's Indian stories about the killing attacks that took place on the Virginia frontier. Years later she said, "we suffered more from fear of the Indians before starting than we did on the plains."[68]

Captivity narratives that reached print also told about wild Indians and their victims. Some of the narratives recounted gruesome deaths in unsparing, discouraging detail. Such stories fed the fear. But many of the tales told how some victims survived and escaped the wild. Those survivors, both men and women, were cast as victors and heroes. Their stories encouraged other aspiring settler-colonists.[69]

Clara and her family, like other Americans, read the Bible often. While the Bible said nothing directly about Indians, a story told in the book of Genesis struck many readers as telling. According to the Bible, once Adam and Eve left the Garden of Eden, people began to labor as farmers and herders. There was no mention of people hunting wild animals and gathering wild plants—which, to those readers of the Bible, meant getting food as wild beasts did. Evidently, hunter-gatherers had degenerated from a way of life that was higher, more advanced. Instead of progressing from that point, they had actually regressed to a lower state—or so many Americans and Europeans believed.

The French scientist and nobleman Georges-Louis LeClerc, Comte de Buffon, detected evidence of degeneracy in North America, and he had a theory about it. The continent's native inhabitants, human and otherwise, suffered from a poor natural environment, Buffon claimed. The mountains were high, and the climate harsh. He had never traveled beyond Europe, but he had read about North America's geography and climate. As superintendent of the Jardin du Roi in Paris, he had seen specimens of North America's flora and fauna while cataloguing the royal collections.

The specimens of native wild animals that he examined struck him as small and inferior in form, but the collection did not include bison, moose, or grizzly bears. The wild animals of North America, he concluded, did not reach the size of the tame animals of Europe. Far fewer wild species of mammals were found in France, of course, a highly civilized land of vineyards and plowed fields and pastures. But their scarcity did not trouble Buffon, and the abundance of North American wildlife did not impress him. Tame, he believed, was far superior to wild.

The native people of North America, Buffon understood, were also *sauvage*, wild. These savages, or wild people, had not progressed to civilization. They could not produce enough children to increase the size of their population. According to Buffon, "le sauvage est foible & petit par les organs de la generation." Not only were their reproductive organs feeble and small, he said, but also the men could not grow beards. *Quelle horreur*! They clearly showed a deficit of manliness. To Buffon, all of the evidence pointed to degeneration due to poor habitat.

The influence of Buffon and his ideas had alarmed Thomas Jefferson. These ideas could prove harmful to the commercial and political interests of the new republic. Jefferson argued against them at length in his book *Notes on the State of Virginia*. He marshaled evidence that Virginia—and by extension the rest of North America—was a rich and promising place, with wild arable lands ripe for colonizing by settlers. His comments about Indians, and their manhood, were cautiously positive, in contrast to his earlier words in the Declaration of Independence about "merciless Indian Savages." The Indian man, he said, "is brave, when an enterprize depends on bravery ... [and] he will defend himself against an host of enemies, always chusing to be killed rather than to surrender." Indian women were "submitted to unjust drudgery," and worked so hard, Jefferson added, that they bore few children. He said nothing about enslaved women and their unjust drudgery.[70]

Clara and the other colonizing settlers had no reason to read *Notes on the State of Virginia*, but they did read a newly published work. Some fifteen years before his death, Joseph Smith, whom they called their Prophet, had recorded the revealed story of American Indian origins. He taught that Indians descended from a scattered remnant of ancient Hebrews, just as many Americans and Europeans had long suspected. That explained their presence on a continent across an ocean and far away from the rest of humanity.[71]

Smith also instructed his followers, called Mormons or Latter-day Saints, to uplift this fallen, degenerated people, and redeem them. They should instruct Indians in their faith, and teach them the ways of civilization. This qualified as a matter of course by then.[72]

A full three centuries earlier, the Spanish had begun converting Indians to their religious faith and to civilization. Puritan settlers had tried to do the same. So had Quakers who formed the Committee for the Improvement and Civilization of the Indian. More recently, the United States Congress had appropriated funds for civilizing missions to the Indians. And just days after reaching the big valley, Clara's husband, the settlers' leader, had spoken about teaching the Indians who claimed that land "to labour & cultivate the earth."[73]

Clara's duty, which she accepted and tried to fulfill, was to civilize the native girl placed in her charge at the fort. While the men set about trying to tame and redeem the wild land around them—rooting out and replacing the native and wild, improving the land by making it more useful, as they saw it—she was to tame a wild Indian. How to begin? The girl did not speak English. She had never eaten food on a proper plate or slept in a proper bed. She did not know how to do useful work.

Years later, people said that the girl was about seven, or perhaps twelve, when Charley bought her, and that his sister proved a good mother to her. A woman who knew her well later in life praised her as "benevolent." Pretty, kind Clara: her sweet face, the woman said, exactly mirrored her character. But that smiling face belonged to someone who was also, by the same account, "very intelligent, prepossessing."[74]

Whatever Clara thought about the young captive at first, she realized that the girl in her care was not a child. Abuse and near-starvation had left her looking emaciated, even shrunken. Clara was short, and she was slight after a long spell of living on limited rations. Still, in comparison to the captive girl, she seemed older, larger. But when the girl menstruated, something that could not be hidden, it became clear that she was more woman than child. Clara thought that she was about nineteen years old, the same age as Clara herself.[75]

Whether the captive girl's family was alive, and exactly where they lived in the uncharted mountains or desert, remained unclear. Only Barney knew anything about that wild country, but he did not go in search of her people or take her to them. Sooner or later, captive Indians usually ran away and headed home. Witness the escape of his Shoshone wife from St. Louis. If this namesake captive, another Sally, ran away, she would no doubt find her way home—as her captors knew. Besides, Charley had given a rifle for her, and a trade was a trade.

CHAPTER 2

The Native Wild

FROM THE MOMENT CHARLEY TRADED his rifle for the girl, a solitary captive, she began a new life alone in the land that Utahs called Tav'-o-kun. For the captive, Place of Sun was a site of darkness. The shape of her new life, and even the prospects for life, looked uncertain. These captors, like the former ones, might withhold food, or torture her. They might sell her—or kill her. At best, she now lived behind walls, trapped by odd-looking strangers from a faraway place.

Only one of them spoke a few words that she knew. And if speaking the same words as her former captors had not helped her, she could not expect much from these people. They murmured in a friendly way to each other, but some of them barked at her as if she could not hear. Were they threatening her?

She kept silent, watching and waiting. She seemed sullen. They did not recognize her impassive manner as a show of courage.

Four months earlier, the men had begun building a fort for protection. Some of the settler-colonists found the valley's open expanse menacing. The valley floor stretched out for miles, uninterrupted, until it met low hills and looming mountains to the east and the saltwater lake to the west. They saw it as a wild wasteland, without houses or roads or fields of crops or any other marks of civilization. One man called it an "uncultivated region and inhabited by Savages." Those so-called Savages who lived in the valley were Chief Wanship and his people.[1]

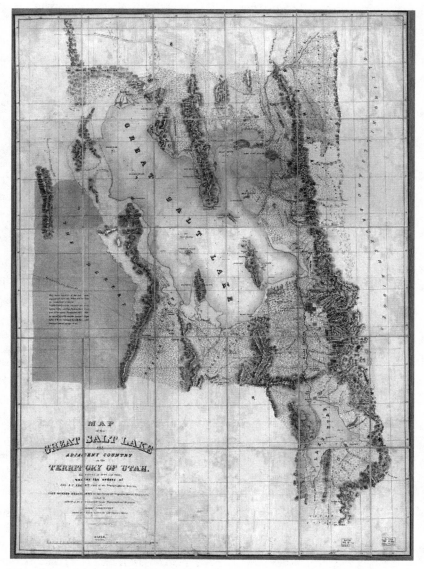

Map of Great Salt Lake and valley. Drawn by John W. Gunnison and Charles Preuss. Used by permission, Rare Books, Special Collections Research Center, William & Mary Libraries.

The new settlers wanted more protection from their neighbors than sheltering in their wagons could provide. They decided to construct small adjoining houses in the shape of a large stockade. The backs of the houses would form a solid wall, "to keep out the Indians, that our women and children be not abused," one man recorded. Some three hundred Indians lived nearby. They outnumbered the newcomers, although they counted fewer warriors than the settler-colonists' force of armed men. The newcomers expected reinforcements, but high walls also gave safety.[2]

They built the walls to keep out everything they feared as native, wild, and dangerous, from howling wolves to Indians. They had read about the howling wilderness in the Bible, and now they lived in it. Chief Wanship's people did yet not seem to pose any threat. Another chief, named Goship, and his Shoshone-speaking people also appeared peaceful and hospitable. The settlers had soon received gifts of food. Even Utahs who lived forty miles away in the next valley seemed friendly, eager to trade with them.[3]

It took months to complete their new home, a settlement fort. Unlike Fort Bridger, a makeshift trading-post fort built to serve commerce, this sturdy fort was meant to protect the colonizing settlers from all wild dangers. The solid walls, made of logs and sun-dried adobe bricks, stood nine feet tall. Small openings, each large enough only for a rifle barrel, dotted the long adobe walls, which were more than two feet thick. The gate closed at nightfall and remained locked until dawn.[4]

When Charley took the girl to the fort and she walked through that gate, she entered a closed, controlled world surrounded by open wild land—although she did not have a word such as wild to describe that land. The world was as it was. Land was neither wild nor tame.[5]

Only one woman at the fort was *Nu'-ints*, Indian. She was married to one of the strangers, a man who was with Charley when he bought her from the captors and who spoke a few of her people's words. Two chiefs and some of their people also came to the fort. They too were strangers, although one of the chiefs could speak her language. None of the men at the fort looked familiar, not like *Nu'-ints* or *Hu-kwots-u*, Mexicans. She had seen many men with *mum'-sŭmp*, whiskers. But some of these strangers had such long hair on their faces, covering their cheeks and chins, that it gave them a dog-faced look. Other men had smooth faces.[6]

The color of the hair on the strangers' heads, and on the men's faces, ranged from dark to light. A few of them had black hair. Most had hair the color of earth, or of grass seared by sun and faded by thirst, or of old leaves before they fall. Some had crooked hair that twisted around instead of falling straight. Most of the men cut their hair short, above the shoulders, instead of letting it grow long. The women bound up their long hair, or let it fall loose on their shoulders. None had short, cropped hair like hers. She saw only a few old ones. The color of their hair made them stand out from the rest, as snowberries stand out against summer green. There were many children.

The strangers' skin, especially the women's, was pale, a nameless color. If they stayed long in the sun, their skin turned bright. Some of the strangers had dark eyes. Others had oddly luminous eyes, which shone the colors of sky.

Their clothing covered most of the body. She saw men and boys wearing *kus* and *tāg*, buckskin pants and shirts. Others wore garments made from soft woven fibers. Her people dressed in sturdy buckskin in winter. In summer, the women wore short skirts made from twined bark. But the garments of these women reached nearly to the ground, and covered most of the body. The colors, faded or not, contrasted with the subtle hues of tanned skins or bark. Some of the people wore *pat-sun*, moccasins, made from supple deerskin. Others covered their feet with a stiff kind of hide. Some wore nothing on their feet, just as her own people often did.[7]

She had never seen so many people camped together in such a big shelter. They had sat down in this valley, and it seemed that they were not going to leave. This was their *kan*, their sitting place, their lodge. They must have put great piles of roasted seeds and pine nuts and dried meats and berries in storage pits so that they could all live together through the winter in this valley. The People, her own people, lived in larger camps in winter than in other seasons, but only a dozen or so small families came together.[8]

These strangers must be planning to stay even when the cold time ended. They had built a shelter so large and sturdy that it could not easily be moved to another place and rebuilt. The big shelter was made from dead trees and earth. The men had killed trees, and cut them into pieces. Then they stacked them high to make a wall. They made the other three sides from earth.

The People did not fell trees very often. It took too much work to split a tree trunk with a wedge made from elk horn, and then to cut it with a stone ax. It was better to find a dead tree, and make a fire at the base, and let the fire burn until they could push the tree over. But they did not need very much wood because they did not make shelters from trees. They never stayed in just one place for all seasons. No one wanted to live in a shelter that could not be moved and that felt like a trap.[9]

Caught inside the strangers' big fort, she could see the sky and sun. Above the walls, a white crest of mountains gleamed, encircling part of the valley. At night, in starlight, a silver line shone in the distance. Even in the high heat of summer, snow held fast to the crest.

Hundreds of women lived at the fort. During the daytime, she saw, many of them stayed inside the walls, and many of the men went outside. Men and boys came in through the gate carrying wood, and carrying water. Among her people, women did not stay at the camp all day. They left to get water. They left to gather plants, and sometimes they went far from camp in search of food.

At night her family slept inside a small willow and brush shelter. It had a round shape, unlike the strangers' big lodge. The rooms of the lodge, she saw, were like caves, but not so sturdy or protected from rain and snow. The thick walls and roof kept out most of the light.[10]

These strangers had *sa-rits'*, dogs, and *ka'-vwa*, horses, as the People did. They kept other odd animals, like those that some of the People saw when they went south to trade with Mexicans. A few of these beasts were larger than ponies, with massive shoulders and heads. As night fell, the men and boys put many of them in corrals. All of their animals were captives—not just the horses that were *spi-kunt*, ridden.[11]

The strangers only liked their own animals. They led the ones that grazed to stands of grass, and they led them to water. They made some of the biggest animals work for them. They also took mother's milk from some of them, and drank it, or used part of it to make a pale grease that they put in their food. Sometimes they killed and ate one of their animals. They cooked meat that they called *beef* in hot grease. It tasted bad to her.[12]

The strangers also had birds that she had never seen in the mountains or the desert. Some of the birds were the size of a *si'-ja*, sage grouse, or of waterfowl by the river and the lake where her family sometimes lived. But these birds did not flee from people. They strutted around them, and spread their wings and jumped, and never flew high or far. Just like the strangers, the birds sat down and stayed. They were captives too.

The women sometimes took *nu-pav'*, eggs, from the nests, but they let others hatch so that they would have more birds. When they took eggs, they cooked them or mixed them with food. The next day they might find more eggs to gather. Unlike sage hens or ducks, some of these birds kept making eggs, even in winter. The strangers liked to eat the new ones. The People liked older eggs better, the ones with baby birds inside. They could find those only in spring and early summer.[13]

There were a few animals prowling around that looked like little *tsum-kuts*, wildcats, but with long tails. They too lived inside the walls of the shelter. These creatures hunted mice that came to the fort. The strangers seemed to hate the hungry mice, and the scurrying, scratching sound of them searching for food in the dark.[14]

Wolves and coyotes, *shin-av'* and *yo'-go-wots*, sang at night, and always the same familiar songs with the long and whining howls. Ever hungry and often bold, some came near the shelter after dark to look for food. Even on starry, snow-bright nights they came close. In daylight, clear tracks in snow showed that they had circled the walls. The strangers disliked their high piercing cries and their tracks. They set out traps and poison to kill the wolves, but they did not want to eat them. They feared attacks by howling creatures, and harm to the animals they led around and fed.[15]

A big gray wolf got caught in a trap one night, and chewed off one leg to get free. The men soon found the wounded fugitive, and killed him. They wanted to kill all of the wolves—they called any animals that howled *wolves*—but no matter how many howling beasts they poisoned or shot, wolves still sang their songs each night.[16]

The People hunted many animals to eat—deer, elk, ground squirrels, rabbits, sage grouse, and ducks—just like these strangers. But they did not hunt wolves or coyotes. They shot them only if they saw them feeding on a fresh kill. It took desperate hunger to drive them to eat a wolf or coyote—or a fox, mountain lion, or wildcat. Those animals did not taste good.[17]

In winter, the old people told stories about Shin-au'-av, Wolf, and Yo-go'-vu-puts, Coyote, animal-people who lived long ago, before humans, and who made many of the things of this world. Wolf was wise. Sometimes Coyote was clever, sometimes foolish. In many ways he acted just like humans, using his wits, using deceit.[18]

When the old people told those stories, everyone listened, and learned how things came to be as they are. One of the old stories explained the origin of people. It went like this:

The creator, Shin-au'-av, Wolf, made the land for people to use. He created buffalo, deer, and other animals for their food and clothing. He caused the earth to produce roots and berries.

In the beginning, there were no people. Shin-au'-av began to cut sticks, which he placed in a large bag. He kept cutting sticks, and finally the bag was full. One day, while Shin-au'-av was away, Coyote opened the bag. Coyote, always curious, wanted to see what Shin-au'-av had put inside. Many people came out of the bag, and scattered in every direction. They spoke different languages.

When Shin-au'-av returned, he saw what Coyote had done. There were only a few people still in the bag; the rest had gone. He got angry at Coyote because he had planned to spread the people evenly across the land.

Because of Coyote, more people lived in some places than in others. The result was war when they tried to take land from their neighbors. Shin-au'-av said that the few people who remained in the bag would be a small tribe. But that tribe, the People, would be "very brave and able to defeat the rest." [19]

This good story told why people fought over hunting grounds. Coyote, as usual, caused the problem. But the story could also explain why these strangers had come to this valley. Too many people lived in their own distant country, so they came across the mountains to this place, where they sat down and stayed. They wanted the land.

The strangers did not know about Wolf and Coyote. If they told stories, she did not understand them. They spoke to her, but most of their words made no sense. They tried gestures. In time she realized that they had given her the name Sally. She did not know what that word meant, and it was hard to say at first because her people did not have some of those sounds. She accepted the new name. Her people did not always keep the same name throughout life. Sometimes they took new ones. She did not understand that for the settler-colonists, naming was part of claiming. They had already replaced the native names of peaks and creeks and canyons with English names. They planned to keep the land with the new names, and they planned to keep her. [20]

Later, when she learned more of their words, she realized that many of their names for people had no meaning. Strangely, they were just sounds. Men and women had different names. Two or three or even more could share the same name, such as John, or Mary. There was another Sally, the woman who was Ku-munts, one of the Others, the Shoshones. She had once been a captive herself. That Sally was married to the stranger called Barney, who spoke some of her words. The short young woman who gave her food had the name Clara. The older woman with black hair and black eyes was called Eliza. [21]

Clara lived for most of the first year in quarters that she shared with Eliza, and then with Sally. The fort had many rooms, each set with a separate door and some with a small window. Clara and Eliza's room had two windows, one with four panes and another with two. Sally had never seen a window before she reached the fort. The People did not need windows in their shelters.[22]

The roof of the fort was made from willow poles covered with layers of coarse grass, dry brush, and earth. After the roof was in place, mice moved into this suitably brushy home. They made rustling noises, and sometimes one fell out of the roof and landed on the floor—or worse, fell on someone who happened to be in the room. Sometimes the mice ran across beds at night. This intrusion by wild nature into civilized space, which was built to keep everything wild and native outside, made Clara and Eliza and the other women unhappy. The settler-colonists had already killed enough of the native wildlife around the fort—snakes and coyotes and hawks—to create a population boom of mice. The task of hunting a multitude of wild mice in the fort was left to a few cats, and to people. They made traps to drown the mice, and set the traps inside the rooms. Dozens could be killed in an evening, one of Eliza's friends recalled.[23]

The valley had stayed so dry, and the weather so mild even during late fall, that the men covered the rooms at the fort with a roof that was nearly flat. There seemed to be no real need for a pitched roof. They remembered late fall and winter on the distant prairie where they had once lived. Blizzards with gusting winds tore in from the north, driving snow into tall drifts. The heavy, pressing cold made breathing painful. Days of leaden skies offered little light. But here the climate, despite the dryness, seemed benign in fall. A warming sun shone brightly in the big sky. In the high desert valley that they called their new home, winter did not arrive early—at least not that year. When cold finally came, the flat roof showed the strength to support a heavy burden of snow.

Clara was away from the fort during the worst storm, in late March. Sally remained there with Eliza. A few days earlier Clara had gone to visit her mother and her stepfather Lorenzo at their log house. Their son, little Lorenzo—a happy, healthy baby, just six months old—had suddenly fallen sick that afternoon. They could not save him. He died eight hours later, a wrenching shock to his parents.

The baby's funeral was held the next day, and people from the fort gathered for the prayers and burial. Anyone could see that they were sad. Some of Clara's people cried, as Sally's people also did when a family member died. Harriet and Lorenzo, mired in grief, listened while a man named Jedediah talked for a long time to them and the others.

What he said was too hard for Sally to understand. She was still learning everyday words.

Some of the men had dug a small hole in the ground, and they put the tiny body there, and then covered it. The body was wrapped in cloth. The People put bodies into rock crevices in the mountains. Deep holes in the ground were for storing winter food, not bodies.[24]

The day after this great sadness, a heavy snow fell, and lay deep on the ground and on the roof of the fort. More snow fell the next day, and the next. Then warmth came, and melting. Clara was still away, still trying to comfort her mother and stepfather, when a furious pelting rain began. It went on for days.[25]

This was just three months after Sally had been "purchas'd," according to a note Eliza made in her journal. Sally had come to live with Clara and Eliza in mid-December, two days after Clara's older brother bought her. In that time she had observed many of the settlers' odd customs: what they ate, and how they ate, where they slept, how they lived, and how they died. And she had learned some of their words. Although she could understand why a baby's death made them sad, now she saw that dripping water inside their shelter also made them strangely unhappy.[26]

Dripping or drizzling water from the roof, as rain fell or snow melted, was yet another unwelcome, unexpected invasion of wild nature into a newly civilized and colonized zone. It seemed to the women at the fort that a barrier built to protect them had failed. They covered their stored provisions and the few pieces of furniture to keep them dry. Some held a thing they called an *umbrella* with one hand, and stirred pots of food with spoons that they held in the other.[27]

One evening during the storm, Eliza welcomed Charley and his wife, refugees from a leaking roof, to her room. They brought their new baby, "a fine daughter," Eliza said. The roof over Clara and Eliza's room had a thicker layer of earth, and at first the room stayed drier than most. But then the drips began. After dodging them for a time, Charley and his wife finally returned with the baby to their own wet room.

Sally wrapped herself in a thick buffalo robe and fell asleep on the damp wooden floor. Eliza went to bed, and covered her head and shoulders with an umbrella. The rest of her, and the bedclothes and feather mattress, got wet. She listened to the drops of water splattering on the floor, punctuated by the sharper sound of falling pebbles. The pebbles dropped, one by one, as rain slowly freed them from the roof. Something constructed from wild willow and brush and earth with human labor had been reclaimed and turned to useless mud by a force of wild nature. Then she heard the wild squeals of mice. They ran to and fro on the floor, seeking shelter from the storm and seeking food. Sally slept soundly.

In the darkness and dampness, the incongruity of it all suddenly made Eliza laugh. A New England Yankee by birth, with a strong sense of correctness and a backbone to match, she had spent most of her life in well-built houses that kept the outside out. But she also had a poet's sensibility. In her room at the fort, "the storm was much worse inside than out," she recalled—and "the Indian girl asleep on the floor, altogether made the situation rather romantic."

In that brief moment she suddenly saw incongruity, the native and wild inside, and laughed. Then her usual point of view returned. Inside was mostly civilized, and outside, mostly wild. At last she fell asleep.[28]

Clara and Eliza had brought little furniture with them. Necessities had crowded out niceties on the long trip west in wagons. Clara had only a makeshift bed, a small trunk, and a looking glass, which she placed carefully on a shelf. The bed, a simple affair made from poles and rope, did have a soft feather mattress, a precious relic of civilized life carried west. Sally saw that Clara and Eliza always passed the night on this sleeping platform.

Clara's trunk sat next to the bed. She and Eliza placed food on top of it and then sat by their eating platform. They never sat on the floor or outside on the ground. Each held a spoon and used it to lift the food from a bowl or plate. Sally knew about spoons made from the horns of wild mountain sheep. The People used them to eat hot mush prepared from seeds. But unlike Clara and Eliza, they held most foods with their hands when they ate.[29]

If she had known more of their words she could have told them that it was good to use fingers, to touch the food and feel the warmth and texture, and then to taste it. It was good to tear roasted and savory meat from a bone to eat, then to chew on the bone until it was bare, and finally to break the bone open and suck out the nourishing marrow. But they did not want her to do that. They did not want Sally to chew on bones "like a dog," Eliza said. And she should not wolf down her food. She should chew slowly and delicately.[30]

Also, she should not drink water like a dog—or wolf. She must never kneel down and drink from the creek. She should not put water in her cupped hand and then drink from her hand. She should always drink from a cup. Sally knew about cups. The People sometimes used *na-ga´-ats*, cups made of horn, or cups shaped from clay or carved from a knot of wood. But that was not their only way of drinking. They had three ways. They drank directly from a creek or spring, or from a cupped hand, or from a cup.[31]

The strangers, she saw, had many customs about hands and food. They wanted her to eat as they ate. She should not touch food with her hands, except dry bread, when she ate. And she should never lick or suck her fingers, or have need to do so, during the meal. Just like their children, the settlers thought, she must learn civilized table manners.

Most of the women at the fort had young children to care for. Eliza, at the age of forty-three, was childless. She and Clara had no men or children in their care. That left them more time to teach Sally how to work and how to live in their civilized way—the same lessons that children had to learn, whether they wished to or not.

Clara and Eliza's lessons began with the basics of everyday life. If Sally sat on the ground, in the eyes of the settlers she sat in the dirt. To sleep on the earth, even wrapped in a soft blanket of rabbit skins or in a thick buffalo robe, was to sleep in the dirt like a wild beast. To eat food without first washing hands, or without using cutlery, was uncivilized, they thought.[32]

Eliza's piercing look and her example spoke as loudly as words, and more loudly at first, since Sally heard most of her words as meaningless sounds. A major principle of Eliza's civilized manners, which she took for granted and could not have explained easily, was the importance of enacting the separation between civilized life and wild nature. It was a matter of tacit knowledge for the settler-colonists, like other Americans, that nearly everything wild and native must be kept apart, removed and segregated, marked as inferior, and dirty. Even many things in tame nature—horses, cows, chickens, and so on—were beneath people, and should be kept separate. Eliza, like others, believed that people had been specially created, and they stood below angels but above everything else. Civilized people stood above savages, but she believed that savages, like children, could be taught, raised up. They could be helped to progress.

She had once made a living as a teacher at "a select school for young ladies," as she put it. Now Sally was her sole student, but not for pay. Eliza sewed for others in trade for what she needed. That usually meant food, because she had arrived in the valley without provisions. Washing and ironing her clothing also occupied Eliza's time. She wore clean, pressed clothing, even at this outpost of civilization—or *especially* at this frontier fort. What she was most prepared to teach Sally was correct English and civilized manners. She would provide religious instruction as well.[33]

Since the fort was so crowded and furniture was scarce, not everyone slept in a proper bed. Some, including Sally, slept on rough wooden floors, but at least they did not lie on the ground in the dirt. Other settlers, whose beds stood on floors of packed earth, suffered until they could get wood for flooring—especially during that first spring when the leaking roof left them living in mud. One woman recorded that she stayed awake for most of a night, dipping up the invading water.[34]

Teaching Sally where and how to sit and where to sleep—not outdoors in the dirt—had begun immediately. At first, she did not want to sleep on a wooden floor enclosed by four solid walls and a sturdy door. She preferred sleeping on the ground and in view of the sky rather than under a thick roof. That was not permitted. It was uncivilized—and she might escape. Then the teaching about how to wash hands and bathe and how to eat correctly began. Clara soon set about trying to teach the basics of housekeeping as well, but that proved difficult at first. Sally did not want to work for her or live inside a walled fort with odd strangers. She wanted to go home. She missed her family.[35]

Eliza saw work not as simply necessary but as morally good. Her parents, Yankees with a strong Protestant work ethic, had taught her, she said, that "useful labor is honorable—idleness and waste of time disgraceful and sinful." She never sat idle, she added. But Sally, in her view, had lived as a wild girl up to that time. Eliza thought that native people did not work. It seemed that they roamed around, searching for whatever they could eat. When they came together, they wasted time racing horses and gambling. Most of the settler-colonists at the fort, like most other Americans, believed that.[36]

Sally already knew about work. Wolf had decided long ago to make people work hard to get their food. Left idle, he said, they would quarrel and fight and destroy each other. Just as Wolf had decreed, her people and others who lived by hunting and gathering worked hard.[37]

If she had known the right words, and if Eliza had asked her, she could have explained how her mother and the other women got food for their families. They dug edible roots, harvested native berries and grass seeds, hunted ground squirrels, and took part in communal rabbit hunts. Women did not hunt large game, but they always went to retrieve the carcasses, which hunters cut into large pieces and cached in trees. The women carried carcasses back to camp, often on packhorses, to skin and to cook. That good work belonged to women, just as most of the hunting belonged to men.[38]

Sally could have explained to Eliza that women worked hard to prepare food for their families, whether food to eat that day or to store for later use. To produce a large basket of winnowed seeds, after spending long hours gathering them in baskets, often took a full day's labor. Next, they roasted the seeds. These could then be eaten as they were, or boiled as mush, or ground into flour and cooked as cakes.[39]

 And whenever the People moved, in order to find replenished game and plants in places they had not visited for months or more, women did much of the work. They packed up the camp gear. Then, at the end of the day, they unpacked the horses, hobbled them, and set up a shelter. The women fetched water. They made food for the evening meal, and something for the morning meal as well.[40]

Still, sitting down to rest and to talk or to pass the time in friendly silence did not strike them as idleness and a waste of time, as Eliza would term it. Time—days and months and seasons and years—simply passed. There were four seasons in a year. There was past, present, and future, or *e'-tis*, *av*, and *pi'-nunk*. There was yesterday, today, and tomorrow, or *kew ki-aung*, *a-ra-va*, and *taik*. At night, stars told whether it was before-midnight, midnight, after-midnight, or towards-morning. But when Eliza assumed the role of teacher, Sally began to learn about wasting time, and about idleness.[41]

In the beginning she did simple tasks, unhappily. Some people judged her reluctance to work as laziness, but it was resistance. Two of the tasks, fetching water and collecting dry wood, qualified as drudgery to the settler-colonists. Although they thought that getting water was a boy's task, Sally could carry water from a creek or spring. There was no young boy to get the water that Clara and Eliza needed. There was just Sally, and this was a familiar task to her. Among the People, women usually fetched the water in basket jugs, which they had woven and coated with pitch on the inside. Women carried water from nearby creeks or springs, and men carried it from distant sources.[42]

Finding wood for fires was another duty of boys and men at the fort. In their former home, that had usually called for felling trees, chopping and splitting green wood, and then stacking it in piles to cure. Much of the deadfall in that humid place had been too rotten to burn well. Here the deadfall was bone dry, and Sally already knew how to choose the best of it to burn for heat or for cooking—if she could find any, and if she was willing to carry it back to the fort. So many strangers had come to live there that dry wood soon grew scarce.

Sally knew other things as well. She knew about plants that the settler-colonists could eat when their own food grew scarce—and which plants should not be eaten because they were poisonous. She knew the kinds of places to find the best food plants, and she knew when they were ripe. There were *ti-va*, pinenuts; *ok*, wild sunflower seeds; *tau-wa-su-guv*, wild onions; *ku-si'-a kûmp*, arrowleaf balsamroot; *pĭn'kapaiäts*, Indian parsnip; and ripe berries from *sūv*, called squaw bush by the settlers. Squaw bush was a generous plant that gave red berries for food and for dye, and branches for weaving baskets. There was also *to-nŏp*, as well as *to-ûmp'*, shrubs that some of the settler-colonists knew in their old home to the east as chokecherry and serviceberry. And there were still more plants that gave berries: *po-gomp*, buffalo currant berries, or wild gooseberries; *ta-ma-nûmp*, silver buffalo berries; and *tu-wi'-is*, wild strawberries.[43]

Other plants gave bulbs. Besides *pim'-ĭ-kwi-ĕts*, which settlers called yellowbells, there was *si'go*, or sego lily, as she heard them call it. The bulbs tasted good either roasted or steamed. The People cooked and ate fresh sego bulbs, or they dried the bulbs to use for winter food. But besides the sego lily bulbs, which were ripe in summer when the plants flowered, there was *ta-bä'-si-gwĭv*, poison sego. Sego grew both in the valley and in the foothills. The poisonous plant that looked something like it grew in the foothills, but the flower differed.[44]

Likewise, *yampah*, wild carrot, was good to eat, and so was wild parsnip. Poison parsnip, or water hemlock, which looked like wild parsnip, was not. Every part of water hemlock, not just the root, was poisonous to eat. To mistake water hemlock for wild parsnip, or poison sego for sego, meant death.[45]

Blue camas lily was another good plant, but death camas was not. The bulbs and leaves looked alike, and the two plants often grew side by side. The only sure way to know the difference was to harvest the bulbs of blue camas in summer, with the flowers in full, vivid bloom. Death camas that grew in the foothills had lacy, cream-white flowers, and the flowers and leaves were as deadly to eat as the bulbs. If grazing animals or people ate death camas, they did not live long.[46]

Most of the dangerous wild plants that grew in the desert and foothills were entirely unknown to the newcomers. Unnamed and barely noticed, they grew among the throng of other nameless native wild plants that seemed to have no use. Water hemlock did grow by marshes in some of the eastern places where the settlers had once lived, but they scarcely noticed it. They did not commonly eat wild roots, only wild berries. They grew carrots, parsnips, potatoes, and other root vegetables in their gardens. The lack of such "garden sauce," as they fondly called that produce, and the lack of wheat for bread—as well as the painful press of hunger—had driven them to harvest and eat native wild plants.[47]

Such were the dangers that the anxious settler-colonists found in the wild land around them. But to Sally, and to the People, the native plants were deeply familiar, with names and recognized qualities. Like good friends, they were profoundly known. Many were useful, and some essential. The People used them for food or medicine, or for making clothing or shelter or tools. They saw that the animals they hunted for food ate some of the same plants, from berries to pine nuts. The animals also ate others that humans did not eat, such as *te-ĕd-kav*, honeysuckle. Deer and elk liked that plant. Even such plants, which the People did not eat, helped to sustain them. Most were good in some way. Only poison sego and a few others were best avoided by everyone.[48]

When the settlers first arrived, they termed most of the native plants *weeds*. Honeysuckle was a weed. Sagebrush, or wild sage as they called it, was a weed. But some of the settler-colonists also watched hungrily to see which of the other wild plants might be edible. They noticed native women, members of Chief Wanship's and Chief Goship's bands, digging up wild roots and bulbs to eat or store for winter—some of the same wild foods they had given as gifts soon after the newcomers arrived in their valley.

Eliza always remembered that they first learned about "the wild 'Sego-root'" from Indians, who showed them how to use the plant. The settler-colonists peeled and boiled the small, smooth white bulbs as if they were potatoes. The sticky result was filling, even if a potato from the garden tasted much better to them. They learned about thistle roots as well. Thistles, gone brown in fall, and bereft of their bristling flowers, were easy to identify. One man dug up two bushels of the nourishing, starchy roots. Along with a small portion of beef, the roots sustained him until winter. But he and the other settler-colonists soon learned that eating some native wild plants brought risk because they might mistake one kind for another.[49]

When a young man who was just twenty-three died suddenly one winter day, Eliza heard people say that he had eaten "poisonous vegetables."

A midwife and healer who was one of Eliza's good friends heard that he "ate some roots," and "it is supposed he was poisoned with the roots." Everyone heard about his death. They knew at once that he was an innocent, unsuspecting victim of the dangerous wild world.

Franklin, the young settler, was not the only one to fall sick on that day. Lorenzo heard first that another man had been poisoned by eating native wild roots. He and Harriet learned about his condition when a neighbor's child came to the door of a friend's house, where they were visiting, to ask for medicine. It seemed to help him, or perhaps he had taken only a small bite of a deadly root. But an hour later they heard about Franklin, who had collapsed on the ground "in a fit" on his way back from a hunting excursion.

They rushed to his side. He managed to speak twice, Lorenzo said, before they carried him to a house where they did what they could for him. They could not stop the violent seizures, the grotesque agony that gripped him and would not let go. They watched over Franklin helplessly until he died thirty minutes later, consumed by poison and writhing pain. "We came home," Lorenzo reported, adding that Harriet "was sick all night."[50]

The next day the settlers held a funeral and buried Franklin. About a week later, Eliza finished composing a poem in his memory. It spoke of the goodness of his short life, and said nothing about the frontier where he died. That place remained alien and dangerous to the settler-colonists. Only by eliminating what was native and wild, they thought, and replacing it with the imported and tame, could they re-create their familiar, safer way of life in this new land.[51]

Eliza copied the finished poem in her journal. If she had read the poem aloud, Sally would not have understood what Eliza wrote about the angel of death. She had never heard of angels, but she did know that a poisonous plant could kill. She knew that everyone would die, one way or another, because of an ancient decree by Wolf. No one could live forever. She also knew that the deaths of friends or kinsmen were never good, even if they did reach the realm of the dead, Na-gun'-tu-wīp, a place of tall mountains and fertile valleys. Everything the People held dear was associated with this life in their cherished homeland where Wolf had long ago created human beings.[52]

Since Sally lived in the same room as Eliza, she sometimes saw her putting marks on paper. Eliza made those marks almost every day, but it was not clear at first why she did that. Even some of the settlers' children learned to make the marks.

Months passed before Franklin's family in faraway Massachusetts finally learned that their son had died from eating wild roots while hunting. It seemed that he had mistaken water hemlock for edible wild parsnip. Except for subtle differences in the leaf, it was hard to tell the plants apart, especially in winter. Worse, water hemlock smelled something like parsnip, and the root had a deceptively sweet odor. Only the inside of the root looked entirely different—but even to touch it while slicing it open held danger. The strange interior chambers, and the sickly yellowish fluid that the cut flesh of the root exuded, betrayed its true identity, but only to those who already knew about the plant.[53]

More heartbreak followed when it seemed that wild nature had once again viciously attacked an innocent victim. A small, hungry child, too young to know about poison parsnips, ate the native wild root and died. He was just two years old. Reports of other such cases led to warnings about eating wild plants, but such deaths continued for years. Still, far more children died from familiar diseases brought from settled places by overland travelers.[54]

However strange her life inside the fort seemed during that first winter, the land outside offered glimmers from her earlier life. Snow covered the mountain crests and blanketed the flanks. In the valley, winter wore dull brown and gleaming white. Horizons vanished in snowfall, pale pearl sky falling into pearly snowscape—that too a scene she knew from Sho-av-ich, her home. Perhaps when the snow left she could escape from the fort, and find her way home. The mountains would guide her.[55]

Just three months after Franklin died, wild nature launched a new attack on the settler-colonists—or so it seemed to them. Killing frost struck long after the early spring planting. With a limited supply of seeds and a dwindling supply of stored food in hand, they had been forced to guess at the contours of the growing season in this untested land. Warm days and strong sunlight in late winter seemed a good omen. Weeks before the spring equinox Lorenzo had sown spring wheat, oats, and beans, and then potatoes, peas, and a half-acre of corn.

Two months later, Harriet appraised the prospects for a good crop, despite spells of unexpected cold. "We have had cool nights with occasional frosts," she said in mid-May, "but we still keep up good courage, hoping for the best." Their provisions were running low by then. With

Franklin's ghastly death still fresh in memory, wild roots held no appeal as food. Along with other settlers, they ate nourishing native fare reluctantly, although wild thistles and wild greens were reliably safe. They waited for the garden plants to ripen.[56]

A week or so later Harriet reported that she and Lorenzo had saved most of the young plants from freezing by covering them. They had not expected any other trouble, she continued, "but today to our utter astonishment, the crickets came by millions, sweeping everything before them." Large native crickets devoured a patch of beans in twenty minutes, then ate the pea plants, and finally finished everything in the garden. "We went out with brush," Harriet said, "and undertook to drive them, but they were too strong for us."

The next day, she and Lorenzo saw crickets eating the field of corn. A day later she wrote, "Today they have destroyed 3/4 of an acre of squashes, our flax, two acres of millet and our rye, and are now to work in our wheat. What will be the result we know not." Another settler lost twelve acres, she added, and still another, seven.[57]

The settler-colonists watched in disbelief as invading armies of the insects devoured new crops in some of the fields and gardens, and nearly spared others. Fences could keep large animals out of the fields. Almost nothing could stop wave after dark wave of crickets from marching across the land, and eating—except igniting dry grass.[58]

Fire could not burn across the six thousand acres of soil that the men had already stripped of wild grass and other native foliage. Only lines of tender green plants stood in the new fields and gardens. Some were vegetables, while others—wheat, corn, millet, and rye—were grasses. Grasses were not the preferred fare of crickets. But sagebrush, one of their staple foods, had been rooted out to make way for the crops. Balsamroot, caviar to the cricket palate, had also vanished under the hoe and the plow, along with other tasty forbs such as wild onion.[59]

A week later, gulls suddenly appeared in the sky and swooped down on ravaged fields to feed on crickets. Lorenzo's young son John watched as they flew overhead and descended, a great cloud that blocked the sun. Many years later he recalled that these "gentle visitors," as he called them, devoured crickets day after day, slowly thinning the ranks. "They were very tame," he said, meaning that they did not flee at the sight of people, and also that the hungry gulls proved useful to the settler-colonists at that moment. The surviving crickets kept eating, but remnants of the crops remained. In mid-July one man confirmed that some fields of wheat had already been harvested, yielding a better crop than expected. But other settlers lost all of their crops, or most.[60]

A few gave up. They left the valley, heading for the trail that would take them east. Others replanted their damaged fields and gardens a full four months after Lorenzo had first sown spring wheat. By late July, as cucumbers and squash and green corn ripened, one woman recorded that she needed "to watch the garden." Native wild fare such as greens and thistle roots did not satisfy the many hungry people at the fort, and she guarded her plants closely. By mid-August, she and some of the other settlers had harvested enough produce to hold "a rich feast," as one man called it. They shared a meal of beef, bread and butter and cheese, corn, melons, vegetables, cakes, and pastries. Sally saw that, like her people, they sang and danced at their feast.[61]

Unlike the strangers, Sally saw nothing menacing about the crickets, or surprising when birds ate them. The People did not fear and despise crickets. No, when the crickets came to the big valley Sally saw bounty, which the settlers could have harvested alongside the gulls.[62]

The People shared this liking of crickets with birds and trout and coyotes and other animals. They had that in common; they all ate crickets. Crowds of trout in creeks gulped them in a frenzy of feeding. Coyotes pounced and swallowed. Prairie dogs fed. Many birds relished crickets. Blackbirds, *pa-gān'-skōp*, and sparrow hawks, *kwi-nau'-ants*, and red-shafted flickers, *un-ka'-kwo-nau-ants*, feasted on crickets. So did crows and magpies and burrowing owls and many other birds—along with gulls. Sally could have shown Clara and Eliza and Harriet how to grind roasted crickets, and how to make dried cakes to store for winter. Those were a favored food of the People.[63]

But the settler-colonists had no intention of eating crickets, even if they were not poisonous, even if deep hunger loomed in winter. They refused to eat insects. To their way of thinking, they had nothing in common with wild birds that ate insects, although some of those birds also liked to eat the grains that they grew for food. It was best to kill them along with other native wildlife that attacked their crops and livestock. It seemed to the settler-colonists that most insects, except their honeybees, were useless at best, destructive vermin at worst.[64]

They already knew that their Shoshone-speaking neighbors in the big valley as well as the Utahs ate crickets. Within a week of arriving in the valley, when large parties of native men and women had come to visit and trade, the settlers had noticed that the visitors carried bags of dried crickets, their food. One man noted that the crickets "appear to be crisped over the fire which is all the cooking required." Soon some of Chief Goship's or Chief Wanship's people had brought gifts of dried crickets and berries to the settlers' camp. They did not realize that their new guests in the valley regarded only the berries as food. To the settlers, eating native crickets was simply evidence of savagery and depravity—certainly not a practice worth adopting. How, and where, their visitors gathered the crickets had passed notice at the time.[65]

They did not pay much attention to crickets until they first attacked the small shoots in their fields and gardens. Those green shoots came from precious seeds and tubers of domesticated plants, which they had imported to this place, carrying them across a thousand miles of wild plains and mountains. Then they had planted the seeds and tubers in new fields and garden plots, wild land cleared of shrubs and plowed with backbreaking labor. But even after the wild gulls did what Harriet and Lorenzo and the others had not managed to do, ridding their fields of voracious insects, the settler-colonists did not revise their view of wild nature. Most of the valley's native wildlife remained an enemy.

The Bible's story of creation, recorded by an ancient, civilized people, told them that they had dominion over the wild: "And God blessed them, and God said unto them, Be fruitful and multiply, and replenish the earth, and subdue it: and have dominion over the fish of the sea, and the fowl of the air, and every living thing that moveth upon the earth." The meaning was clear. The colonizing settlers were to subdue, to conquer and control, the wild land.[66]

Plowing the soil had already helped to eliminate large stands of native plants, so-called weeds. The men rooted out sagebrush and rabbitbrush, snakeweed and greasewood, and other wild plants that seemed useless or, worse, noxious. Plowing also drove away snakes and burrowing owls from their nesting sites and homes. Hunting would kill out many more wild animals that they regarded as vermin. The number of native game animals favored as food had already plummeted as the number of colonizing settlers grew. By the first winter of settlement, deer and other game animals were "very scarce in the country," an explorer remarked. Some of the men had intruded into the Valley of the Utahs, to take fish from their lake.[67]

During the settler-colonists' first winter in the valley, and Sally's, they set traps, put out poison, and shot wolves and other wild predators. During the second winter, they held a competitive hunt like those once held in eastern places. Unlike the People's communal hunts, when men and women and children worked together to get food, the settlers formed two teams of men for their hunt to kill out pests. In a few short months, the eighty-four hunters killed 1,299 wolves and coyotes; 647 foxes; fifty-one weasels; two wolverines, two bears, and two wildcats; thirteen eagles; 403 magpies, hawks, and owls; and 1,465 ravens. The men collected animal "scalps" as proof of killing some 3,900 wild animals. And they collected quills from the wings and tails of the dead raptors, highly useful for clerks who kept careful records.[68]

Chief Wanship and his people routinely hunted some of these animals because they ate them, but their new neighbors' communal hunt left their valley larder nearly empty. Many of the hunted animals had often fed on crickets, which swarmed in force again after the hunt—and again, and again. The settler-colonists did not notice which animals, besides gulls, ate crickets. They just wanted to rid the valley of whatever held no use for them, or worse, imperiled their plants and animals. Only then could they cultivate orchards of useful domesticated trees, plant fields of wheat and other grains, and safely raise livestock. Only then would the desert "blossom as the rose," they often said, quoting scripture.

They did not mean the wild rose. They meant the cultivated rose, which they soon imported for their flower gardens.[69]

Sally knew about wild rose, *tsam'-piv*, which liked to grow near creeks in canyons and valleys. That good plant gave food and medicine. She knew nothing about wheat, one of the grasses with big seeds that the settlers planted in straight lines. But she did know how to get nourishing small seeds from native grasses that did not need much water, or protective fences, and that lived in the desert and the foothills.[70]

She also knew how to grind the roasted seeds by hand, using a *mar*, a flat stone mortar, and a *mo'-a*, a small grinding stone. She could easily learn how to sift cornmeal through fine cloth, as the new settlers did, separating flour from bran. That too was a familiar task. Her mother and the other women had made winnowing baskets, and used them, patiently and skillfully, to separate small seeds from chaff.[71]

But the settler-colonists showed no interest in gathering native grass seeds or grinding seeds by hand. They let their cattle and sheep and horses eat all of the native grasses, even those with the best seeds. They let them graze on balsamroot, sego lily, and other edible food plants as well. The settlers only liked the seeds of wheat, buckwheat, rye, and corn that they had brought with them from a foreign place.[72]

No one showed interest in what Sally knew about native wild plants and animals. Despite so much record keeping, such knowledge went unrecorded. It seemed useless and best forgotten. The sooner she gave up her wild and savage ways and became civilized, the better, they thought.

When Sally first began to live with Clara and Eliza, and the time came for her to sit apart and rest, she had no place to go. There was no *wap*, native juniper, nearby, and very few willows. She needed branches and brush to make a small shelter. She needed soft juniper bark to staunch the blood, and a buckskin string belt to hold the pads of bark in place.

She saw that Clara and Eliza and the other women at the fort did not sit apart, either alone or in company with other women. They did not make brush shelters, and rest inside for a few days and nights each month— and perhaps receive a suitor, for a flirtation or something more. They did not use soft bark. They used pieces of cloth, called *rags*, which had to be washed and used again. And they kept working.[73]

Clara liked to read, and to think her own thoughts. But she also had a deeply practical side, and the usual liking for her own way of life. She valued the comforts: the sturdy houses, soft featherbeds, sweet desserts, and books. If Sally was going to live among the settlers, Clara needed to teach her how to live a civilized life. She needed to show her how to earn her bread by the sweat of her brow. "Clara taught her to work," said a woman who lived at the fort, not understanding that Sally already knew how to work. Clara showed Sally how to do tasks that settler-colonists, including Clara, found useful. She demonstrated how to sweep, how to launder clothing, how to wash cooking pots and pans.[74]

She patiently instructed Sally with words and with example, although Sally remained aloof, and showed no interest in working. Clara's method was the steady drip, drip, drip of cheerful kindness—never threats or force, not even the warning looks that Eliza favored. And she fed her. Food remained limited the first winter and spring. But Clara, unlike Eliza, had a store of provisions, food to share. Eliza cooked now and then, but she often took her meals with friends. She recorded details of two exceptional meals. At a dinner, the guests "feasted on 2 roasted geese." At a supper,

Eliza ate biscuits with "butter, tea, dried beef, peach-sauce, sweeten'd fried cakes & custard pie."[75]

One of the other women at the fort—one of those with the name Mary—long remembered the monotony of the daily diet as well as the short rations. But everyone had enough, or nearly so. Mary recalled making cambric tea with water and some milk. That drink, she said, "was found to be one of the best remedies for hunger—taken hot, and with a little spice or aromatic herbs to flavor it." Tea and coffee had soon run short, and remained scarce, along with sugar and flour.[76]

Over time, Sally's visible wounds—the burns, the cuts—healed. The stabbing grief did not subside. She wanted to go home. She wanted to return to the high valley, Sho-av-ich, a place of tall cottonwood trees, *sho-av*. A river that ran down from mountains known as Tu-sha'-kaivw flowed through a steep canyon and into the valley. Many creeks fed the river, and beavers had long flourished with this wealth of water and cottonwood trees. Her family and her people cherished their homeland, where men hunted and women found good seeds and roots.

She did not like Clara's food, especially the fried beef. Still, she ate enough each day to lose her famished, gaunt look. Her body slowly filled out, and her thick hair grew long. She wore only cloth garments. She learned more and more of Clara and Eliza's words, and after a time began to speak to them, haltingly.[77]

To stay in one place—not to move with the seasons to other known places, and then back again—seemed at first a strange way to live. It was good to leave a place when no more game animals or other food could be found there, and to return later, to see it renewed by rest. But weeks and months and then whole seasons passed, and still Sally stayed at the fort, and ate Clara's food, and slept in her room. She tolerated Clara's tiresome teaching and Eliza's sharp glances. She wanted to leave but she needed to stay, at least for a time.

She did not have to stay with Clara in order to eat. She knew how to get roots and berries and ground squirrels for food if she left the fort in summer—but there was no safe route home. It had not taken her long to grasp the lay of the land called Tav'-o-kun. She understood that walking south through Place of Sun meant passing through part of the Kumumpa homeland. Chief Wanship and Chief Goship and their people were the settler-colonists' loyal allies. They could capture her and return her to the fort. Even if she eluded them, and the thousands of strangers who had come to live in the valley, she could not go directly south, to the valley with the big freshwater lake. The captor who had sold her, the much-feared Utah warrior named Baptiste, frequented that valley and lands beyond.[78]

Heading toward the rising sun, finding a way through the wall of mountains, would take her into unknown land. Skirting the mountains and walking north would lead to other lands and people she did not know. Walking west, toward the setting sun and broken lines of mountains, and then turning south and east, would take her home. But that meant crossing open desert, with little cover. People who spoke the language of Chief Wanship's tribe lived there. She would meet unknown men, alone. They could capture her to sell to other strangers for a rifle. They could mistreat her. Or they could hand her over to Baptiste. He might sell her for a better price the second time, now that she knew some of the settlers' words and something about their ways.

And if she did find her way home safely, she would surely see the man who sold her first. He too could sell her again. Only when she learned more of the new words would she know how to explain this to Clara and Eliza. Only then could she tell them about her family, and speak about the man who had betrayed her.

In the meantime, she remained with the two strangers who grew more familiar as each day passed. The one with black hair was old enough to be her *pi'-ats*, mother. The other, who gave her food, seemed to be the age of a *pats*, an elder sister. They offered nourishment and shelter. Each day she chose again to stay with them, not to run away. She had nowhere safe to go.[79]

CHAPTER 3

Forts

A MONTH OR SO after the crickets swarmed and the gulls feasted, Charley, Lorenzo, and Lorenzo's young son John went to meet colonizing settlers who were on the way to the big valley. They were expecting Lorenzo's older brother, and Charley and Clara's sister, Lucy, the eldest of Harriet's daughters. The men took extra teams of oxen and some cattle. Harriet decided to go with them on the trip, and Lorenzo drove the wagon while she rested as best she could. Charley and John herded the loose cattle. Clara and Sally remained at the fort.

This was seven months after John had first seen the captive girl, and five months after Lorenzo and Harriet's infant son suddenly died. Harriet's health, never good, had declined after the loss of her little son. Then came the loss of their crops to crickets, a leveling blow inflicted by wild nature as the settler-colonists saw it. Despite the rigors of a long trip by wagon, Lorenzo and Harriet thought that the cool, fresh air in the mountains might help her—and it did.[1]

They reached Fort Bridger and stayed for two weeks, waiting. The Shoshones at Fort Bridger were friendly, and enjoying some favorite sports. "Every day," John later recalled, "I watched Indians run horse races and gamble." One day Jim Bridger gave him some money to bet, and he won. If Jim had counted on John learning a life lesson by losing the money, he was disappointed. Instead of offering congratulations, he advised him never to gamble again, saying, "I have noticed that gamblers nearly all die with their boots on, and you are too fine a boy to die that way."[2]

To Shoshones at Fort Bridger that summer, who did not wear boots, gambling and horse racing were established customs—not a vice or a mark of idleness or a waste of time. The men had good reasons to hone their skills as horsemen and risk takers. Hunter-gatherers, unlike farmer-settlers, did not make a living by staying in one place. They did not engage in a daily, monotonous fight with wild nature, the ceaseless effort to bend it to human will, to transform and control it. To hunters, the land was useful largely as it was. The risks came with hunting, and with defending their hunting grounds from armed and mounted intruders—including hungry overland travelers on the way west to colonize new lands. The travelers depleted their land of wild game.

Life seemed good that summer, at least for a time at Fort Bridger. That was about to change, and quickly, especially for Utahs who held fine hunting and gathering grounds to the south. The change would have nothing to do with the risks of racing and gambling, and everything to do with the flood of colonizing settlers arriving from eastern places. When Harriet and Lorenzo left Fort Bridger to return to the big valley, so did more than two thousand new settlers.[3]

Despite the size of the valley—more than five hundred square miles—some of the earlier settlers had already gone thirty miles north to colonize new land for grazing. That part of Shoshone country had been first settled by a young trapper, turned trader, and his Utah wife and two young children. He sold the trading-post fort to the newly arrived settlers, and left for California.[4]

Sally saw the crowd of new settlers arrive at the fort just nine months after she entered it as a captive. The newcomers had traveled in long wagon trains, bringing thousands more livestock to the high desert valley. There were far more of the imported animals than people. Like the people, most of them had walked for a thousand miles.[5]

Some of the livestock died from overwork before they reached the valley and the fort. They were killed by the wasting fatigue of pulling heavy wagons mile after mile, day after day for their masters. Teams of tame oxen toiled on through heavy, pressing heat—June, July, August—beneath a blaze of sun that burned a broad path across the sky. An ox stumbled, and fell down dead on the trail, and then another animal took that place. Sometimes tired milk cows were forced to pull.

Other animals died from mishaps. Wolves killed a few, including one woman's favorite ewe, a pet. The sight of the bloody ruin moved her first to tears, then to anger. "I feel like waging a war of extermination against those ferocious beasts of prey," she swore. But then she felt remorse for her poor sheep's painful death, "occasioned by neglect or carelessness," she confessed.

Later, when settler-colonists told stories of their journeys west, they often spoke of suffering in the wilderness, and of battles with the wild. Few spoke about how their livestock suffered daily under the yoke, but many did recall that wild and hungry wolves sometimes came near in the night. One man recorded in his journal that "the wolves struck up a most doleful melancholy howling," and that "they are found here in greater numbers than they have been." He feared for the cattle, so weakened by the journey. A kindly woman remarked that "the only pay they have for their hardest labor" was water, but even that had grown scarce along the trail.[6]

The travelers worried not only about wolves devouring their animals but also attacking men. The woman whose pet ewe died feared for her husband's safety a few days later when he passed through a place said to be beset with bears and wolves. He saw none, and soon returned to camp. The settler-colonists dreaded the native, the wild wolves and Indians, far more than the familiar and lethal diseases of civilization, such as measles and cholera. Those diseases proved the true killers on the trail, and later—but when settlers told stories of their hardships, they said less about deadly sickness than wild threats and terrors.[7]

When the new settler-colonists, who happened to be carrying measles with them, at last reached the big fort, Sally saw that more horses, mules, oxen, cows, sheep, goats, pigs, and dogs had trudged along with them to the valley. She saw more cats, as well as chickens, turkeys, pigeons, geese, and doves. The strangers had brought their honeybees as well. They carried the non-native bees in small shelters that they called *hives*. Many bees lived together in a shelter—just as these strangers did.[8]

And just like those who had earlier reached the valley, these newcomers sat down and stayed. They belonged to the same large tribe, and had decided to gather in this place. It seemed that this prosperous tribe numbered in the thousands, and that all of them were Clara and Eliza's relatives.[9]

Sally heard Clara and Eliza call others by names that used the words *Brother* and *Sister*. Many people called Eliza by the name Sister Snow. Eliza reported happily one day that another sister had prepared and shared a lavish supper with her. Such sharing came as no surprise to Sally. The

People thought that sisters and brothers should share food. It was especially good to share food with relatives in times of need. When Clara gave
Sally the same food that she ate, she acted like an elder sister.[10]

Since Harriet was the *pi'-ats*, mother, of Clara and Charley, they were
clearly sister and brother. Other men called Brother, who were not Harriet's sons, must be Clara's cousins. Sally could understand this because the
People called cousins by the same terms that they used for brothers and
sisters. But when they encountered others who were not known relatives
yet spoke their language and followed the same ways, they used a term
that meant *we are far away relatives*. They were all related in one way or
another.[11]

Clara had not seen her older sister for more than a year when Lucy arrived
with the large wagon train. The leader of the colonizing settlers—Clara's
husband, who was Lorenzo's older brother—returned at the same time.
He had been absent for more than a year.[12]

Sally heard Clara's people call him by an odd name, *Brother Brigham*,
which belonged only to him. The words were very hard to say because the
People did not have some of those sounds. It was easier just to avoid saying
the words—not that she would address him by that name. He was *ni-av'*,
the chief of Clara's tribe. Many of those people called him the Leader.[13]

Anyone who saw Clara and Lucy together could tell at once that they
were sisters. They had the same short, slight build, the same dark eyes
and dark hair and small, even features. Now Sally saw that they shared
something else as well. Clara's husband was also Lucy's.[14]

Sally had no way to know that the practice of sharing a husband,
or having multiple wives, had provoked conflict in the former home of
Clara's people. It had not abated even when their leader, her husband,
took his followers west to colonize northern Mexican territory. For a man
to claim more than one woman at a time as a wife was seen as immoral
and criminal, as a form of adultery or unlawful cohabitation or bigamy—
or worse, polygamy. Most Americans and Europeans viewed polygamy as a
depraved practice of savages, or of once-civilized people who degenerated
and fell into barbarism. It recalled the notorious Kingdom of Münster,
where radical Anabaptists with millenarian beliefs had practiced polygamy—not that Sally had ever heard of the German city of Münster or
Anabaptists or Europe.[15]

There was something else as bad, or even more depraved, than polygamy to most Americans and Europeans. That was for a man to have sexual

relations with sisters. At worst it qualified as incest. At the least it was seen as a grievous breach of decency. Eastern newspapers rarely reported anything about the Leader and his followers without also condemning the practice of polygamy.[16]

Sally knew nothing about newspaper stories or conflict over polygamy. It did not surprise her to see that Clara and Lucy had the same husband. No one needed to explain this to her. Among the People, some men, especially chiefs, had more than one wife, and they too were often sisters. The old people said that a man and woman who were brother and sister to each other should not act like husband and wife. To do so would be incestuous. But for a man to marry sisters who were not his own sisters was good, and had nothing to do with incest.[17]

Other men besides the Leader, Clara and Lucy's husband, had more than one wife. Some of those men were members of the Leader's council. As Sally knew, a chief always had a council of advisers. In these few ways the strangers' tribe seemed familiar.[18]

Five months after the Leader returned to the fort, Barney and two other men left in mid-winter on an expedition south to trade with Utahs—"the wildest of wild Indians," as one of the men put it. They took tobacco, gunpowder, and other wares of civilization to offer in exchange for horses and for goods from the wild, especially furs and tanned skins. Barney went along to serve as interpreter. His wife and the children stayed at home. Adelaide, at the age of ten, had begun attending a school at the fort.[19]

Soon after that trip, Barney joined an expedition of the colonists' militia, again serving as an interpreter. He went south this time to punish Utahs who had captured some horses. Sally had lived at the fort for more than a year by then, and she had no reason to regret the purpose of the expedition. She knew that many of the Utahs who lived in that valley, the Timpanogos, were allies of her captor, and allies of Chief Wákara who captured horses as well as children.

Some of the settler-colonists said that Timpanogos men had taken horses belonging to the Leader, but that the missing horses had returned to the herd a few days later. Others said that they had taken cattle or sheep. The stories varied. Still, many people believed that the Utahs were guilty of theft, whether or not they agreed about exactly what had been taken, or understood why.[20]

The Utahs told different stories. They told about capturing, not stealing, horses, or about hunting cattle for food to compensate for the loss of game animals. To capture horses from an enemy was an old tradition. It always brought prestige—as well as valued horses.

Chief Wákara was famous for capturing horses on raids in California. His people took pride in their prowess, and later often told the story of a successful raid by acting it out, performing for onlookers. Just months earlier, the chief had taken hundreds of horses to the big fort and sold them for good profit. The buyers did not object to paying for such horses brought from faraway places, but they did object to losing their own.[21]

When the militia reached the valley to search for culprits who had taken livestock, they sought out a Timpanogos leader named Little Chief. He told them where to find the alleged thieves. One of those men, known to some of the settler-colonists as Blue-shirt, "always appeared very hostile," said a young man who had earlier met him. He recalled the sharply carved features of Blue-shirt's face, and his unflinching manner. He had tried to intimidate Blue-shirt by reaching suddenly for his gun. "I had no sooner got mine than he had his, and cocked ready to shoot," he said. The young man left, unharmed and, as he later conceded, probably the more frightened of the two.[22]

Little Chief could not have foreseen the result of his words to the militia. A year earlier, men from the fort had gone to the Valley of the Utahs to complain about the loss of some cattle and a horse. An unnamed chief—Little Chief or another man—had listened to their complaint. Then the chief punished some of his men, the supposed culprits, "and they all promised to do better." The episode had ended there.[23]

If Little Chief expected the same outcome again, he was disappointed. The militia, numbering thirty armed men, located the small camp of three lodges near a creek that the Timpanogos called Pa´-sa-so´-its. They launched an attack at daybreak. Within hours, Blue-shirt and three other Utah men, who had defended the camp with bows and arrows and just one gun, were dead. "They fought with the most determined resolution to die rather than yield," a militiaman recorded. He had heard them encouraging each other as they shot back at their attackers. Thirteen of their women and children survived the gunfire by hiding near the banks of the creek in icy water.

"The morning was clear and calm as God ever made," another militiaman said of the aftermath, a cruel contrast to the bloody scene. Blue-shirt's body was torn by eighteen bullets. When Little Chief reached the site, he cried out, anguished at the deaths of the four men. "He blamed himself," the militiaman recalled, offering no comment to the contrary.

But Little Chief also cursed the settler-colonists and warned them to stay away.[24]

More woe for him and the other Utahs followed. A colony of the intruders soon arrived in the valley, and built a sturdy settlement fort near the river and the freshwater lake. The new settlers had admired the land and lake since first reaching the big valley, when a small exploring party had gone south. One of the men, standing on a rise, glimpsed water shining in the distance, a beacon of wild plenty in a fertile land. They reported to the Leader, who recalled Bridger's warning about intruding into the Utahs' valley—and also his enticing words. Surveying the large number of armed men in the wagon train, Bridger said that they could easily drive out or enslave the Utahs. Four months after arriving in the big valley, a party of settler-colonists had made a swift foray to take fish from the Utahs' freshwater lake, which stretched twenty-five miles in length. Their reconnaissance included prized land near the lake. Just a year and a few months later, the Leader sent the militia to the Utahs' valley.[25]

The colonizing settlers named their newest settlement Fort Utah. The Valley of the Utahs, as trappers called it, became Utah Valley. The old name clearly referred to Utahs as a people and to their homeland. The new name made singular what had once been plural and possessive. Settler-colonists now spoke of the valley without making clear reference to the longtime inhabitants. They had already begun to call Utahs by a shorthand name, Utes, which trappers sometimes used. They had heard Jim Bridger and then Barney speak of the Utahs as Utes. As that usage spread, it too began to obscure the link between a people and a namesake place.[26]

The colonists who claimed and occupied the Valley of the Utahs again rewrote a landscape, replacing many of the native names with English names. They called Pa´-sa-so´-its, where Blue-shirt died, Battle Creek at first, and then Pleasant Grove. The later name helped eliminate their memory of a violent conquest, but the Utahs did not forget. Tum-pai´-uv became Springville. Maps bristled with the new English names.[27]

Some of the Timpanogos stayed in their valley home after the new fort was built, despite more episodes of killing violence. Other Utahs remained in wild country south of the valley, even after settlers arrived to colonize those lands. The settlers built houses and planted crops near a creek that they called Salt Creek. One of the Utah men had a Shoshone wife known to the newcomers as Peggy, and she soon found work with them. An Englishwoman named Mary—the same Mary who recommended drinking cambric tea to ease hunger—hired her to do the laundry for her growing family. Peggy did the work to get food for her family. Native wild seeds and roots had grown scarcer, along with wild game, as more and more settler-colonists arrived.[28]

Peggy was hardworking and friendly, but her Utah husband made the settler-colonists wary. Baptiste seemed fearless, and his shows of courage alarmed them. Some people, including the Leader, said that he was the man who traded the captive girl to Charley. Sally knew that Baptiste still trafficked in slaves, and that he sometimes came north to Tav'-o-kun. At least she lived there in the midst of the strangers and, better, with the Leader's family. That gave some safety—as long as she stayed near Clara and the others.[29]

She also knew that Clara's husband had dealings with Baptiste. Once, he gave Baptiste a letter that he had just dictated to take to the colonists at Fort Utah. The Leader's letter instructed them to gather up their possessions and to leave the fort and their fields. He also told them to buy and bring with them any children offered for sale—presumably by Baptiste as well as his ally Chief Wákara and others.

Conditions remained dangerous in the Valley of the Utahs. Months earlier, the militia had launched another attack on the Timpanogos. The attack left many Timpanogos warriors dead, and afterwards the militia took dozens of the women and children north to the big valley. The survivors, brought to the city, spoke a dialect that Sally understood. She longed to see her mother and sisters, but she had not left with the women who soon fled from Tav'-o-kun. Baptiste had allies in the Valley of the Utahs, the place that those fugitive women called home.[30]

The settler-colonists regarded Baptiste as one of the most notorious traffickers of captive children. They called him cruel, and told stories about how he and Chief Wákara killed any captives who remained unsold. They always said that Charley's offer of a rifle had saved Sally from a brutal death at the hands of savages. Sally heard that again and again.[31]

She and Peggy were learning to do useful work, the settlers thought. The children that they purchased could also learn to help with the hard labor of colonizing and taming the land. Teaching the little captives of Baptiste and others was part of the civilizing effort. The children would grow up, and make good laborers—unless they left, or died. Some of the Utah women and children taken north to the big valley by the militia after an attack had soon run away but others had died, "not being able to stand our way of living," a militia commander later said. Sally, who had not yet run away, or died, was slowly, and still unhappily, learning the new way of life.[32]

The settler-colonists often said that as a matter of duty they taught wild Indians how to do civilized labor. Taking Indian children into their homes, in order to teach them to work on farms and in houses, qualified as a well-known practice in some of the eastern places where they had once lived. It helped them to get work done.[33]

A few years after Sally arrived at the fort, one of the leading men explained the practice this way. They had the duty, he told his fellow settler-colonists, to bring native children into their homes and "to teach them to till the earth, and earn their bread by the sweat of their brows." These children, he said, should also be instructed in "the principles of civilization," with the aim of eliminating their native ways. "I have a little Indian boy and girl," he continued, "and certainly it is repugnant to my feelings to have to put up with their dirty practices. . . . In a short season we shall be rewarded for all that we do to civilize this lost and fallen race." The little boy, he added, still had "some of his Indian traits, and I presume it will be some time before they are all erased from his memory."[34]

Sally, unlike that little boy, was too old ever to forget her family and the People and her homeland. She recalled other times and places, and with a bitter sense of loss. Clara and Eliza would have to convert her to their way of life, show her the error of her former ways. They would have to teach her the better way to live, their way, and tell her their stories to explain the past, and the present. That would take time. She did not yet seem to understand that she had been saved from savagery, as they saw it, lifted up and given the blessings of civilization. But Sally did not want to do Clara and Eliza's work. She did not want to be *pai-yu'-go-tsits*, a slave, or live with strangers at the fort. To them, she still seemed moody, sulky, and reluctant to work. She resisted.[35]

Eliza and Clara, undeterred, continued with their civilizing lessons, just as the men continued with their work of taming the land. It took hard labor to transform the waste and the waste places, as the colonizing settlers called wild lands. Those terms came from the Bible. "As I live, verily they that are in the waste places shall fall by the sword," they read. Such words boded ill for native people, Utahs and Shoshones and others, who lived on wild lands.[36]

On a day in June, a few months after a colony of settlers built Fort Utah, Chief Wákara and some of his men met with the Leader. Mountains still shone spring green beneath white crests, but the hot dry season had settled into the big valley. The sun's gathering force had already burned the foothills brown.

Chief Wákara and his council wanted to learn the Leader's intentions about settling on their lands. The chief and twelve of his men met with the Leader and eight of his councilors. Men such as these visitors had brought Sally to this alien place, Tav'-o-kun. Baptiste might be with them. He was Wákara's close ally. An anxious thought, but there was the visible and comforting fact that the chief's people numbered few to the strangers' teeming thousands. The sheer number of Clara's people gave Sally safety from the men on horseback.

A settler-colonist named Dimick served as interpreter when the Leader and Chief Wákara met. Dimick had spent time with Utahs, not always peacefully, in the two years since he arrived in the big valley. Along with Barney, he had gone with the militia as an interpreter on their first raid into the Valley of the Utahs, the attack that killed Blue-shirt and three other men. Just weeks after that first attack, Dimick had moved south with his family and others to build Fort Utah and establish farms. Although he was still learning the Utahs' language, at the meeting he interpreted the visitors' words, and the Leader's, as best he could. It happened that Chief Wákara could speak some English, as well as Spanish. He had also mastered sign language, or "the graceful alphabet of pantomime," as one man put it.[37]

Dimick had learned words and phrases and certain statements in Chief Wákara's language, but the chief knew more of Dimick's and his people's words than they knew of his. So did Sally. She heard English spoken each day, all day, once she began to live with Clara and Eliza. The people at the fort wanted her to learn their language. By that point, Sally could have understood what the chief said as well as what the Leader said, but she had good reason to avoid Chief Wákara, an ally of her captor. As custom dictated, only men took part in the meeting.[38]

The Leader and Chief Wákara spoke about their mutual interests, land and trade. The Leader said that he would send some of his men in the fall to the chief's territory, to see if it might be good for settlement. He asked the chief to send a few of his men to act as guides for the trip. "We are a poor people now, but in a few years we shall be rich," he promised. "We will trade cattle with you." When the meeting ended, he gave the chief and his men a gift of half an ox. Then the usual avid trading began.[39]

In the years after colonizing settlers built Fort Utah, others went to valleys where they built new settlement forts. Some bands of Utes resisted their presence, refusing to give up their best hunting and gathering grounds and

water sources for small gifts and promises. The new colonizers thought
that they needed the protection of high walls. One of their settlement
forts, called Fort Fillmore, stood a hundred miles south of Fort Utah,
on lands that Sally's people had long claimed and occupied as homeland.

Once Sally had learned enough of Clara and Eliza's words, she told
them that she was Pahvant Ute, and that her name, as Eliza heard and
recorded it, was Pidash. Pahvants, who numbered a thousand or more
when colonizing settlers entered their homelands, claimed and occupied
a spacious territory. A range of mountains formed an eastern border, but
their lands also stretched into the high desert west of a saltwater lake
some twenty-five miles long. Pahvant Utes called the lake A-vwa-pa, and
other Utes called it Pa-vwan, Big Water. *Pa* meant water, and *a-vwat*, big.
The Pahvant homeland, where the People lived by hunting, fishing, and
gathering, encompassed thousands of square miles.[40]

Sally and her family and other Pahvants occupied the southernmost
part of the territory, including the valley called Sho-av-ich. But they and
their relatives to the north shared the lake's name. They were known as
Pahvandüts and Pahvantinunts, the Water People or People of the Big
Water. Settlers and travelers heard and spelled their name in a multitude
of ways, from Pauvan and Parvian and Parvain to Pauvante and Pibandy.[41]

The first trappers and traders to reach Sho-av-ich had seen what it
offered, aside from frost and snow. They found pure and plentiful water
in creeks and in the willow-lined river that ran west from the mountains
through the fertile valley to the desert, and north toward A-vwa-pa, the
saltwater lake. Wild ducks and other waterfowl abounded, and beavers
thrived in the creeks and river until too many trappers and traders arrived.
Lush stands of native wild grasses covered much of the valley, food for
horses and other grazing livestock.[42]

Sally was still in the early years of exile from her family and her people
when the Leader and a party of companions crossed that large and level
valley where she had once lived. The Leader and other English-speakers
called it Beaver. He called her people the Pi-Band tribe. One of his companions recorded what they saw in Beaver Valley in spring. "The land is
dark and rich," he wrote, "grass abundant, and the Cedar groves are truly
beautiful." The river abounded in trout. It could also provide a rich supply
of water for thirsty livestock and for irrigating farm fields. "This will make
a good place for a settlement," he summarized.[43]

Three years later, when a French traveler named Jules Rémy passed
through that high valley, Pahvant Utes still occupied it. Colonizing

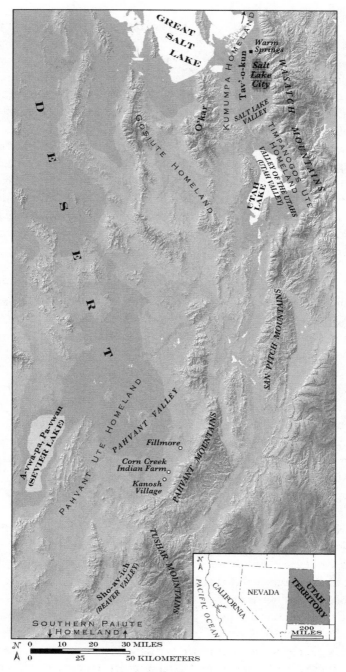

GREAT
SALT
LAKE

D E S E R T

GOSIUTE HOMELAND

O'kar

KUMUMPA HOMELAND
Tav.-o-kun

Warm
Springs

Salt
Lake
City

SALT LAKE
VALLEY

WASATCH MOUNTAINS

TIMPANOGOS UTE
HOMELAND

VALLEY OF THE UTAHS
(UTAH VALLEY)

UTAH
LAKE

SAN PITCH MOUNTAINS

PAHVANT UTE HOMELAND

PAHVANT VALLEY

A-vwa-pa, Pa-vwan
(SEVIER LAKE)

Fillmore

Corn Creek
Indian Farm

Kanosh
Village

PAHVANT MOUNTAINS

TUSHAR MOUNTAINS

Sho-av-ich
(BEAVER VALLEY)

SOUTHERN PAIUTE
HOMELAND

N

PACIFIC OCEAN

CALIFORNIA

NEVADA

UTAH
TERRITORY

200
MILES

N 0   10   20   30 MILES
A 0   25   50 KILOMETERS

Map of Sally's World, 1847–1878. Drawn by Chelsea McRaven Feeney.

settlers had already taken their northern lands, at Fort Fillmore and farther north, and they were about to take the Pahvants' best southern lands.
That included the valley that Sally had left as a captive years earlier.[44]

Winter had not yet set in, at least by the calendar, when Rémy and his
party of travelers passed a night in Beaver Valley. They made camp in a
foot of snow. The next morning they awoke to gripping cold, but the sun
soon shone so brightly in a high blue sky that the snow began to melt.[45]

Around midday, the travelers spotted some women leading a string of
packhorses loaded with heavy carcasses of wild game. The women walked
in bare feet, and wore tanned skins that left parts of their bodies exposed.
They seemed unperturbed by the bracing cold that Rémy and the other
men felt as such hardship. The bright sun gave heat at that altitude.[46]

The men tried to speak with them, but the women kept walking.
"They passed by us," Rémy said, "without condescending either to give
us a look, or reply to our questions and signs." Hunters were nowhere in
sight. "What especially struck us," he added, "was their having no man
with them, from which we inferred that the men belonging to their party
were following at a distance, shooting along the ridges above the valley."
A cover of snow brought prime conditions for hunting. Fresh, clear tracks
in snow led hunters straight to prey.

At least one Pahvant man was watching these intruders when the
women passed by, carrying carcasses that they had retrieved from caches.
Later, he passed close by Rémy and his party. They could see that the
man on horseback, a warrior on patrol, carried two rifles, and that his
face was painted red and black. If he was hunting for something, it was
not solely wild game. Red and black signified war. The travelers did not
try to engage him. They watched him ride by in silence, a dignified and
solitary figure who grew smaller and smaller and finally vanished into a
blank snowscape.[47]

If Sally had evaded capture and remained in the valley, Rémy might
have seen her with the other Pahvant women, walking through the snow
and leading horses. Instead, she had been lost to the People for years. But
she had not vanished completely.

A young chief of the Pahvants, called Kanosh by the settler-colonists,
knew where Sally's captors had taken her and Baptiste had sold her.
He knew that she lived with the Leader's family, and among thousands
of his people, in the valley with the big saltwater lake, the home of the
Kumumpa. By taking the girl two hundred miles north to sell, her captors
had spared themselves hundreds more miles of hard travel in winter to and

from a New Mexican slave market. The girl's presence, by happenstance, in the Leader's family might prove useful to him in some way.

By the time Rémy reached Beaver Valley, settler-colonists who lived nearby had already begun going there to cut whole stands of native wild grass to use as winter feed for livestock. Pahvants who arrived later, planning to graze their horses and to gather grass seeds to eat and to store for winter, found stubble. Blades, not hungry horses, had clearly done the work.[48]

Just months after Rémy's trip, the floodgates opened to colonization of the valley by hundreds of people, on orders from the Leader.

Adelia Hatton arrived at Fort Fillmore a year or so after the palisades and first houses were erected there by colonizing settlers, and shortly before others entered Beaver Valley. She and her husband and children had made a long overland journey from Illinois, and planned only a brief stop there. William had "California fever," as Adelia later put it. Their original route would have taken them by Fort Hall, a trading-post fort hundreds of miles to the north. Barney had helped to build that fort years earlier. Reports of trouble with Indians along the northern trail had led William to shift course at a fork, to take the southern route to California. As it happened, that detour gave Adelia a chance to see her mother and family again. She had not seen them since they left Illinois to go west.[49]

They had recently settled at Fort Fillmore, and Adelia had a joyful reunion with them. But some of the other settler-colonists regarded her husband William with suspicion. He was not a member of their faith, and showed no interest in joining them. He seemed determined to take his wife and children to California.

Just weeks after the Hattons reached the settlement, a newspaper reported William's death there, along with what seemed to be related incidents elsewhere in the territory. The brief article named the suspected killers of William as Pahvant Utes, Sally's people, although her family did not live with the accused band. The fort and nearby fields and pastures stood on Pahvant land. The newspaper report stated:

> About 3 o'clock on the morning of Sept. 13th, William Hatton was killed by Indians, while standing guard at Fillmore. It is supposed that the Pauvans committed this deed, as they have been quite saucy at times, and have stolen much wheat from the fields at that place. Five Indians have been killed at Manti; date not learned.

There has also been some Indian chasing done in south part of Utah valley; dates and particulars not known here.[50]

When Adelia finally recorded the story of William's death years later, some memories remained sharp and painful. On the night of his death, she recalled clearly, he went to bed early. He had to get up at midnight to take his turn standing guard because "all had to stand guard then," Adelia explained, "on account of the Indians being so hostile."

Hours after she went to sleep, she suddenly heard a noise, and someone said, "Hatton is shot by an Indian." Adelia jumped up, dressed quickly, and was about to go outside when some men brought William's body into the kitchen. "They would not let me see him until they had washed, dressed, and laid him out," she remembered. After they had cleaned the body and the wounds thoroughly, they allowed Adelia to see him.

"He had been shot twice in the left breast and in his upper lip," she said. "It looked like he had been hit with an arrow." No one showed her the three arrows said to have wounded William in three places. If he had been hit with something else—bullets from a settler's gun, as others later alleged—the evidence was not visible. The rest of the night had dissolved into a gray blur by the time she recorded her memories. She could not even recall whether they buried her husband immediately or waited a day.[51]

Pahvants were later brought to the fort and questioned about the murder. They examined the spot where William Hatton had stood, and the direction of the shooting, and the course followed by the missile that killed him. That evidence indicated that someone in the fort, not outside the walls, had fired on Hatton. It was an inside job, they concluded, not their work. This went unreported in the newspaper, but the story of the Hatton murder did not die.[52]

Weeks later, Adelia and her parents traveled sixty miles north toward Salt Creek, the site of the closest settlement. Some men stopped their wagon on the road, telling them that Indians had just killed four settlers. The bodies had been laid out at the fort. With her husband's death still fresh in her mind, Adelia did not go to view the bodies "for I did not feel I could stand the sight," she said.

The next morning, eight Pahvants—six men, a young boy, and a woman—appeared at the settlement. Pahvant Utes knew the nearby creek as U-av-kaiv Nu-kwint, not Salt Creek. The party of visitors included Early Dawn, Brave One, Little Summer, Red Shirt, and others. They were known to people who lived at the settlement, and the presence of a woman in their party signaled their friendly intent. But a local leader from another valley ordered his men to shoot all but the woman at once, Adelia said, "without even considering whether they were the guilty ones or not." It was "a sickening sight," she remembered: "They were shot down like so many dogs, picked up with pitchforks, put on a sleigh and hauled away." The settlers took the woman prisoner but she was later released, Adelia recalled. The city newspaper gave other details in a terse, one-sentence report about what was called "a skirmish."

"It was afterwards learned," Adelia said, "that the seven men murdered ... were Lake Indians from Parvian [Pahvant] Valley." Those Pahvant men "had no hand in the murdering" of the four settlers, she added. She recorded the whole sad story late in life, still haunted by ghostly figures from the past, trapped in memory.[53]

Sally could not read the newspaper. But like nearly everyone, she heard story after story of Indian attacks, from William Hatton's murder by Pahvant Utes to the so-called skirmish near Salt Creek, to the murder and mutilation of a U. S. Army surveyor. Captain John W. Gunnison and some of his men had died just six weeks after Hatton was killed. They were traveling, and had made camp alone by a river when Pahvant warriors attacked. No one she knew contested their guilt.[54]

The Indian stories she heard, including tales of violence by her own people, were unnerving. By the time of the Hatton and Gunnison murders, she and Clara and Eliza, along with many others, lived outside the protective walls of the big fort. A few years earlier, the Leader had judged the valley to be safe enough for them to leave the fort and move into houses. As more and more colonizing settlers arrived in the valley, a small city took root in a place where, as a trapper and explorer had once said, wilderness stretched for a thousand miles in every direction.[55]

PART II

The Heart of Civilization

CHAPTER 4

The City

THE FIRST COLONIZING SETTLERS had begun to survey and claim land within days of arriving in the valley, a few months before Sally walked into their fort in Tav´-o-kun. They laid out streets and city squares and house lots, one step in their plan of colonizing and taming the land, planting civilization in a place they saw as raw wilderness. But most of them lived in the fort during the first year, for safety, except Lorenzo and Harriet and a few others who built houses outside the walls.[1]

One man had reported at the end of that year that "several tribes of Indians" lived nearby. He implied that they lived at peace with their neighbors. Chiefs Wanship and Goship and their people remained in the valley even as thousands more colonizing settlers arrived in a startling surge. There had been violence, but not with the newcomers. Chief Wanship's old enemies in the Valley of the Utahs had killed one of his grown sons, known to the new settlers as Jim. Eliza noted Jim's death in her journal.[2]

A year after his son's murder, Chief Wanship and his men retaliated. They raided Little Chief's camp, capturing dozens of horses. Then they headed north. Little Chief and his warriors finally caught up with the raiders, and he died in the ensuing fight. The violence did not spread to the settler-colonists, who had chosen not to intervene despite Little Chief's plea for help. By the second year of settlement, and the time of Little Chief's death, many had already built houses on their city lots. As an early visitor reported, they had "never been bothered by the Indians; consequently they have spread out over the country."[3]

After living with Eliza at the fort for nearly a year, Clara had moved happily to other rooms when her sister Lucy arrived in the valley. Sally stayed with Eliza. Six months later, Clara and Lucy moved about a mile away to the center of the emerging city, and into a newly built long row house known as Log Row. It stood near Lorenzo and Harriet's log house. Clara shared a room with another young woman who, like her, did not yet have children. She was called Lucy B., to distinguish her from Clara's sister Lucy.[4]

Eliza briefly shared her room at the fort with Sally and a young woman named Margaret. She moved to Log Row, and a separate room, a few months after Clara and Lucy left to live there. Sally remained in Clara and Eliza's old room until, after two winters at the fort, she left for quarters outside the walls. New settlers took vacated space, briefly, until they too moved to houses on city lots. Wave after wave of newcomers filled the fort, and then moved on. And so the city grew, and the fort fell slowly into ruin, yielding day by day to wild forces: sun and wind and rain.[5]

Clara and Lucy's husband, the Leader, had lived at first in a small house that he bought, but he soon built a large adobe-brick house near Log Row. The plastered white walls, shingled roof, and French doors were luxuries without rival in the valley. The two-story house stood on high ground. A visitor saw it from a distant vantage point across the valley. It overlooked the low, dull-colored cottages of the city. Another visitor called the house "elegant," in contrast to Log Row, "a poor, miserable log adobe affair" as she described it.

A long line of steps led up to the house, through grounds planted with ornamental trees and flower gardens. A wall, eight feet high in front, soon surrounded the house and grounds, a silent sentry standing between the Leader above and the masses, the colonizing settlers, below. This was civilization, where leaders stood above and apart—unlike Chief Wanship and leaders of other hunter-gatherer bands, including those known to Sally earlier in life.[6]

Log Row, where only women and children lived, had adjacent but separate sets of rooms, each with windows and a front door that faced the same direction. The roof, with a pitch that shed rain and snow, proved sturdier than the fort's. The windows, made larger, coaxed more light into dim rooms. Quarters remained cramped. Still, Log Row did offer an improvement over the rooms at the fort, however poor it looked to one visitor.[7]

On a day in June, a midwife went to see Clara. The midwife happened to be a younger sister of Dimick, a settler-colonist who served as an interpreter with Indians. Just a week after her brother had moved to "the utaw valley," as she called it, to help build Fort Utah and colonize wild land, she noted a dream in her journal. "Dreamed of the Indians &c.," she wrote. The midwife was often guided by the true spirit, as people put it, and that spirit had moved her to seek out Clara and her friend Lucy B. in their rooms at Log Row. Clara was pregnant with her first child, and due to give birth in a few months. Lucy B. still had no children.[8]

Sally was with Clara and Lucy B. when the midwife arrived that evening. First the visitor spoke good words, called *blessings*, to Clara and to Lucy B. Then, still inspired, she turned to Sally, who sat nearby. She put her hands on Sally's head, and at once began to say words that neither she nor Clara nor Lucy B. could understand.

This was called the gift of tongues, or speaking in foreign tongues, or simply speaking in tongues. Some said that the words spoken came from the language of Adam and Eve in the Garden of Eden. The speaker served only as a channel, and someone else needed to interpret the words. The interpreter was inspired to understand the words, just as the speaker was to say them.[9]

Clara did not understand what she had just heard, and neither did Lucy B. But then Sally told the three women that she *did* understand. The visitor, she said, had spoken words from her language.[10]

Sally heard a word that sounded to her like *piats*, mother. She heard other words that sounded like *namints*, younger sister, or *pats*, older sister, and *ut*, good. She thought the visitor said that her mother and sisters were coming. She thought the woman said that in the meantime she "must be a good girl." This news brought relief from a lonely, heavy despair, the fear that she would never escape, that she was forever lost and would live always among these strangers, far from family and home. Her captivity "was a great cross but the Lord crowned it with joy," the midwife recorded later that night in her journal.[11]

Sally could not safely make her way back home. But she could choose to trust the words she had just heard. This *po-a´-gunt*, shaman, or medicine woman, clearly had Power. Shamans often spoke in strange voices that slid over words, bending and twisting the sounds. Sometimes they shouted angry words. But this *po-a´-gunt* spoke comforting words, and she spoke them gently, quietly.[12]

Sally understood the instructions. She wanted to leave, but she should wait for her family. She should be a good girl until her mother and sisters arrived. Even if they had not known at first where her captors took her, she had just heard that one day they would find her and take her home. This gave her hope, at last. She would wait.

Clara gave birth to her first child, a daughter, three months after the summer evening when the midwife blessed her. The baby, named Jeannette, was called Nettie. When Nettie was two, Clara gave birth to a second daughter, named Nabbie. A few months later she took two stepchildren into her care, a two-year-old girl and her infant brother. Their mother had died just days after his birth. Three years later, Clara gave birth to another child, a son called Jeddie. That name, like the others, seemed to have no meaning—at least to Sally, who was still learning the puzzling ways of the strangers. In just a few years, Clara had become the mother of three daughters and two sons. This was good. Sally liked small children. Earlier in her life she had never seen such a young mother with so many children.[13]

Visitors to the city noticed large families with up to a dozen sons and daughters, or more. Those young people, and wave after wave of arriving settler-colonists, fed the uprush of population, which helped the newcomers gain ground in the big valley, and beyond. "Be fruitful, and multiply, and replenish the earth, and subdue it," the settlers read in scripture, in the biblical story of creation. This was wild/civilized discourse that qualified as sacred narrative knowledge. They must fill the land, and work to subdue and tame the desolate wild waste—in order to feed more and more people. That took hard labor by many.

The women did their part. One visitor remarked that many of the houses "swarmed" with children, as she put it. Others later joked they were the biggest crop in that desert valley—and the only crop that did not need irrigation. But children did need care, and Clara's got a good share from Sally.[14]

She already knew how to take care of small children when she arrived in the valley as a captive. She knew how to comfort them, how to distract them. The People indulged small children with kindness and generosity. They held them, and amused them with leaf cutouts and stories and songs. What Clara called *dolls* they called *ki-up'-i-swav*. The tiny figures formed from clay were hardened in the fire.[15]

The settlers' children had different kinds of dolls, and they played different kinds of games. They raced, and they chased each other, but they did not seem to know about a favorite game that the People called Wolf and Deer. In that game, a child who could run quickly played the part of the deer. The rest acted as wolves, chasing and howling and trying to catch the deer with their teeth. They ran on hands and feet, scrambling over rocks and leaping over bushes, chasing for hours on end. A tired, slow deer got bitten. But Clara and the other women would not like that game, with the howling and the biting. They would not like their children to play at being wild beasts, crawling around in the dirt. That seemed as bad to some as sitting on the ground in the dirt.[16]

Once Clara entrusted Sally with the children, she had more time for other tasks. Another servant, a woman named Susan, helped her. Sally was willing to hold an infant or comfort a small child while they attended to other children, or sewed, or cooked. Unlike the People, they did not lace infants to cradleboards, which mothers carried on their backs, or gave to an older girl to carry. Sally simply held the infants. Anyone could see that she liked that. To hold and amuse a small *pi'-shots*, a child, was not work but pleasure. It also gave her time to watch how Clara and Susan and the other women cooked.[17]

Most of them cooked food on small stoves or in fireplace hearths, using heavy iron pots and skillets. The baking skillets for hearth cooking had rimmed lids that allowed hot coals to be placed on top as well as underneath. Women baked bread in the covered skillets, and cooked other food in large iron pots. They had many trade goods that Sally had never seen before she began to live with them.[18]

She observed the varied ways of cooking, watching how Clara and other women prepared the strange foods that had slowly grown familiar to her. The new fare lacked the vivid, earthy tastes of the People's foods. It lacked the sharp tartness of wild rose berries, the bracing bitter taste of ripe chokecherries, the coarseness of roasted wild seeds, or the robust flavor of deer meat. At first the new foods had tasted oddly mild, even bland, except for the intense and lingering sweetness of some. But as she ate meal after meal, day after day, she grew used to muted flavors and softer textures.

At least the new food was filling. She had sometimes known hunger as a child. Later, as a captive on a forced march, she reached the edge of starvation. The claw of deep hunger dug into her, leaving scars. Even after the captors sold her to the strangers who fed her well, she had not forgotten that hunger.[19]

Cooking and baking, feeding and caring for children, and cleaning up after meals amounted to just a small part of a day's work for most women.

But Clara had the benefit of help from Sally and Susan, and her sister Lucy had a servant named Caroline. Their wealthy husband also provided for many of their daily needs, from food and drink to candles. This also spared them work. Most women needed to tend gardens, look after chickens, milk cows, churn butter, make soap, dip candles, sweep and scrub. Clara and Lucy, like nearly all of the women, did knit and darn, and sew and mend. Keeping the children clean, and dressed in clean clothing—looking civilized, as they saw it—also preoccupied them. Clara and her children created an ever-growing stack of laundry, from bedding to clothing.[20]

Sally, by then in her early twenties, qualified as a full-time laundress and servant, although she did not sleep in Clara's quarters. She shared a room with two other young women named Ellen and Margaret—the same Margaret who had moved into the room at the fort with Eliza and Sally after Clara left. Neither had children, and unlike Clara they did not need her help.[21]

Sally already knew something about laundering when she arrived in the valley as a captive. The People used the roots of wild yucca for soap. Women washed buckskin clothing with yucca soap. They did not wash bark clothing or the soft bark that they gathered for bedding. Clara and the other women seemed to think that everything must be laundered, using soap that women made from wood ash and lard. But just when everything was clean, it was time to start washing again—and starching, and ironing. And then the soap ran out, and women spent time making more. Doing laundry counted as drudgery.[22]

Earlier in life, before Sally began to live with people who wore cloth garments, and before she began wearing cloth herself, she had not needed to spend hours at a time laundering. She had never ironed, but now she spent time at that tiresome task too. The pressing iron was a flat, heavy object made of cast iron, heated on a stove, and then applied firmly, but carefully and quickly, to cloth. Clara also showed Sally how to darn socks, yet another foreign and tedious task that held no interest.[23]

Women made the socks from something they called *yarn*, Sally learned. She watched them weave the socks by using thin sticks. The People knew about other kinds of weaving. Women wove baskets from pliable branches of squaw bush, which they gathered in spring. Sometimes they used the coarser branches of willow. They gathered wild blue flax, which grew in most of the valleys, to make cordage for nets. Women gathered and twined sagebrush bark to make clothing for summer.[24]

Sally saw that Clara's people used different fibers, but they did not gather them. They had to grow those fibers, and that took months of hard work. To produce their tame flax, they prepared the soil, planted seeds, weeded, irrigated, tied up the plants as they grew, and harvested the flax. Then, at last, the cloth making began. First, they spent long hours at a wooden spinning wheel, making threads of flax. Next, they wove the threads into cloth, which they called *linen*, on a wooden loom. But eventually Clara and Lucy's wealthy husband filled a storeroom with trade goods that included linen. This spared his wives the hard work of making that cloth. As Sally noticed, the storeroom held other kinds of cloth as well, the ones called *calico* and *gingham* and *flannel*.[25]

The settler-colonists also wove cloth called *wool* from hair that they took from their animals, the ones that looked something like *nag*, wild mountain sheep, but without the big horns. They worked hard at breeding and caring for those captive sheep. They needed to guard them constantly as they grazed, to keep them from straying and to keep them safe from wolves. Finally, when the sheep's hair was long and thick, they cut it. The women carded and washed the hair, then spun it, exacting work that Sally learned to do. After dyeing, the wool was finally ready to be woven into cloth on large wooden looms.[26]

Then came the sewing. Clara and Lucy and Eliza and all of the other women knew how to sew clothing, everything from shirts and pants to skirts and blouses and dresses. Sally first saw Eliza sewing a cloth hat, which she called a *cap*. Eliza made this cap by sewing together small pieces of cloth with tiny stitches, using a thin needle and fine thread. She made a cloth string for each side of the cap so that it could be tied under the chin. Then it completely covered a woman's head, and her hair. Eliza gave the cap to a friend.[27]

Sally already knew about sewing. The People sometimes wore buckskin clothing, which women sewed. They tanned the skins of deer, and then they sewed a dress or a shirt or pants. Making a dress from two doeskins required time and skill as well as special tools, a needle and an awl, each made from a piece of a deer's hind leg bone. Women usually carried two awls, one large and one small, in rawhide cases. They used awls to punch holes in the pliable but tough skins. Then they sewed.

When Sally began to sew cloth, Clara and Eliza and the other women thought she was clumsy. She found it hard at first to use such a small and slender needle. The People used large bone needles. And she needed to learn how to sew cloth so soft that it fell into folds, and some so soft that it tore easily.[28]

Making cloth, and taking care of cloth, took time. Many women worked at it. And these people always seemed to need more cloth, more cloth. Their tribe was so big, and growing so quickly that they could not use the skins of animals. There were just too many of them and too few animals. They also needed a lot of cloth because they wore large garments. They covered the entire body. No one wore just an apron of buckskin or bark, or only a skirt of twined sagebrush bark.

Clara and Lucy and the other women even made young children cover their bodies. That meant more spinning and weaving, sewing and mending, washing and ironing. For their children to look civilized meant keeping them "respectably covered" in cloth as one mother put it. As a small child, Sally had gone without clothing in summer. Later she put on a bark apron, or wore a skirt of twined bark that reached her knees. Her upper body remained bare. She was dressed in a bark skirt when Charley bought her.[29]

She had learned from the start to keep most of her body covered. Clara's mother, Harriet, had washed her and covered her in cloth before Charley took her to the fort. Months later, in the steady heat of high summer, the cloth garments felt heavy and hot, and grew damp, and stuck to her skin. A bark apron felt better. But for some reason, the strangers did not want her or any other woman to expose *pi-av'*, a breast, or *pun'-ka-vu*, a leg.[30]

And so Sally had begun to wear clothing like Clara and the other women wore, and to learn about their housekeeping tasks, including the care of cloth. To them, she was beginning to look and to act civilized, sharing the household work with Clara as well as the helper named Susan. Even Clara, who had the benefit of their labor, had work to do each day. But during the years after they left the fort, more and more of it fell to Sally. Clara instructed her carefully in the basics of housework.[31]

Unburdened by pregnancy and childbirth, and refused the few days each month to sit apart and rest, Sally had little respite from the daily round of heavy work—except when she sat down to hold a baby or a small child. After moving from the fort, she found moments of solitude by going to a nearby canyon to fetch water from the creek for Clara. When she first went alone to that creek, she had lingered, savoring a few moments of refuge from the strangers and their tedious work. In the eyes of settler-colonists, she *ma*lingered. But she soon learned that going alone to the creek for water carried risk. At least once she fled back to avoid recapture. After that, she preferred to go in company.[32]

Clara's directions left her little time for what Eliza and others called idleness. Sitting apart would qualify as idleness. For some reason unknown to her, the pleasure and comfort of holding Clara's small children did not. More and more, Sally worked. She washed, ironed, darned, mended, and spun, and helped take care of the children. She watched how the women cooked and baked. This was her daily life. She had stopped resisting, choosing instead to be a good girl as directed by the medicine woman's prophesy. She continued to wait for her mother and sisters.

One of Eliza's good friends was a midwife named Patty. Sally had known her at the fort. Eliza often sewed caps for Patty, and Patty shared food with Eliza. She was fifty-two years old when she drove a team of oxen and a wagon across the plains and mountains to colonize wild land. She and her husband arrived in the big valley with one of the first wagon trains.[33]

At the end of each day while Patty lived at the fort, and after she moved to a house on a city lot, she recorded her day's work. She did not have small children to care for, and she did not bother to record the humdrum chores of everyday life, from making fires in a stove or hearth to cooking meals. But she had no end of other work, the endless round of housekeeping in civilization. She usually summarized the day's work with a word or a phrase: "washed," "ironed," "washed bed quilts," "commenced making soap," "cleaned," "scoured," "sewed all day," "quilted all day," "mended," "made shirts," "made curtains," "cut carpet rags," "twisted carpet yarn," "sewed carpet rags," "carded wool," "spun," "finished a pair of socks," "mended sox," "butchered an ox," "sift[ed] over two beryls of flour," "baked mince pies," "baked bread," "baked sweet cake," and simply "baked."[34]

The milled wheat that she sifted and baked came from the farm her husband carved out of a few acres of the wild high desert south of the city. He had dug out sagebrush and other stubborn wild shrubs and plants from the land, and then replaced them with roots and seeds imported from his old home. He and other men had also dug out ditches for irrigation channels in the Big Field, as the surveyed land was known. He labored hard at the farm for nearly a week at a time, leaving his wife to care for their home and garden.[35]

One day when he was at home Patty helped her husband lay down a wooden floor, "the first floor that I could set my foot upon as my own for more than two years," she remarked. "I have lived on the ground all the time," she added, meaning that she had stood on a dirt floor indoors, just as she stood on earth when she went outdoors. But she had slept in a bed, covered with quilts, every night. A civilized woman, she believed, did not lie in the dirt.[36]

She often worked outside, whatever the season. Long before spring reached the nearby mountains and dressed the flanks in dazzling green, Patty set to work in her garden. It covered a full acre. She looked down at the brown sandy soil as she hoed, not up at a sky that on some spring days shone lavender. If she noticed the sky, or the mountains, she did not bother to record what she saw. Making a garden, transplanting her old way of life in a new place, took her attention. She sowed seeds, and tended tiny green shoots of lettuce, radish, corn, cucumber, and squash. She planted peas, potatoes, onions, and melons, and set out beet and cabbage plants, all brought west. She replanted after a killing frost in late May.[37]

When planting ended, weeding and irrigating began. As she recorded again and again, "worked in the garden," "watered the garden," and "hoed the garden." Weeks passed without rain, and sunburned garden plants collapsed with thirst unless she rescued them. "Wattered the corn all day got very tired," she wrote at the height of the dry season. In a good year, her hard work produced a "plenty," as she put it. "I picked my garden strawberys," she recorded on a day in late June, adding that she gave some to an acquaintance who was "very sick with consumption."[38]

The burden of gardening ended in fall ("dug my beets"), but winter brought a new round of exhausting chores. "Melted snow to wash," she wrote at the end of a long and tiring day. "I have fixed the cow pen and hen coop," she recorded on another snowy December day. Her husband was absent. "I have shoveled snow 2 hours before I could feed the cow and mare, then I shoveled out the wood," she wrote on a cold day in January when her husband was away. "I am tired out," she added. When she needed firewood, and he was absent, she set to work on logs he had felled and carted from a canyon. First she had to saw the logs into lengths, and then split them. "I have had to cut wood all this week for the stove," she recorded unhappily, adding that her back felt "very lame."[39]

She delivered babies at all hours of day and night. She made medicine, and visited the ailing and infirm. Barney Ward was "very sick," she reported one day, but he recovered. Her husband did not. She recorded his final illness, noting "quite sick," "he is worse," "has not spoke since Friday but I think he knows what we say," and "ten o'clock he died very easy."[40]

In the three years after they reached the valley and before her husband fell sick and died, Patty sometimes recorded her deep fatigue, an exhaustion that could spiral into illness. "I have worked in the garden untill I am allmost done out," she wrote, and "I was so tired I could not sleep last night." "I have worked hard all the week to take care of cows calves and garden," she recorded one day. Then, a few days later, "I have been sick all night" and "I am very weak." Two days later, "I sit up but little today." A week passed, and she recorded, "worked so hard I could not sleep." Three months later she wrote, "I am not well" and "I have to work hard."[41]

Patty recovered then, and again, and again. She married a second time ("I feel to thank the Lord that I have some one to cut wood for me"), and she kept working. But the grinding labor of colonizing the wild left marks on her life and health. Her first husband and others died early in the effort, or from the effort. She recorded their names and sometimes a cause of death, everything from childbirth to "numb palsey," a stroke.[42]

Colonizing the wild meant eliminating native wildlife, all of the so-called pests and weeds, and cultivating imported domesticates. It meant forcing the land to yield more and more of just what was needed to feed and clothe more and more colonizing settlers, including thousands of their babies ushered into the world by Patty as a midwife. Colonizing the wild and populating it could consume a man's life, and a woman's.[43]

As more and more settler-colonists arrived and built houses, the shape of the new city emerged. This planned and highly ordered city had uniform features, from the size of house lots to the width and placement of streets. The first visitors—explorers and overland travelers headed to the goldfields in California—estimated that it was at least two miles wide and three to four miles long. It seemed surprisingly large since it had just sprung to life, yet dwarfed by the size of the big valley and by towers of mountains east and west. Hundreds of small houses, most built of adobe bricks, lined the wide streets.[44]

The streets formed a grid and ran straight, north to south or east to west, without deviation. Sally had never seen anything quite like this new and strange creation. Now she had to walk on the straight trails when she left her room each day and went to help Clara, who had moved from Log Row to a small house with her children. Each trail was as straight as a young aspen fallen to ground.

She could no longer simply take the most direct route to a nearby place, just as she could no longer walk along *nūm-po*, the People's word for the ancient trails that their ancestors had followed. But now Sally

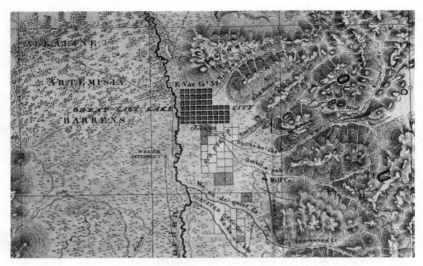

Map of Great Salt Lake City in 1850. Used by permission, Rare Books, Special Collections Research Center, William & Mary Libraries.

learned that she should not walk across house lots and through gardens. The People thought their land was for all of them, and they could go where they wished. But the men in Clara's tribe had cut up the land into little pieces, and fenced the pieces, and now everyone must walk on the straight trails. A long fence surrounded the city too.[45]

Beside the trails flowed straight creeks, the narrow tame creeks that men made by digging. These carried water to house lots. Here and there the men had placed a flat piece of wood on the ground, crossing the water, so that people could walk over it instead of jumping from one side to the other. Sally saw that men took precedence at these crossing points. Women stepped to the side, and waited for men to pass.[46]

Horses and oxen moved along the wide straight trails. People walked along narrow ones on the side, next to the water. When Sally turned to walk in a different direction, she needed to wait again for men to pass. Those men held the reins of massive animals that pulled loaded, lumbering wagons. Then she stepped carefully across ruts and over piles of pungent steaming waste that the animals left behind.

These straight trails of hard packed earth had deep ruts that collapsed into slick mud after rain or as snow melted. In winter and spring, the mud caused trouble for walkers, including her, as well as for riders and wagon drivers. By summer, the mud had long since dried. Clouds of choking dust rose up behind the horses and oxen, and settled lazily on passers-by.[47]

Unlike the old trails that meandered through canyons and across mountains, following the contours of the land, the city boulevards followed the dictates of the planner. Streets imposed order on open space that in the eyes of the settler-colonists, and most travelers, had a chaotic, wild look. After spending months on rough or winding trails, overland travelers at last arrived in this place of mandated order and control. Streets, like the linear fenced fields of crops, marked yet another step in colonizing the wild and transforming the waste—as most Americans viewed it.

One day a party of overland travelers, approaching the valley from the east, reached a vantage point where they suddenly saw cattle, horses, and sheep grazing in every direction. The trail took them past fields of wheat and other grains and vegetables, and lines of small, neat houses. "At the first sight of all these signs of civilization in the wilderness," one man said, "we were transported with wonder and pleasure. Some wept, some gave three cheers, some laughed, and some ran and fairly danced for joy ... happy to find themselves once more amid scenes which mark the progress of advancing civilization."[48]

The city offered other such scenes of settler society transplanted, created anew on expropriated lands. The commercial area—with a newspaper office and hotel as well as workshops and stores filled with imported goods—had no rival in the two thousand miles between St. Louis, Missouri, and the goldfields of California. It drew thousands of customers, a growing number of overland travelers as well as the settler-colonists. A flood of hopeful men reached the city in a rush. In her journal, Eliza noted the first to arrive, a week or so before she moved from the fort to Log Row. "People with pack animals arrive from the States going to California," she wrote. They had just reached lands recently taken over by the United States after a war with Mexico.[49]

Travelers made such haste toward the goldfields of California that for five hundred miles east of the valley the road was strewn with dead bodies of oxen and horses and mules. The overlanders paused briefly in the city to rest and to buy or barter for supplies. Those supplies would enable them to cross the wild desert that stood between them and, as they dreamed, a bonanza of gold.[50]

Within two months, stores lined the streets, and served thousands of travelers. "Merchant shops are open in every direction," Eliza recorded in her journal. Some of the men sent letters about their journeys to friends and family and newspapers. They used a new place name, City of the Great Salt Lake, as their temporary address. The first colonizing settlers, planning on permanent occupation of the valley, had agreed on a name for their city within days of arriving at their destination.[51]

A few of the travelers remarked on the landmark that gave the city and the valley their names. Long before colonizing settlers and those overland travelers arrived, Jim Bridger and other explorers had seen the immense saltwater lake. It spread over so much of the land that when they stood on the shoreline and looked west, they often saw no horizon. Blue sky dissolved into blue water. At first they thought they had reached an arm of the Pacific Ocean. Following the shoreline they discovered what Gosiutes and Kumumpa and other Shoshones, as well as Utes, had long known. The saline water filled a shallow lake, by far the largest lake in the vast high desert. Explorers had named the Valley of the Great Salt Lake for its most remarkable wild feature.[52]

One of the travelers, who paused at the city before hastening on to California to seek his fortune, called the lake "a great curiosity," with water much saltier than seawater. The shoreline was about twenty miles from the city, he reported, and people went there to gather salt. "Salt is so plentiful about the shore," the traveler told newspaper readers in the East, "that it is shoveled up by wagon loads like sand, and drawn to the city. It is coarse and clear, and is very clean." He explained that boiling the coarse crystals in water produced a very fine salt. "They have the finest salt here you ever saw," another traveler confirmed. The useful salt helped compensate for what was otherwise seen as useless waste, the saline water.[53]

The settler-colonists harvested still more from the lake and wild marshland. In the marshy flats, boys filled baskets with eggs they gathered in late spring and early summer from the nests of wild geese, ducks, curlews, and snowy plovers. Sometimes they rowed out to islands in the lake to raid the nests of gulls and pelicans, cranes, blue herons and brants. They returned with a rich harvest of eggs. Men also hunted geese and ducks around the lake.[54]

Despite the bounty of wild nature near the saltwater lake, few of the travelers or city residents saw its value or showed much regard for it. They did notice the wild and soaring mountains that ringed much of the valley. Who could not? But most Americans and Europeans, visitors and residents alike, deeply admired something else. They praised the transformation of anything native and wild by means of human labor, along with all signs of human order and control. They welcomed the displacement and decline of the native, and replacement by the imported—the favored plants, animals, goods, and practices that the colonizing settlers brought with them. These were marks of settler colonization, of settler society taking root in a new land, of life in civilization.

The valley's "improved land," as visitors called the fenced city lots and farm fields, mostly rid of native wildlife, impressed many of them. So did the irrigation system, a novelty to travelers from the well-watered eastern states and Europe. As they soon learned, this land of little rain was by luck a land of rushing water. Snowmelt and spring water filled creeks that cascaded, gushed, or merely flowed, depending on season, from high in the mountains down through canyons, and into the valley's irrigation channels.

One visitor to the valley estimated that twenty miles of channel took water from the canyon creeks to outlying farm fields as well as city lots. "The water is very pure," he said, "and conducted to every acre of ground in the city." He saw men cutting wheat from fields that spread over thousands of acres in the valley. Other travelers noticed irrigated fields of corn, wheat, buckwheat, potatoes, and other crops—all products of intensive labor and water control.[55]

A U.S. Army officer from the East also admired the network of small irrigation channels. The channels reached all of the city lots, "spreading life, verdure and beauty," he said, "over what was heretofore a barren waste." No one told him about the richness of the tall wild grasses and rushes that covered the valley bottom when the first colonizing settlers arrived. Hungry livestock had soon grazed the grass short.[56]

Water flowed through the channels toward saplings as well as gardens and fields of crops. The newly planted trees, like the beds of flowers and garden vegetables, were thirsty tame transplants to the high desert, and needed irrigation. Some of the first colonizers, who had brought seeds of peach trees and locust trees, planted the imported seeds on their new city lots just two weeks after arriving, one step in transforming the wild land to serve their purposes. The non-native trees would offer flowers in spring, and nectar for the imported honeybees. In summer, the trees would provide shade and fruit.

Lorenzo had soon planted the seeds that Harriet brought from their old home, hoping to cheer her with the prospect of green leaves and shade in summer. Most of the other settler-colonists did the same, creating small orchards by their houses. Some bought young saplings from Patty, the doyenne of peach trees. The enterprising midwife delivered tiny trees as well as babies, for a fee.[57]

The colonists labored on, taming more land, as they saw it. They turned more soil and planted more wheat. They dug more channels to control and carry more water. They felled more stands of native trees in canyons, and took the wood away to build more fences and to heat more houses. The Leader urged them on with lofty words about the mastery of wild nature by the labor of civilized man, a staple of wild/civilized discourse. "It is the bone, sinew, nerve, and muscle of man that subdue the earth, make it yield its strength, and administer to his varied wants," he told them. "This power tears down mountains and fills up valleys, builds cities and temples, and paves the streets." "In short," he concluded with a rhetorical flourish, "what is there that yields shelter and comfort to civilized man, that is not produced by the strength of his arm making the elements bend to his will."[58]

A few years after the first surge of travelers passed through the city, two visitors, husband and wife, arrived from the East in late October. Cornelia's husband Benjamin, a lawyer, had been appointed to a high-ranking federal post in the territory. They stayed in a well-kept boardinghouse, which offered the only suitable lodging for a genteel woman such as Cornelia. Hotels, with flimsy partitions rather than solid walls between beds, gave no privacy.[59]

When Christmas arrived, their hostess, Mary Farnham, prepared a sumptuous feast of wild game for her guests. By then, in the fifth year of settler colonization, the supply of wheat and other crops produced on farms in the valley had grown, along with the herds of cattle and sheep. A few types of native game still appeared on the table. Reaping from the wild brought the benefit of sparing tame animals from slaughter. For the Christmas meal, Mary "loaded her dinner table with all kinds of game," Cornelia recorded, from duck and goose to pronghorn antelope and jackrabbit.

Great flocks of wild ducks and geese gathered in the lake's wetlands during spring and fall migration, and the desert jackrabbits—well, they bred like rabbits. Their numbers soared after settler-colonists killed so many wolves and coyotes, which preyed on them. Mary had also planned to serve a sirloin of grizzly bear, Cornelia added, but deep snow in the mountains kept hunters away from the bear's winter refuge.[60]

On a fine spring day a few months later, Cornelia and her husband took a long walk in a nearby canyon. They planned to leave the city soon and go to California. Wildflowers already bloomed in the canyon, bursts of purple and yellow among the greening wild grass, but snow still hid the rocky contours of the mountains in the distance. Snowmelt fed the rushing creek, and Cornelia and her husband saw the flashing forms of trout darting in the clear cold water. In the wild upper reaches of the canyon, they passed by lingering patches of snow.

They seemed to be completely alone, but then they encountered a young hunter carrying a rifle. Cornelia identified him as Ute. "I was childish enough to feel timid," she confessed, "as we were at least a mile and a half from the mouth of the cañon, and out of all sight or hearing of the city." She and Benjamin spoke to the man, and he, "with apparent good humor, entered into such conversation as we could hold, with a few words and many signs." Cornelia, who had taken along pencil and paper, signaled that she wanted to make a drawing of him. He assumed a graceful pose, leaning on his rifle, as she made a hasty sketch. He seemed pleased with the result.

The hunter's dignity impressed Cornelia, but she did not like the look of Utes in the city. She often saw them in the street, dressed in wild skins, squatting on the ground, and eating food with their hands, in their accepted manner. But in her eyes they were "devouring their food like dogs." They did not use dishes and cutlery. They did not sit on chairs at a table. As she saw it, they sat on the ground in the dirt.[61]

Sally no longer showed much outward evidence of her Pahvant Ute origins in the way she ate and dressed. The longer she stayed with Clara, subjected to daily civilizing lessons, the more she conformed to the colonizers' ways. As the years passed, she became "delicate in appetite," Eliza noted with approval. That is, she learned how and what she was expected to eat. According to Eliza, she also grew "neat and tasteful in dress."[62]

Sally wore clothing sewn from gingham fabric, and favored red checks, the brighter the better. She knew that squaw bush, which grew wild, had berries that yielded a pale red dye. Certain kinds of red rock, if soaked in water, produced a red paint, which the People used to decorate hides. But the red of gingham cloth was especially bright, the threads dyed with a cultivated plant named madder. Sometimes Sally wore a shawl with red stripes, which she folded to make three corners, following the style of Clara and other women, instead of wrapping it straight around, Indian style.[63]

Her liking of red did betray her cultural origins. *Un'-kar*, red, was a good color, a color of strength and success and joy. She preferred it. With her dark hair and eyes, red suited Sally. But black-haired Eliza, who favored dark dresses with dazzlingly white collars, avoided it. The Puritan heritage of Eliza and many of the other women led them to see bright red as suspect, an unsuitable color for a respectable civilized woman to wear. Except for her liking of red, Sally conformed in the clothing she wore.[64]

For a time she wore her hair loose or braided, as the People did. But then she began to pin it into a knot, following Clara and Lucy's habit. Her hair was so much thicker that it made a large knot, which looked unshapely to some. But what made Sally stand out most of all was the color of her skin, which the settler-colonists called tawny or dark. They could not see beauty in her appearance. Dark skin signified a curse, they believed. Dark-skinned people, the wild people, were not "delightsome" according to their scripture.[65]

The color of Eliza's hair and eyes nearly matched Sally's, but her skin remained suitably pale. Most of the settler-colonists, especially the women, had pale skin. One of Lucy's daughters always remembered that her mother had "the loveliest, whitest skin I have ever seen." Women tried to avoid the sun or wore sunbonnets outdoors to protect their fair complexions. A few of them had olive skin, which was cause for comment, as was Sally's brown skin—and Chief Wákara's, recorded as "reddish olive not dark." She heard Clara and others speak of two people by names that referred to their dark skin. A man known as Black Isaac worked for the Leader as a coachman. His wife was known as Black Jane.[66]

In the view of those who knew her, Sally grew ever more civilized in both conduct and appearance as time passed. Her complexion, like her preference for bright red, did reveal her native origins. But it seemed to some that living in civilization caused skin to lighten, at least to a certain point. She became somewhat lighter and far more delightsome to settler-colonists the longer she lived with Clara, the better she learned their language and their ways, and the harder she worked. As time passed, she worked more and more indoors, out of the strong sunlight.

Sally was still living with Clara at the fort when the new settlers held the first celebration to mark the success of their colonizing effort. They memorialized the day in late July when colonists reached the valley. The earliest to arrive included the Leader, Clara, Lorenzo, Harriet, and more than a hundred others. The celebration of that event soon spread, and became an annual holiday in the city and throughout the territory.[67]

In a remote settlement where Barney had moved with his family, Indian neighbors attended one celebration as invited guests. Several years had passed since Barney and other settlers had arrived to colonize their lands, but they still seemed friendly for the most part. Festivities began early in the morning with music and a rifle salute, followed by a parade. A martial band with members dressed in uniform stood first in line. They carried a banner that read "Our Mountain Home," asserting the colonizers' claim. A rifle company, also in uniform, followed—a display of strength that showed how the claim would be enforced. The armed men did not need to carry a banner. Everyone present knew the meaning of guns.

Next, Barney led a procession of twenty-four young men who wore blue shirts with buckskin pants and moccasins. The buckskin announced their identity as native people, so-called wild Indians. But the cloth shirts, as well as their willingness to form a line behind a settler-colonist who led the way, signified that they were marching on the road to civilization. This wild/civilized performance expressed hope for the peaceful and complete assimilation of native people into civilization. The parade anticipated the elimination of the native.

A banner, which the young men carried but could not read, said, "We shall become a white and delightsome people," the last four words taken from scripture. The banner's wording, like the cloth shirts the young men wore, held out the promise that the civilizing project would succeed. They would be tamed, and their skin would lighten. Civilization would prevail.

Other groups of marchers followed, including young boys who wore red sashes, white shirts, and blue pants. Next came a group of women dressed in white, with blue sashes and wreaths of flowers. They carried parasols that protected their fair skin from the strong sun. Their banner read, "We instruct our sisters of the forest." Those native sisters watched, but none joined in the parade. Little girls, wearing pink dresses and green sashes, and carrying a banner—"Let Virtue abound"—fell into step behind their mothers.

After the parade ended, the assembled crowd prayed and then listened to speeches. Then a procession formed again, and the people marched to large tables and sat down to a splendid feast. The menu included chicken and other meats, and vegetables, from potatoes and peas to beets. There were loaves of bread and pies, puddings, custards, cakes, and coffee. The appetites of the guests alarmed the hosts, but the guests did say politely that it was the best meal they had ever eaten. One of the settlers explained why they had offered so much food. "This is quite a tax on us," he said, "but we are on their land & wish to be at peace & give them no cause of complaint against us."[68]

Sally did not see a parade with Indians. Most had already been dispossessed and displaced from the valley and nearby canyons by settler-colonization. Few remained, and they did not figure in the festivities.[69]

Three years after Adelia's first husband mysteriously died inside the walls of a fort, she married a prominent associate of the Leader and moved to the city. Her new husband had a grown son named William who had traded a horse for a little Gosiute boy sometime in the first years of settlement. William called the boy Dave. Whether or not the trade for Dave resembled the earlier trade for Sally—whether the seller threatened to kill the captive, or simply offered the child in exchange for a horse—William took possession of Dave.[70]

A year or two after William made the trade, Dave's mother chanced to see her son while passing through the city. "She was so overjoyed at finding him that William's heart was touched," his brother later said, "and he let her have her darling boy." Dave returned to his people's ancestral homeland in the nearby desert, a place they called Yo-gūmp' and settler-colonists called Skull Valley.[71]

The trade in Indian children had grown routine over time. William's family purchased three. Many of the leading families had at least one child, and some had more. One of the Leader's brothers had acquired a girl who was given the name Lilla, and another had a girl named Lucy. As William's brother recalled years later, a well-known trader sometimes loaded a pack train with goods favored by Indians, and visited Indian camps where he bought the captive children he later sold.[72]

Adelia met one such child after she moved to the city. A young girl known as Kate lived and worked in the household of Adelia's new husband—in order to be made civilized, it was said. Someone gave her to the family, Adelia noted. Kate was about thirteen years old at the time, and, according to a new law, an indentured servant rather than a slave.[73]

But when an Indian boy suddenly disappeared, a notice in the city newspaper carried the same heading and promise of reward as notices in Virginia and other southern states used for missing slaves. Under the heading "RAN AWAY," a settler wrote: "From this subscriber, an Indian BOY about twelve years old; speaks a little English. Supposed to have gone back to Parowan. Anyone giving information where said Boy may be found, or returning him to me, shall be liberally rewarded."[74]

Procuring Indian children as indentured servants had been made legal five years after settlement. The stated purpose of the new law was to end the abuse of Indian children by their captors. Settler-colonists should buy the children, and indenture them for up to twenty years. They should clothe the children well, teach them to read and write by sending them to school between the ages of seven and sixteen, give them religious instruction, and teach them useful work. In a word, they should civilize them. The children would pay for their purchase and the other benefits with as many as twenty years of labor. This conformed to Spanish precedent. Colonists in New Mexico paid so-called ransoms for Indian captives, who each then owed ten or twenty years of service to their so-called redeemers.[75]

Sally's legal status remained ambiguous, even under the new law. Clara's brother had bought her, not as a young child, five years before the law went into effect. By the time that the involuntary servitude of Indian children became legal in the territory, she was in her mid-twenties. No one seems to have signed papers at that late date spelling out her terms of indenture. There were no stated terms.[76]

Unlike the young boy who escaped, she had not run away from Clara. No one took her away as Dave's mother had taken her son. Her father had died, she told Clara and Eliza. She lost the man who would have protected her from captors, or searched for her and rescued her from captivity. Then her mother remarried, and her cruel stepfather sold her, she said. If she explained why he did that, Eliza said nothing about it later. Sally's mother had not managed to prevent the sale or trade. She had not found her daughter, despite what Sally had heard from the medicine woman, the one with Power who said that her mother and sisters would come for her and take her home. Sally had remained with Clara, waiting, as a year passed, and then another, and another.[77]

Sometime during these years a boy named Jack ran away. Some people said he was Gosiute, and others said Ute. He worked for a family named Norton, but no one seemed to remember the term of Jack's indenture, or if he had one. He drove an ice wagon, someone claimed, until the day when Mrs. Norton struck him. Or was it Mr. Norton? Later, few people besides Jack could recall exactly what had happened—except that there was violence, angry words, and hitting. And then he left.

He did not go west to nearby Gosiute country in the desert. Heading east, deep into Ute country, took him far away from the colonizers and their straight trails and wagons filled with ice. He found a home in the high mountains where peak followed peak followed peak for more than five hundred miles. He joined a band of Utes, courted a young woman during the annual Bear Dance in spring, and married her. Colonizing settlers in Colorado Territory later knew him as Ute Jack or Captain Jack. His people called him Nicaagat, Green Leaf, or Leaves Becoming Green, after the color of willow and cottonwood leaves in early spring.[78]

In the eyes of settlers, when Jack ran away from civilization, when Jack became Nicaagat, he went wild. He reverted, as it was said. He joined people of the wild in the remote interior of the mountains, a place where wild wolves and bears also lived. He had left city life and settler-colonial society for good.

CHAPTER 5

Plagues

BY THE EIGHTH WINTER of Sally's new life with Clara and the Leader's family, Chief Wákara and his people had nearly lost their old way of life, along with much of their homeland. Many had lost their lives, dying from alien diseases with frightening symptoms and odd names: *mumps*, *scarlet fever*, *pneumonia*, *cholera*. Colonizing settlers, as well as travelers headed west, had brought plagues into their country, killing thousands. Children lost their parents, and parents lost their children. People who lived by hunting and gathering often went hungry. And trade with the Leader and his followers had not proved as lucrative as he at first seemed to promise.[1]

Some of the new settlers had grown richer, just as the Leader predicted. They colonized the best lands, near rivers and creeks and springs that had always drawn deer and other game animals. When armed conflict finally erupted, the Leader blamed it on Chief Wákara. The short war proved costlier to Utes than to the settler-colonists, who built a thick wall of adobe bricks around the city for protection. It stood twelve feet high.[2]

Chief Wákara died suddenly in January after the conflict ended. Some people thought that he died from pneumonia. He had been sick for ten days with "a cold [that] settled on his lungs," as one man put it. But his close ally Arapeen at first charged the Pahvant Utes with making "bad medicine," using sorcery, supernatural means, to kill Wákara. Sally had no reason to regret the death of Baptiste's ally. But the power of certain people, Pahvants and others, to practice bad medicine, *po-av'-kai-um*, and to take the life of a chief so commanding and strong, was disturbing.[3]

One night soon after the chief's death, Arapeen had a powerful vision. Wákara appeared to Arapeen, and said that he had died a natural death, and that he wanted his people to be at peace with the settlers. Guided by that vision, Arapeen, Wákara's successor as chief, tried to keep the peace.[4]

On a Sunday in winter, he addressed a large assembly of the Leader's people in the city. He spoke to them in Ute. Eliza's friend Patty, the hardworking midwife and gardener, listened carefully to him. Patty sometimes spoke in tongues or interpreted for others. She thought that she understood Chief Arapeen's words. His remarks that day resembled what the settler-colonists heard from their leader and his loyal lieutenants, and what the chief's own people often heard from him. He exhorted the crowd to follow their leaders and to do no wrong.[5]

Just months after Chief Wákara's death, the French traveler Jules Rémy reached the city with a small party of men. Two Indian guides, who rode in front of Rémy and the other men, dropped behind as soon as they caught sight of the streets and houses in the distance. They had never seen a settlement of such size, with so many people gathered in one place.

Unlike American travelers from the East, the two guides did not laugh or dance for joy when they glimpsed the city. Rémy recalled the moment. "Struck with astonishment at the sight of this immense group of houses laid out in rows which were suddenly revealed to them, they passed, by an instinctive movement, from the front to the rear," he said. They did not want "to be the first to venture into this unknown labyrinth," he explained, "to them a peopled desert, doubtless more alarming than to us the desert which had just been crossed."[6]

From that distance, the two guides could not see the city's commercial district, where shops filled with alluring goods attracted Utes and Shoshones as visitors. The place that Utes called Tav'-o-kun had grown into a busy trading center where they brought furs, tanned skins, and buffalo robes to exchange for a wide range of trade goods, from coffee and sugar to cloth. Tens of thousands of American overland travelers and colonizing settlers, and a few explorers, also stopped in the valley on the way west. The city had become a trading post par excellence, with wares imported from eastern and international markets. Shops stocked a range of goods that far surpassed those ever offered at Fort Bridger and Fort Hall.

Louis Vásquez, sensing opportunity in the city, had soon opened a store there. When he sold it, he and Narcissa and the children returned to Missouri, where he spent the rest of his life. There he and Jim Bridger and their families lived as near neighbors for a time, although Jim returned often to the western plains and mountains as a guide.[7]

Just before Rémy had reached the city, parties of Shoshone and Ute chiefs and warriors met there to make a peace treaty. Several Ute chiefs—including Tintic, Pe-teet-neet, and others—represented their people. Sally lived only a short distance from the place where they assembled. Baptiste was with them.

Some of the men with Tintic appeared unwilling to make peace. They carried arms, and wore black paint, "as if for battle," according to Dimick, who acted as interpreter. When he told them to put down their arms, Baptiste refused to give up his war spear, and two other men kept their guns. Others put down their guns but concealed bows and arrows under their blankets. Then, as one of the Shoshone chiefs made a sign of peace, Baptiste began dancing the war dance, and thrusting his spear toward the ground. Finally, order prevailed, the treaty ceremony took place, and at last Baptiste and Tintic and the others mounted their horses and left. About a week later, thirty more Ute warriors came to the city with Chief Arapeen for a second treaty ceremony with the sixty Shoshones.[8]

It seemed then that Baptiste's visits to the city had no end—like a bad dream that came back again and again, stalking Sally. At least the powerful Chief Wákara was dead. But the presence of so many warriors, for days on end, gave a sense of impending danger. Most of those armed men were strangers, and the Utes among them were Baptiste's allies. They walked freely through the streets, and stared at the houses. It was better if they did not see her.

After so many winters with Clara and Lucy and the other women, Sally no longer viewed them as strangers. Their presence meant safety. She had not forgotten how she came to live with them, the nightmare journey that stole her home and family from her. She had not forgotten who threatened to take her life, and took a rifle instead.

When Rémy and his companions reached the city, they learned of the treaty, and saw some of the treaty signers camped in a large square across from their hotel. Rémy noticed that during the day the men walked through the streets, looking at the houses and studying the array of trade goods displayed in shops. "They were to be seen moving about sometimes singly, sometimes in small groups," he said, "all dressed in skins, and uniformly armed with their bows and arrows, some even with rifles."

He thought that they looked longingly at the goods, but he saw no direct sign. "Their admiration was restrained and silent," he recalled, "and it was a matter of surprise to us to mark the care they took to suppress all appearance of astonishment."

That changed when night fell. They grew vocal and expressive then, in the darkness and among themselves. They were no longer the silent and impassive figures city residents saw during the day. "As soon as evening brought them back to their bivouac, they set to work playing, dancing, singing, yelling," Rémy said. Accustomed to European music—civilized music to his ear, with orderly and restrained rhythms—he thought they sounded like "enraged animals" when they sang, their voices rising and falling wildly. He did not know why they sang, or what the words meant. The singing went on for hours at night. These "discordant concerts," the weary hotel guest added, "were often prolonged until daybreak."[9]

When Ute and Shoshone visitors left the city, they usually carried valued trade goods, gained in exchange for fur pelts and tanned skins. Sometimes, after spending days in the city, they carried away contagious diseases as well.

A signal test, and milestone, in Sally's life with Clara and her people, came months after the treaty signing that drew so many Ute and Shoshone warriors to the city. That winter, seventeen children in Lucy and Clara's family fell sick at the same time. So did Sally. She was twenty-eight when she suffered the sickness.

A kind woman named Zina helped take care of them. She was the woman with Power who years earlier had spoken in tongues and, as Sally heard the words, prophesied that her mother and sisters would come for her. They had not yet come when Sally grew ill. That was in December, in the ninth winter of her life with Clara. The Leader's family had just moved to a new house.[10]

Zina's young daughter did not have the sickness, but Zina took care of those who did fall ill. The children wore something called asafetida bags, filled with the resin of a root that smelled repellant, like the strongest garlic or onion. Sally also heard Zina say special words, blessings. When she said those words, Zina always put her hand on the patient's head. Sally saw that Zina and Clara often held their hands up in the air, and kept them there, as if they were reaching for something.[11]

Zina's healing techniques resembled some of those that Sally knew from her earlier life. Zina used plant medicine, laying on of hands, and special words, spoken or sung. But she had other healing methods as well. She wanted Sally and the sick children to stay in bed inside the house, resting and keeping warm. The sturdy new house kept them well protected from the wintry cold outside.[12]

The Leader was away from the city, but some other men came to the house one morning in early January. They put a special oil on some of the children who remained desperately sick with the deadly disease. Then they left. Lorenzo, the Leader's younger brother, had come to see the family earlier, and stayed for a week. His wife Harriet, Clara's mother, had also come, and stayed for nine days, helping to care for the sick.[13]

Sally saw that many others helped, but Zina cured. As she had learned long ago in her life with the People, a woman could heal others. A woman could have Power, and Zina was a strong *po-a'-gunt*, shaman. By January, when the men brought oil, Sally was already recovering from the sickness. She survived, along with sixteen of the seventeen children. Even Lucy's son who had been so sick survived.[14]

The single death was unexpected. Zina had thought that all of the children were doing well by then, after a long struggle to heal them. Even Clara's baby son was improving, although "rather more slowly than the rest," she said. But Lucy described him as "a very sick boy, yet." Two days later, he died.[15]

Sally had helped to take care of little Jeddie from his birth. The mournful loss came just as she recovered from the disease with the strange name, the disease that took his life. She knew that other people had died from measles over the years. Some settler-colonists had died, along with many of Chief Wákara's and Chief Wanship's people—but not Baptiste, a strong medicine man known to have great Power. He had withstood that terrible sickness. But no Ute medicine man, not even Baptiste, could cure others of it.

Only Clara and her tribe appeared to have good medicine for the bad diseases. They had Zina, the *po-a'-gunt*, the skilled medicine woman with Power. Others too had some ability to heal. With Zina's help, and the close care of other women, Sally lived. It seemed by then that Clara's people had twice saved her life, first from her captor Baptiste, and then from killing sickness.[16]

Measles, a highly civilized disease, had entered even the far corners of Ute country with Europeans and Americans eight years earlier. Colonizing settlers who entered the big valley, and overland travelers who passed through on the way west, carried deadly illnesses with them from the East: whooping cough, mumps, chicken pox, cholera, diphtheria, scarlet fever, typhoid, pneumonia, and tuberculosis, as well as measles. Those dreaded diseases of civilization thrived where great numbers of people traveled or lived together. Measles, one of the first diseases to arrive with the colonizing settlers and one of the most contagious, proved among the deadliest. Clara's good friend, Lucy B., who reached the valley at the same time as Clara's sister Lucy, had fallen ill with measles on the overland trip, but survived. Few had died.[17]

But by December a year later, in the third year of settlement, and Sally's third winter with Clara, the disease had reached Chief Wákara's band. Some settler-colonists on an exploring trip reported that the chief and dozens of his people visited their camp. Many were desperately sick, aflame with fever, when they entered the camp. They were on horseback, with their dogs trotting beside them as they rode into gusting, cutting wind. It swept snow from drift and slope, flinging sheets of shining sharp crystals against exhausted riders. Wind tore into trees, tossing clouds of snow toward flat white sky.

"Much sickness prevailed among them," one of the explorers reported, "which we found to be meazles." He said that the men tried praying and laying on hands. They also "nursed the sick," he added, by giving them bread and meat, as well as coffee, tea, and sugar. But the men soon gave up on nursing the sick, and made haste to complete their exploring trip. They wanted to reach home before their reduced supplies gave out, and before winter descended with full freezing force.[18]

Chief Wákara's people had time-tested methods for dealing with sicknesses long known to them. They held curing ceremonies, or they used plant medicine, or sweating, to treat a person who was ill. Their sicknesses did not afflict a dozen or more people at once. They did not need a nursing tradition like the one that helped Sally and all but one of the Leader's young children survive measles. That nursing regimen saved lives during epidemics, but Chief Wákara's people had no experience with epidemics and no resistance to those diseases. In desperation, they had moved the sick and dying on horseback through a blizzard, riding in search of food, and hoping for help with the alien disease. Finally, famished and spent, they made camp in deep snow and deep cold. People died.[19]

Arapeen fell sick but recovered. He lost his only daughter, just nine years old, to measles in that killing time. She was sick when they came down from the mountains for the winter, Dimick remembered years later.

He called Arapeen "a hard-hearted man" with a cruel streak, and gave vivid examples. He did not say whether Arapeen showed such brutality before his child and so many of his people died, or only after.[20]

A few months later, near the end of that winter, Zina's young son had also fallen ill with measles. With her good care and bed rest and warmth, he recovered, slowly. The deadly plague had spread quickly through the big valley. Sally escaped measles that time. Years passed before it caught her. But the epidemic that killed so many of Chief Wákara's people, and missed her, had soon reached Chief Wanship and Chief Goship.[21]

According to the Leader, he had "an understanding" with the two chiefs about their valley homeland. By the time measles arrived, the chiefs and their people had shared the valley peacefully with their guests and presumed allies for nearly three years. "It is not good to fight the Indians," the Leader said, and indeed the settler-colonists had no reason to fight their friendly hosts and neighbors. As it happened, a disease, not bullets, proved fatal to them.[22]

Sally knew about the deaths. Everyone knew that the chiefs and many others died at a mineral spring, just a mile from the center of the city. She had reason to suspect that the deaths were due to bad medicine, sorcery. Chief Wanship's old enemies in the Valley of the Utahs could have used bad medicine to cause his illness and death. No one with Power had been able to cure the sickness. The chief and others had sought healing at the spring.

Some of the first colonizing settlers had seen the spring and pools of water within days of reaching the valley. They soon began to bathe there. Eliza had gone to the spring in a carriage with friends just four days after arriving at the fort in fall. She reported feeling "quite refresh'd" by the warm water. Patty pronounced it "a splended place."[23]

The new visitors did not know that the site had a long history as a place of healing. Warm water flowed into shallow pools, where people soaked in soothing sulfurous warmth. The bracing fumes of sulfur, and the heat of crystalline, mineral-filled water, often restored health. Chief Wanship and Chief Goship and their people had sought healing there when the ominous signs of sickness gripped them in late winter. They did not know any other way to cure this new disease, which brought raging fevers and alarmingly mottled skin.

One woman always remembered that killing epidemic. She and her family had just moved into a new log house in a still-sparsely settled part of the valley near the mineral spring. Her husband soon left for work that took him hundreds of miles away from their new home. She was alone with her children when the frightful sounds of the measles epidemic first reached her. She heard the despairing cries of sick and dying people on the way to the spring, and then the keening wails of survivors. The crying and wailing went on for days and nights. She did not know those people who passed by her door. Her fear made it hard to sleep alone, even protected inside a sturdy log house.[24]

Finally, the cries and wails stopped. The old curing practice of soaking in the warm waters of the spring had not saved Chief Wanship and Chief Goship and others. Men, women, and children died at the spring. The survivors interred some of the bodies. Settlers buried dozens of others in a mass grave, and they killed and buried an even greater number of dogs. They thought that the dogs had belonged to the people who died, and that the killing was customary.[25]

Six months later, a large bathhouse stood at Warm Springs, as English speakers called the site. It served city residents, including the Leader and his family, for many years. Befitting his position, he bathed apart from others, in a pool with a private entrance. He thought the water had medicinal value, and helped to relieve his rheumatic pain.[26]

Just a month after Sally survived a bout of measles, her old captor Baptiste was shot in the head. This happened at Chief Tintic's camp, located many miles north of the growing settlement near Salt Creek, where Baptiste's Shoshone wife Peggy had once worked as a laundress. Although accounts of the conflict varied, Sally soon heard that the man who had threatened to kill her, and then sold her as a slave, was dead. Perhaps he had also caused her sickness—and the children's. He had regarded their father, the Leader, as a dangerous enemy who wanted him dead. It seemed at first report that Sally no longer had to fear Baptiste or his bad medicine.

The settler-colonists knew him as the powerful medicine man who had once cured Chief Arapeen after riding fifty miles, at speed and with a relay of horses, to reach his camp. He was known even in the city for making powerful medicine. The Leader and others sometimes called him a chief. Baptiste not only healed his people but also tried to protect them from the foreign intruders on their lands. He seemed unyielding and without fear.

One of the early residents of the settlement near Salt Creek recorded that he stormed into their church on a Sunday morning, "in a great passion," she said. He accused the men of asking the Leader to have him killed, and then he demanded food for his people. On another Sunday, his men surrounded the church and Baptiste entered it alone, doing a war dance. He had removed his clothing, a customary practice for Ute men performing a war dance. But to the churchgoers, who knew nothing about that, his actions seemed startling and made no sense. They resolutely ignored him.[27]

He and Chief Tintic had later joined Chief Wákara in the short-lived war against the colonizers. After peace was made, Wákara and Baptiste protested the wall that soon surrounded the village near Salt Creek. Why did the people who lived there want to keep them out? Were they not friends now? Baptiste insisted that they put a gate in one corner for his special use, so that he could come and go as he wished. He demanded entry to the very settlement where seven innocent people had been shot down only months earlier, a sight that Adelia could not shake from memory. More recently, the Leader, who was trying to keep a fragile peace, had directed the settler-colonists to build a house for Baptiste nearby, and one for Wákara "where he wants it." Baptiste appeared so fierce and alarming that the Leader urged his people to give him food "and keep him there in peace."[28]

Just months later, Chief Wákara had died suddenly at his camp, still without a house. Baptiste had withstood yet another deadly sickness, which took the chief's life. Later in the same year, the Leader and his men worried once again about Baptiste, when his show of belligerence seemed to threaten the treaty ceremony with Shoshones. The people who had colonized the land around Salt Creek also remained wary of Baptiste. To their relief, he and the rest of Tintic's band moved north, and made camp on the western side of the big freshwater lake.

Soon enough the new neighbors of Chief Tintic and his men accused them of stealing cattle. If any settler-colonists had ever given food to Baptiste as ordered, they had stopped when drought and a plague of grasshoppers brought famine. Conditions grew worse during a hard winter with deep snow, when many cattle, horses, mules, and sheep died. Even settlers with farmland and surviving livestock suffered—but they did not face such deep hunger as Baptiste and Tintic's people, who lived on diminished wild lands. By that time, the territorial legislature had begun hearing petitions from men of means, and granting large tracts of wild land for their exclusive use as herding grounds. More and more of their grazing livestock intruded into ancient hunting and gathering grounds, damaging the land for wildlife, and leaving hunters and their families hungry.[29]

A large posse of armed men arrived one day at a fort that stood close to the place where Chief Tintic was camped. While they argued among themselves about how to proceed, Baptiste rode into the fort alone. He refused their demand that Tintic come to the fort. Instead, he asked the interpreter to go with him to his camp. Since he had shown courage by riding into the fort alone, surely the interpreter could ride alone with him to the camp.

The two men galloped away on Baptiste's horse. The interpreter spent hours at the camp, sitting in Chief Tintic's lodge, and listening to him and his men, uneasily. As the day wore on, the men in charge of the posse at the fort grew more and more worried about the interpreter's safety. They decided to go to the camp, rescue the interpreter, and arrest Tintic. The sun was low in the sky when they reached the lodge.

Two men rushed inside, and one grabbed Chief Tintic by the hair and drew his revolver, shouting that the chief was his prisoner. As the interpreter told the story years later, when Tintic tried to wrest the gun away, it went off, shooting him through the hand. Then the posse opened fire, he said, and Baptiste aimed a rifle at one of the men. Someone pushed the barrel aside, and Baptiste missed his mark. At that moment another man shot Baptiste in the head. Outside the lodge, the posse killed a woman and some men. One of the women grabbed a spear and threw it at an attacker, striking him in the leg.

The posse had run out of ammunition, and they retreated to the fort, taking the wounded man with them. Some of the women and children at Chief Tintic's camp had already fled, finding cover in a nearby stand of trees. The interpreter, left for dead in the empty lodge, had not been wounded. He rode away under fire, he later said, mounted on Tintic's horse and leading a second one that belonged to Baptiste. Tintic's men ran after him, shooting carefully, trying to miss the horses and hit the rider. The interpreter escaped, but the settler struck by a spear did not survive the night. Mournful cries from Tintic's camp reached the fort, and then subsided into silence. Tintic and his people carried their dead and wounded away in darkness, leaving a trail of blood in snow as they went west into the desert.[30]

Reports published in the city newspaper offered only sketchy details of the attack. Chief Tintic, named as a casualty of the conflict, did not die that year, or the next, or the next. Nothing was said at first about Baptiste. But then one of the Leader's associates publicly announced his death, as a triumph for the settler-colonists. He called him Battuze, this man whom they also called Battees, Batteste, Battese, and Battice. They knew very little about him. Baptiste's actions in the city, and inside a church, implied that he was a war chief, not solely a medicine man who did battle with spirits. "Battuze," a "chief so long famed for his brutality in murdering prisoners and Indian children with the coolest cruelty, has met his fate, and settled his last account in a fray with a posse," the Leader's associate said. He had not witnessed the shooting or seen a corpse.[31]

Baptiste was shot at dusk on a cold day in February. That happened in the ninth winter after he traded the captive girl to the newcomers for a rifle, and in the third winter after he entered a church to demand food for his famished people. But Sally did not know if this powerful man had truly died. The newspaper had reported Chief Tintic's death, yet he remained alive and at large. Chief Arapeen had heard about his escape. The Leader learned of it too.[32]

Some settler-colonists thought that Tintic's band had gone west and then south seeking refuge. Sally knew that country. The People went there to hunt and fish and gather. She knew that many of them had died from the new diseases. Their healers could not save them from such sickness.

By the time Baptiste was shot, she had reason to doubt that the few Pahvant survivors of the plagues included her mother and sisters. In those first years of colonizing settlement, far more of her people had died than survived. When she fell ill with measles, sixteen epidemics of deadly diseases had already swept through the territory. Smallpox reached the city a few months later, brought by colonizing settlers.[33]

The Pahvant Ute chief named Kanosh, an ally of the Leader, often rode to Tav'-o-kun, to visit him at his office in the city. Chief Kanosh knew exactly whom among his people still lived. He, like other chiefs, also knew that Baptiste had not died in the violence at Tintic's lodge. Chief Arapeen had told the Leader two months after the fight that Baptiste wanted to make peace. Two months later there was a report that Chief Tintic had offered to return cattle and horses. He too wanted peace. For Sally, their survival seemed to spell danger. Still.[34]

CHAPTER 6

The Mansions

SALLY HAD MOVED to one of the Leader's new mansions just months before Baptiste was shot in the head, and survived. The new *kan*, her home, clearly offered greater safety than the small house where she lived after she moved from the fort. It offered more protection than the city walls.

Clara and Lucy's husband had built two new houses, each far larger and grander than his previous home. The two mansions stood together on a street in the heart of the city. They occupied the very spot where Lorenzo and Harriet's small log house had once stood, the place where Charley took Sally after he paid Baptiste the sum of one rifle for her life and her labor.[1]

The mansions had no rival in the city or anywhere else in that part of the Far West, as visitors noted. More and more emissaries from eastern places had begun to arrive, and to report back on the progress of civilization, including such telling signs as mansions and other monuments of wealth and power. Sally lived with Clara and Lucy in the fine home known as the Lion House. The name came from the carved stone lion placed above the front portico. The lion, a biblical symbol of varied meaning, here gave clear warning. Clara and Lucy's husband, known to his people as the "Lion of the Lord," was also a vigilant guard of his family, the many women and children who lived inside the mansion.[2]

At the age of fifty-five, he retained a lion-like build, with short legs, powerful shoulders, and a massive chest. A rather tall man, he loomed over diminutive Clara and Lucy, and Sally too. He spoke in a forceful way but rarely roared unless addressing a multitude about their enemies, who ranged from some of the Utes to federal authorities.[3]

Sally had never read about lions. She still did not know how to read. But like anyone else she could see that the carving over the front portico of the new mansion looked something like a *tok*, a mountain lion of the high country. Those stealthy predators struck suddenly, with great force, and often with deadly force. The People feared *tok* as clever and dangerous animals. They did not hunt them. The settlers, fearing for their livestock, and themselves, did kill mountain lions. But they respected the ancient and powerful lions of a foreign land, the lions that that they read about in the Bible.[4]

Eliza, Margaret, and Ellen, who had earlier lived with Sally in cramped, shabby quarters, moved to the spacious Lion House along with Clara and Lucy and their children. Zina, who had given Sally hope of seeing her mother and sisters again, and who later gave her good medicine to cure measles, lived there too. Clara's close friend Lucy B., a woman named Emeline, and still others had also moved into the new mansion with their children. The women of the Lion House—Clara and Lucy and all the others except Sally and the hired helpers—were the Leader's wives. They shared him as a husband, and the mansion as a family home.[5]

Clara and Lucy's husband lived next door in the stately Beehive House where a large gilded beehive, symbol of cooperation and industry, adorned the top of the roof. He spent workdays in an office that stood between the two mansions. The Leader had prospered in the years since he and the first colonizing settlers entered the big valley where the small city now stood. The city spread out across more land with each passing year, as more and more people arrived and built new rows of small adobe-brick houses. The size of their houses and lots only magnified the scale of the Leader's houses and estate and other holdings. His enterprises—a farm here, a gristmill or sawmill there—were scattered across the valley, in the canyons, and beyond.[6]

His spacious city estate covered twenty acres of land. It measured sixteen times the size of the city lots owned by common folk, and it suited his stature as leader of a thriving settler-colonial site. To his people, he was no mere chief such as Wákara or Arapeen, who showed their importance by giving gifts, or by leading warriors on raids, or both. Like most high leaders in civilization, he showed his power by amassing and displaying, and by sending other men to do the fighting. No one known to Sally rivaled him in wealth or power—or in family size.[7]

So many wives and children! She and a few hired women, working under Lucy's direction in the kitchen, prepared their meals. Sally helped to

The Lion House and estate wall. Used by permission, Rare Books, Special Collections Research Center, William & Mary Libraries.

cook and serve a feast each day. This leader far surpassed Chief Wákara and all the others she had ever heard about or known. She lived and worked in the big house of the supreme chief of the world as she knew it. As long as she remained at the Lion House, she ate well at his table, and lived in safety under his protection. She was also subject to his authority.[8]

He had once said while giving testimony in court that she was free to leave. Years had passed, and still Sally stayed with Clara, her guardian and protector in daily life. Clara carried some influence with her husband on matters of home and family. Clara was like a good *pats*, to use that old word, the People's word, which no one at the Lion House understood. Like a good elder sister, Clara always shared with her. She shared her food, her shelter, and her children.[9]

When Sally walked outside the house, in the garden and orchard, protective barriers greeted her. A massive cobblestone wall, ten feet high and three feet thick at the base, surrounded the estate. Guards stood, day and night, by the heavy gate. And the carved *toq*, the stone lion, gave warning to all who passed by on the other side of the broad street and glanced above the wall.[10]

Even from the inside, when Sally looked out through the windowpanes she could see that the house, her sanctuary, looked fortified. The thick walls of the mansion, which framed the windows, offered yet another layer of protection from the violence. She heard story after story about killings in the territory, a few of them attributed to Baptiste or his known allies. Clara and the other women read reports in the newspaper, or learned about them from the Leader.

Within the walls of the Lion House, Sally witnessed a peaceful and absorbing daily drama played out by members of a complex family. More than a dozen women and some thirty-five children lived together there. She had come to know them well after so many years of watching and listening, a quiet presence always on the margins. She had known all of Clara's, most of Lucy's, and many of the other women's children from their births. She knew almost everything about them.

They knew nearly nothing about her, the "Indian girl," the servant who lived in Clara's rooms and worked in the kitchen with Lucy. The children did know the story of how Charley had saved her life. They heard how he rescued her from cruel savages and gave her to Clara, who civilized her. That story of wild and civilized became part of family lore, often told to the children and to visitors, sometimes in her presence.[11]

For Sally, who knew so much about them, the women and children of the Lion House formed a kind of band, a small group of familiar kin, a local community within the Leader's large tribe of settler-colonists. Some fifty people lived together, and they were closely related to each other. She had lost one band when captors took her away, and now she lived with a different one. But unlike the earlier band, no men lived in the Lion House, and few ever entered it other than the Leader or his brother Lorenzo or the rare workman. Most men met the Leader in his office. The guards at the gate saw to that.[12]

The Lion House had just been built, the lion carved, but the wall not yet constructed, when the Leader issued a public warning. An English visitor to the city heard him tell an assembly of several thousand people that they should come to his office, not his home, to transact any business. Then the Leader added that "he wished to give warning to all present that he had just received from London a new pair of boots with particularly strong toes, and that he should not scruple to use them on intruders."[13]

Guards and a high wall built around the estate soon took over from the boots. The men who guarded the sturdy gates were not simply enforcing privacy—or protecting the family from Indians, as Sally and the children heard. The guards and the wall protected the Leader from his enemies. He feared for his life. Murder was common enough, but most of the victims were not powerful men. They were outsiders or dissenters or petty

thieves, men on the wrong side of authority if not the wrong side of the
law. Some died at the hands of stealthy assassins dressed as Indians.[14]

In the hinterlands, a stock verdict-by-rumor about murder was "Killed
by Indians," although some people privately suspected certain men as the
main culprits. They whispered names, and pointed out those who played
"sham Indians." Suspicions lingered for years, even for generations. But
Sally did not live with people who voiced such doubts, and she had no
reason to question the accusing stories she heard.[15]

Ever since her arrival in the valley, she had listened only to the settler-
colonists' tales of attacks and killings. Many centered on the People, Pahvant Utes, who were once her people. Besides hearing of the murders of
William Hatton and Captain Gunnison and his men, she learned about
the massacre of more than a hundred overland travelers—men, women,
and children—at a place called Mountain Meadows. Everyone had heard
about the attack, which was blamed at first on Pahvant Utes and then on
Paiutes.[16]

A party of armed settlers had gone to their rescue, the Leader always
said. It seemed that those brave "pioneers of civilization," as they were
called, arrived too late to stop the massacre. They managed only to rescue
a few children spared by the attackers. In this wild/civilized narrative,
as Sally heard it told, wild and violent people had won a gruesome battle.
Other people, in other places, told the story differently, but Sally never
heard their version.[17]

There seemed to be few places of safety aside from the Leader's estate.
Elsewhere in the city violent men had entered a house, and committed an
unspeakable mutilation on a man who was alive, not dead. The four men
were dressed as Indians.[18]

She heard an endless, gruesome litany of violence, and no dispute
about guilt in any case. And she had her own tale of terror and suffering
at the hands of violent men who held her captive, burned her, forced her
two hundred miles north to the alien land of Tav'-o-kun, threatened to
kill her, and finally sold her to strangers from an unknown place. Those
men who hurt her were also relatives. Whether far away relatives or not,
they spoke her language.

Even before she knew that she would stay with Clara, Sally had learned
to speak the strangers' words. She studied their ways carefully, and
learned how to live with them. She survived. Now she lived peacefully
in a mansion with Clara and the children and others, the Leader's family. This was her home. The Lion House, like the big fort, defended her

from the dangerous men who had sold her, and others like them who attacked Clara's tribe. Nearly all of the violence came from them—or so she learned from hearing story after story of Indian attacks, tales of brave settlers and their battles with wild Indians.

Narratives of wild versus civilized taught her about wild villains and the good people who fought them. No wonder a high wall circled the Leader's estate. As he said, it kept dangerous wild Indians out. The only zone of peace and safety, it seemed, lay behind that wall.[19]

One quiet evening Clara sat alone in her suite, alone with her thoughts, and with only a piece of handiwork to take her attention. The Lion House stood nearly empty on that day and at that hour. She heard a knock at the door, and without raising her eyes from her work she invited the visitor to come in. A man entered the room, a stranger, and asked to see her husband. No such intruder had ever managed to penetrate the walls and gates of the estate, and to evade the guards. It was later said that he was a tall man in torn clothing, his hair unkempt, with a fierce look in his eyes. He was not Indian. No Indian man had ever entered the estate uninvited.

When Clara said calmly that her husband was not there, the intruder demanded to know where he was. Clara offered to find him. Taking the light into the dark hall she led the man out of the Lion House and to a room next to her husband's office, where she knew a guard was posted. "There," she said politely, "if you'll step in and wait a few moments, I'll inquire if he's here." But when the guard entered the room, he found it empty. A thorough search yielded nothing.

Clara returned to her rooms, relieved that the intruder had fled. She closed the door to the hallway, and had just sat down when she heard a knock. It must be the guard. "Come in," she called out. The door opened. The intruder again! This time he was bleeding from an injury. But the guard was close on his trail, and he secured the man and led him away.

Who the man was, why he wished so desperately to see the Leader, and what became of him—none of that remained in memory. What people liked to remember later when they told the story was that Clara did not betray fear, that she quietly led the "maniac," a wild-eyed intruder, out of her rooms and toward a guard. They said that she showed great bravery.[20]

When people told the story of Sally as a young captive, they said nothing about her stoic courage even if they spoke of her ordeal at the hands of wild captors, her starving hunger and the burns. They said nothing about her grievous loss of home and family, or her later resolve and effort to build a new life in an alien world. They spoke instead of her good fortune in living with Clara and the Leader's family, living in the heart of civilization.

A breach of the estate was rare. As Sally knew, the guards admitted only family members and friendly visitors. That meant no disaffected settlers or unknown Indians or suspicious people from other places. She lived and worked and ate and slept in a sturdy fortress that kept dangerous men out.

Behind the high wall of the estate, one day followed another, each much like the other, in a steady, soothing rhythm. She worked long hours in the kitchen under Lucy's firm direction. She ate three times a day without fail, not just twice as the People did—or as they sometimes did not, during lean times, when supplies of pine nuts and berries and game grew scarce. Even in a year of famine, when food was rationed in the city, and hungry people broke into a bakery to take flour, she still had eaten well each day. The Leader's family did not go hungry. She had grown to like their food. She ate her fill, just like everyone else at the table.[21]

She lived safely in a place of warmth and nourishment, among familiar women and healthy growing children. Now and then in the daily drama of life inside the house, an angry little boy demanded more dessert and brandished a sharp fork—but not at her, never at her. She liked to give food to hungry children. And those threats with forks came to nothing. They counted as mere ripples in calm water.

Snow fell, and snow melted. Spring slipped past the canyons and paused to rest in the city before moving on, and up, to mountains still smoothly draped in white. The air turned soft, and exhaled the scent of warmth, reminding everyone that they had forgotten how spring smells. Orchards flowered, and blizzards followed as pale silken petals fell to ground. Beneath the wind-blown drifts, tender shoots crowded damp soil.

Higher up, in the steep canyon above the Leader's mansions, bare cottonwood branches still glinted gold and copper in the sunlight, without a trace of green. A few fugitive oaks, not yet felled for firewood, stood shoulder to shoulder, twisted and gray. Slender bigtooth maples held smooth silver limbs aloft against blue sky. Clear, cold water rushed by the patient trees, falling down the narrow rocky creek.

Now and then some men with tools passed through a gate, and walked purposefully up the canyon on the trail by the water. Sally stayed at home, working in the kitchen. She no longer went to the creek, her old refuge from the strangers. They were no longer strangers, and the big fort where she had once lived was no more than a memory. The creek's old names, Nah-po-pah and Pa-sho'-wit, had been nearly swept from memory in the city. She heard everyone use the new name, City Creek. The Leader owned the canyon where the creek flowed, and could keep people out. Everything had changed.[22]

She never needed to fetch water again after she and Clara moved to the Lion House. The Leader's big houses had piped water and every other luxury. He saw to that. The women, including Sally, had no daily need to go outside the house or to leave the estate. Even a well-stocked family store was at hand.

Sally had never seen so many trade goods before she lived with the family. Clara often got cloth and yarn, medicine, food and drink, and sundry household items at the family store. Now and then she gave Sally a piece of cloth for a skirt, or a pair of shoes. Sometimes Sally, like the other kitchen servants, chose a small item for herself at the store. She asked the clerk for a measure of Epsom salts or bergamot oil. The Leader paid the women with goods as well as with room and board.[23]

One spring, a year or so after they had moved to the mansion, the Leader invited Clara and Lucy and Zina to join him on a grand excursion to a new fort nearly four hundred miles north. A large party of travelers left the city in late April. More than a hundred men as well as some twenty women and three boys, eleven and twelve years old, went with the Leader. The Ute chief Arapeen and his wife Wispit also joined the excursion. Dimick, Zina's brother, served as their interpreter. Some fifty carriages and wagons carried the travelers and supplies over a rugged track that took them north to Shoshone and Bannock country around the Salmon River.

Sally knew Chief Arapeen as one of Wákara's close allies, and the man who succeeded Wákara as chief. He had once counted Baptiste as an ally. She wanted to avoid such men. She stayed at home, and took care of Clara's two young daughters, Nettie and Nabbie, and the children Clara fostered. Lucy's children also stayed home.

Since Sally did not go on the excursion, she did not see how the men who lived at the northern fort conducted their colonizing and civilizing mission to Shoshones and Bannocks. A few of them had married Indian women, as the Leader advised. Intermarriage offered one means of assimilating and eliminating native people. The children would grow up among settler-colonists.

The men at the northern fort preached, and baptized a Shoshone chief and some of his people. They raised livestock and tried to make a farm.

Shoshones seemed friendly, the Bannocks less so. Anyone could see that Clara was enjoying far greater success in civilizing Sally. It seemed that she clearly wanted to live with the Leader's family, and to learn their language, customs, and skills. But no one knew much about Sally's circumstances: what she had lost, why she stayed.

A month after leaving on their journey, the travelers arrived back in the city. Clara always relished company, but she had shared some daunting moments with the other travelers. They braved chill winds and snow flurries in early May. They survived the danger of crossing wild rivers a-rush with frigid snowmelt. Once back at the Lion House, she and Lucy and Zina again embraced the comfort and safety of their life in civilization. They rarely left the city.

A year later, Bannocks attacked the northern fort. They killed a few men, wounded others, and captured hundreds of cattle. Some people later said that a young American man with a Bannock wife, a Virginian who preferred "the wild life to civilization," had encouraged the raid. That ended the colonizing effort and the civilizing mission to Bannocks. The story was often later told as a battle bravely waged in the war between wild and civilized. The settlers had suffered a setback, not a defeat, by people of the wild. Survivors had escaped, and that qualified as a small victory.[24]

In the eyes of people who lived in cramped cottages or rough log houses, and who carried water from creeks or canals, the women of the Lion House and Beehive House lived in splendid mansions. Some visitors to the city disagreed. One of them, the well-born Englishman who reported on the Leader's new boots from London, pronounced the Beehive House "pretentious." Still, it looked "well enough," he conceded, because of its large size, and the freshly painted white walls and green shutters. The newly built Lion House looked like "a sort of harem," he said, and he saw no beauty in its Gothic façade. "I felt a pity," he added, "for those who had to live between the gables."[25]

Like other visitors, the Englishman spoke from one side of an unbridgeable chasm. The narrow front side of the house, with the carved stone lion that warned passers-by, stood merely feet away from the street, but those feet were as miles. He knew nothing directly about the interior of the house, or about Clara and Lucy and the other wives who lived there. He knew nothing of Sally and the other servants. Nor did most men, including the federal census taker who compiled an official list of residents of the Lion House.

The census taker worked with great haste, paid according to the number of names that he recorded, and paid little at that. He listed the full names of several unmarried women who worked at the Lion House, without noting "domestic servant" beside their names. He ignored the heading on the printed census form—"Profession, Occupation, or Trade of each person, male and female, over 15 yrs. of age"—and gave only the occupations of men. Women who worked as servants at the Lion House went nearly unnoticed in the census, as in the house.

The census taker recorded Sally, without any surname, as "Indian," thirty-two years old, and born in the territory. She was the only woman at the Lion House and Beehive House who had been born west of the Mississippi River. A few of the hired servants came from Britain and Denmark. Otherwise, the women were nearly all of American origin, mostly from New York and New England. Only one wife came from a southern state. Her place of birth was near the Blue Ridge Mountains of Virginia, in the green and sheltered Shenandoah Valley. Clara and Lucy's birthplace was in the state of New York, and Eliza's, in Massachusetts. Those lands were as utterly foreign and unknown to Sally as her own place of origin, Sho-av-ich, remained to most of them.[26]

A month or so before the census taker set to work, a famous Englishman arrived in the city. Richard F. Burton—later called Sir Richard Burton after Queen Victoria knighted him—was a celebrated explorer and author, known for his daring exploits and discoveries in foreign lands. In Africa, he had searched for the source of the Nile River. He had spent years traveling and exploring the wild mountains and deserts of India and Arabia and then writing popular books.

Burton had a special fondness for kingdoms ruled by despotic sultans with harems. In Arabia, in disguise, he had managed to penetrate two holy cities—as well as harems in Egypt, he told his readers. He had become an avid reader of old Arabian tales, which he planned to translate into English. *The Arabian Nights' Entertainments*—also known as *A Thousand Nights and a Night,* or *A Thousand and One Arabian Nights*—featured stories of women who lived behind walls, captives of various sorts in remote and mysterious places. He had already started planning the translation project years before traveling to the United States.[27]

Now Burton wanted to visit, and write a book about, what he regarded as an exotic new kingdom in the wilds of a remote North American desert. He had an interest in all things that he, and his readers, found exotic. That meant, in the case at hand, that he hoped to learn about a mysterious new religion and an autocratic leader with many wives. In a recent book, the visiting Englishman who preceded him had claimed that the wives lived in a harem. Burton also wanted to write about Indians, "wild men," as he called them in print. They too seemed suitably exotic.

Sally might have taken his interest if he had managed to see her, but only as a minor curiosity, a tame Indian who lived in a mansion. In her plain blouse and skirt and apron, she had a civilized look, the look of a lowly servant. From what he had seen on his trip west, he judged that Indians did not wear civilization well. Wild Indians, especially those who scalped their victims, fascinated him. He had his hair cut very short, hoping to lessen his appeal as a candidate. Later, he wrote a few learned pages in his book on the subject of scalping.[28]

He stayed at a hotel in the city, took many of his meals there, and spent time touring wild sites around the valley. On a fine late-summer morning, he went with companions to see the big saltwater lake. On another day and with a different companion, he rode toward a canyon on the eastern edge of the valley. Big Cottonwood Canyon was carved into a rocky wall of mountain, merely miles from the city but a world apart.[29]

From the road Burton watched some Indian women sweeping wild grass seeds and crickets into large conical baskets. Then a settler, an Englishwoman, crossed the fields to speak to Burton and his companion. She complained about four Indian men who had frightened her, galloping by in hard pursuit of a stolen horse. The four men, and the few women with baskets, held no deep interest for Burton. Living just seven miles from the city, and in such small numbers, they did not seem to qualify as wild. By then, Indians had nearly vanished from the valley, replaced by crowds of colonizing settlers.

As Burton continued on horseback up to the canyon's mouth, he passed groves of native trees, quaking aspens. He took note of the singular leaves. They were "absolute green, set off by paper-white stems," he recorded. The leaves showed shiny green on one side and pale, dull green on the other. The barest breeze set long-stemmed leaves a-shimmer, and then pale green flashed silver in the sunlight.[30]

Some of the namesake trees in Big Cottonwood Canyon still stood, spared from burning in the settlers' hearths and stoves, or from serving as fence posts. Burton thought that the English name of both canyon and creek was a translation of an Indian name, but it was not. The early colonizers had eliminated and replaced most of the native place names they heard. They chose new names for canyons, for the creeks that flowed down from the mountains, and for most other sites in and around the big valley.[31]

The clear water of the creek glinted that day as it flowed across pebbles and past boulders. The rush and roar of snowmelt in spring had dwindled to babble and murmur. On the canyon's upper slopes the two riders saw stands of other native trees. Mountain maples wore autumn red. Looming spruces, ever green, cast a bluish light. The canyon's lower slopes were bare, completely cleared, the timber taken miles away for building and for firewood.[32]

In the city, Burton saw other sorts of sights. He surveyed Main Street, where newly built stores and workshops lined a long block across from his hotel. Just thirteen years earlier, only tall stands of wild grass and shrubs had occupied that ground. So many colonizers and overland travelers had soon arrived in the valley that the new stores had struggled to keep a supply of staples and other goods on hand. Coffee, tea, sugar, and flour had sold out quickly, and the selection of other merchandise was small. Now a vast range of goods from mundane to de luxe, imported from the East and from foreign lands, were offered to customers with money to buy them.

Burton did not see one of civilization's most ancient and time-honored wares, human chattel, on Main Street. He knew that Indian indenture was legal in the territory. He had read the law soon after he arrived in the city, and planned to include the entire text in his book. With slight effort he could have found Indian children who lived with prominent families. But those children, like Sally, qualified as tame and held no interest for Burton. He saw no wild child for sale on Main Street.[33]

General stores sold everything else, from mousetraps to shoes to gold lace, imported from distant places across the mountains and plains. Barbers and tailors, gunsmiths and locksmiths and blacksmiths plied their trades in small workshops. The purveyors of food and drink ranged from a bakery and a butcher shop to a liquor store and an ice-cream parlor. An apothecary, or drugstore, carried pills and bottled medicines that promised to bring health or kill pain. Some contained a secret ingredient: morphine or another opiate. No prescription was needed.[34]

A block from Main Street, Burton entered the Leader's office. The governor of the territory escorted Burton, and introduced him as Captain Burton of the British Army although his military career had ended years earlier. The office, "a plain, neat room," Burton said, held the usual furnishings. He saw a large desk, a safe, sofas, chairs, and a table. Unexpectedly,

a pistol and rifle hung on a wall, in clear view and within easy reach. Someone told him, politely if pointedly, that one of the firearms was a twelve-
shooter, newly invented.

The brief meeting lasted scarcely more than a half hour, and a clerk
summarized it as just "a pleasant conversation." Burton told the Leader
about his explorations in Central Africa, and the large lake seven hundred
miles from the sea that he saw while searching for the source of the Nile.
This was a story of European civilization encountering unknown wilds
and unwelcoming native people who lived there. He did not circle the
lake, one of the Leader's associates recorded, because "it would have taken
500 men" to fight their way through "the natives."[35]

Despite his celebrity and charm and compelling physicality—
or because of it—Burton did not manage to set foot in the dining room
of the Beehive House, where honored guests were invited and where he
might have seen Sally. He was a tall, dark, and exceptionally muscular
man in his late thirties who left a lasting impression on those who met
him. Some felt a vague sense of unease, even danger, in his presence. Some
women, drawn by his look and the slight whiff of disrepute, found him
disturbingly attractive. He had spent so much time traveling in foreign
lands, often alone. No one knew exactly what he had seen, and done,
in those wild places, even if they read his books.[36]

As a visitor of note, Burton did have the privilege of touring the
grounds of the estate. Fruit- and nut-bearing trees, grown from imported
seeds, stood on soil once claimed by native grasses and sagebrush.
He walked through an orchard of peach, plum, quince, apple, apricot,
cherry, and walnut trees. He saw three types of grapes, and learned of plans
for homemade wine. Strawberries, currants, raspberries, and gooseberries
flourished in the garden. Rows of hardy vegetables grew nearby, obedient soldiers standing at attention. The ranks included white potatoes and
sweet potatoes, squash, cabbage, cauliflower, broccoli, beets, and peas.
The steady hum of imported honeybees at work, and a scattering of hives,
gave promise of sweet honey. After admiring the garden, Burton walked
through the mills and workshops.[37]

He learned much about foods grown on the estate, but nothing about
those who cooked and ate the harvest. So mysterious did the mansions
and their occupants remain that he confused the Bee House, as he called
it, with the Lion House. "There is a Moslem air of retirement," Burton
remarked, "about the Bee House; the face of woman is rarely seen at the
window, and her voice is never heard from without."

Most of the women in the city, he complained, lived in "semi-seclu-sion." So it seemed to a man who wished to meet women who did not necessarily want to meet him, or whose husbands and fathers forbade it. Burton was, after all, an outsider, not of the faith. He was an oddity, even a threat, as an unmarried man, and a handsome one at that. He surveyed young women with his eyes, noting "the clear, transparent complexion, the long silky hair" of the few he saw. His gaze lingered, alerting the men.

Burton managed to speak at length with just one woman, a middle-aged Englishwoman named Mrs. Stenhouse. Burton did meet many men, and conversed with them on a range of subjects. He concluded that the men regarded themselves very highly, as "creation's cream," he said. The English visitor who preceded him had reached the same conclusion. From what he saw and heard in the course of two months he had judged that boys were more highly valued than girls. Men thought any deference to women "a humiliation of the superior sex," he said, and women obeyed their husbands and bore a great many children as matters of strict religious duty. He did not meet Zina or Patty or the other midwives who helped so many women do their duty. In a moment of piercing insight, Zina had once perceived that the word woman should be written wombman.[38]

Burton finally gave up his futile quest for a thrilling glimpse of a harem in the English-speaking world, and he left the city after three weeks. Other men who made shorter visits reported similar results. They saw nothing of the women who lived at the Lion House, and little of those who lived elsewhere. None of those women bore a resemblance to Sally, who wore the humble dress of a servant, and lived and worked in the safety of semi-seclusion behind high walls.[39]

Few visitors from faraway places received invitations to meet the Leader. Famous New York City journalist and newspaper editor Horace Greeley was one of the few. The two men met in the office next to the Beehive House, where Greeley spent two hours conducting an interview. He wore his signature white suit. One of the Leader's associates who met him said, "He was middling well dressed [in] white but bald headed." Then he added, "Looked as though he had not washed his Head since he came off the plains." White cloth seemed to wear dust well, unlike Greeley's head. The fine film of grime no doubt came from his walks along the unpaved city streets, where churned-up scurf rained down as dust on dry summer days.[40]

Greeley met many men, but saw few women, and Sally was not among those few. He finally concluded that the women occupied "the single office of child-bearing," as he put it. He saw no visible evidence that they did anything else. There were no signs in the streets or notices in the newspaper about events that women organized or attended. This stood in marked contrast to New York City and other cities and towns in the East. And he heard nothing about the women. None of the men Greeley met spoke of "his wife's or any woman's opinion on any subject," he reported. None "voluntarily indicated the existence of such a being or beings."

So far as Greeley could tell, women were, if sometimes seen, certainly not heard. The Leader confirmed that impression with a single statement. He told Greeley, "If I did not consider myself competent to transact a certain business without taking my wife's or any woman's counsel with regard to it, I think I ought to let that business alone."[41]

Two years later, an obscure young man from Missouri who spoke in a lazy drawl slouched into the same office. His brother Orion Clemens, a lawyer, was on his way to Nevada Territory. He had just been appointed to a federal post there. Sam, Orion's younger brother, was traveling with him. The two men and some companions talked to the Leader "principally about this Territory," a clerk at the office recorded blandly. "The improvements in the valley far exceeded their expectations," he added, and "after the conversation they politely took their leave." Sam, unlike Orion, held no official position, and the clerk made note of his presence only as an afterthought.[42]

Sam did not encounter Sally, and he would not have given a favorable account of any such encounter. He did not think highly of Indians, wild or otherwise. As a child he had listened closely to the Indian stories his mother told. Those family tales of bloody Indian attacks were narratives of the battle between wild and civilized. She came from a line of settlers who moved west from Tidewater Virginia to colonize remote backcountry, which took the name Kentucky. Indians would serve as imagined villains in some of his best-known books, written under the name Mark Twain. Narrative knowledge fed his fiction and fueled some of his cruelest satire.[43]

If Burton had ever gained entry to the Lion House, whether by invitation or deception, his readers would have been disappointed by the report. The long, rectangular house and estate grounds did not compare well with the palaces, harems, and perfumed gardens of an Arabia they imagined. It did not look sumptuous and exotic, either inside or outside. The interior, with lace curtains and heavy dark furniture, followed the conventions of Victorian taste. Most of the residents of the Lion House were young children. And their mothers and the other women were "far from resembling Sultanas of an Eastern harem," one woman said in pointed rebuke to the fond imaginings of Burton and others. Clara and the other women wore ordinary dresses, not the clinging costumes of lounging sultanas. Most of them had household duties.[44]

Daily life at the Lion House centered on the prosaic. The women cared for children, sewed, knitted, darned and mended, washed and ironed, dusted furniture, and swept the floor. Still, their daily burden was far lighter than that of most married women, including Eliza's friend Patty, the midwife. They did not need to cook three meals a day. Just one of them oversaw the kitchen, with the assistance of Sally and the other servants. They did not tend a vegetable garden and fruit trees, or milk cows each day. Hired workmen took care of the garden and orchard, and butter and cheese arrived fresh from the dairy of the Leader's nearby farm.[45]

Many of the wives did wash their own clothing in the Lion House laundry room, and they ironed in scheduled shifts. Eliza had only her own clothing to launder and iron. With her usual meticulous care, she reached dizzying heights of crisp and white. Others admired and aspired, but with a higher volume of laundry they could not achieve Eliza's results. Clara had as many as seven children in her care, and Emeline had eight—but also, as a special privilege, the full assistance of her own servant. Sally still helped Clara, even when her duties in the kitchen grew to full time.[46]

A weaving room stood across the hall from the laundry room. Some of the women did not know how to weave cloth, but they did spin and color thread. Spinning thread for cloth took many times the labor of weaving that thread into cloth. Manufactured cloth, imported from distant places, soon arrived, relieving them of that work. But the women still sewed clothing for their children, as well as their own everyday clothing— at first by hand, and later with a sewing machine.[47]

These few duties left them time to see the many friends who visited at the house. Clara, Lucy, and Emeline shared the privilege of entertaining guests in the parlor. The others, including Eliza, invited guests to their rooms.[48]

The most striking exterior feature of the Lion House, as many visitors to the city noted, was its gabled length. Twenty gables lined the mansion's upper story, ten to a side and each with a window. Inside, a long central hall divided the living space. The twenty doors on that hall each opened into a small bedroom. The kitchen servants, other than Sally, shared rooms at one end of the hall, closest to the street.[49]

The rest of the women who lived upstairs were wives of the Leader. Most of them, like most of the servants, were childless. Eliza lived there, and so did Ellen, who had once shared rustic quarters with Sally. Each of the women had a room furnished with a bed, chairs and table, and a mirror. A fireplace or stove provided heat.

Eliza's room stood out because of the books and papers, which were nearly absent from the others. A stand covered with books stood in the center of the room. She spent time writing as well as reading. Besides composing hymns, she wrote poems, which had been published recently in London in two volumes titled *Poems: Religious, Historical, and Political*. Eliza was widely regarded as the most intellectual woman at the Lion House. She had little to do with most of the others—or so someone said.

Ellen lived across the hall from Eliza. Her room at the Lion House qualified as the most tastefully furnished. She spent much of her time on embroidery and other fine needlework. She had once shown the strength to cross a thousand miles of plains and mountains. But now, in poor health, she did little besides her sewing. She led a sheltered, quiet life in the narrow confines of her room, spared daily labor by Sally and the other servants as well as by her ill health.[50]

On the main floor of the house, a richly furnished parlor occupied one corner. This long and narrow room had a large window on one end and four more windows along one side. Heavy curtains provided privacy at night. On summer days they shielded the room from blazing brightness and heat.

A large and costly wool carpet covered the floor. An admirer described it as "a beautiful Brussels carpet," with a floral pattern against a light background. Matching tables of solid mahogany, also costly, stood at each end of the room. There was an elegant and expensive rosewood piano, and a melodeon, a type of reed organ with piano keyboard. A sofa, covered in dark crimson velvet, stood near a bureau that held silver candlesticks and decorative objects. A large stove in one corner heated the parlor in winter.[51]

The rest of the main floor was divided into suites with sitting rooms as well as bedrooms. A few wives with young children each lived in a separate suite on that floor. Lucy and her children occupied a corner suite for several years. Clara and Sally and the children lived in the one beside it. Clara's friend Lucy B. and her daughters were in the next suite, and another housed a woman and her six children.[52]

Emeline, the mother of even more children, lived across the hall in a large suite by the parlor. An expensive rug covered the floor, and red and white curtains covered the windows. A high-post bed, sofa, table and chairs, and wardrobe filled the room.[53]

Clara lived with Sally and the children—three daughters, a young son who was born two years after Jeddie died, the brother and sister Clara fostered, and another foster daughter—in her suite of three rooms. Sally helped with the children except when she was at work in the kitchen, and she slept with them in the suite. The bedroom where Clara slept—with the Leader when he visited for the night—was furnished with an ornately carved bedstead enclosed with heavy damask curtains. An oil portrait of the Leader, along with a large mirror, adorned the walls, and a colorful rag carpet covered the floor.[54]

Clara possessed a small private library, but unlike Eliza she did not display her books. She read novels. Her husband did not approve of fiction, not even uplifting tales by Charles Dickens about plucky orphans who outwitted cruel masters. He recommended reading selected works on religion, and practical works on geology. The furnishings of Clara's suite led someone to conclude that "from its superior furniture it is easy to infer that its occupant is a woman fond of show, as well as a favorite" of her husband. What the occupant read and shared with others remained discreetly out of view in a closet.[55]

There was so much for Sally to learn inside the two mansions, even apart from her kitchen duties. Consider the things called carpets. Clara and Lucy and the other women taught that the smooth wood floors needed coverings made of cloth. O, the labor! They spent tedious hours cutting up rags and sewing strips, assisted by their daughters, and by Sally, who did not sew rags cheerfully. Then they spent more time weaving the strips into colorful carpets. These covered most of the floors in the house. The trouble was, the rag carpets collected that thing called dirt, which was the same term used for the soil in the garden and orchard, or the earth in the nearby canyon, or the smears on young children's clothing after they played outside the house.[56]

Dirt was something that belonged outside, in the wild outdoors, but found its way inside, stealing into civilized spaces. More work! Women had to remove this unwelcome intruder from the house by means of brooms and mops and rug beaters as well as soap and water. At least once a year, and sometimes twice, the carpets were taken up and thoroughly cleaned. Then there was still more labor. Workmen put small piles of clean straw on the polished wood floors, and tacked each of the carpets in place over its own bed of straw.[57]

Sally had learned something else about dirt long before she moved to the Lion House. One of the lessons taught during the first year at the big fort was that she should never sit directly on the earth, or "sit on the ground in the dirt," as Clara's husband put it. No, she should always find a chair or bench to sit on, to separate her body from the earth, or rather, from the dirt. That was the best way to sit outside a house—and also inside, even with the wood floors and carpets.[58]

Besides learning about dirt and cleaning, and the names of countless objects, Sally had learned how to use or care for many of those things. She saw more and more trade goods enter the mansions as the years passed, from the one called a sewing machine to new chandeliers fitted with coal oil lamps. By watching carefully, she had also learned who should, and should not, handle those goods, called stove, clock, sofa, piano, candlestick, dishcloth, broom. The list went on and on. She handled the broom and dishcloth, not the piano.

CHAPTER 7

The Kitchen

SALLY'S DAY USUALLY WENT like this. Wake up early. Get dressed and get ready for the day. Help Clara with the children. Go downstairs to the kitchen. Help Lucy and the kitchen staff prepare breakfast and set the dining room table for the fifty women and children of the Lion House. Eat breakfast with them, and then help clean up the dining room and kitchen. Fifty sets of breakfast dishes and silverware must be washed and dried and put away in the dish room. Pots and pans must be scrubbed clean and made ready for the next meal.

Prepare the main meal, set the dining room table for fifty people, and serve the food at midday. Eat with the family, and then help clean up the dining room and kitchen. Fifty sets of dishes and silverware must be washed and dried and put away in the dish room. Pots and pans must be scrubbed clean and made ready for the next meal. Do other housekeeping duties as needed in the afternoon.

Help prepare supper, and set the dining room table for fifty people. Eat with them, and then help clean up the dining room and kitchen. After fifty sets of dishes and silverware, along with pots and pans, have been washed and dried and put away, join the family in the Lion House parlor. Sing and pray with them, and listen to the Leader's talk. Help Clara put the children to bed. Go to sleep. Wake up early, and begin again.[1]

The heart of the Lion House, as a community of women and children, was located downstairs where Sally worked. The basement ran the full length of the house, and the kitchen and a family dining room filled part of that

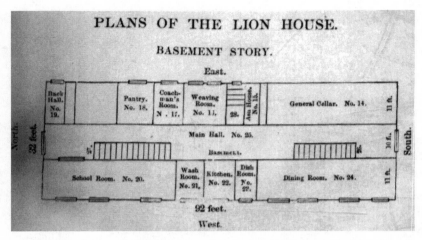

The Lion House basement. Used by permission, Rare Books, Special Collections Research Center, William & Mary Libraries.

space. A pantry, a schoolroom where the children had daily lessons, and a room for the coachman called Black Isaac, stood nearby. Small windows, cut into the walls at ground level, near the ceiling of the basement, admitted light. In summer, the basement stayed cooler than the rooms upstairs, which stood in direct line of the sun's daily assault. In winter, a comforting, fragrant warmth from a large cooking stove and baking oven spread from the kitchen into the schoolroom and dining room.

The women and children gathered in the dining room three times a day. Breakfast, served at eight o'clock, was usually a meal of eggs, toasted bread, and fruit. Sometimes the kitchen staff prepared buckwheat cakes with maple syrup. They made the syrup from maple sugar, imported from a faraway place called *Vermont*. Sally had not heard that name before she lived with the Leader's family. Vermont was the Leader's place of birth, but he had left his homeland forever and led his tribe to Tav'-o-kun.[2]

As soon as breakfast was finished, and the kitchen clean, the staff began to prepare the most complicated meal of the day. The sun gave good light to the kitchen at that hour. The large meal that the family called *dinner* was served at noon. Sally and the other members of the kitchen staff often prepared beef or mutton, or *pa-gu*, fish, especially mountain trout. Or they cooked poultry, sometimes *un-wan'-unk*, wild goose, or the bird called *chicken*. For certain special meals in winter they roasted the big birds known as *turkeys*. They did not prepare the meat called *pork* because the Leader disliked it. Fragrant loaves of light bread, served with rich sweet butter, always appeared on the table, along with generous helpings of creamy potatoes and other filling foods, and vegetables. At the end of the meal came a sweet dish of juicy ripe fruit, called *pie* or *cobbler*, or sometimes cookies or a pudding. The soothing sweetness lingered in Sally's mouth.[3]

In keeping with a set daily schedule, the Leader joined the women and children at the Lion House for supper at the end of his workday, five o'clock. Supper, sometimes prepared in dim light on late afternoons in winter, was a simple meal. The kitchen staff often made cornmeal mush, and served it with milk. They also carried platters of cheese, bread, and fruit to the dining room—the fruit fresh or baked or stewed, depending on season.

The Leader ate with his family at a long T-shaped or U-shaped dining table. The shape changed as the family grew. He sat at the head, at the shorter and so-called upper table. Clara, ever cheerful, sat beside him with her children. Emeline, whose arresting beauty brought her favor, sat on the other side with her children. Lucy presided at the lower dining table where the rest of the wives and children were seated, along with Sally and the other kitchen servants.[4]

As part of a fixed weekly schedule, Sally helped prepare the biggest meal of the week on Saturdays. The cold meat left over from that dinner provided part of a meal the next day. On Sundays, she helped prepare only two simple meals. That was a day of rest at the Lion House, except for Lucy and Sally and the hired servants.[5]

In the kitchen, Sally took daily lessons from Lucy. She had not darned socks cheerfully for Clara, but she willingly cooked. No reports of sullenness issued from the kitchen. Food was life. To the People, an abundance of meat and seeds and berries meant prosperity. The good work of preparing food belonged to women. Giving food to others, and especially to children, brought affection and respect.[6]

Everyone agreed that Lucy was a fine cook, a superior housekeeper, and a very practical person. Sally spent each day learning the many specific skills that Lucy taught, from cookery to housekeeping. As most people saw it, she learned those skills because she needed to earn a living—not because, as happened to be the case, she wanted to be part of the Leader's family, to help them by doing the good work of preparing and serving food.[7]

The kitchen had a hierarchy and a division of labor, and Sally started at the bottom. At first, alongside the least skilled of the hired women, she scrubbed the stove and oven, and kept the stone-flagged floor clean. She washed and dried the large cooking pots and frying pans. She learned to wash plates and glasses carefully, to dry them with a clean cloth, and to return each to an assigned place in the dish room between the kitchen and dining room.

Sally had already learned about correct dining before she started to work in the kitchen. She knew how to wash her hands before eating, and how to handle a ceramic plate—which is to say, very carefully. She knew how to sit in a chair at a table while eating, with her back straight, and elbows held close. She knew what to eat with a spoon, and what to spear with a fork. Once at work in the kitchen, she learned some finer points about serving food at the table. Some foods should be served in a bowl, others on a plate or a platter, and always with the correct serving utensil.

Sally reached the next level in her apprenticeship when she began to prepare food. She peeled, sliced, boiled, baked, or fried all manner of garden produce. She cut, seasoned, boiled, stewed, fried, or roasted poultry, beef, fish, and wild game. She learned not only how to roast a chicken, or beef, or other meat in an oven, but also how to make gravy to serve with it. She already knew how to boil roots, but in Lucy's kitchen she also mashed the cooked potatoes, and arranged them in a mound topped with a tiny lake of sweet melting butter. Then began the lessons about puddings and simple desserts. She rarely made bread. That usually came from a bakery on Main Street, which spared the kitchen staff hours of labor.[8]

The unspoken aim of the settlers' cooking, as she learned by doing, was to transform something raw—vegetables or part of a carcass or both together—into something cooked that bore little resemblance to the raw. The greater the transformation, the better the dish, the more refined or civilized.[9]

This transforming not only required a series of steps, some of them difficult to master. It also required an intricate supply of ingredients, nearly all of them imported domesticates, not native and wild. Most of the meats and grains came from the farm, and fruits and vegetables, from the orchard and garden. The small, dried pieces of plants, called *spices*, were imported from faraway and unknown places. Sally had never seen these ingredients when they were growing. There was the sweet thing called *sugar*, which looked like grains of sand, and the fragrant nuts named *nutmeg*. The thin brown sticks or fine powder known as *cinnamon* had a faintly musty smell and a subtly sweet taste. Since each of the dozens of dishes that she prepared had a special name, she learned those as well. Some of the names gave clues about ingredients, but others were mysterious. She learned *summer squash with cream, strawberry shortcake*, and *doughnuts with hot syrup*, but also *royal favorite*, a dessert.[10]

The children loved her doughnuts. A special kind made with nutmeg was also a favorite of the Leader. There were ten ingredients, always the same, which Sally committed to memory, along with the steps in preparing doughnuts. She started by putting a large measure of flour into a big bowl. Next came half as much sugar, and small amounts of baking soda, baking powder, salt, and ground nutmeg. Then she added eggs, butter, and finally the buttermilk, a little at a time, stirring and kneading the dough until it was soft but not sticky. When the texture was just right, she rolled out the dough on a clean board sprinkled with a little flour.

She cut large doughnut rounds from the dough, and then cut out the center of the dough with a small cup. After heating lard in a pan, she carefully lowered the doughnuts one by one into the sizzling hot fat, and fried each side until it reached a tender golden brown. Then she removed the doughnuts from the pan and placed them on plates. She repeated the process, making dozens of doughnuts to feed fifty people. Finally, she drizzled the warm doughnuts with hot syrup—and served this treat to a crowd of excited, hungry children, and their mothers, in the family dining room.[11]

There was still more to learn in the kitchen besides how to make and serve doughnuts and all sorts of other food, from meats and vegetables to grains and fruits. Even before she began to make pies, Sally learned that a pie must always be cut into six pieces of equal size, and each piece served on a plate. She also learned when to serve meals. Lucy looked at something called a *clock*, and insisted that the first food be ready at exactly eight o'clock and more food at twelve o'clock, and then again at still another o'clock. She was very particular about all of the details, including the schedule. These treasured customs about what and when to eat were not simply practical but also deeply meaningful. They were symbolic markers of what the settlers saw as a civilized way of life.[12]

Sally had grown up with a very different culinary tradition. What a raw food was—wild berries, roots, seeds, fish or game—often remained clear even after cooking. She had acquired some of the berries and roots and seeds herself when she went with her mother to gather food. She knew how they looked, where they grew, when they turned ripe, and how to cook them. Her mother and the other women often roasted the food. Or they cooked with stones heated in the fire, and then put with food in a basket, or in a pot, or in a pit in the ground. The cooking was simple. Gathering and processing took far more time, effort, knowledge, and skill.

As a child, she had eaten many different foods, but rarely all at once. Sometimes the People ate only one food for a meal. The particular plants they ate depended on season and supply. The particular animals they ate depended on season, supply, and the skill and luck of hunters. When they had a great variety of foods at one time, the women made a stew or soup, *u-wap'*, and put everything in it. It was never exactly the same twice. The People relished those meals.[13]

Sally soon learned that such meals drew scorn from Clara and Lucy's people. In their world, good cooking required hours of labor as well as skill and control. A stew should always be made in the same way, with the same ingredients, not with everything that happened to be at hand. It would not be good to add dill pickles to roast turkey, even if Lucy had a generous supply of pickles on hand.

As time passed, she grew more and more proficient in preparing food in the new way. Her tastes had slowly changed, and she did not miss the old ways of eating and cooking.

After directing the kitchen at the Lion House for four years, Lucy had received a promotion of sorts, a reward for her skills and service. At the age of thirty-eight, and just months after she bore her tenth child, Lucy took charge of the Beehive House, the Leader's official residence. She moved next door with her seven younger children. Sally still lived with Clara and the children at the Lion House. She still cooked there, supervised by Lucy's replacement in the kitchen, a woman named Twiss.[14]

Eventually she began working with Lucy again, spending her days in the Beehive House kitchen where her daily workload lessened slightly. She helped prepare meals for twenty-five people instead of fifty. Lucy directed the kitchen staff in cooking breakfast, a large midday meal, and supper for the eighteen hired men who worked at the estate. On most days she made breakfast and sometimes a second light meal for her husband. Her family ate their meals separately. Lucy also planned and helped prepare formal meals for her husband's important guests.[15]

Besides Sally, Lucy's assistants in the kitchen at the Beehive House, as at the Lion House, included a few young women, or hired girls as they were generally termed. One of Lucy's daughters remembered being told not to call them servants. Instead, the workmen and hired girls were supposed to be called "the men or girls who helped with the work." But later in life, she referred to Sally as one of the "maids."[16]

The young women who helped in the kitchen were "strong girls," another daughter recalled. They had the physical stamina to work hard—like Sally, although she was twenty years older. One, named Mary Ann, came from England. Another, Emma, had arrived from Denmark, and still another, Sophia, from Norway. Some of the young women did not know how to speak English when they reached their new home. In Lucy's kitchen, they learned to cook, and they also learned English by listening to instructions about mundane matters such as how to clean the stove, or cut the vegetables, or set the table. Lucy's daughter thought that the hired girls learned English even more quickly by listening to children. So had Sally.[17]

It might have seemed to Lucy's daughter that these servants from foreign lands followed Sally's path of assimilation, learning to speak a new language as they learned their new work. But Sally had made a far longer journey from a birthplace just a few days' travel from the city. The servants, speakers of various European languages, learned English, a related European language. She had grown up speaking an American Indian language entirely unrelated to English.

She had also needed to learn far more about the world of the kitchen and dining room than did the hired girls. Mary Ann, Emma, Sophia, and the others knew about forks and plates and clocks long before they entered Lucy's kitchen—even if they knew little about cooking and sewing and housework because they had only worked in factories. One of them, employed in a button factory, had learned how to make buttons, but not how to sew them on a shirt. Lucy tried to train her and the others, as she trained Sally, in all of the housekeeping arts, not just cooking. Then they could help her with housework as well as cooking.[18]

Lucy took it as a matter of both pride and regret that these kitchen servants married and left once they had learned English and mastered some of the skills that she taught. Sally did not marry and she did not leave, even as years passed. She held a nearly unique status, not only in the Lion House but also in the city and territory, as a woman who was socially eligible to marry, but who remained unmarried in her twenties, then in her thirties, and even into her forties.

Very few of the settler-colonists had married Indian women. But barriers of language and culture did not exist with Sally by the time she reached her mid-twenties. She spoke English and knew how to live as Clara and

her people lived. Moreover, she lived with the leading family of the territory, an advantage to any man who married her.

Some people said she discouraged a suitor. She did not want to leave
the peace and safety of the Leader's walled estate. Years earlier she had felt
confined by walls at the fort. To someone who had never lived behind
walls, not even in a sturdy house, the fort felt like a trap. But over time,
as the violence of settlement and resistance continued, walls and gates and
guards had come to feel protective.[19]

She stayed with Clara and Lucy in their sheltered community of
women and children, and continued to learn and practice the higher culinary arts. She worked so hard and made herself so useful that her value as
a dependable, skilled cook in a busy kitchen assured her a place with the
family. When she was not at work with Lucy in the kitchen, she worked
for Clara. At a time when hired labor—or at least men's labor—was expensive, hers came at slight cost. She did not receive wages.[20]

After years of service in the kitchen, and training under Lucy's firm
direction, Sally finally reached the highest position of the kitchen staff.
As chief cook, she prepared the most prized dish. In the kitchen, even
food formed a hierarchy. What Lucy and Clara called *dessert*, she learned,
stood at the top. Everyone prized dessert. This special sweet dish was only
served once a day, and always at the end of dinner. That was the custom,
at least for people who had the means. The many poor settler-colonists
who lived on wild greens and jackrabbits could not afford such daily
luxury.

Desserts required more labor and skill to prepare than meat or vegetables. Most contained a complicated mix of ingredients, usually some
combination of flour, leavening, sugar, cream, butter or lard, eggs, spices,
and fruit. Some of the ingredients, especially the sugar and spices, were
scarce and costly. The cooked product looked nothing like the raw ingredients that went into it. There were so many desserts, each with its own
special name, which might have nothing to do with the ingredients. She
learned the names pound cake, Washington cake, pain-au-ris, Charlotte
Rushe, transparent, blanc mange, and fancy mange, as well as raspberry
pie, mince pie, cherry pie, custard pudding, ice cream, and many more.[21]

Directions for making these tempting, complicated desserts were
sometimes recorded. A recipe, Sally saw, was a set of marks on paper. The
marks told which ingredients were needed, and exactly how much of each.
The marks also told how to mix them, how long to keep the dish in the

oven, and how much heat was needed. Since Sally still could not read or write, she learned each recipe by heart.

Lucy taught her how to make apple pie, a dish that she mastered along with many others. A generation of children always remembered the flaky, delicate crusts, the taste and texture of the sweet, soft slices of apple when a forkful of Sally's pie reached an eager mouth. Bliss! The doughnuts that she made rivaled the pie with their warmth and sweetness, inside and out, with a crust so soft yet slightly crisp. And the size always delighted the children. Sally made the largest doughnuts, just to please them. She knew about the family's strict limit on sweets served to children. Since each child was allowed one portion only, she increased portion size.

As a pastry chef who prepared desserts, she held an honored place in the kitchen—and in the hearts of tiny diners. She indulged children, as her elders had once indulged her. When she baked cookies and pies, a soothing fragrance spread throughout the house. If the children were not in school, the sweet aroma often drew a few of the bravest. Hungrily, hopefully, they crept into the kitchen—despite the family ban on eating between meals, and despite the risk of sharp words if they were caught with sweet contraband in hand. They looked for Sally, who was good-natured, they thought, and always kind to children.

Sally knew that it was good to give a hungry child a warm sweet cookie, fresh from the oven, although it was best to make sure that no one else saw. It was also good to let the child take one and run away before the other women noticed. They would chase the little scofflaw, but Sally stayed in the kitchen and kept cooking. She saw no mischief when a hungry child bravely captured a cookie. That was not stealing. It took courage and skill to raid the kitchen for a cookie, and to avoid notice, and escape.

For a hungry child to eat was always good. Giving food to hungry children was one of the good things in life. She could not think of refusing to give a child a cookie when she saw so much food always at hand in the kitchen of the Leader's house. To hear children cry because they were hungry, because there was no food to give them, that was bad. Long before she began to live with Clara at the fort she had learned that, and she never forgot it.[22]

Years later one of the Leader's children, by then an old woman, remembered herself and the others as "little ravenous wolves" who devoured food, and who prized dessert most of all. Sally's apple pies and custard pies, her crullers and molasses gingerbread, were the "acme of culinary delights," she said. One of her sisters still recalled fifty years later the melting pleasure of eating Sally's fare. "What good bread she could make! And what cookies!"[23]

Lucy, of course, stood above Sally at the top of the chain in the kitchen. She trained, directed, and supervised the help as they prepared meals, but Lucy also found time to cook. She sometimes baked pastries and made other desserts, displaying her own culinary skill and her stamina. One of her daughters remembered, "She thought nothing of making fifty mince pies at one baking or of freezing ten gallons of ice cream." Sally usually worked beside her, whether her daughter noticed or not.[24]

Like the other kitchen servants, Sally took directions from Lucy about her daily duties. The directions came from a woman who was devoted to her husband's comfort and to good cooking and good housekeeping. Sally knew better than to interrupt Lucy when she was busy with kitchen and household tasks or tired. She had such a sharp tongue that it kept some children away from the kitchen. There was an old word for someone like this, *nam-tum-po'-a-gunt*, a scold. But Lucy was Sally's elder by nearly ten years, and Lucy's husband, an elder by thirty years. She listened carefully to them.[25]

Joining Clara and Lucy's tribe had meant learning many things over again, and doing as they did. Joining had meant entering a world of hierarchy, inequality, separation, and highly specialized labor. And Sally had entered it at the lowest level, as a captive, a mere woman, a servant, and—in the view of most Europeans and Americans of the time—as a dark-skinned wild Indian, "a genuine savage," as one man later said.[26]

A great gulf divided higher and lower, even when they lived in the same place. Men and women, rich and poor, master and servant, free and captive, light-skinned and dark-skinned, civilized and so-called savage—all enacted the firm boundaries that divided them. Higher had privileges that lower lacked. Higher told lower what to do. Lower was supposed to listen when higher spoke. When lower disobeyed or presumed to take any privilege, lower acted saucy, to use the settlers' word. They often complained that Indians were sullen or saucy. Sally did not know any of this at first. No one had explained it to the captive who did not understand English and who struck them as sullen and sulky. These were matters of tacit knowledge, which she learned as best she could by watching and listening.[27]

In the beginning, she had remained silent because she could not understand or speak the strangers' words. Later, after learning the words, she still said little, in part because she was studying their ways, especially those of her elders. When someone older than Sally talked to her, she always listened. She had learned early in life that the words of her elders deserved attention, and that they often made good sense. To listen to her elders and the chief, to defer to them if possible, was virtue. They in turn earned the affection and respect of those younger by helping them, by giving to them. That was the good way to live, as the old people often reminded everyone. She had never forgotten this.[28]

Every evening at seven o'clock, an hour or so after supper ended, and after Sally and the other servants had finished their last chores in the kitchen, the family gathered in the parlor of the Lion House. On stormy nights, wind hammered at the windows, and sheets of rain or sleet slid down the glass. The curtains, drawn, shut out the storm. In the parlor, the family sat together in comfort, sheltered from wild forces outside.

Sally and the kitchen servants always joined the wives and children in the parlor. Clara and her children were there, and Eliza, and Zina, and all the others—each deeply familiar to Sally who had lived among them for many years. The Leader sat in the center of the room, with Eliza next to him. He led prayers. Afterwards he talked. This, like the meals the family shared in the dining room, was part of a cherished daily routine at the Lion House.

All chiefs, as Sally had learned long ago, were *um-pa'ta-wi-unt*, talkers. Among the People, the chief talked early in the morning, exhorting them to live well together and advising them about the work they should do that day. Sometimes he also talked at the end of the day. At the Lion House the Leader always talked in the evening. But first, everyone prayed.

Prayers, as she had learned years earlier, were special words said, or heard, sometimes after assuming a special posture, with knees bent, back straight, head bowed. This posture, she understood, was meant only for prayers. It seemed important also to keep eyes closed while the special words were said, words such as, "Bless the church and Thy people, the sick and the afflicted, and comfort the hearts that mourn."[29]

What those words meant, especially about hearts, was not entirely clear, but it seemed that one part of the body felt sad. Mourning had once meant something else to her. When Clara's baby son died from measles, the death came as a terrible blow to Clara—and to Sally, who had helped take care of little Jeddie from his birth. But she had seen enough of death by that time to know that Clara would not cut her hair short, or cover herself with ashes, or wear ragged clothing, or cry each day for a year. Instead, Clara's heart mourned.[30]

The People held different beliefs about death, and followed other practices. They thought that it was better not to speak about the dead, especially close relatives. But Clara's people not only told stories about the dead, they also named their children after them. Clara's second daughter, Nabbie, bore the name of the Leader's beloved, long-dead mother and sister. Clara's second son, Albert Jeddie, shared the name Jeddie with her first son. Jeddie had died a few years before Albert Jeddie's birth. The name had originally come from a man named Jedediah, the one who spoke special words when Harriet and Lorenzo's baby was buried years earlier. Now that man too was dead. The People knew that it was not good to name a child after someone who had died.[31]

After evening prayers, or sometimes before, the family gathered around the piano to sing. By then, Sally had not heard the old music, the old songs, for years—except outside the house, when Utes traveled by horseback to Tav'-o-kun, and camped in the city. But that had grown rare as time passed.[32]

Many of the new songs, the ones she heard in the parlor, had words such as angels and Heavenly Father. She could only try to imagine what they looked like, just as she had once tried to imagine Wolf and Coyote and other animal-people. Such songs were termed hymns. Others, which did not have those special words, were just songs. "Hard Times Come Again No More" was one favorite. Another was "Auld Lang Syne," whatever that meant.

Eliza had written a good hymn that began: "O, my Father, Thou that dwellest / In the high and glorious place / When shall I regain Thy presence / And again behold Thy face?" The hymn spoke of heavenly parents. Sally had never heard about them before Eliza told her about Heavenly Father and Heavenly Mother. She had only heard the elders tell how Shinau'-av, Wolf, created the first humans.[33]

Eliza's stories included some about life after death that Sally had never heard before she knew Clara and Eliza. When these people died, she learned, their spirits went to places known as the three kingdoms of glory. A few went to the highest one, which they called the celestial kingdom, a realm of glorious light. Clara's and Harriet's baby sons had gone there. People who died in great pain also went to a kingdom of glory—including poor Franklin, who ate the poison parsnip. It did not matter if Franklin acted brave when he died, or if he cried out in pain. He went to a kingdom and lived happily there, at home forever with others who had died but lived again. Eliza was certain of that.

Sally learned that she would also go to a kingdom of glory when she died. That was thanks to the ritual that Eliza and the others called baptism. And in that eternal home she could again see her mother and father and sisters—if only they were baptized in the special ritual for the dead.[34]

No one had ever told Eliza about Na-gun'-tu-wīp, a home for departed spirits who show courage. She did not know that the dead arrive there only after a harrowing journey through an underground passage. Animal-people, including Wolf and Coyote, and Kwi'-ats and Pat'-suts, Grizzly Bear and Bat, also dwell there. They are the Ancients, E'-nu-ins-i-gaip. Eliza had never heard of the Ancients, and she did not understand that many spirits of the dead live together in a beautiful and fertile valley on one side of tall mountains. When Eliza's people died, they did not go through an underground passage even though their bodies were put into the ground. Eliza said that their spirits passed through a veil into the light.

Dimick had long ago translated Wolf's name as Devil, perhaps because Wolf lived below the People, not above them. Sometimes he seemed to think that Coyote was the Devil. Dimick did not want to translate Wolf's name as God even though Wolf had created people. He and the others did not understand exactly what the People believed. They wanted Indians to believe what they believed. They told stories to persuade them, tales about once-civilized people who came across the ocean to this land and degenerated, went wild. Those people wore animal skins and fought battles against opponents who were good people and who wore cloth. The ones who wore skins were the Indians' ancestors, Dimick and the other settler-colonists said.[35]

In the parlor Sally heard other stories as well. Sometimes the Leader talked about the past, and sometimes about what had happened that very day. He liked to tell Indian stories. He told about the terrible Wákara, Baptiste, and others, who took children captive and sold them as slaves. He told the frightening story of her captivity, too. He talked about brave men he sent on missions to convert wild Indians to their faith and to civilization. The ungrateful Elk Mountain Utes, like the Bannocks, had attacked and killed some of the missionaries.[36]

It was better for the children not to hear the worst Indian stories, such as one about the poor overland travelers massacred at Mountain Meadows. She had not heard such stories before her captors sold her to Charley. She had never listened to tales about wild people who attacked and killed settler-colonists or travelers, or about heroic settlers who defended themselves against their wild attackers. She had not known any settlers when

she was growing up, only the People. But now she heard again and again
that the People and others like them, including her captors, were wild. She
understood from the stories that wild meant bad, cruel. Her stepfather
and her captor Baptiste and other men like them were clearly wild.

In most of those narratives of wild against civilized, the colonizing
settlers won the battle, at least in the end. So she heard as she sat with the
family inside a fortress, the Leader's walled estate. She heard the frightening stories in the comfort of safety, surrounded by women and children,
and in the presence of the Leader, a man of great power who protected
his family.

As a child Sally had sat with her family in a shelter, near the warmth of
a small fire, listening as an elder told tales in winter. That was the season
for telling stories. Some of the stories were alarming, and others made
everyone laugh. In one of them, Coyote flies through the air, and crashes.
In another, Coyote, wearing an elk head that got stuck on his head, says,
"I always wanted to be an elk," and goes on his way. The tale about the elk
head spoke of acceptance, making the best of what cannot be changed.
Taking such wisdom to heart, she had finally accepted that she would
spend the rest of her life with the Leader's family. She had set about learning all of their words and their ways because she wanted the most human
of things. She wanted to have a sense of belonging, a sense of safety, a family and home.[37]

The stories of wild versus civilized that Sally heard at the Lion House
differed from tales she had heard as a child, yet the nightly storytelling
in the parlor felt deeply familiar in some ways. On cold winter nights,
the family always gathered by the warm Franklin stove in the shelter
of the parlor. There she listened to another elder and gifted raconteur,
the Leader.

Sally listened to the words of the Leader night after night. He told
stories in all seasons, not just in winter. Unlike the other women, she could
not read the newspaper, another source of stories. But many of the stories
that reached print were just the same as those she heard in the parlor.

She rarely talked to people outside the Lion House. They told the same
stories in any case. Her daily work in the kitchen, along with other duties,
left her little time for visiting or errands, but she never complained about
that. She preferred to stay at home. Whenever she walked through the
gate of the estate, she went in company, never alone.

She did once go to the house of the midwife named Patty, Eliza's friend.
She went there with a woman who came from a distant place called Wales,

and who had recently married the Leader's brother-in-law. Her name was Phebe. That was one of many names shared by the women of Clara's family and tribe. Sally knew other women called Phebe, or Mary, Fanny, Jane, Clarissa—and even Sally. There was another Sally who worked in the Lion House kitchen, and who came from the faraway place called England.[38]

As time passed, and she listened only to Clara and her people, who spoke English, some of the words Sally knew from childhood began to fall away. She seldom heard the old words except when the Pahvant Ute chief visited the Leader, and wanted to speak to her. She did not care to speak to him. He had not brought her good news about her family, and at the Lion House and the Beehive House she heard only bad news about the People. She heard again and again that they attacked and killed innocent travelers. No one she knew suggested that they took the blame for the violent acts of other men.

Now she lived with Clara and her people. She spoke their words, cooked their food, ate that food, and lived in the house of their leader with Clara and the children. She had made her home with them. The way she had once lived with the People was finished. Gone.

CHAPTER 8

Resistance

WHEN ARMED CONFLICT BEGAN again with Utes, who were led by the formidable chief known as Black Hawk, Sally heard the story about how Barney died. He had moved south to lands that Utes had long claimed and occupied as homelands, and that colonizing settlers had quickly seized. Utes remembered Barney, the trapper and trader they knew before colonizing settlers reached the big valley. They remembered that he later guided armed men to the fertile land by the freshwater lake, and joined in the deadly raid against the Timpanogos Utes.[1]

Sally heard that his killers had come upon Barney and a companion in a remote canyon. The settlers who recovered the bloody bodies found them lying in the dirt—scalped, riddled with bullets, and bristling with arrows, a nightmarish scene. The civilized way to die, Sally had long ago learned, was in a bed with pillows and clean linens, inside a house with proper floors, and surrounded by a grieving family.

Barney's young daughters, Louisa and Polly, were not with him when he died in that wild place. At sixteen and seventeen, they were nearly Sally's age when she was taken captive. Now they were orphans too—and the chief of the Sanpete Utes wanted one or both of them as wives. The Leader refused. He had them brought under heavy guard to the Lion House. Sally had first seen Polly and Louisa years earlier, as small children at the big fort. Now she heard the story of their narrow escape from the clutches of Chief Sanpitch, saved by the Leader. Polly joined Sally as a servant for his family, and lived at the Lion House.[2]

A year later, Sally and Polly heard that militiamen had captured and jailed Chief Sanpitch and eight of his men. The militiamen then shot seven other men and a woman and child, as alleged accomplices of some sort. Chief Sanpitch and his men escaped weeks later, fearing for their lives. It took just two days for the militiamen to track them down and kill them. Despite what the Leader suspected, they were not allies of Black Hawk. And allies or not, they had no power to capture Black Hawk and hand him over, despite what the Leader had hoped.[3]

By the time she heard of Barney's death, Sally had stayed with Clara, anchored in her sunny sphere, for nearly eighteen years. She had lived with Clara and the children at the Lion House, her adopted home, for the last ten years. Inside the walls of the estate, life still passed peacefully in a daily round of cooking and eating and cleaning and helping with the children. But she heard story after story about violence outside the walls. Still the violence: it seemed the bloodshed had no end outside her home and refuge. Now there was the new war with Black Hawk and his warriors. The Leader blamed Utes again—but not the Pahvant Utes. Their chief, Kanosh, his close ally, had not joined Black Hawk.[4]

There had been no recent sightings of Baptiste. After recovering from the gunshot wound to his head, he had remained at large for years, in company with Chief Tintic. Reportedly, an order for his arrest and Tintic's had finally been issued, but to no effect. A few months passed, and then, as Sally heard, Tintic suddenly died.[5]

Two winters after he died, Sally learned of the death of Chief Arapeen, Chief Wákara's successor. Arapeen was the Leader's ally, but Sally had no reason to regret his death. She had heard stories told about his murderous brutality to captive children. She could have come to that kind of end herself at the hands of Baptiste, but for Charley. Or so she heard whenever her own story was told.[6]

Perhaps Baptiste was finally dead, too, and she no longer needed to fear recapture or his powerful bad medicine. Or perhaps he had only vanished once more, for a time. Even if she heard a report of his death from the Leader or someone else, he might suddenly reappear—just as happened years earlier after he was shot and assumed to be dead.

The settlers often spoke of what they called the blessings of civilization. No one needed to name those blessings because everyone understood. This tacit knowledge was also narrative knowledge, embedded in stories

they told each other about wild people and efforts to convert them to civilization. It was embedded in stories told about Sally. Those narratives of
wild and civilized implied, if they did not directly state, that the unnamed
blessings must be protected and extended.

But people of the wild, the native people who were subjects of these
stories, did not enter gladly into civilization. Many openly resisted control.
Chief Wákara and Black Hawk and their warriors fought, and some died.
Baptiste opposed the settler-colonists until he was shot in the head, but
survived and took refuge in the desert. The boy who ran away and joined
Utes in the mountains became Nicaagat, a warrior, and then a war chief.
Even Sally, the captive who did not run away, at first refused to work as
told, and then darned socks and laundered glumly.

They resisted because entering into life in civilization meant losing
their homelands forever to invaders, colonizing settlers who intended to
make a new, permanent home on their ancestral lands. It meant losing
liberty, the freedom to go where they wished. It meant entering a kind of
captivity that the settler-colonists, and most Americans, accepted as part
of life, and even as protective. Theirs was a world of walls and fences, locks
and keys, gates and guards, corrals and cages, prisons and chains, rules
and regulations. It was a world of orders issued, taken, and enforced. Sally
had only entered fully into that way of life when she accepted that she
could not return home with her mother and sisters. They were no longer
alive. At least Clara's world, which had grown familiar with time, offered
protection from the ongoing danger and violence.[7]

Although Utes had resisted the settlement of their hunting and gathering grounds for years, colonizers kept arriving in wagon trains. Some came
from the eastern United States, and others, from Britain and Scandinavia.
Many were poor and landless. Like those who had preceded them, they
wanted land and they planned to stay.

Just twenty years after settlement, the settler-colonists already numbered more than fifty thousand. They had conquered by means of weapons
and violence and the diseases they carried. They had conquered by fencing
and farming, destroying the hunting and gathering grounds of Utes and
other native people. They continued the conquest by means of their sheer
numbers. "We shall increase, and we shall occupy this valley, and the next,
and the next," the Leader warned Ute chiefs during treaty talks when they
resisted giving up their ancestral lands.[8]

Most of the Utes, only hundreds of people by then, had soon gone
unhappily to a new reservation many miles east of the city, across the wall

of mountains. The Uintah Reservation stood on wild land that none of the colonizers wanted—yet. A surveying party termed that stretch of wild land waste. The place seemed too cold and rugged for farming. To the north, the jutting High Uintas tore great clouds to shreds. To the south lay red rock plateau.

The tract of land set aside for the reservation could not support the Utes' old life of hunting and gathering, even for the few people sent there. Their numbers had plummeted from thousands to hundreds after years of violence, hunger, displacement, and disease. Hunger and hardship settled in with them when they could no longer move with the seasons. The survivors felt caged at the reservation, held captive, and exiled from their sacred and familiar homelands.[9]

Some of the Timpanogos sought permission to return to their old home near the big freshwater lake. They wished "to live as they formerly did," the Leader told settler-colonists in that densely populated valley. "This is the land that they and their fathers have walked over and called their own; and they have just as good a right to call it theirs today as any people have to call any land their own," the Leader conceded. "They have buried their fathers and mothers and children here; this is their home, and we have taken possession of it," he said. "We are not intruders," he hastened to add, but "here by the Providence of God." The exiled Utes did not receive permission to return home.[10]

Sally still lived in the city. Her life, once spent under open sky on the western edge of mountains, had come to this: a settled, ordered, and confined life inside two mansions with lace curtains at the windows and carpets on the floors. The home that kept her safe also held her in place. Surrounded by high walls, she saw the shining crest of mountains to the east, and overhead a swath of sky. The summer sky was often still—purely, blankly blue. Now and then a wisp of white appeared, then paused, dissolved, and vanished from sight. In winter, pearly clouds raced by, rushing on their way to somewhere else.

People came and went. Emeline, the famously favored wife, moved with her children from the Lion House, unhappily, tearfully. A young woman named Amelia took the suite that Emeline vacated across the hall from Clara's rooms, where Sally still lived. By then Emeline was in her late thirties and had borne nine children. Just weeks before she gave birth to the ninth, a son, her husband married a new wife—a bitter blow to the longtime favorite. Amelia stayed at home with her parents for three weeks while Emeline recovered from childbirth, but not from the shock of the wedding. The infant died, the only child she ever lost.[11]

Lucy B.'s daughter Susa never forgot Emeline's renowned beauty. She recalled her violet-blue eyes, sculpted features, and wavy hair, her elegant manners and grace, which had once drawn the appraising gaze of an artist. He studied Emeline carefully from a distance, this "accomplished and beautiful woman," as he called her. A French visitor, who glimpsed her in a garden, called her "strikingly beautiful." She was in her twenties then. Anyone could see now that she was no longer young. The Leader's new wife, who had captured the title of favorite, was in her twenties, thirty-seven years younger than her husband.[12]

Emeline's despair ran deep. She cried. She was often ill. Her older daughters watched helplessly as she soothed the pain with laudanum, morphine, whiskey, and brandy from the family store. Some of the other wives also drank spirits, but only Emeline used morphine. Susa remembered that she grew hopelessly addicted.[13]

Clara, two years younger than Emeline and ten years older than Amelia, took her own fall from favor with more grace. Better to accept this new reality than to become an object of pity, or to annoy her husband and be sent away. Better to make herself useful and to dwell in sunny uplands than to descend into darkness. Resolutely smiling and always busy, she remained at the Lion House with her young children and Sally.

Like Emeline, she drew heavily on the family store for small but costly luxuries, not only simple needs. Sweet desserts and imported black tea and coffee, well sweetened with imported sugar, brought Clara comfort and greater girth. She enjoyed a sociable life, and a life of ease, at the Lion House where the other women and their children formed part of her large extended family, and where Sally and the other servants did the heavy work for the household.[14]

Her closest family ties—as Harriet's daughter, Lorenzo's stepdaughter, and Lucy's sister—gave her a measure of protection and support that Emeline lacked. She kept her troubles to herself, even after her second son died, the year after Amelia's entrance brought Emeline's departure from the Lion House. Clara lost that son in December, the winter dying time, just a month before his seventh birthday. Her first son had died on a January day eight years earlier, while the Leader was away from the city, presiding over the territorial legislature, and in the company of Emeline. Clara had confronted the grief of her baby's unexpected death without the comfort of a husband's presence.[15]

The two deaths left her with three birth daughters and three foster children. It seemed a small family to some. Clara "could have mothered whole multitudes," her niece and namesake, Lucy's daughter Clarissa, later said, without any mention of the help Sally gave. Instead, Clara mothered a somewhat smaller multitude, the girls of the Lion House who were growing up. There were ten older girls, with another five following close behind.[16]

Susa always remembered the attention that Clara gave to the older girls. They outnumbered the boys, and had a greater presence at the Lion House. The boys spent their time at school or working outside, often away from the estate. The girls passed much of their time inside the house when they were not at school. They were not at liberty to go where they wished, when they wished, outside the walls of the estate. They had to seek permission. They needed to go in company with each other as chaperones, a matter of proper conduct for respectable young women. Like other young women, they lived under surveillance and greater control, without their brothers' freedom of movement.[17]

The oldest girls were fifteen and sixteen when their father married Amelia. They were about Clara's age, as it happened, when she had married him. The girls witnessed Emeline's shattering distress, and her removal from the Lion House. They also saw that Clara retained influence with her husband, who seemed to respect her more than most women. She assumed the role of confidante with the girls, and interceded on their behalf with their father. She always listened with sympathy to the girls' petitions, whether for a new sash ribbon to wear with a dress or for permission to go on an outing with friends. Susa recalled that Clara "knew the 'psychological' moment" to approach her husband with a request. She saw him each day at supper and in the parlor for evening prayers.

Clara stayed so busy that she seemed to have no time to appear in public with her husband. She took no part in public life. She was always too "engaged" with duties at home to spare the time, she said, even when she finally had only one small child in her care. Sally still lived in Clara's suite and could help with little Lulu when she had finished the day's work in the kitchen. The other daughters—Nettie, Nabbie, and her foster daughter Eva—had already reached courting age.

Clara did leave the house on "missions of mercy," as Susa called them. She visited the sick, and did other good works of her own choosing. She did not attend church. But while she kept far too busy to appear in public as one of the Leader's many wives, the door to her room always stood open for the girls.[18]

No matter how late the hour, Susa said, when the girls returned to the house after an evening social event they found Clara awake and waiting for them. The fire in her sitting room stove still burned brightly when others had dwindled to embers, and most of the women and children in the house had already fallen asleep. Sally had gone to sleep earlier in a back room of Clara's suite because she needed to wake up early for another day's work in the kitchen. But there sat Clara, "quiet, sweet, sympathetic, and cheery," Susa said, waiting to hear a full account of the evening, and of their young suitors, from the girls.[19]

Clara, so generous with her time and attention, also shared her books with the girls. Susa borrowed every book she owned, including a copy of *The Arabian Nights' Entertainments*. The Leader would not have recommended this book. Better to read edifying works, including Eliza's poems, than romantic fantasies about Ali Baba and the forty thieves.

Susa read the book again and again. When she returned it, on her thirteenth birthday, she told Clara that she had read it thirteen times. Something in *The Arabian Nights' Entertainments* resonated deeply. The stories pulled her back again and again, and kept her attention through those many repeated readings.[20]

The book was a loose collection of tales held together by a framing device, the story of Scheherazade entertaining her tyrannical husband by telling him linked tales night after night in order to evade death. Schahriar, the sultan, had not just put aside his previous wives, but had ordered them killed, one after the other. So long as Scheherazade could keep the sultan's interest, so long as she could tell her husband what he wanted to hear, she could resist their fate. She could live, and so could other women.

The stories captivated Susa—not that she saw her beloved father in the figure of Schahriar. Emeline had of course been put aside, but certainly not killed. When Susa read the tales, Emeline was still alive, sick and addicted but not dead from despair. She was halfway through her painful exile from the Lion House, although no one knew that then. No, the story surely had nothing to do with Susa's father or with Emeline. And Amelia was no Scheherazade. She had nothing to fear.

Still, there was something compelling about *The Arabian Nights' Entertainments*. Anyone who heard or read the stories, including Susa and the other girls who borrowed Clara's book, learned something about how to resist control and survive as women in a male-dominated world. The stories contained all of the familiar elements, in the most extreme form, starting with a powerful man who must be obeyed, placated, entertained.

The stories also told of rich men and the poor—the rich with often ill-gained treasure, the poor with no recourse but magic. And finally, along with slaves and other captives, there were women who must live by their wits, and magic, or perish at the hands of dangerous men. Those men had the power to harm or to protect—as they chose.

The only sure means of escape seemed to be magic carpets or the help of genies.

Sally did not read Clara's book of stories. She still did not know how to read. By the time she began to speak English with some ease, she was more than twenty years old. She did not attend school at the fort or later at the Lion House, where the school at first occupied a room in the basement near the kitchen. The Leader soon had a schoolhouse built on the estate grounds. By then Sally had reached her thirties, and worked long hours in the kitchen.[21]

She remembered many stories, even if she could not read. The People told stories, but not about powerful rulers and captives and treasures in faraway places. They never spoke of genies and magic carpets. If anyone needed to escape, they just left as quickly and quietly as possible.

Eliza and some of the other women told longer stories than some of those she recalled about Wolf and Coyote, and they always wanted her to listen. They liked to tell her the story about people who left a place known as Israel. Sally heard that name in their songs. The people who left belonged to a lost tribe who found their way to a new land. They were the ancestors of Sally's people, Eliza said, and of all the Indian people. She heard the story again and again.

She learned that Wolf had not created people and put them in a bag, and Coyote had not opened the bag so that they scattered in all directions. Instead, her ancestors had long ago crossed an immense stretch of water. So said Eliza and the others, and they gave her the book about it. The marks made no sense to her. But she listened carefully when they told her the story. Learning their stories was part of learning to live with them.[22]

Clara and Eliza's people were not descendants of those who scattered in all directions when Coyote opened Wolf's bag. They had come from another place to make a new home because, they said, they had a right to the land, and the duty to improve it. They were turning a wild wasteland into a garden, and making the desert bloom. They wanted to civilize Sally and the other so-called wild people, to redeem them. That was how they saw it, and so did many other Americans. After a time, so did Sally.

During these years, a famous man who cherished civilization and who lived more than two thousand miles away made a short entry in his journal. He wrote a few words about the very place where Sally lived. Ralph Waldo Emerson, then sixty years old, had not seen that land. He had never seen a desert, although of course he had read in the Bible about those waterless sites of desolation and waste in the Holy Land and Egypt.

Emerson lived in eastern Massachusetts, a green and wooded place, and had not traveled far west from his home. It had been so long settled that only traces remained of what a Pilgrim, one of the first colonizing settlers to live there, had called "a hideous & desolate wilderness, full of wild beasts & wild men." Emerson had read about the new city on the fringe of a great western desert, a city his son had recently visited, and he believed that the changes there were for the good. He thought that the Leader deserved the credit.[23]

"Good out of evil. One must thank the genius of Brigham Young," Emerson said, for creating a city from the waste. That effort provided "an efficient example to all men in the vast desert, teaching how to subdue and turn it to a habitable garden." Wild land, it seemed, was evil. It was not under human control. Colonizing the wild desert valley, and building a city there, had redeemed it and turned it good.[24]

"Good out of evil." His words about a distant city he had never seen, a city said to be a veritable garden in a desert, borrowed from those of Saint Augustine. Fifteen hundred years earlier, he had written, "God judged it better to bring good out of evil than to suffer no evil to exist."

Many of the settler-colonists, like other Americans, thought that they were doing sacred work by making a garden from the wild, bringing good out of evil. Eliza seemed to think of Sally as something like a garden that she and Clara had created. Under "our mutual care and cultivation," she said (picture Eliza and Clara hoeing hard, stubborn ground, and planting good seeds), Sally "very soon became disgusted with her native habits." She turned away from her life as a useless weed and toward a life as—well, if not a blooming rose, a useful cabbage.[25]

As more and more daughters of the Lion House approached womanhood, Clara watched and listened. Susa, an admiring little sister, also watched. She was seven or eight years younger than the Ten Big Girls, as she called them. Years later, looking back, she realized how little work the girls did at the Lion House other than some sewing and light housework. This left them time to think about parties, and how to style their hair and how to dress. Lucy B. acted as their hairdresser, and their mothers or a dressmaker sewed their gowns.[26]

The daughters of the Lion House were "giddy and gay," Susa recalled. They wanted "nothing but fun and frolic," she said. They shared a sense of importance as daughters of the Leader, and a strong sense of kinship as half-sisters who claimed that powerful, wealthy man as their father. Their young suitors, as well as older ones, understood the advantages of joining the family as sons-in-law of the Leader.[27]

One of the girls, Susa remembered, became engaged to a young Englishman who worked in the Leader's office as a clerk. It was an open secret that she was adopted. Nearly everyone, including the other girls, knew that, but the clerk and his fiancée did not. When he learned the truth, he broke off the engagement. When his former fiancée learned the reason, Susa said, she fainted from the shock. She had always received the same treatment as the other daughters, but in their eyes she was not one of them. Later she married someone else, and in Susa's telling of the tale she lived happily ever after.[28]

Sally kept working. Years earlier, in sworn testimony about Indian slavery, the Leader had said that Sally lived just as his children lived. True enough, in that she lived in the same house, and she ate the same food, and she heard the same stories and sang the same hymns each evening. Yet here was a difference: she wore an apron and worked long days in the kitchen while his daughters, by birth or adoption, went to school, studied music, read books, talked about their beaux, and attended parties. There were other differences as well. The special religious ritual that would join her to the Leader's family for eternity had not been performed for Sally. And she still had no surname. She was just Sally, not Sally Young.[29]

Clarissa spoke for others in the family when she later called Sally the "Indian girl" who worked for her mother in the kitchen. She did not regard a brown-skinned servant as a member of the family. Sally did not qualify as a foster daughter of Clarissa's father, which would have made her Clarissa's foster sister or perhaps, because of her greater age, a courtesy aunt. "She was obedient, took her orders well, and did her duties as she was told," Clarissa said firmly.

Sally had known Clarissa and Susa well, watching them grow from infancy onward. But they, in contrast, seemed to recall very little about her life at the Lion House and the Beehive House. Sally seldom spoke, Clarissa said years later, adding, "She had the reticence of her race to an extreme degree."

Clarissa did not understand why she often chose silence. Sally did not question Lucy's orders or ask for her attention or help. It was better not to disturb Lucy while she supervised novice helpers in a crowded kitchen. Lucy was apt to speak sharply as mealtime loomed and she tried to time the cooking precisely. Unlike Sally, few of the helpers spoke fluent English. They did not readily understand Lucy's directions.

Sally stood silently in that kitchen, just as she later stood mutely in the shadows in family memory.[30]

As the years passed, more of the women and children Sally knew well moved from the Lion House to smaller houses in the city. Lucy B. and her younger daughters moved south to a remote settlement. Other women and children took their places at the Lion House, sometimes in desperate circumstances. Polly, Barney's daughter, had stayed at the Lion House and worked with Sally for years after her father died. Clara's much younger half-sister, who was slightly older than Lulu, came under her care. Mary Farnham, who had long run a successful boardinghouse in the city, also lived with Clara for a time during these years. Clara's niece remembered Mary as under Clara's "protection" at the Lion House. Mary had divorced her polygamous husband by then. She was an outspoken, implacable opponent of polygamy.[31]

It seemed odd that Clara had given shelter and protection to a woman who so openly resisted polygamy. Her presence at the Lion House bordered on rebuke, and set a bad example for the daughters who lived there. Few of the girls had yet entered a polygamous marriage although their father encouraged, consented to, and even arranged such marriages for his associates with his daughters and other young women. He believed that such marriages had a special sanctity, besides their value in strengthening his alliances. And he held great power over his followers and his family, and could generally do as he thought best.[32]

He did not always succeed. Some of his daughters resisted. Lucy B.'s oldest daughter eloped with a young suitor. Clara's oldest daughter, Nabbie, tried to elope with a young man but was thwarted. A third attempted to escape by train—call it magic carpet—rather than marry an older man of her father's choosing.[33]

Sally did not want to marry. She did not want to leave the safety of the Leader's walled estate. Since she had so little contact with men, as she entered her forties marriage grew increasingly unlikely. Lucy, in charge of a busy kitchen, counted on her daily help. By then, Sally had become the senior cook at the Beehive House.

Unidentified servant (in apron), probably Sally, in front of the Beehive House. Used by permission of Utah Historical Society.

Kind Clara, part genie and part sphinx, smiled and laughed and nod-ded sympathetically as she listened to the older girls. "I remember Aunt Clara best for her loving, sympathetic nature," her niece Clarissa later said. Along with her sympathy for not-yet-married young women went great discretion. Clara was "safe to tell secrets to," Susa recalled. She always showed interest in what they said about their young friends and suitors, their courtships and romances.[34]

There had been so little of that in her life—except for the time long ago when she traveled across the plains and mountains with her husband, the Leader. The other wives stayed behind when he took the first party of settlers to colonize the big valley. He built a small house for his young wife at the fort, and then left, planning to bring more of his wives and other people to the valley. Clara, lonely for him, sent a letter of tender intimacy, one meant "for your eyes alone," she said. "I often dream of you," she wrote, "generally living my happy days over again, but when I wake I find nothing but a dream and like a sunny morning the remembrance passeth away." Still, she continued, "your kindness to me this past summer will never be forgotten. It shall live while memory lives with me."[35]

He had given her instructions, telling her to share the new house with one of his older wives, Eliza, when she arrived with the next wave of col-onizing settlers. "I will endeavor to do as you requested me in all things," Clara told him obediently. She even added that she felt "much pleased" to share her quarters at the fort with Eliza. Life went on, but without his daily, and nightly, presence and the bright glow of his attention.[36]

Later, some of the stories Clara read in books spoke to what she had briefly lived, and then lost. Many novels told happily-ever-after stories of youthful and lasting romantic love between one man and one woman only. The wreckage wrought by Emeline's dethroning, painful to behold, also had parallels in fiction, in melancholy tales of grand passion that ended in betrayal and deep suffering. Novels, and even the girls' accounts of courting by young suitors, were a source of narrative knowledge for Clara. They clarified an intense but fleeting moment in her life. She knew how it felt to fall in love, and to feel loved by her husband as his only wife—until he returned to the fort with the others. And she knew how it felt to bear a great sorrow, her baby's death, while he was absent, and in the company of another wife.

For the girls, Clara's warmth and enthusiasm about their courtships and young beaux offered a kind of emotional applause that urged them on. And Clara encouraged them not only by listening, and by sharing her books, but by helping them as well. She could make small wishes come true. Petitioners could also count on good counsel if they asked for it. Susa claimed years later that Clara was uncommonly wise, and that "she understood human nature as few women have ever done." Although she usually kept her thoughts to herself, when Clara did give an opinion, she spoke decisively. No one missed the meaning, including her husband. Few doubted the wisdom of what she said—and certainly not the girls.[37]

Emeline died at the age of just forty-nine, ending her long exile from the Lion House. She was worn out by loss and pain. The funeral, a quiet affair, took place at the Beehive House. A friend recalled Emeline and, as always, her beauty. She was "tall and graceful, with curling hair, beautiful eyes"—and also a broken heart. Her husband reportedly shed no tears at her funeral. After the eulogy ended, he stood up and told her bereaved children, in a startling breach of custom and in front of other mourners, not to follow their mother's example but to follow his instead.[38]

Weeks later, when one of the Leader's sons was buried, he again shed no tears, but he did cry a month later at the funeral of one of his oldest associates. People always noticed what he did. It became the stuff of stories told about him by admirers (he was so strong, he did not cry), and by detractors (he was so heartless, he did not cry). After he died, the old stories continued to be told, along with new ones. Narrative knowledge about the Leader grew.[39]

Winter days: gauzy gray clouds sank to the valley floor as snow fell fast, veiling the long line of mountains. When clouds shifted, sun burst through, lighting up the winter-smooth white flanks of mountains. Then the clouds closed up again. The world looked blank once more, white shading to pale gray. But this was visible only from high windows in the Lion House, and only if someone looked out at the mountains and sky, and if she turned away from her sewing, or her conversation, or her thoughts.

The kitchen of the Beehive House became a warm refuge on cold days, filled with steamy fragrance from the simmering and the baking. Lucy and Sally worked intently with the hired women, preparing midday meals for the estate workmen. Now and then hungry visitors interrupted them. Many were Kumumpa women who could no longer find much wild food to gather in the valley, but who resisted going to a reservation for Utes. They were Shoshones, and they wanted to stay in their homeland. They came to the gate and asked in English for food. The guards always called Lucy.[40]

Her daughter Clarissa remembered that the women often wanted sugar. They had so little in the way of sweeteners, she said, but of course sugar had many virtues besides taste. It was a rich source of energy for its weight. It was easy to carry and to store. It did not spoil.

For all those virtues, sugar did exact a toll. Lucy had lost all of her teeth by then. She wore false teeth, and so did her husband, the Leader. His were gold plated. Clarissa remembered that one of the women who asked for sugar stared with fixed fascination at Lucy's face. Lucy returned the gaze, and finally asked the visitor why she was staring. "You take 'em out," the woman said. She realized that Lucy's teeth were false, and wanted to have a close look at them. Her own people had kept their teeth, as trappers and settlers had noticed with some wonder. But then sugar arrived.[41]

These visitors held no interest for Sally. She would not see her mother and sisters again, at least in this earthly life. They had never come for her, despite what she had heard long ago as Zina's prophecy. The visitors who stood at the gate were strangers, and hungry, but years had passed since Sally last felt the sharp jab of hunger. The women walked from house to house in the city, collecting what they could in old flour sacks while she prepared genuine feasts each day. She did not have to ask for food, and she did not eat scraps. She had come to feel deeply at home at the Lion House and the Beehive House, and attached to Clara and the children.

CHAPTER 9

Reports

A SURGE OF TRAVELERS BEGAN to arrive in the city once the transcontinental railroad reached completion. Some came to visit, and colonizing settlers by the tens of thousands came to stay. Journeys from the East by train suddenly took just days, not months. Passengers traveled in comfort along smooth rails and in enclosed cars, some with plush seats—not in the jolting wagons and carriages that had carried hardy travelers, from the first colonists to Richard Burton, over dusty, rutted trails.[1]

Emerson, who had once praised "the genius" of the Leader in his journal, was one of the many visitors. Despite his age and failing health, he crossed the continent by train with friends, and stayed in the city for a day. Along with the men in his party, he went to see the Leader at his office. The two had little to say to each other. When one of the friends gave the Leader credit for building a city in the desert, he waved the words aside. Just one clerk at the office seemed to know anything about their eminent visitor. Emerson did not receive an invitation to dine at the Beehive House, and he did not see Sally or the other women who lived at the estate.[2]

Other travelers interrupted cross-country trips by train in hope of having a mere glimpse of the Leader. Curious tourists walked by his city estate or rode past it in carriages, craning their necks and trying to look over the wall to see him or, better yet, his many wives. Some of them had read the newspaper stories about the family that began to appear often in New York and Chicago newspapers as soon as the transcontinental railroad was completed. Journalists from the East suddenly found it easy to reach the city, and to report on one of the nation's most famous families.[3]

Like Emerson, many of the travelers also wanted to see the progress of civilization at a new settler-colonial site. Their dispatches about the city and hinterlands ranged from newspaper and magazine articles to books and government reports. The steady flow of print included commentary on Utes and other native people. Only one of the visitors saw Sally and reported on her progress, as she saw it. The estate's high walls kept nearly all outsiders out.[4]

Among the eminent visitors to the Beehive House during these years were General Thomas Kane and his well-born wife Elizabeth. General Kane, the scion of a wealthy and powerful Philadelphia family, had served as a brigadier general in the Union Army during the Civil War. He had been badly wounded in two battles in Virginia, one in the Shenandoah Valley where Union troops engaged General Stonewall Jackson. Despite his credentials, he did not impress Lucy's daughter Clarissa.[5]

Three years earlier, at the age of nine, she had met General and Mrs. Tom Thumb when they visited the Beehive House as invited guests. The diminutive General Thumb bore a made-up title and name, invented to entice crowds of paying customers. But there was no contest for Clarissa between the two generals called Tom. She saw nothing special about her father's old and trusted friend. A slightly built man who still suffered from his war wounds, he limped and used a cane or crutches. Her father had invited him to visit. Perhaps the dry, western air would help his alarmingly poor health. Cold, damp winters in northern Pennsylvania, where he lived, had done nothing to help him heal.[6]

General Kane and his wife arrived by train in early December. Elizabeth was a serious-minded woman in her mid-thirties. In the early years of her marriage, she lived in the Kane family mansion in Philadelphia and spent summers at their estate in the country. She had always lived with servants, and brought one of them, an African American man named John, to help with her husband on the trip.[7]

When Elizabeth visited the Beehive House and the Lion House, she saw Sally. She was intrigued to see an Indian woman who lived and worked in a mansion in the city. That woman, captured by the notorious Wákara, had been bought and "adopted into" the Leader's family—or so Elizabeth understood. Chief Wákara still held a commanding place in memory, while fewer people in the city recalled his ally Baptiste.

Sally offered living proof, Elizabeth thought, that the civilizing effort could succeed. "She seemed to me a very respectable and sedate, good woman," Elizabeth wrote a few days later in a letter to her father. Then she added that this same Indian woman "was said to entertain a 'morbid' horror of Indians." By then, Sally had lived completely apart from the People and with the Leader's family for twenty-five years. She had been subject to their unceasing efforts to erase her past and civilize her, and she had heard gruesome stories of Indian violence and mayhem, of wild against civilized, again and again. Repetition built conviction.[8]

When the Kanes left the city, they traveled south with the Leader and a party of other people, including Lucy B. and her youngest daughter. The travelers' destination, the Leader's winter home, lay three hundred miles away, in the small town where Lucy B. had moved when she left the Lion House. It offered a warmer and drier climate.

On the third night of their journey the Kanes stayed with a family who years earlier had bought a young Southern Paiute boy. Her hostess told Elizabeth the captive's sad story. He had been captured by Wákara, she said, probably hundreds of miles to the south. The captors had burned the little boy so badly that the scars on his back and legs and feet remained visible, Elizabeth reported. The family named him Lehi, gave him their surname, and always identified him as their adopted son and brother. Whenever any Indian had come near the house, they claimed, Lehi hid under the bed. Indians were no longer in evidence when Elizabeth met Lehi because they had been forced to leave, sent to the Uintah Reservation.[9]

This tale of brutality, and another about Baptiste, were two of the frightening stories that her hostess told. The Indian stories, as she called them, did not surprise Elizabeth, but did make her nervous, she confessed. She had brought firm attitudes west, based on old narrative knowledge. In Pennsylvania, captivity tales abounded, but those tales of wild and civilized came from long ago. That made them less alarming than these more recent ones.

There was the well-known story of poor Mary Jemison, stolen when she was just fifteen, after Shawnee Indians killed her family. She bore children by a Delaware Indian husband, and after he died she married a Seneca man. She chose to stay. In the eyes of most Americans, she went wild. Mary, called Deh-he-wä-mis for most of her life, had reached her eighties when she finally told her life story to a minister who recorded and published it. The book became a best seller, and remained in print some fifty years later.

There was yet another Mary, taken captive just twenty years earlier in the desert south of Elizabeth's destination. Mary Ann Oatman's family, dissident Mormons crossing wild lands alone, were attacked by Indians. Mary Ann and her sister Olive survived the attack, but little Mary Ann soon died. Olive was later ransomed from Mohave Indians, who had adopted her, treated her kindly, and did not want to give her up. It was not certain at the time that Olive wanted to leave her adoptive family. Still, to many Americans her story ended more happily than that of Mary Jemison because she returned to life in civilization.

Olive's narrative, at turns horrifying and heartening, and also written by a minister, left no doubt about the blessings of civilization. The author asserted the blessings, with no need to name them directly, as opposed to "the degradation, the barbarity, the superstition, the squalidness that curse" the people of "the caverns and wilds," as he put it. *Captivity of the Oatman Girls: Being an Interesting Narrative of Life among the Apache and Mohave Indians* sold tens of thousands of copies in several editions.[10]

Unlike Mary and Olive, Sally's life after capture had gone unrecorded. Because she was Indian, not American, her life held no interest for the reading public. Only Elizabeth mentioned her—in a letter, in passing, and without using her name.

Two days later, and sixty miles south, the Kanes and their traveling companions reached a small town where a settlement fort had once stood. Twenty years earlier, when Adelia Hatton stayed there with her husband, the walls and gate had not protected William from a deadly shot, likely fired from within the fort. It had since shed its walls and grown into a town, the county seat.

On arrival, the Kanes were directed to one of the houses for a meal. As they waited, their hostess's son arrived at the house with five Pahvant companions. Elizabeth watched as their hostess spoke a few words of Ute to them. The son explained that she had told them that she only had enough cooked food to serve the Kanes but that she was preparing a meal for the men. Looking pleased, they squatted on their heels, folded their blankets around them, and prepared to wait outside the house.

"Will she really do that," Elizabeth asked the son, "or just give them scraps at the kitchen-door?" "Our Pah-vants know how to behave," he replied. "Mother will serve them just as she does you, and give them a place at her table." "And so she did," Elizabeth reported. "I saw her placing clean plates, knives, and forks for them, and waiting behind their chairs, while they ate with perfect propriety." The settlers' civilizing efforts had borne fruit—at least at the table, she thought.[11]

That scene, of the five men dining, pleased Elizabeth. Twenty years earlier, a visitor had complained about Utes she saw in the city, squatting on their heels in the street and eating with their hands. Now they had good table manners, Elizabeth concluded. They sat in chairs, not on the ground in the dirt. They used forks and knives, and ate properly—just like Sally.[12]

After dinner, Chief Kanosh arrived at the house to see Elizabeth's husband. He and Tom were old acquaintances who had met years earlier. Chief Kanosh had sought out the general, the Leader's good friend, because the Leader had just refused to see him, a puzzling rebuff. The Pahvant chief counted as an old and close ally of the Leader.

Elizabeth remarked on his arresting appearance. "Kanosh has bright penetrating eyes," she said, "and a pleasant countenance. He cultivates a white moustache, and carries himself with a soldierly bearing." He and his people were sometimes called Bearded Utes, or *Barbones* in Spanish, because of the men's facial hair. It clearly betrayed some Spanish or other European ancestry.[13]

Unlike many chiefs, Kanosh cut his hair short, in the style of his non-Indian neighbors, and he customarily wore at least one fitted cloth garment. Elizabeth took note that day of his dark blue jacket with bright brass buttons, part of a military uniform of some sort, which enhanced his soldierly look. With this tailored jacket, he wore buckskin pants and moccasins. He had thrown a small blanket over one shoulder. Chief Kanosh did not wrap himself in a large bright blanket, Indian style. His was a dark carriage blanket, a type used by settlers. Altogether, Elizabeth found his appearance "prepossessing," she said. It seamlessly merged two styles of dress for a man who bridged two different worlds, and who mediated between them.

His men, in contrast, "wore Indian costume," as Elizabeth put it. One of them did wear a hat, but he had put a wild turkey feather at the back of it. The directness of his gaze took her aback. He stared at the party of visitors, she said, "like some newly caught, but unscared wild beast." He showed no sign of deference or servility.[14]

The world of civilization seemed more familiar to Chief Kanosh than to his fellow Pahvants or most Utes. Some settler-colonists claimed that he had been born at a Spanish mission in California, the son of a mission Indian woman and a Ute father. Others said only that he had spent part of his childhood at a mission, or that his mother had some Mexican ancestry. That could explain why he spoke Spanish so well, and why settler-colonial

Chief Kanosh. Used by permission of Utah Historical Society.

life, and all that it entailed, did not seem so alien to him as to Chief Black Hawk and many Utes. It might explain why, unlike so many chiefs, he did not openly resist them.

Still other people thought that the chief lived in the place of his birth, his homeland. Chief Kanosh made that claim. He tried to keep the peace so that he and his people could remain on ancestral lands, and that meant living near the colonizers and understanding their ways. When they offered a meal, he knew the importance of following their rituals and other customs. Those customs included washing hands before the meal, sitting on chairs by a table, saying the special words called a blessing, using utensils, placing saucers under cups. He did not hesitate to reprimand his men for any lapse in the table manners that their hosts prized.[15]

He had once been an ally of Wákara and other Ute chiefs, who were long dead or dispossessed of much power. Because he had formed a close alliance with the Leader, he and his people still occupied a small piece of home ground between the mountains and the desert. All of the Utes, including Pahvants, had been sent to the Uintah Reservation east of the mountains, but some of the Pahvants resisted and returned home. The settlers who colonized and farmed the land that Pahvants had been forced to vacate had named their village after Chief Kanosh, an honor reserved for friendly chiefs. They tolerated the Pahvants' return, and the Leader did not object. He had long regarded the chief as an ally and loyal lieutenant. But now, in what seemed an act of rude caprice, he refused to meet with him.[16]

The chief spoke mournfully to Elizabeth's husband of changes since the two men had last seen each other. So many people had died. He had lost all of his children, six sons and four daughters, each dead by the age of twelve. He counted the dead on his fingers, and said "all gone, all sick, no *shoot*, die *sick*." Most, it seemed, had died from the alien diseases brought to their land, but some of his people had also died from bullets. He did not tell Elizabeth and Tom that some people suspected settler-colonists of using bad medicine, sorcery, to kill them with sickness. Instead, he spoke with the extreme tact of a master diplomat who faced stiff odds in any negotiation.

He peppered Tom with questions that he wanted to ask the Leader. He asked to be told the truth. Had the government sent any food or money for his people? Were the government's agents cheating them? And why had he and his people been forced from home, and sent to the distant reservation under armed guard? Why had they "been poked off with guns" to that alien place?

Tom had no answers, but he asked Chief Kanosh to dictate a statement, and he asked his wife to record it in her pocket diary. The chief enumerated what he had not received. Elizabeth wrote down his statement, given mostly in English but with a few Ute words as well. His formal complaint about the government was summarized in the last five words, "good talk, but no give." Not trusting that Elizabeth had recorded his exact words, he insisted on having the statement read back to him, but not by her. "The astute old fox made three persons read it to him to make sure I was not cheating him, before he made his X mark," she said, piqued.[17]

Years of false promises and betrayal, including the current refusal of the Leader to see him, had left him wary and also weary. He and his people lived on a meager remnant of a homeland more than two thousand square miles in size that Pahvants had claimed, occupied, and defended before colonizing settlers arrived, and after. Now they farmed a small piece of land in the shadow of the Pahvant Mountains. Fewer than a hundred Pahvants lived together in a community that bore the English name Corn Creek. This was just twenty years after the first Pahvant lands had been seized and colonized.[18]

Elizabeth later heard stories about the chief from her traveling companions, including the Leader. One story centered on his marriage to a young woman named Mary, his "civilized wife," she noted. Some people claimed that Mary was Cherokee by birth or that she came from the far north, but she was probably Ute. None of them knew much about her origins except that she had lived for some years with a settler family in a fortified village near the big freshwater lake.

The family heard her name as Tanequickeup, but called her Mary. They did not know the meaning of her name, Root Gatherer. The father of that family, who owned the village store, had traded blankets and flour for her. His young daughter, Betsy, disliked Tanequickeup, and sometimes fought with her. Betsy's father punished Tanequickeup, harshly, for infractions such as walking away from the house and leaving chores unfinished. Before living with them, she had not taken orders or spent days behind walls. Her people did not live that way. Finally she ran away. Betsy thought she married a Spanish-speaking man, but after a time she returned alone to the family. Later she met Chief Kanosh. The details about how they met, if known, slipped from memory.[19]

Everyone did recall clearly the stated cause of Mary's violent death. Chief Kanosh had another wife, Elizabeth learned, and she grew jealous of her rival. Mary was young and pretty, people said. She was civilized, they added, and kept house as they did. Mary knew how to milk cows, and make butter. She grew vegetables in a small garden. She knew how to sew, and how to launder and iron clothing. To their great satisfaction, Chief Kanosh wore a clean, crisp shirtfront and high collar every Sunday. They liked Mary so much that they built a cottage for her, one with doors and windows, at Corn Creek. The furnishings included six chairs, a high-post bed with a feather mattress, and a standing cupboard for plates and dishes.

Thus equipped, she could show the Pahvants how to live in a better way, as settler-colonists saw it.[20]

Chief Kanosh seemed to favor Mary. The two went riding together on fast horses, and they made a fine pair. But then, one summer day, the simmering jealousy of the other wife finally erupted. Some people claimed that she killed her rival while Mary knelt in the garden, digging in the soil. Elizabeth heard that story three years later. Other people said that the murder took place when the jealous wife and Mary went gathering, a few miles from the settlement, and Mary knelt down to dig a sego lily bulb. Still others said the two women were hunting ground squirrels. Whatever the exact circumstances, each story of the murder ended in the same way. The older woman cut Mary's throat with a knife, and dragged the body away. In the version told to Elizabeth, the murderer buried the body in a cornfield.[21]

Weeks later, when Chief Kanosh returned from a long trip, he learned that Mary had disappeared. Suspecting murder, he told the older wife, the alleged culprit, that she would soon die. "And she gradually faded away," Elizabeth heard, and died within a year. Some people said that she confessed to the crime before her death. Chief Kanosh was left to mourn Mary and to live without her civilized ways and housekeeping skills. "He wore his shirts, however, faithfully and honorably," Elizabeth reported in a mocking tone, "till the buttons, the sleeves, and collars, all deserted him." So ended this unusual story about the battle of wild against civilized, a story of an attack by one woman against another, which led to the untimely death of each.[22]

Twelve miles south of the county seat, the travelers passed near Corn Creek, or "what Kanosh pompously called *his city*," Elizabeth recorded. Just as the Leader had a domain centered in the capital city, the chief claimed one as well. Elizabeth's few words, like the several stories she had just heard, had a diminishing tone. Truly, the size of the Pahvant chief's domain, in land and in people, had shrunk proportionally as the size of the Leader's had grown.

The chief had invited the travelers to visit, but his small house stood off the main road. They had a long journey ahead, and the Leader still wished to avoid his old ally. "We could not see the Kanosh mansion from the road," Elizabeth noted with heavy irony, and then turned her attention to the landscape, which looked dry and empty to her, completely wild and forbidding. The day felt so cold that when they stopped for lunch they ate in closed carriages, not in the open air.

The Leader's party of travelers carried water for their horses that day, taken from the creek by Chief Kanosh's community. Elizabeth did not recall passing any more settlements or creeks until, just before sunset, they reached a fort that served as a way station for travelers. Inside the walls, she found welcome comforts of settled life, from warm fires and warm food to warm beds. The night air at that high elevation, she reported, felt "stingingly cold."[23]

When the Kanes and their companions left the fort the next morning, the cloudless sky shone brilliant blue, but the sun gave no warmth. The frigid air sparkled with ice dust. The travelers crossed hills and plains for hours before descending into a valley intersected by a river. The valley floor, with an elevation two thousand feet higher than the city, qualified as decidedly "frosty," Elizabeth said. The travelers finally reached a small town. The valley, river, and town shared the same name, Beaver. That name memorialized the native wildlife that had drawn fur trappers there. They had killed out most of the beavers.

Sally, as a child, had lived in that high valley with her family, but she would scarcely have recognized Sho-av-ich when the Kanes saw it. Clearing, fencing, planting, and building had begun to transform the valley years earlier, just months after the first colonizing settlers arrived. Only the look of the snow-swept Tushar Mountains to the east remained the same. Tushar was a Ute word for white. Chief Kanosh and his people called one of the tallest peaks Tu-sok-av-kaiv. Settlers used the English name Mount Baldy because of the bare and sculpted rock that rose above tree line.[24]

Rows of small houses, or "shanties" as Elizabeth called them, lined the streets of the town. Colonizing settlers had arrived in the valley just sixteen years earlier, but already some had prospered far more than others, a standard feature of settler-colonial sites. She saw that as she stepped out of the carriage. Their host for the evening lived in a fine house with his wife and daughter. They struck her as Virginians—and "F. F. V. Virginians, too," she added, alluding to the so-called First Families of Virginia.[25]

To that point in the trip, class-conscious Elizabeth believed that she had mingled only with social inferiors. But she had finally encountered a family whose inherited class position might approach hers. Or so she thought. She showed no animosity toward highborn Virginians, despite her husband's unhealed war wounds. A sense of shared class seemed to override the regional prejudice she might have harbored, just as her

husband's code of honor and his ties with Virginia cousins had led him
to treat Confederate officers as fellow gentlemen, not mere enemies.[26]

Their host family lived in a large two-story house that appeared rather
imposing against the backdrop of humble, unpainted cottages. The style,
which recalled houses of the upland South, conveyed a sense of refinement
and comfort. A daughter named Julia served as hostess, and she looked
like a bona fide southern belle to Elizabeth. Julia was "as much of a little
lady as any belle of the James or Rappahannock River plantations," she
concluded. Her hostess wore a gray frock and a purple jacket braided with
black, not the usual plain dress sewn from homespun cloth. Elizabeth, as a
lady of quality married to a gentleman, knew the difference between fine
wool and soft cotton broadcloth, on the one hand, and rough homespun
on the other. She saw in Julia the very image of an FFV belle manquée.[27]

The FFV formed a faux aristocracy. These patricians possessed not only
wealth but also pedigree. They descended from a few Englishmen, early
colonizing settlers in Virginia, who had displaced and dispossessed native
people, amassed great tracts of their land, and grown rich as planters and
slaveholders. Elizabeth's host had in fact grown up in Missouri. What she
heard as a refined Virginia accent was a Missouri drawl. And she knew as
little about FFV surnames as about accents. The host family's name did
not qualify. Moreover, their money came from success in local business,
not from inherited wealth. Still, they did show their guests a gracious
hospitality, assisted by several women. Elizabeth could not decide if the
women were helpful neighbors or hired help, a pressing question for her
since servants indicated wealth.[28]

The next morning as she waited for breakfast she heard noise outside
the house, and when she looked out the window she saw twenty Pahvant
men dismounting from their horses. Her host stood nearby. After confer-
ring with one of the men, he threw open the gates of a yard where a tall
stack of hay stood. And then—"shall I use the civilized phrase?" Elizabeth
asked with amused irony—"a Committee of savage citizens proceeded to
demolish half a haystack" to feed their horses, picketed nearby.

The men soon went inside the house at the host's invitation, and took
food from a table that had just been spread with a lavish breakfast for
Elizabeth's party of travelers. She waited hungrily. Only half an hour later,
heaping platters of food again graced the table. The platters held "hot rolls,
coffee, chickens, and other good things," she said, "from an apparently
inexhaustible larder."[29]

The Pahvants' wild larder, in contrast, was nearly exhausted from colonization of Sho-av-ich, Beaver Valley, by thousands of the Leader's people. Farm fields had replaced wild meadows. Herds of livestock grazed on the native grasses and shrubs that remained. Pahvant women, such as those Rémy had passed seventeen years earlier as they led packhorses through snow, were no longer to be seen. Elizabeth saw only their men, all on horseback.[30]

They still had good reasons to roam, as most Americans insistently termed it. They needed to hunt for native wild game, which grew ever scarcer and more scattered. They needed to hunt for new settlements, which kept springing to life on their most fertile lands, near creeks and rivers in Pahvant Valley and Sho-av-ich. They needed to hunt for the Leader, who encouraged the colonization. He seemed to flee from place to place to avoid them when he passed through their homeland.

Giving hay to Pahvants to feed their horses that morning helped them survive in a fenced and farmed land. But true coexistence—and providing enough food for people and horses whose hunting and gathering grounds had been destroyed—cost more than the colonists, or the federal authorities, consented to pay. The government, as Chief Kanosh had told the Kanes with great eloquence, offered fine words and little else.[31]

Elizabeth's host seemed to have a greater sense of noblesse oblige, befitting his imagined social origins. But on the morning of the Kanes' departure, he simply made strategic use of food to divert the unwanted visitors. It would take time for them to eat, and more time to feed their horses. He gave the Pahvants food, which they valued and needed, but not what they sought, a chance to talk to the Leader.[32]

The travelers hurried away from town after breakfast, trying to avoid the twenty Pahvant men who had got hay and hot rolls instead of an audience. A small escort of townsmen on horseback left with the party. In the early hours of a cold, gray morning, brooding clouds clung to the white crest of massive mountains to the east. A few lonely snowflakes fell aimlessly from a low leaden sky.

Elizabeth saw more Pahvant men waiting along the road, posted there to intercept them. Two of the men had painted their faces, one in hues of red and the other in yellow. They wore colorful Navajo blankets, supporting Chief Kanosh's claim that the government had failed to give his people any blankets that year. These came from Navajo traders who traveled north.

The Pahvant men approached the Leader's carriage. When he failed to stop, most dropped behind silently as the travelers passed. Just one joined the escort of horsemen from Beaver, and rode beside those men for a few miles. Elizabeth saw him leaning forward in his saddle as the horse cantered along the rough road. A heavy Navajo blanket lay draped on a saddle strap. His long black hair and the fringe of his buckskin leggings fluttered in the wind as he rode. Finally the horsemen, including the lone Pahvant, dropped behind, waving farewell as each carriage passed.[33]

That was the last the travelers saw of Chief Kanosh's band. The Leader had managed to evade first the chief and then his men, running a gauntlet across some sixty miles of Pahvant country. Their determined efforts to speak with him had failed completely. A Ute chief and petitioners tried to see him when the party stopped at the next settlements along the road, but he avoided them as well.

He did not want to give federal authorities any reason to think that he was "in league with disaffected Indians," Elizabeth concluded after leaving the Pahvant horsemen behind. Just three months earlier, soldiers escorting a large government exploring party had killed nine Ute warriors near Beaver. "Fight Between Utes and a Calvary Escort—Nine Savages Killed," the *New York Times* reported. That followed news reports of armed conflict between Utes and settler-colonists during the summer. The Leader of those Utes had complained of promises made and not kept by the government, and of rations so scanty that his people went hungry. They refused at first to return to captivity on their reservation. "They said they had left it because they were starving," a reporter stated. "They thought they might as well be killed by the soldiers." The headline for the news story read, "The Hostile Savages."[34]

Chief Kanosh had no clear connection with the "outrages" that the *New York Times* had reported during the summer, from capturing horses to attacking a telegraph operator and others. But the chief had reportedly attended a Ghost Dance a few months earlier, in spring, hosted by Utes, which drew thousands to a Ute sacred site. The famished people refused to return to the reservation until federal officials provided them with promised supplies. Then came the conflicts with settler-colonists. Chief Kanosh had been a good ally of the Leader and his people for years, but the Leader now faced myriad problems with the federal government. He decided to avoid his old ally. He could make amends later.[35]

After a few more days of hard travel, the Kanes reached their destination near the northern border of Arizona Territory. In the balmy and mild winter climate, Tom improved at first, and then relapsed. He narrowly skirted death, but finally recovered. After two months, with their hope for a full healing dashed, the Kanes and a party of travelers retraced their steps, heading north.[36]

Elizabeth's dislike of the Leader, and her scorn for the nouveaux riches of the city, remained unchanged. When he fixed his gaze on her, the shrewdness and cunning that she saw in his blue-gray eyes made her flinch. "His photographs, accurate enough in other respects," she said, "altogether fail to give the expression of his eyes."[37]

Her view of Indian people, as cruel savages, had changed only slightly. The bloody tales Elizabeth heard about Chief Wákara horrified her. His narrative presence remained strong nearly twenty years after his death. It seemed that settler-colonists could not stop telling stories about him. She heard the tales again and again, recounting bloody conflicts. She heard many other Indian stories as well. Most narrators reported only violence and depravity. Very few mentioned skills and virtues, although she did hear admiring words about Navajos who showed great skill in taming the wild, reportedly as "wonderful horse-tamers."[38]

If her views of Indians changed at all, despite the terrible tales she recorded, it was only because she had seen some effects of the civilizing effort, which impressed her. She had witnessed Pahvant men dining politely at a table inside a house. She had heard Chief Kanosh speak English. She had encountered the thoroughly civilized boy named Lehi, who lived with a settler family, and a "sedate, good woman," Sally, who lived in a mansion with the Leader's family.

Just a year earlier the Leader had said publicly, "There is a curse on these aborigines of our country who roam the plains and are so wild that you cannot tame them." But by then, nearly all of the so-called wild Indians had been taken captive, compelled to live on reservations far away from settlements, and under the control of government agents with civilizing goals. The Pahvants and Chief Kanosh lived near a village of settler-colonists, in close range of their civilizing efforts. But only Sally and Lehi, who lived with settler families and completely apart from Indians, had grown wholly civilized and assimilated—as Elizabeth saw it. So she reported to the American reading public a year later when the letters she wrote to her father were published as a book.

Elizabeth did not name Sally or Clara or any other woman who lived at the Lion House. In her journal, she wrote that she spent a week at that house as the wife of a trusted friend of the Leader, the sole outsider "to whom every door was set freely open." That "very fact seals my lips," she added. Such silence no doubt disappointed Richard Burton and the many others who had sought, and failed, to gain entry to the Lion House, hoping to report on the women who lived there.[39]

Just months after Elizabeth met Chief Kanosh, Major John Wesley Powell singled him out in a report to the federal government as "a man of great ability and wisdom." Powell had official business with the Pahvant chief, but he also took time to ask him questions about the Ute language. The questions reflected Powell's scientific interests more directly than his official purpose in meeting the chief. A geologist by training, he had a growing interest in a new science called anthropology.[40]

Powell had recently gained fame as an explorer-scientist after crossing a swath of wild country, one of the last large blank spaces on maps of American territory. Those wild lands had not yet succumbed to colonization by settlers. The land and the native people remained poorly known to Americans.

Powell's exploring trip began on the Green River in Wyoming Territory, near landmark bluffs and buttes. The river carried his exploring party to the wild whitewater of the Colorado River. Powell's journey ended nearly a thousand hazardous miles later in the Grand Canyon, in Arizona Territory. Powell tested his skill and his luck when he returned to the Green River again, two years later, on another expedition. He planned to carry out a scientific survey of the country along the same perilous route.[41]

The northern part of that route—terra incognita to most Americans, including Powell and his men—was the homeland of Utes. Their ancestors had lived in that country from the beginning, when Wolf created the People, who stayed there, and other people who scattered in all directions. Utes told Powell what they knew about the river country, and much more, just months before he set out to explore it.[42]

He had spent that winter in a valley in northwestern Colorado Territory, near a camp of Utes on the White River. He recorded the name of the river as A-vwīm'-pa, White Water. Cold, clear water rippled over stones and ran beneath a skim of ice. Winter-bare cottonwoods lined the riverbanks, and winter-white mountains framed the broad river valley.[43]

Quinkent, also known as Chief Douglas, was the leader of the White River Utes. As it happened, Nicaagat, also called Captain Jack, had joined the White River Utes after running away from the Norton family and heading east into the mountains. Settler-colonists in Colorado Territory called him a war chief.[44]

Powell, his wife, and a dozen or so companions—college students and sundry others, mostly from Illinois—spent the winter in cabins they built as soon as they reached the valley. They had made a collecting trip to get specimens of native wildlife, fossils, and rocks for schools and colleges in Illinois. Powell was then in the last year of his short career as a professor of science.[45]

Chief Douglas and his people lived nearby, in a winter camp. Their tents stood just a few hundred yards away from the cabins of their new neighbors. Almost every day some of the Utes visited the people they called Merrekats, Americans.[46]

Powell was the rare American who asked questions about their way of life, and recorded words from the Ute language. He showed interest in their stories of the past, and their beliefs about spirits, and sickness and healing. At the invitation of Chief Douglas, he attended some of their healing ceremonies.

In some instances of sickness, Powell learned, the medicine man could not dislodge the harmful spirit from the patient's body with ceremonial measures, including smoking and chanting. Then a medicine man might try to drive it away with knives. Using sharp flints, the shaman would make cuts on the back, sides, arms, and legs of the afflicted. Or, Powell reported, he might resort to burning, placing hot coals on the patient's back, and creating a line of ten or twenty blisters. In cases of chronic disease, the treatment would be repeated. Powell had seen people proudly exhibit such scars, boasting, he said, of "the fortitude with which they bore these cruelties." Such healing practices struck him as a kind of torture.[47]

When he met Chief Kanosh, a few years after witnessing the healing ceremony by the White River, Powell was no longer an obscure professor of science from a small college in Illinois. Americans knew him as the famed explorer of a capricious river that cut through arid wild lands in the West. But to Chief Kanosh and his fellow chiefs who met him a few years later, Powell had a different identity. He was a visitor to their homelands, sent by Washington.[48]

The chiefs and their people gave him a polite welcome. They called him Ka'-pu-rats, Stump of Arm, because he had only a remnant of his right arm. This warrior, they learned, had lost his arm in a bloody, deadly battle called Shiloh. The name meant nothing to them, but they could well understand the circumstance. His stump of arm was not so much an odd deformity, a grievous absence, as it was a warrior's credential. The man must have courage.[49]

Eight years after the Civil War ended, when Powell met Chief Kanosh, he was not only a warrior whose terrible wound announced that he had shown courage. He was also, importantly, an emissary from Washington. Utes had long thought of Washington as the powerful leader of the Mer-recats. Over the years, many emissaries had told them what Washington wanted them to do, and what gifts Washington was going to give them.

The wealthy leader had sometimes sent them supplies of food, as well as canvas tents. They had once made their lodges from the skins of elk. When herds of elk dwindled, canvas took the place of skins. But Washington, despite sending these gifts, had proved to be unreliable and even treacherous. He often did not keep his promises.[50]

Now Washington had sent another emissary. By that time, Utes had come to understand that the famous leader was long dead, and that the current American leader lived in a distant eastern place called by Washington's name. Chief Douglas, along with Captain Jack, or Nicaagat, had gone there with others just a year before Powell met him in Colorado Territory. The chief and his companions traveled to the federal capital by train to take part in treaty talks. They returned home with a treaty that recognized the western part of Colorado Territory as their land.[51]

This new emissary from Washington, Ka´-pu-rats, was supposed to find out where Utes lived west of Colorado Territory. Federal officials knew that wave after wave of colonizing settlers had taken the best of their country. Because of settlement, Utes went hungry. Yet the officials seemed unable, or unwilling, to give them enough food to survive, as Chief Kanosh had complained to Tom Kane just months before he met Ka´-pu-rats. Elizabeth had written down his words. "One snow-time since, I got blankets," he said; "no flour, no beef, but a little last spring; no flour, no oats, no wheat, no corn, no bullets."[52]

Powell and a fellow commissioner set out to survey not only Utes but also other Indians living in the western Rocky Mountains and the Great Basin. They planned to report the names of all the groups and their chiefs, to determine the size of each group, and to learn more about their circumstances. They would then advise the federal government on where to send these people, and how they should live once sent there. The government wanted to remove them from the best western lands, and to open their homelands to colonization by settlers, from farmers and ranchers to miners. This was for the progress of the nation and for the good of Indian people, officials said.[53]

Powell met first with Utes. A young man from the Uintah Reservation served as his interpreter and as a linguistic and cultural guide. Richard Komas, known to his people as Ai-po-up, was about twenty years old. He not only spoke English but also knew how to read and write. Richard was enrolled as a student in the college preparatory program at Lincoln University in Pennsylvania, where he studied Latin and Greek as well as English grammar, composition, history, geography, and arithmetic. Nearly all of the other students at Lincoln University were African American.

Richard wore his hair cut short and parted on one side. When he posed for a portrait photograph, he dressed in a dark suit, white shirt, and bow tie. He seemed to offer visible evidence to Americans who met him or saw his photograph that education, as well as labor, served as a path for assimilating, and thereby eliminating, the native. That old idea had given rise in the seventeenth century to schools for male Indian students in Virginia and Massachusetts. New schools were being established in Virginia and Pennsylvania.[54]

When Powell met Chief Kanosh, he learned that the chief was the "elder brother" of Pi-an-nump, a Gosiute chief. It would be good to hold joint talks because the two men were close allies. Goshiutes had given Chief Kanosh the name Mo-a-gai'-tūp, which Powell understood meant playful spirit, although settler-colonists rarely saw the chief laugh and never heard him joke.

Powell sent a messenger to Pi-an-nump, and then held talks with the two chiefs. He learned that Pahvants numbered only 134 people, and Gosiutes, 256. He spoke with the chiefs about going to live with Utes on the Uintah Reservation to the east, and the prospects of living there as farmers. Washington would help them with tools and seed. As it happened, Pahvants and Gosiutes were already growing wheat and corn, and in places more suitable for farming than the reservation.[55]

Powell asked Chief Kanosh a series of questions that had to do with his scientific interests, but also bore on the official purpose of his journey and survey. He recorded Pahvant Ute words, including more than thirty kinship terms. His word list showed how closely the Pahvant dialect was related to other dialects of Ute. Gosiutes, in contrast, spoke a separate language. He thought that their language was related to Shoshone.

Powell came to understand that Gosiutes and Pahvants, while linguistically separate, were socially and politically affiliated. They maintained friendly relations, intermarried, and sometimes hunted together. This evidence offered support, he thought, for the plan to send them all to the Uintah Reservation.[56]

Resuming the journey and survey, Powell headed south into the red rock region, Southern Paiute country. The other commissioner went west into the desert valleys and mountains to meet Western Shoshones. After long talks with Southern Paiutes, Powell traveled north again. In Beaver Valley he happened to meet Chief Kanosh and some of his men, who were on a hunting trip. This gave him the chance to have another long talk with them about the future.

Powell detected great shrewdness in the chief, not only from what he said but also from what he had managed to get for his people. Relative to their numbers, Powell said, Pahvants had received four times more from the government than had other groups. Even with those supplies, he admitted, they barely eked out a living. Still, Chief Kanosh's success had gained him the admiration of other chiefs. They consulted him for advice about how to deal with government officials.[57]

When Powell and his fellow commissioner submitted their report months later, they summarized their findings and then made recommendations. Far fewer hunter-gatherers survived than had been estimated, they stated. In some cases, the survivors amounted to just 10 percent of the population before colonization by settlers began some twenty-five years earlier. In many places, the newcomers had already taken most of their homelands. As always, they had destroyed hunting and gathering grounds with farm fields and grazing livestock.

The native people must learn to be civilized, the two commissioners affirmed. They should settle permanently in one of four places suggested as reservations. They should farm there, although in truth most of the land was, in the commissioners' own words, "sandy desert and mountain waste," so ill-suited for farming that it had no value for most settlers. The land might be better suited for ranching, but giving seeds and tools was far cheaper than providing livestock.

Tents should no longer be offered, the report advised. Tents supported the old habit of moving from place to place. Instead, the government should build houses, to encourage the stubborn hunter-gatherers to stay in one place. Each family should also be given a cow so that they would begin to value private property. Thus would they enter into civilization, and come under settler-colonial control. They finally understood the "hope-lessness" of resisting "the tide of civilization," according to the report.[58]

Two more American visitors arrived in Pahvant country by train a year after Powell left. Captain John Codman, a former New England sea cap-tain, had turned traveler and writer. Years before Powell launched his small boats in the Colorado River Codman had sailed south to Brazil and other far-flung places. Now, at the age of sixty, he preferred the comfort of the transcontinental railroad, traveling with his wife Anna, and dispatching reports on frontier life. He was writing a series of articles for *The Galaxy*, an eastern magazine.

The couple traveled slowly south of the city on horseback, through mountain valleys. In early November, Anna wrote a long letter to their daughter about the journey, still in progress. She told her about the sage-brush plains ("barren and desolate"), the mountains ("sublime"), and then a sudden, raging storm. That "whirling tempest of rain, snow, sleet, hail, and wind," Anna said, tore across the land and ripped the sky. She and John rode through the storm for hours. She heard wolves howling in the mountains, and feared for her safety in what was still, it seemed to her, the howling wilderness.[59]

A few days later John and Anna reached a village in the vicinity of Corn Creek. They stopped for a meal, prepared by a village woman who did not impress them as neat and orderly. She complained, to the Codmans' surprise, that her neighbors at Corn Creek were not neat and orderly. They learned that Chief Kanosh lived there in a small adobe-brick house, but spent his time "roaming" in the mountains and valleys. John had earlier reported that settlers regarded Indians as "troublesome wild beasts." Reports of "roaming," even by an unusual chief who lived in a house instead of a tent or lodge, and other reports as well, led John to conclude sadly that the civilizing effort had so far come to nothing. Every attempt had ended in failure, he told his readers, although he did refer to Utes who showed an interest in farming as "half-tamed."[60]

In any case, it was well known, many Americans said, that Indians were dying out. It was only a matter of time, some claimed, in a cascade of published reports on western wild lands and Indians. Many of those reports qualified as wild/civilized discourse. The wild, and all that was native, was allegedly going or gone, eliminated by settler-colonization and replaced by the tame and civilized.[61]

PART III
Exiles

CHAPTER 10

The Civilizing Mission

YEARS LATER, NO ONE REMEMBERED how long Chief Kanosh courted Sally. Some people did recall that she showed complete indifference when he appeared in the kitchen of the Beehive House. She knew that he had once been an ally of Chief Wákara and Baptiste, her captor. That raised suspicion, although he had long ago become a loyal ally of the Leader.

She ignored the chief as he talked. She kept at her work, pouring, mixing, stirring, and baking. Someone said that he once approached Sally while she was ironing, and that she burned him. True or not, it did add drama to the story years later. In any case, he came back again and again, after meetings with the Leader in his nearby office. Finally, about five years after Elizabeth met her, Sally left the city. She left her longtime home at the Leader's estate dutifully, unhappily, as a newly married woman.[1]

The Leader had told her, after thirty years of daily service to his family, that he wanted her to perform one last act of service. She was to marry Chief Kanosh, live with him and his people—who were also her people— and convert them to civilization. He knew no better candidate for that task. Sally was a fine example to all of the superiority of civilized life. She offered living proof, he and others thought, that civilization could tame the wild and eliminate the native.

When he told Sally his wishes, he talked and talked. All leaders were talkers, and he was of course the supreme leader. He used the term *mission* to explain where he wanted her to go and what he wanted her to do. This was confusing. She had heard of men going on missions, usually in groups. Most did not marry someone chosen for them, someone they did not wish to marry, as part of the mission. And they usually spent no more than a few years on the mission. Then they came home—unless, that is, they died first. She had heard the gruesome tales of attack and murder.[2]

The Leader had just asked her to do something entirely different, even if he did not say that. This meant entering an unwanted marriage and permanent exile. It meant danger. She had heard the stories that blamed Chief Kanosh's warriors for attacking and murdering travelers, and the story about the murder of the chief's wife Mary by a rival. She had not expected to suffer a long exile in a dangerous place. Again.

Could she refuse the Leader? She had a long habit of keeping silent when listening to her elders. She had also listened carefully in order to learn the ways of Clara and her tribe, which were complicated and often puzzling. The habit of listening had only deepened over many years of working with Lucy in the kitchen, and listening to daily instructions. She occupied a certain place in the family as the Indian woman who worked in the kitchen. They expected her to listen. Her daily life centered on assigned duties, a series of set tasks. When Clara or Lucy asked her to darn a sock or iron a dress or make a pudding, she complied. She did as they asked, and helped them. That was her life with the family.

But this duty differed. And what the Leader had told her to do, without warning, came as a deep shock and betrayal. He had never sent away any other woman in the family on such a mission. The Leader had even protected Polly and Louisa, Barney's daughters, from Chief Sanpitch who wanted them as wives. Polly had worked with Sally and lived at the Lion House for years until she finally left to marry a settler.[3]

But now the Leader had ordered Sally to marry another chief who wanted *her* as a wife. He was sending her away for the rest of her life, and she did not want to go. She did not want to leave the safety of the walled estate. She had lived there with Clara and the children for many years, and had slowly, silently adopted them as her family. It seemed that the Leader's family had adopted her, too, just as someone had told an important visitor, the general's wife, a few years earlier.[4]

Clara, who long ago at the fort had given her food, and then slowly gained her trust, had become a kind of elder sister, a substitute for the sisters she lost, the sisters who never found her. She would never see them again, or her mother, in this life. Fatherless as well, she was completely orphaned. But growing up among the People, she had learned that everyone was kin by blood or marriage, or a kind of kin by mutual agreement or adoption. There were no orphans. Even young captives taken by the

People, and kept by them, came to regard their captors as kin. The People's understanding of kinship had early become part of her, and remained with her.

Treating Clara as an elder sister had made her a younger sister. Then she knew how to behave toward Clara, with a measured reserve that showed affectionate respect. Regarding herself as a younger sister had also given her a sense of belonging, and a sense of connection to the children. It had long ago made Clara's daughters and foster children *shi-nan'-sin*, the People's word for older sister's children. Her anguished sense of belonging to the strangers as chattel, a captive and slave, had faded as the children were born, and as Clara slowly became an elder sister. And Lucy, as Clara's elder sister, also qualified as her elder sister in Sally's way of thinking. Lucy's other helpers in the kitchen were not members of the family, not sisters by adoption. They stayed for a short time and then left.[5]

Sally had lived with Clara and the family for decades, but she had never fully grasped the cultural nuances of their naming and kinship practices. Clara and the other family members did not address her or refer to her as a sister or daughter or aunt. They always called her by her English name, just as they called the servants by their first names. But she also heard the women of the Lion House call and refer to their children by name. And she had been given a name that other women shared, which seemed to mean that she belonged. She had no way to know that the family had identified her as a servant to census takers, and one without any surname. She was counted as a member of the Leader's household, not his family.[6]

But to her way of thinking, even the Leader, as Clara's husband, had qualified for a kind of kin status. He was sister's husband, or *naim'-pi-won*, to use the old word. More to the point, he was much older, old enough to be her father. And he was the paramount leader, not just a chief. After living with Clara's people for so many years, she knew that she could not easily refuse a man with such power. Few women did. He taught that women must obey men, something she had not learned from her own father and the People.[7]

She did not understand why he was sending her away, and she did not have the means to refuse. Where would she live? Despite thirty years of daily labor for the Leader's family, she was destitute. She owned nothing of value, and had nothing to sell but her labor, which had never brought her a wage. She had no social connections except to Clara and Lucy and a few other members of the Leader's family. None would openly oppose him.

His fixed gaze was unsettling, his eyes the color of fair sky but with a gray cast, as if warning of a coming storm. She accepted his order sadly, as a final duty.[8]

Clara seemed to have remarkable powers of perception about the daughters of the Lion House. She had known them from their earliest years, and she listened closely to them. But she did not have the same means of understanding who Sally was by virtue of her upbringing among the People. Clara had known only, from the beginning at the fort, that she had a civilizing mission with the captive girl, a mission to be carried out at home.

The settlers always gave Clara credit for teaching Sally how to speak, how to dress, how to eat, how to clean and keep house. But Sally had finally learned everything, and learned it to perfection, because she wanted to stay with Clara and the children. She had no other place to go, and she wanted a home and family, and the safety of belonging. And yet . . . she had grown up speaking a different language, among people who saw the world, and lived in the world, in a far different way. It could not all be eliminated and replaced.

Clara could easily see that Sally loved her children and treated them, and other young children, with exceptional kindness. But she did not understand that Sally's early upbringing was a source of that admirable quality and others, including the quiet deference she paid to her elders and her willingness to work so hard for the family. And even if she understood that Sally had long ago adopted her and the children, Clara had not in turn adopted Sally as a sister. She already had three sisters—as well as parents, two brothers, three daughters, the foster children, and, too briefly in this earthly life, two sons. She had nieces and nephews and cousins, half-brothers and half-sisters, step-brothers and step-sisters and step-children. They numbered far more than a hundred, and most of them lived nearby.

Clara had wanted not an adopted sister but someone to help with the children and the laundry and housekeeping. Then her boys died and the girls grew up. Finally only Lulu remained, and Clara no longer had as much need of Sally's help. Lulu, at sixteen, was slightly older than Clara when she married the Leader as a plural wife. Some girls still married at that age, often to older men with other wives—but not Clara's daughters. She used her influence as a mother to discourage that, quietly and successfully.[9]

The Leader had long advocated polygamy, instructing women "let your Daughters Marry Good men [even] if they have 40 wives." Any who opposed it, he threatened, would suffer eternally. Clara had heard all of that.[10]

She also knew that Sally did not want to marry Chief Kanosh and leave the family and the estate. But at least Clara had prepared her well to carry out the civilizing mission that lay ahead. And Sally was entering marriage as the chief's only wife, and as a mature woman, not a vulnerable young girl. That was worth something—to Clara.[11]

To the Leader and to Chief Kanosh, unlike Sally, the impending marriage solved problems and brought benefits. The chief saw advantage in having a wife who knew the settler-colonists' ways and who spoke their language, a woman like his late wife Mary. As an Indian man, he was not permitted to marry a settler. That would be "against law," as the Leader put it, a violation of an unwritten code. But Sally was eligible. She was also one of the few Pahvant women who survived, and nearly the only one who remained unmarried, available as a wife.[12]

Giving Sally to Chief Kanosh would help the Leader to repay him for many favors and years as a helpful ally. And yet it cost virtually nothing, financially or politically. A marriage involving an Indian servant would not attract the notice of federal authorities who had long watched the Leader closely. They regarded him as the leading advocate of an illegal practice, polygamy. They did not want him to interfere in Indian affairs or any other matters of governance.

He had long ago given up the policy of encouraging his men to marry Indian women as polygamous wives. It had seemed a good strategy at first, and the fastest way, he thought, to civilize wild people, to assimilate them. But few men sought marriages of that sort. Even worse, news of his policy had reached the East almost at once, where meddling newspapers, as he saw them, denounced that policy in print. The *New York Daily Times* accused him by name of promoting "intermarriage" with Indians, a practice that remained anathema to many of its readers.[13]

The marriage of Chief Kanosh and Sally was not intermarriage, and would be nearly invisible to prying eyes in eastern places. It would also serve to strengthen the Leader's alliance with the chief. That was an age-old strategy, and one he had already pursued with great success among his own people. With his counsel and consent, some of his daughters had married his associates, older men of means with other wives. They usually married without incident, although one had tried to run away by train.[14]

From his earliest years of leadership he had instructed women—clearly, repeatedly—that their religious duty was to obey men and to bear children. Men should obey God. For women to disobey men, or God, had a fearful consequence, he said. It threatened their eternal lives.[15]

There was nothing worse, he thought, than disobedient women—except wild Indians and wild wolves. They were all out of control, it seemed, roaming around and making trouble. Black Hawk had died, but some of his followers wandered about for years, threatening the peace and prosperity of the settler-colonists, always with complaints about loss of their homelands or lack of food. And the wolves, those roving packs of hungry wild beasts, gave the poor livestock and their owners no peace.[16]

But there were fewer wolves and wild people now in the settled lands. Of the surviving Utes, fewer than six hundred lived on the Uintah Reservation and a hundred or so at Corn Creek with Chief Kanosh. They did not always stay where ordered. Some still left the Uintah Reservation to hunt and to visit their old homes, their ancestral lands.[17]

Sally, in contrast, stayed at home. She rarely left the estate. She was a good girl, compliant and obedient. He could trust her to follow orders. As a longtime member of his household she had a strong connection to his family, the most important in the territory. Chief Kanosh stood to benefit in prestige and influence by marrying her, as he well knew.

Once Sally had learned to work well, after careful training by Clara and Lucy, her labor as a highly skilled and reliable cook had proved very useful. Yes, she worked hard for the family, but that was woman's lot. She was not indentured, and had worked long past the twenty-year limit. But in return, she received room and board, and goods from the family store now and then. She lived in far greater comfort, even luxury, than most of his followers enjoyed, to say nothing of her own people. Anyone could see that she was well fed. She had received other benefits as well, such as the blessings of civilized life, and teachings about salvation and eternal life. She was a true convert to civilization.[18]

Sally had been a great help to Lucy at the Lion House and the Beehive House, but Amelia would preside as hostess in his new mansion. He was having a stately home built, a veritable castle, with a tower, four floors, and some forty-five rooms to be filled with fine furnishings. The once-splendid Beehive House looked small and plain now that so many rich merchants had built ornate, even opulent mansions of brick or stone. In this Gilded

Age, and among these new mansions, the house looked drab, and no longer fitted his stature. Even tourists noticed.[19]

Lucy was to stay at the Beehive House as housekeeper and caretaker. She held legal title to the house, an effective way during troubled times to keep it out of federal hands. But it also seemed a just return for her years of faithful service, and a means of future security. She was no longer young. Soon she would have few guests and no need of kitchen help, including Sally, who had reluctantly left Clara's old suite at the Lion House to live in servants' quarters at the Beehive House. Lucy's youngest daughter Clarissa, at seventeen, was surely old enough to help her mother, if only Lucy taught her. Clarissa of course had never had any reason to learn how to cook or keep house. The "maids," as she called them, did that work. She regarded Sally as one of them, but now Sally was leaving.[20]

Clara no longer needed Sally's help either. She and Lulu had moved to a small cottage a few blocks from the Lion House. The cottage stood next to the Social Hall, a popular venue for parties, plays, and dances attended by young and old. The location suited Clara, highly sociable as she was. The Leader had deeded the cottage to her to provide for her future, although at a more modest level than the Beehive House ensured Lucy's. He no longer saw Clara each day at supper, sitting at the long table, always in his field of vision. She had fewer chances to make requests on behalf of daughters, or to intercede now for Sally.[21]

Clara still saw the daughters, including the married ones, when they visited at her cottage. She welcomed them, always willing to listen, still able to soothe troubled hearts with her counsel. Most of the unmarried daughters had also left the Lion House, and lived with their mothers in other houses. Zina had moved from the Lion House several years before Clara left. Fewer people sat at the dining room table these days. With nearly all of his sons and daughters now grown, or almost grown, there was simply less need for Sally's help in the kitchen, and no need for her help with small children.[22]

There was something else to consider about Sally, the question of her future. He had nearly reached the venerable age of seventy-six, exceeding the biblical threescore and ten. His health was failing, and his mortal life, waning. He needed to plan for the earthly care of his many dependents.

A few years earlier, during the Kanes' visit, Tom, a lawyer by training, had advised him about making a will. Untangling his complex financial dealings, drawing up an inventory of his holdings, and then constructing a legally sound will had taken time and skilled assistance. He was a wealthy man with many wives and children, more than fifty beneficiaries in all. He made no provision for servants. They had received fair compensation, in his view. He gave food and wages to men who worked at the estate, and food and lodging to women who worked in the Lion House and the Beehive House.[23]

This marriage and mission settled the question of where Sally would spend the rest of her earthly life. She would live near her old home and with her people. That seemed fitting. Her most cherished hope had been that her mother and sisters would find her and take her home with them. But Zina's long-ago prophecy had not come to pass. Her mother and sisters were not among those ragged women who came to the gate over the years, holding empty sacks in their hands. They had asked only for food, not for a lost daughter or sister.

Thousands of Indian people had died since settlement. As he had often said, and continued to say, they were doomed to extinction. Many had died from measles at Warm Springs. "I do not suppose there are three of that band left now," he had told his followers a few years earlier. Yet he recalled seeing some three hundred when he first arrived. In little more than twenty years, their numbers had plunged nearly to the vanishing point. "There was another band a little south," he added, "another north, another further east; but I do not suppose there is one in ten, perhaps not one in a hundred, now alive of those who were here when we came."

Many of the indentured children had also died. "We brought their children into our families," the Leader reminded the assembled crowd, "and nursed and did everything for them it was possible to do for human beings, but die they would." Children were still dying from the foreign diseases.[24]

Although Sally, a remarkable survivor, could not return to her own family, at least he could send her back to her people, somewhere near her old home. That would honor Zina's prophecy even if, strictly speaking, it did not fulfill it. But perhaps the prophecy had meant that Sally would be reunited with her mother and sisters not in this earthly life but after she died. Her intended husband, the chief, would no doubt see his deceased family members and three wives in the afterlife because he had recently had the necessary ritual performed. It promised that the deceased, once baptized, would live together in a kingdom of glory, eternally at home with other baptized family members. The same had been done for Sally's family.

In the meantime, he thought, she could do some good for the surviving Pahvants who lived under the leadership of the chief. She could uplift them by sharing the benefits of her many accomplishments. Perhaps she could teach them to follow the same path to a higher moral and spiritual plane. She might have greater success on a civilizing mission than the men he had sent long ago.[25]

O, those hard first years after settlement when he called group after group of men to preach to wild Indians, to baptize and civilize them. The cost was dear, the gains slight. It remained so hard to redeem their fallen wild brethren, he said. As he had preached in a rousing address, "God cursed them with this dark and benighted and loathsome condition; and they want to sit on the ground in the dirt, and to live by hunting, and they cannot be civilized." If only federal officials would listen, he would tell them, "You need never fight the Indians, but if you want to get rid of them try to civilize them." "There will then be no stain on the Government," he explained to his followers, "and it will get rid of them much quicker than by fighting them." "They have got to be civilized," he concluded, "and there will be a remnant of them saved."[26]

Sally's civilizing mission did not seem quite so daunting as the earlier ones that ended badly. The Pahvant Ute remnant had already been baptized. They already knew how to farm although the men left their fields of corn and wheat to make long hunting trips. Chief Kanosh provided both a good and a bad example to his men. Admirably, he produced enough grain to sell a small surplus. Regrettably, he too retained the bad habit of hunting wild game—or roaming and wandering in the mountains as settler-colonists saw it. More to the point, he and the other hunters were armed with guns and beyond surveillance or control when they hunted.[27]

Zina's brother Dimick had recently ordained the chief as an elder in the church, but that had not yet led to his complete reform. Still, it did mean that Sally had a worthy husband. He was authorized to preach to his people, and his new wife could instruct the women in the arts of civilization. She could show them how to keep house and how to cook in a highly refined way.[28]

Keeping house well was one of the most important skills for women, the Leader often said. Lucy, the consummate housekeeper, knew how to make his daily life comfortable. "I have seen women pretend to keep House," he had once declared, as an associate recorded his words. "Make tea first then fry meat then Boil potatoes & at last make Bread. There are but vary few good House keepers," he told a group of women. "But when you find one you find a woman that knows what to do." He advised any woman who knew how to teach school to offer lessons in housekeeping. "Have a place for Evry thing & Evry thing in its place," he also counseled.[29]

Sally could show Pahvant women how to cook and sew and darn socks and iron. She could encourage Chief Kanosh to stay home, to tend his crops, and to preach. Perhaps the other men would follow his good example and give up hunting. She could not preach to them. Only men had that authority. But by her own example she could encourage her husband and the other men to attend church, and to learn about their eternal salvation.

This marriage of Sally to Chief Kanosh also resolved the question of who would provide for her for the rest of her earthly life. She was no longer young, and she might one day fall into infirmity. The chief, her husband, would be her provider and protector—assuming he lived as long as she did. If the required ritual was performed to seal her to her husband for eternity, she would remain forever at his side. That was the correct place for a woman, the Leader believed. She had stayed unmarried for so many years. She must be nearly fifty by now, like Clara, far too old to bear children for a husband. It seemed unlikely that any other man, besides Chief Kanosh, would want her at that age.[30]

No one had performed the special ritual for Sally that would join her to Clara and the rest of the family for eternity. In truth, Sally was not a member of their earthly family, but rather a loyal and hardworking servant who had lived with Clara for many years. She was clearly the right helpmeet for his old ally Chief Kanosh, and well suited for this civilizing mission to the Pahvants—even if she failed to understand that, even if she looked sad when he told her. She would just have to overcome her "morbid horror," as the family called it. Time had not yet healed that wound.

This mission would test her capacity for obedience and great sacrifice, which he expected of his people. Of course she had already demonstrated that capacity during years of daily service to the family. This mission would call for even greater sacrifice. Sending her back, he decided, was best for all concerned.[31]

On an evening in early June, Sally married Chief Kanosh. Dimick officiated. Her name was recorded as Kahpeputz, and also as Sally, without any surname. The new Ute name given to her, which meant Red Drum, seemed auspicious for the impending mission. It suggested success in communication. Drums can speak, and red is the color of good fortune. The marriage certificate identified Sally by race, as "an indian," not as Pahvant Ute by origin. Her thirty years of cultural assimilation went unrecorded.[32]

By family custom, a wedding was a private affair, and usually took place in a church building called the Endowment House. The ritual that sealed a husband and wife to each other for eternity was performed there. But Sally did not want to be the chief's wife for eternity. She did not want to marry him and go far away to live with him. She had heard too many stories about murders in Pahvant country, and she did not want to leave the protection of the Leader's walled estate.

Three of Chief Kanosh's earlier wives had already died. They, along with his family members, also dead, could be with him after he died. The rituals that she and the chief had taken part in a year earlier promised that. They promised the same for her and her family, and she wanted to be with them. The short marriage ceremony, a bitter moment, was held not at the Endowment House but at Clara's cottage.[33]

On the day of the wedding, Clara had gone to the family store at the Beehive House to gather household goods for Sally. These supplies for her civilizing mission also made a serviceable trousseau for the unhappy bride. The total cost was $39.35, or slightly more than a dollar for each year of Sally's service. It added up to a small part of Clara's annual expenditure at the store.

The household goods included table service for six—plates, forks, spoons, and knives—as well as a sugar bowl, cream pitcher, and a large water pitcher. These would help Sally set a good table, a matter of importance on her mission. She could show the women how to cook, what to cook, and how to eat at a table—even if none had a table, or a house. The chief's people preferred to live in tents and lodges.

Clara added some precious sugar, a few ounces of whole nutmegs, and a pound of tea. To help with good housekeeping, she picked out a broom, stove polish, and a few bars of soap. Next came some candles, a gallon of kerosene, and two boxes of matches. In case of sickness, there were three boxes of pills. Clara selected two pounds of stocking yarn, twenty yards of calico, ten yards of coarse gray linsey, and some needles, pins, and thread. She had already got a parasol for Sally from the store, and the day after the wedding she returned for a pair of gloves and a pair of shoes. Sally needed to dress well for her mission—and that would console her, too. Clara had donated some silk dresses for that purpose.

She returned to the family store one more time, for a rocking chair. As Clara knew, Sally had long ago grasped the importance of sitting in chairs, and she needed to have a good one for this mission. She would never again sit on the ground—or as the Leader and others put it, sit on the ground in the dirt. Showing the Pahvants how to live properly in a house included showing the importance of sitting in a chair.[34]

Before leaving the city, the unhappy bride sat in a chair and posed
alone, not with her husband, for a formal portrait photograph. Gone were
Sally's plain garments and apron, her daily uniform for so many years.
Instead, she wore a dress of black silk taffeta with a white collar. The narrow wedding ring on her left hand announced a new, unwelcome status
as the chief's wife. Her thick hair was pulled back, confined in a silk net.
She looked worn, older than Clara, who wore a black wig, and fine dresses
of heavy silk trimmed with velvet and lace, and who maintained a brisk
social schedule. After years of daily orders and toil, Sally now faced an
order to enter permanent exile. She stared gravely at the camera, returning
the gaze.[35]

Sally and her new husband boarded a train for their journey south,
a suitable means of travel for a woman of the Lion House. The train pulled
away from the station and the city, from quiet streets lined with poplars
and shady elms and maples, and small adobe-brick houses bordered by
orchards in flower. Harriet's old dream of a tree-shaded home and orchard
had come true for all city-dwellers, even those who lived on the farthest
outskirts. On a bright and windy spring day, only fluttering light broke
through the deep shade of green canopies. Harriet had lived long enough
to see native grasses and shrubs on open land nearly replaced by imported
trees and flowers in a growing city. In gardens by the houses, where blooming lilacs and bright tulips had earlier announced spring, crowds of daisies
still presided.

Then, as the train passed the city's edge, came the first glimpse of cultivated fields. The big valley, which the first colonizing settlers, and Sally,
had reached just thirty years earlier, was now home to nearly thirty thousand people. The once-open land beyond city limits, where some fifteen
years earlier a visitor had seen a few Indian women gathering native wild
seeds, had been plowed and fenced, planted with crops and with houses.
Only on the slopes of the valley, in the foothills, did native wildflowers,
grass, and sagebrush still stand their ground. Streaks of violet, white, and
yellow brightened pale gray-green.[36]

After twenty miles, the train entered another valley, once the beloved
Valley of the Utahs, where the big freshwater lake blazed silver on still,
bright days. A dazzling path, flashing points of sunlight on water, ran
straight across the surface. Farm fields and grazing livestock filled what
had been wild country when her captors took her north to Tav'-o-kun,
where strangers lived behind walls in a fort.

Sally's wedding portrait. Used by permission of Utah Historical Society.

Twenty years earlier, some ten years after Charley bought her, she had come to the Valley of the Utahs with Clara and the rest of the family when they sought refuge there. She had come reluctantly, dreading the destination. Chief Wákara was dead by then, but not Baptiste, and some of his old Timpanogos allies still lived in the valley. Nearly everyone in the city had moved south during those anxious times to avoid the approach of federal troops. Soldiers were escorting the newly appointed official who was to replace the Leader as governor of the territory.[37]

Now, in this more peaceful time, the sun-struck land wore colors of late spring, the tender young green of new leaves on native willows and cottonwoods, the emphatic yellows and purples of scattered wildflowers. But few settlers took notice of wild nature and the so-called waste. Everyone was busy with civilizing work in the warm month of June. Farmers and their families were planting and tending new crops, and looking after irrigation canals that carried water from creeks to fields. They were caring for livestock, including new calves and tiny lambs. But to Sally this route took her through a landscape of violence, the setting for countless Indian stories. She had heard those tales of turmoil, violence, and murder again and again over the years.

She and Chief Kanosh left the train where the tracks ended, seventy miles south of the city. A wagon stood ready, loaded with the rocking chair, household goods, clothing, and other trappings of her former life. The wagon looked nothing like the fine carriage the Leader had put at the disposal of the Kanes for their journey, or even the one that Clara had ridden in years ago on the long trip to the northern fort in Salmon River country. It was unthinkable to Sally that she, a well-dressed woman who had lived in the Leader's fine houses in the city, should ride in a loaded wagon. She insisted on traveling by stagecoach to their destination.[38]

When they finally left on the next leg of the journey, the road took them through a landscape of remembered violence. A branch led over the mountains to the remote canyon where Barney had died twelve years earlier, one of the first casualties of Black Hawk's warriors. Perhaps his killers were still alive and at large. She knew that a few of Black Hawk's followers, even after his death, still attacked colonizers who destroyed hunting and gathering grounds with their farm fields and livestock.

A crowd of curious people greeted the couple when they reached Fillmore, the county seat near Chief Kanosh's home. The two already enjoyed a certain celebrity as a well-known chief and his bride—she dressed in finery, she a longtime member of a famous household in the city. The town was the last stop before their final destination, Corn Creek, twelve miles farther south, and a hundred and fifty miles from the city.[39]

Pahvants called the creek that coursed down from the mountains Un'-kar-tum Nu-kwint, Red Rock Creek. Colonizing settlers who first explored the region had given it the name Corn Creek. They noticed not the tumbled red rocks but something tame that they valued, the small patches of corn planted by Indians on the banks above the water. Some twenty-five years later, a new village of settlers stood nearby. The Leader had urged them to move from another place that was not so favorably located and to colonize this site.

The settler-colonists used the name Corn Creek both for the creek and for the nearby site where Pahvants lived. Corn Creek was just two or three days' journey by horse or wagon from A-vwa-pa, the long saltwater lake to the west known to the settler-colonists as Sevier Lake. It was the same distance north of Sho-av-ich, Beaver Valley, Sally's old home.[40]

But truly, the Leader had not sent her home. He had sent her away from her cherished home in the city. Even after she had lost her living quarters with Clara and the children at the Lion House, she at least still had the comfort of the daily routine in a familiar place and with familiar people. She still spent long days beside Lucy and her helpers in the steamy, busy kitchen. She still lived safely inside the walls of the estate. But then the Leader wrenched her away from that as well.

Corn Creek was a mere splinter of the Pahvant homeland, and fewer than a hundred remaining Pahvants lived there. They had dwindled nearly to the vanishing point. As Chief Kanosh had told the Kanes about his family five years earlier, "all gone, all sick." A few of the survivors, taken under armed escort to the Uintah Reservation, had stayed there. Others, in resistance, had returned home to Corn Creek with their chief.[41]

The nearby village that bore the chief's name was a drowsy, rustic place, far from the city with its Gilded Age mien of grand mansions, splendid flower gardens, and new gaslights illuminating broad boulevards. Several hundred villagers lived in rows of small houses built of logs or adobe bricks. Farm fields and pastures surrounded the settlement, an orderly and linear zone, which had replaced the chaos of the wild waste, as settler-colonists saw it. The rules of uniformity and order prevailed in the village. Build houses in rows. Lay out streets on a grid. Keep houses in order. Keep children in line.[42]

Corn Creek had just one house, the chief's, and a scattering of thirty tents and lodges. There were no streets, and no other construction, to distract Sally's gaze from peaks in the Pahvant Mountains. Beyond them, to the east, stood other ranges in the Rocky Mountains. Open desert lay to the west.

Perhaps it was fitting to wear a black dress in this deep exile. Black, unlike red, was a hard color. Red boded well. It signified joy and success. Black was the color of ashes and dried blood and mourning.

Still, Sally wore this dress with pride, just as Clara and Lucy and all of the Lion House women wore their elegant clothing. It gave the look of a lady of quality. Eliza had posed for a portrait photograph in such a dress, made from the same dark, stiff fabric. It had the same long sleeves and full skirt, the same prim white collar. But it was not the same dress, passed on to Sally. Eliza was too small and delicate in build.[43]

Sally had looked small, even shrunken, when Clara and Eliza first saw her. She entered the fort as a famished captive, but she left the Lion House as a woman of substance. She had lived in the house of the supreme leader. She wore a fine dress such as the People had never seen, and sometimes she wore a fine hat as well. And she returned as the wife of the chief.

At Corn Creek, nearly half of the Pahvant men still identified as warriors, no comfort to her. The rest identified as hunters. All of them bore arms for hunting, and none called himself a farmer. One of the men, Moshoquop, was known as the Pahvant war chief. Moshoquop and his warriors had allegedly murdered Captain Gunnison and his men by Pi-au-wip Nu-kwint, the Sevier River, on a cold autumn day twenty-four years earlier. They often hunted along the willow-lined banks of the river in autumn. But they usually hunted for waterfowl, not men.[44]

Few of the settler-colonists doubted that Moshoquop and his men bore sole responsibility for killing the captain and seven other men in his company. Everyone had heard the ghastly tale of murder and mutilation. Now Sally found herself living in a den of murderers who might also have killed William Hatton. After all, he had died inside the walls of a nearby fort just months before Gunnison died by the river.

The thought that Moshoquop and his men killed Hatton as well as Gunnison was chilling. It mattered little that no one was ever charged with Hatton's murder, and that his killer must have been inside the fort. Decades later, his widow, Adelia, still harbored doubts about who murdered her husband. She had willingly lived near Pahvants, the supposed killers, for years. Some of the settler-colonists even liked Moshoquop. "He had a dignified bearing, and his face showed strength and a fearless nature," one of them said. Befitting a warrior, he looked "as lithe and wiry" as a mountain lion.[45]

Josiah Gibbs and his father William held Moshoquop in high regard. They lived in the nearby county seat, and they were carpenters by trade. Some years earlier, before moving south, William had built a farmhouse for the Leader outside city limits, miles from the Beehive House. He and his son were also trusted guards who stood by the gates of the Lion House one night each week. Josiah had come to regard gentle Zina as "a second mother," he said. But then the Gibbs family moved away from the city.[46]

A few years after they left and before Sally arrived at Corn Creek with Chief Kanosh, Josiah and William had gone into the Pahvant Mountains on an exploring trip to the north fork of Chalk Creek. They wanted to search for "accessible timber," as Josiah put it. Despite the distance, it might be profitable to cut down stands of native trees in the mountains and turn the felled trees into useful lumber. Such trees in the valley had already been removed by ax, and the wood put to use. The demand for wood only grew as the number of colonizing settlers increased. Sawmills consumed more and more of the native trees.

Father and son left the valley on horseback on a sweltering day in early July, with their dog, loyal Victor, lumbering along beside them. He was a big shaggy dog, a Newfoundland mix. The two men rode for miles along a rough track, ascending the south fork of the creek to the point where the road ended. Then they followed an ancient trail that led to an open, grassy summit in the mountains. Just an hour or so before sunset they approached the summit, and saw Indian ponies grazing in the distance. They realized that the ponies' owners, who had followed the same ancient trail or others that crossed the mountains, could not be far away. To reach the north fork of Chalk Creek required passing by these people, whoever they were.

With stories of recent attacks by Black Hawk's followers fresh in his mind, Josiah felt a sinking stab of fear. He suggested retreat. William wisely pointed out that their presence had no doubt been detected. It seemed better to proceed and show their faces than to turn around and expose their backs. Besides, he said, the ponies might belong to friendly Pahvants who were not Black Hawk's allies.

When they reached the summit, they heard shouts of welcome. A few Pahvant families on a summer hunting trip in the cool mountains had camped near a spring. The children ran to see the visitors and their *sa-rits'*, their dog with the thick dark fur, a dog that was as big as the biggest wolf. Friendly Victor, wagging calmly, was happy to be greeted by these small people who crowded close around him. He was happy to sniff, and happy to lie down and rest.

Beyond the Pahvants' camp, in a separate camp to the northeast, Josiah spotted men, and only men. If they were Pahvants, he wondered why they had camped apart. And where were the women and children? Their absence struck him as strange.

Moshoquop greeted Josiah and William. His companions at the camp included Narrient, whose Ute name meant strong, and a man called Nimrod by settlers. That name came from a biblical figure, known as "a mighty hunter." Moshoquop's wife, Ruth, and other women and children had also come along with the three men. They knew this country well, including the rushing, singing water they called U-wi-ats Nu-kwint. The settler-colonists, who valued the useful chalk deposits, had named it Chalk Creek. It lay within the Pahvants' ancient hunting grounds.[47]

Moshoquop's wife was, in the view of some, a once-tame woman. Like Chief Kanosh's late wife Mary, Ruth had lived with a family of settlers. But she had reverted, or gone back to the blanket, as they put it. Josiah later concluded, romantically, that her love for Moshoquop explained why Ruth gave up the blessings of civilized life and reverted. Others claimed gloomily that it was nearly impossible to civilize the wild people.[48]

Josiah's father wanted to hobble the horses, but Moshoquop insisted on picketing them securely. Then he turned to Ruth and asked her to cook deer meat for the two guests. After they ate the fragrant roasted venison, and as dusk descended, Josiah's father asked where they should put their blankets, saddles, and rifles for the night. Moshoquop showed them a place not far from his shelter, and suggested that they sleep facing north, with their backs against a large log. He asked them to tie the big *sarits'* to an upright limb on the log so that he could not steal deer meat. The children had petted and fed Victor so well that Josiah wondered at Moshoquop's odd instructions, but he and his father complied. Last of all their host advised them to sleep in their clothing because of the morning chill.

William fell asleep quickly, but Josiah lay awake ruminating. Why had Moshoquop given them such detailed instructions about where to sleep? Why had he advised keeping the rifles and Victor nearby? Why had he said nothing about the men in the other camp? There were twice as many of them as at Moshoquop's camp.

Moshoquop's instructions all added up to preparations for fight or flight, Josiah thought. Finally he fell asleep, but slept fitfully. He woke often in the darkness to find Victor's cold nose pressed against his cheek. Sometime before daybreak he heard Moshoquop speaking loudly in the darkness, with great eloquence, about protecting his friends and guests. Josiah and his father and Victor left the camp later that day without incident.

A year passed before Josiah fully understood the events of that night, before Nimrod told him that the men in the other camp were Utes, but not Pahvant Utes. They had come from the other side of the mountains, he said, and they were followers of Black Hawk. The men had proposed to Moshoquop in the night that they should kill the two visitors, and take their rifles and horses. Moshoquop declined. Anticipating this proposal, he had made careful plans for his guests' escape.[49]

Until the end of his long life, Josiah remembered that uneasy night with his father in the Pahvant Mountains when he was twenty-five. He always gave Moshoquop credit for saving their lives.

Moshoquop, Nimrod, Narrient, and others at Corn Creek also remembered how they had saved the lives of the two men at their hunting camp in the mountains. But if anyone told Sally the story when she arrived at Corn Creek six years later, it did not change what she had earlier heard in the city about the brutality of Moshoquop. She knew that long ago he had been found guilty of killing an Army surveyor and his men. She knew that Moshoquop had walked away from the prison farm with no one in pursuit. The stories about the murders were well known, even if details varied from one version to the next.

Sally could see that he still went wherever he pleased in the mountains, armed with a rifle, and that his wife Ruth had shrugged off much of what she learned from a settler family. She willingly slept in a wickiup, a brush shelter, on their hunting trips. She gutted and butchered wild game and cooked bloody cuts of meat over open fires. She sat on the ground in the dirt. She who had once lived in a house! She who had learned to speak English![50]

Sally would have none of that. She had lived for years inside a mansion with sturdy walls and a proper roof and fine furnishings, including chairs. And she did not rest easy in the place where Mary had so briefly lived, the chief's small adobe-brick house, which was leaning toward ruin after years of neglect. Poor Mary, a woman who had learned to live properly, and who knew how to speak good English, like Sally. But Mary had been brutally murdered by another wife of the chief.

The jealous rival was dead, but that gave small consolation. Worse, Chief Kanosh had reportedly told a previous wife, the accused killer, that she would soon die, and she had died—perhaps from his bad medicine, his sorcery. That knowledge, which settlers did not grasp, was disturbing. Few of them knew of the accusations against Pahvants, made some twenty years earlier, for causing the death of Chief Wákara with sorcery. But Sally knew, and she lived uneasily in their presence.[51]

It did not help her, after spending so many years in safety with only women and children, that men outnumbered women at Corn Creek. It boded ill for the Pahvants' future that there were far more men than women, and more than twice as many adults as children.[52]

Still, she understood her duty. She made some effort to show the Pahvants how to live as she did, properly, as she saw it. But the futility of teaching the skills that she had mastered soon became clear. She had learned about housekeeping in a well-appointed mansion. She had learned to cook in a well-equipped kitchen with an abundant supply of food. Pahvant women, who spent long hours acquiring the food that they cooked over campfires, had their own prized skills, learned from their mothers and grandmothers. They showed no interest in learning hers. Just as she did not accept the women as they were, they did not accept her.[53]

Far from following her example of how to live on a higher, civilized plane, as some people put it, Pahvants just laughed at her squeamishness. They did not mean to be unkind. But the humor of it! Sally, who had once lived as they did, now shuddered at everything. They knew something about how their neighbors in the village lived. They knew how to sit on chairs at a table and use cutlery, but they had no need for tables and chairs in their lodges and tents. They knew about washing hands before eating, and saying special words, the blessing. They dutifully performed those rituals in the presence of villagers. They knew about farming, but they farmed in a casual way because they preferred hunting, and they needed wild game for food. They understood that the villagers called Moshoquop's wife Ruth, but they also knew her by a native name.[54]

Chief Kanosh's new wife did not want such a name. She was not Kahpeputz, Red Drum, as he had told Dimick. She was Sally. She remembered some of the old words, but she only wanted to speak English. And she liked to spend the day inside the house, not outside. They could say about her, and about women in the nearby village: *Ma'-mōts kan-in'-ya ka'-ri*, The woman stays in the house.

Unlike this Sally who now rejected their ways and words, Pahvants lived in two worlds. As a practical matter, they followed the ways of the settler-colonists when they went to the village, but their life at Corn Creek and on hunting trips in the mountains belonged to them. They valued the old ways, what remained of their old life. Their ears could not listen to tiresome words about dirt and soap and sitting on chairs. And they could not help laughing whenever they saw Chief Kanosh's wife refuse to sit on the bountiful earth or touch it, as if it held danger.[55]

Sally had lived for so many years with Clara and the Leader's family, and only with them, that Pahvants were nearly strangers to her. They were like figures from a hazy, half-forgotten dream. She had slowly, long ago, entered into another world, a world of women and children, laughter, filling food, and protection. In this second exile, she could not stop mourning her loss. She felt the loss of home and family, of safety and a sense of belonging. Again.

Just three months after Sally arrived at Corn Creek with Chief Kanosh, the Leader suddenly fell ill at home in the city. In his mid-seventies, he had seemed suddenly to turn old and frail. His rheumatism worsened, making it hard for him to walk or to travel. Then came the illness, and he died.

Everyone knew about his grand funeral from the newspaper stories. Tens of thousands of people viewed his body as it lay in state in the city. Under a cloudless blue sky on a day in late summer, a band played as thousands walked in the funeral cortege to his gravesite in a small family cemetery near the Beehive House.[56]

His children, most of them grown and married, and his wives assembled the day after the funeral to hear the will read. Then they waited for the settling of the large and complicated estate. Like Clara, many of the women lived in houses that their husband had already deeded to them. Eliza and the few others who lived in the Lion House retained the right to remain there. Sally, of course, was not a beneficiary. Seven of the Leader's children, including three of Emeline's daughters, contested the will.[57]

News of the Leader's death had spread quickly to the most remote corners of the territory. For Sally, the sad news brought an opportunity. His death made it safer for her to resist his last order, to try to interrupt her hapless, unwanted mission. His death made it safe to contact Clara. She knew that over the years Chief Kanosh had sent many letters to the

Leader, dictated by him and recorded by Dimick or others. She could ask the village schoolteacher to help her with a letter. She wanted to return to her old life or some semblance of it, even if briefly, and only as a visitor.

The villagers had set up a small school for their children. Their teacher, Emily Crane, was English, born and bred. Her family had arrived in the village when she was fourteen. Living on the outskirts of London had not prepared Emily for her life in a new country. On board a ship to America, she had worn her best clothing, including a hat and dainty black shoes. Her journey ended in a remote village where women wore simple sunbon-nets and cobbled shoes, or went shoeless. Emily put away her best clothes and entered into village life.

She started as an assistant teacher in the school at the age of fifteen. Now twenty-two, she had paying work as the teacher. True, the salary was low, and a good part of her payment came in the form of room and board with her students' families. One student had paid for his schooling by making a wooden chest for her. Still, she felt proud to teach the children to read and write and do numbers—and to earn money, and spare her father George the expense of her food.[58]

The village school occupied a small log structure. It bore no resem-blance to the fine schoolhouse the Leader had built on his city estate, to replace the old schoolroom in the basement of the Lion House. The schoolhouse had matching child-size desks painted bright green, high windows to admit good light, and a belfry and a sonorous bell to ring in the school day. Emily's students did not have desks. Instead, they sat on boards that rested on boxes. When they needed to write, they knelt on the floor. But with Emily's patient help, her students did learn to read and write and figure.[59]

School began in fall, a few months after Sally reached Corn Creek, and after children in the village helped their families with the harvest. Aspens shimmered in autumn light, the dry leaves a-murmur in the wind. Sum-mer's silver-green had gone, leaving trees that shone chartreuse and gold against a dark blue sky. Wild geese honked, sailing southward overhead, and flocks of boys and girls fell silent as they filed into the schoolhouse. Each school day commenced when they went indoors to learn their letters and numbers. Each ended when kind Miss Crane dismissed them, and they burst out the door and into sunlight.

At the end of one such day, as Emily was clearing her desk in the empty schoolhouse, she looked up to see the figure of a woman standing in the doorway, blocking the light. As the visitor advanced into the room, Emily saw that she wore a fine black dress and a hat, and that her dark hair was bound up in a silk net. It took a moment to register this startling sight. Emily had been laughed out of a public gathering for far less—the English girl in her hat and stylish black slippers, putting on airs, while the other girls wore sunbonnets and homespun.

"You are Miss Crane, the schoolteacher, are you not?" the visitor asked. Who was this woman? Emily still could not see her clearly in the dimness, with bright sunlight behind her. This visitor who spoke in a cultivated way, with quiet dignity, must be a parent who wanted to enroll her child in school, Emily thought. She affirmed that she was indeed the teacher. Then, to her great surprise, the woman asked if she would write a letter for her.

How, Emily wondered, could someone who dressed so well and spoke so well not know how to read and write? Sensing her confusion, the visitor explained that she was the new wife of Chief Kanosh. The Leader had sent her on a mission to the Pahvants. She wanted to write to Clara. She explained that she had lived with Clara and the Leader's family after arriving in the big valley long ago as a captive.

Emily thought that she spoke wistfully of her old home in the city, and concluded that her visitor must be homesick. Emily understood homesickness and loss. She had lost her mother, who died after giving birth to her fourth child when Emily was just five years old. Her father left his motherless children with their grandparents in Bedfordshire, and worked in London, fifty miles away. Then she had lost her grandparents and her home in England when her father converted to a new faith, remarried, and took his new wife and children to a foreign land thousands of miles away.

Yes, she would write the letter. Sally told Emily that she wanted no word of complaint or sadness in it. The letter to Clara was to consist simply of questions. How was each member of the family? Who did her duties now that she was gone? Were any beautiful flowers still in bloom in the city gardens?[60]

Time passed, and then a letter arrived for Sally. Lulu had written to her. Emily read the letter to Sally, who dictated a reply. As Emily wrote this letter and others, details of Sally's new life seeped out, one by one, but Emily honored her wishes and said nothing of them in the letters. The adobe-brick house had fallen into disrepair because the chief rarely used it after Mary died. Sally found it filled with vermin and dirt. The sad, violent tale of Mary's murder disturbed her. She disliked the way people lived at Corn Creek. And the food they ate . . . She longed to see her old home and Clara and the children again.[61]

Sally had not fully understood when she left the Lion House and the Beehive House that the way of life she held dear had already entered its last days, many of the women scattered to other houses in the city, most of the children grown. She did not know that the Leader's death had brought the complete collapse of that old way of life. There were no longer any fine meals to prepare and serve to distinguished guests at the Beehive House, no longer the crowds of workmen to feed each day. Even the kitchen servants were to be dismissed.

Lucy and Clarissa, along with Eliza and a few other aging women, remained in the two mansions. A visitor to the Lion House, who had seen it five years earlier when Sally still lived there, thought it showed signs of dinginess and neglect. The women of the Lion House lived in fading elegance and deepening silence, amidst the restless ghosts of memory—the Leader, Emeline and her poor baby, Clara's two little sons, and more.[62]

Emily wrote a series of letters for Sally. Lulu, not Clara, replied to each of them. That served to remind Sally, gently, that Lulu, the last of Clara's children, was nearly grown. By this means Clara also avoided any direct petition for help from Sally, from one mature woman to another, as it seemed to her, not from one sister to another. By then, Clara's long tenure as self-appointed genie had ended. Her ability to make small dreams come true, by interceding tactfully and discreetly with her powerful husband, vanished forever with his death.[63]

It was clear why Sally asked who did her duties now. She knew how much she had done for the Leader's family, for their comfort, whether they noticed or not. No one else would work as hard as she had worked day by day over the years to help keep dozens of people well fed, clothing washed and ironed, and the parlor clean and in good order. The Lion House had slipped into neglect after Sally moved to the Beehive House.

Still, Clara could not invite her back to the city and her old life with the family. The Leader's family had dispersed, and Sally's services were no longer needed by the few women who remained at the Lion House, or by Lucy at the Beehive House, or by Clara who lived so simply in a cottage with Lulu. And if Sally came for a visit, she might ask to stay. Clara had limited means as a widow. The Leader's estate, not yet settled, appeared smaller than expected.[64]

She had dutifully taught Sally how to work and earn her keep. That had taken years of daily attention and patient instruction. Sally needed to learn so much, but she had learned everything well. She had helped Clara and Lucy beyond measure, but now her duty was to teach her people. Besides, Sally was married, and belonged at her husband's side.

When Sally first sought Emily's help, the young teacher was lodging with the family of the local church leader. Without betraying exactly what Sally had confided, she made it clear to the bishop that Sally lived unhappily at Corn Creek in a crumbling house. She would prefer village life, Emily told him. The bishop finally offered Chief Kanosh and his wife the use of a small, sturdy log building, an empty storehouse that stood on his lot, and they moved into it.

The chief saw advantage in living beside the bishop with his new wife. The bishop and his people knew about Sally's civilizing mission, and regarded her presence as promising. They could see that the dilapidated house at Corn Creek was not suitable for her mission. She and the chief needed a better house.[65]

Sally saw advantage in living miles away from Corn Creek, the site of the unwanted mission. The village offered other advantages as well. She valued living near people whose way of life and language she had adopted. The women followed familiar daily routines, centering on cooking and housekeeping and child care. And she found deep comfort in the presence of so many young children.

CHAPTER 11

The Village

SALLY HAD ALWAYS BEEN KNOWN as Sally, or Indian Sally, at the Lion House and the Beehive House. A few years before she married and left the city, the Leader mentioned her name in public. He exhorted his people to be better organized in daily life at home, to make a place for things so that there would be no need for Mother to ask, "O, Sally, where is the dish cloth, I want it in a minute?" Those passing words recalled his own home, with Lucy and Sally at work in the kitchen of the Beehive House.[1]

But when this Sally of the dishcloth married and became the wife of a dignitary, when she wore fine clothing in a village where most people dressed in homespun, she gained a title and surname. As Sister Kanosh, she attended church each Sunday with her husband, who was always attired in a freshly laundered shirt with an ironed collar. She saw to that. Villagers recalled that Chief Kanosh wore a black suit as well. In the village he often wore a tan duster, a long, western-style riding coat split on both sides.[2]

Sally, as Sister Kanosh, joined the local branch of Relief Society, a women's group. The new head of the village branch was Sister Kimball. Adelia Hatton Kimball was slightly older than Sally, and twice widowed: first by the long-ago murder of her husband William Hatton, and again by the death of her third and last husband, a longtime associate of the Leader. Years earlier she had moved south to live with a grown daughter, William's child. Living in the village with her married daughter placed her just miles from the site where William died.[3]

Adelia knew some of the women at the Lion House. She had lived in the city for years before moving south, and she and Sally shared many influential acquaintances in common, in contrast to most of the villagers. There was prestige in knowing those people of influence, including Eliza, president of Relief Society. The Leader had appointed her to oversee the society's hundreds of branches.

Eliza was without doubt the most prominent woman in the territory, in part because she held high office. She was also well known for the many poems and hymns she had written over the years. Of all the women in the village, only Sally knew Eliza well. She had known her since the first winter at the fort. By the time Sally left the city, she had lived nearby that important woman for nearly twenty years. Even after she moved to the Beehive House, she saw Eliza every evening when the family assembled in the parlor of the Lion House.[4]

The village branch of Relief Society, like others, engaged in good works to help the poor. Most of the members were middle-aged or older. Sally attended weekly or biweekly meetings where the women gathered to sew rag carpets and quilts and to knit socks. They gave these to families in need or sold them to raise money for the families.[5]

At one of those meetings, as the story was told years later, two women sang a popular ballad called "Do They Miss Me at Home?"

> Do they miss me at home, do they miss me?
> 'Twould be an assurance, most dear,
> To know that this moment some loved one
> Were saying, "I wish she were here."
> To feel that the group at the fireside
> Were thinking of me as I roam,
> Oh yes, 'twould be joy beyond measure,
> To know that they missed me at home,
> To know that they missed me at home.[6]

When the song ended, the plaintive question unanswered, Sally murmured tearfully, "I wonder." Or so the story went. To express pain so openly seemed counter to her early upbringing and her usual demeanor. But the point of the story rang true. Emily knew that Sally missed her old home in the city, and the family, and those evenings in the parlor. In such a small village, everyone knew. Emily noticed that her face still looked drawn even though she had gladly moved to the village.[7]

Sally set about making a new home and a new life there, which held faint echoes of her old life with Clara and her children and the others who lived at the Lion House. She joined the community of women and children, and made friends. Besides attending meetings of Relief Society, she visited some of the village women. One of them, a young mother named Alice, had a baby boy. She was young enough to be Sally's daughter.

Alice's brother Edward, known as Ted, later recalled that Sally visited Alice more often than anyone else, and helped her with her little son. She had a lifetime of experience in taking care of other women's children. Alice, just twenty years old and a new mother, surely needed some guidance—and Sally liked the familiar comfort of holding a baby or small child, the sense of connection and acceptance.

One day Ted arrived at his sister's house to find Sally changing the baby's diaper. She had just removed the wet diaper and was about to replace it with a dry one when she picked up the baby and dangled him in front of nine-year-old Ted. "Look at his teapot," she teased. "I went out of that house like a shot," Ted claimed years later. "Believe me, I was on my way home when I heard Alice and Sally laughing."[8]

Sally's sly joke and laughter struck a blow to his male dignity, but Ted had more serious cares. At the village school, there was high turnover in teachers. Some of those who preceded or followed Emily were kind, others not. The pay was low, and a few of the men who served as schoolmaster for a year or two seemed to regard teaching children as hard duty, a trying way to earn a pittance. They showed no patience with the least sign of mischief or disobedience. Wild children must be tamed. The worst teacher, according to Ted, had a favorite painful punishment. He would lead an errant student around by the ear, lifting high as he pulled.[9]

Such were the cares and woes of schoolchildren. When they left school at the end of the day, some went to visit Sally at her small log house where they always found a welcome. "Her home was clean and neat," one said. "We thought her quite refined," another added, "and she had nice silk dresses." Sally spoke uncommonly well, and she had impeccable table manners. She wore silk proudly each day. She often had something sweet for the children to sample when they visited her.[10]

Giving food to children was good. Treating people who were younger in a kindly and generous way, helping and guiding them, was good. Sally had learned long ago, as a child, how older and younger should treat each other. At the Lion House, where most of the women were older than she was, she had paid them due deference. But now she was one of oldest women in a village of mostly young people. Her seniority brought greater responsibility.[11]

If the schoolchildren had spoken of their fears, she could have given them some guidance. The elders of her childhood had taught her about courage and fortitude. She learned how to face hardships and suffering in life, and without showing open fear or despair. Settlers often mistook such stony silence in the face of pain and loss, or even terror, for indifference, a lack of human feeling. They did not know that it was a sign of courage.

Even Adelia, who had lived near Pahvants for many years, and who had known her own share of fear and suffering—beginning with the brutal murder of her first husband—never understood how Utes faced fear. Near the end of her life, when she recalled the long-ago murders of the seven Pahvant Utes, the image of the sole survivor remained sharp. The woman had seemed completely impassive after the sudden execution of her companions, her kinsmen. She did not know if her own life was about to end, and if the dark tunnel of death, Tu-wĭp pu-ru'-kwa po, lay before her. Yet she walked past the onlookers, Adelia said, "as if nothing had happened."[12]

Sally shared that demeanor, which Emily recognized as quiet courage and dignity in a lonely exile. Yet Emily did not understand the source. She knew nothing of Sally's early life lessons, and thought those qualities belonged uniquely to her.[13]

Most people noticed what Sally had learned later, in the Leader's mansions in the city. Everyone agreed that she had mastered the civilized arts of cooking and housekeeping. Her skills were superb, they said. Of course, she knew far more than she needed in order to keep house in a one-room log building.[14]

From the schoolhouse each day, Ted saw Pahvant women walking by with their children, who did not attend the village school. Their mothers were on the way to ask their neighbors in the village for food. They had walked three miles to the village, and would walk three miles back to Corn Creek. This was a new form of food gathering for the women. On these foraging trips they sometimes collected flour or bread, or dried fruit, or meat.[15]

It took courage and resolve to walk from Corn Creek to the village in order to forage there. Look what had happened to those men who walked into another settlement years ago in a friendly spirit, only to be shot and killed. It was always safer to gather food in the old way if any native wild food could be found. They still went to the mountains for pine nuts during the fall, and collected wild grass seeds in the summer. They still gathered up crickets. The villagers often made that easier by putting straw in the path of cricket hordes headed toward green farm fields for a

summer feast. Then they ignited the straw to kill the crickets. Pahvants
gathered the roasted remains in baskets and carried them away. And of
course Chief Kanosh and Moshoquop and the other men still hunted in
the mountains.

Trading offered yet another way to get food. Sometimes Pahvants
traded pine nuts to the villagers for flour, meat, or eggs. The women also
traded the large baskets that they wove from branches of wild willow. Villagers liked to use those as clothesbaskets. Pahvant men and women also
traded their daily labor for food. Men worked as farm laborers. Women
worked as laundresses, in exchange for bacon and flour or for wages of
twenty-five cents a day. The villagers counted on their labor.[16]

One of Emily's sisters recalled that a Pahvant woman known as Jane
washed for their family once a week. Her husband was Narrient. "She
was a handsome girl," said one man, who recalled first seeing Jane when
she was in her early twenties and he was a few years younger. "I distinctly
remember the blue circle in the center of her forehead," he added. "It must
have been a tattoo mark." Women made the tattoos with cactus thorns
dipped in the ashes of juniper leaves.[17]

Sally showed no such visible marks, and her clothing hid any scars
from burns inflicted long ago by her captors. She who dressed in silk no
longer did laundry for other women. She did not gather native foods from
the wild. She did not pick up roasted crickets and grind them with dried
wild berries to make what settlers mockingly called desert fruitcake. She
had not cooked or eaten Pahvant fare for decades. Instead, Sally prepared
the foreign dishes that she had learned to make in Lucy's kitchen, the
finest in the land. Lucy's fruitcake contained flour, sugar, spices, and dried
fruits from the garden and orchard, not wild berries and crickets.[18]

Some of the land surrounding the village remained wild, but damaged
by settlement. An ever-growing number of settler-colonists had grazed too
many livestock on native grasses and shrubs, felled too many native trees,
diverted too much water from creeks for irrigation, and taken too many
fish and game animals for food. This impoverished the land and creeks,
and thus the Pahvants, who found their supply of wild foods dangerously
depleted. Harm sometimes came to settler-colonists as well. Their livestock went hungry, bare slopes yielded mudslides, and too much irrigation
ruined the soil.[19]

If Sally ever left the village—the colonized, tame, and settled zone—
no one remembered. Some villagers did later confuse her with Chief
Kanosh's murdered wife Mary, a fine horsewoman who had often ridden

beside him. But a woman who wore a silk dress had no reason to venture out on horseback into the wilds. Unlike Moshoquop's wife, Sally did not go with her husband on his hunting trips in the mountains. She stayed at home and kept house, just as the Leader had expected.[20]

Chief Kanosh had married Sally a few years after Powell and his fellow commissioner submitted their report to Washington, which advised moving the Pahvants who remained on their homeland to the distant Uintah Reservation. That plan, if put into effect, would have meant an even more bitter exile for Sally, forcing her to live far away from settlers and their familiar way of life. But Chief Kanosh had made different plans. He did not intend to live on the reservation, as Powell came to suspect and reported to Washington.[21]

The chief understood the strategic importance of having a wife who knew the settlers' language and so much about how they lived. They seemed to welcome highly assimilated women such as Mary and Sally, who spoke English well, wore cloth dresses, lived in houses, and had learned to keep house. To the villagers, they embodied successful assimilation. Perhaps the example they set would spread. That prospect, the chief understood, might help to insure that he and his people could remain on land where they had been born and where their ancestors had long lived.

Chief Kanosh seemed to understand more about his neighbors than they understood about him. They remembered later that he liked to travel alone. Some thought that he rode across the desert to California, hundreds of miles away. No one knew why he went there, or where else he went when he left the village for long spells of time. Think of him on those solitary journeys. Did he wear the duster and his flat-crowned Mexican hat? Did he ride the big bay horse named Jim?[22]

Chief Kanosh's prized horse had run and won many a race, often with a crowd of visiting Utes as spectators and supporters. Sometimes they rode west across the mountains from the Uintah Reservation to spend time at Corn Creek, where they played the hand game, raced horses, and gambled on the outcome. These were the favorite old sports and entertainments.[23]

Chief Kanosh, a good judge of a fast horse, acted proud of Jim. He led the big horse around, showing him off to the villagers and his fellow Utes, praising his strength and speed. Surely they could see that splendid Jim had no equal. Some of them took the bait, convinced that their horses could beat the chief's.

He was in his fifties by then, and wise in the ways of the newcomers to his land, and of his own people. Instead of asking one of his men to ride for him, pitting Pahvants against settlers or Pahvants against other Utes, he often asked a villager he called Georgie George. But this young man had grown wary of trouble with the owners of fast horses that lost races against Jim. Some of the owners were sore losers and "revengeful," he said. When the chief asked him to ride in yet another race, he said no. He kept saying no. When he finally gave in, Chief Kanosh promised him, "Now, Georgie George, I will send the Indians with you any place you want to go so as to protect you."

He soon rode Jim in a half-mile race, trying to outrun a horse that another Pahvant owned. For that high-stakes race, Chief Kanosh and others bet their guns, ammunition, buffalo robes, and more. Jim did win that day, and so did the people who bet on him, but Chief Kanosh never raced that horse again. He sold Jim to a wealthy man who happened to visit the village.

When Georgie told this story years later, he had this to say about Chief Kanosh: "He was sure smart."[24]

Word from the city reached Sally now and then. The most tantalizing news arrived in Lulu's letters. Lulu passed on welcome news of the family to Sally, and to Emily who read the letters aloud. The two young women soon forged a warm friendship by mail, which Emily treasured. Her friendly correspondent was not only the age of a younger sister but also the daughter of the revered and recently deceased Leader, a member of his famous family.

Lulu's oldest sister was Nettie, the very child Clara was carrying long ago when Sally heard Zina prophesy that her mother and sisters would find her. Nettie had married a young man named Henry as his only wife. As Sally knew, she did not have children. The middle sister, Nabbie, had married a young man called Spencer the year before Sally married Chief Kanosh. She too was her husband's only wife. A few months before Sally left the city, she gave birth to her first child, a daughter named Clara. If Sally had stayed in the city, she could have helped Nabbie with baby Clara, as she had once helped Clara with Nabbie. Instead, she helped Alice in the village.[25]

Some news of the family also came to the village by word of mouth, with travelers. Susa visited Sally when she made a trip south to see her mother. Lucy B. remained in the remote settlement where she had moved seven years earlier. She and her youngest daughter still lived in the house that the Leader had used as his winter home.[26]

Susa had followed the lead of her older sister, Dora, by marrying at a young age, unwisely. Two years after Dora eloped and married her first husband, Susa married his brother. Like Dora, Susa bore two children and then divorced her husband a few years later, as Sally no doubt heard, whether from Susa or someone else. Stories about the Leader and his large family circulated widely, even after he died.[27]

Eliza kept on with her work as president of Relief Society, assisted by Zina and a cadre of other hardworking women. Lucy led a far quieter life at the Beehive House with her youngest daughter. Clarissa had not yet married, but was finally learning how to cook, in a kitchen empty of servants. Years later, she recalled that before her wedding she "made cakes for three days—white cakes, gold cakes, layer cakes, cream cakes, and sponge cakes." Lulu helped her.[28]

Sally welcomed all news of the family, and especially the letters that Lulu wrote and that Emily read to her. But just months after the first letter arrived, and after the school year ended, Emily suddenly left the village. She moved to the county seat to teach. Lulu's letters stopped, and Clara kept her silence. In what seemed a puzzling betrayal, she had never written to Sally and invited her to visit.

There were other events that summer that some people saw as ominous signs. Daylight nearly disappeared one day, replaced by a disorienting glare of light—a "sickening," even "deathly" glare, some said—that covered village and land as far as the eye could see. Heat ebbed along with light. In the cool dimness, chickens began to roost, but full daylight and full summer heat soon returned. People called the strange event an eclipse. It was unsettling, at the least, to see the moon block the shining sun.[29]

Worse, Sally learned that she would soon have to leave the new home she had made in the village and return to exile at Corn Creek, to live there always, and fulfill the unwanted mission.

A few months after Emily left the village to teach at the county seat, Sally moved back to Corn Creek, or the Indian Farm as villagers called it. She had lived away from the Lion House and the Beehive House for more than a year by the time the village interlude ended. She and her husband moved into the small house built for them at Corn Creek, which replaced the adobe-brick house where Mary had once lived. She passed empty hours inside the new log house.[30]

Chief Kanosh and Sally's log house at Corn Creek. Oil painting by Dean Robison, not drawn from life. Undated, after 1960. Used by permission of the Territorial Statehouse State Park Museum.

The return to Corn Creek marked the end of a year of quiet resistance, of peaceful homemaking amid the crowds of village children she welcomed to her house. A few women—especially Emily and Alice—had become her friends. But better, on her civilizing mission, to live among Pahvants than apart from them. So it seemed to someone. They must assimilate. Sally had shown that was possible. Now she must teach the women what she had learned, what the Leader had valued: how to keep house.

The bitterness of betrayal and exile, again. A new life and home that she had made once again reduced to dry, dead ash. O, the blank silence and the darkness of the new house. The Lion House had been home to so many children, a house bursting with their laughter, a place of light. The village too overflowed with young children, unlike Corn Creek, nearly without babies and small ones.

The distance from the new house to the village made it hard to visit Alice and her little son. A trip to the village, three miles away, required a ride in a wagon or a long walk on a dirt track. On cold days the track stayed mired in mud or smothered by snow. Sally would not ride a horse astride as Ute women did. Women of the Lion House rode in carriages. Her fine clothing, like theirs, anchored her. Stiff silk taffeta helped hold her in place, alone.

After Sally moved to the new house, village children could no longer stop to see her on the way home after school. And Emily was gone. Lulu's old letters, folded papers covered with marks, went silent when Emily left. Sally faced a joyless life she did not want, far from her old home at the Leader's estate. Abandoned.

Grief crowded in as winter drew near, and darkness overtook light. The low sun, often veiled by cloud, shone the color of dull nickel, casting a moon-like glow. Time seemed to slow as the month moved toward the winter solstice, an end that marks a beginning. The end of hope marked the beginning of despair. She had no hope of ever seeing Clara and the family again. No hope of ever returning to the safety and familiar comfort of her old life at the Lion House and the Beehive House. No hope even of living again near new friends in the village. No hope. She belonged nowhere.

Sickness seized her in the cold short days of December, the season when disease stalked prey. The skillful healers who had cared for Sally when she fell sick, in the years when she lived among them, were days away by stagecoach or carriage. Zina, the powerful medicine woman who cured her of measles, lived in the city. Eliza, who knew how to lay on hands and to bless, lived in the city. Clara, who offered herbal remedies and the close care of a good nurse, lived in the city. Lucy B., who cured with herbs and prayer, lived days away to the south. Too far away, she knew, all too far away.[31]

The People had time-honored healing techniques, and deep knowledge of plant medicine for treating illness and injury. But they had only a short, brutal history with the foreign diseases of civilization. Before the infectious diseases arrived, they had not needed a nursing tradition like the one that colonizing settlers carried west. The regimen of bed rest, warmth, nourishing food and drink, and attentive care was suited to those diseases.[32]

Still, the best nursing care could not always save a life. It had not saved Clara's small sons long ago. It had not saved the Leader a year earlier. Even the pills that Clara gave her from the family store could not cure this sickness, or lift her from the chasm of aloneness. If her few friends in the village heard of her sickness, they did not find time to visit and to help her. Or the news reached them too late.

When she knew that she was dying, Sally told her husband what to do with her belongings. He needed instructions because the old way was to burn most possessions at death. She did not want to follow the old ways. Later, no one recalled who got her silk dresses, or her hat, or the rocking chair. Emily always treasured a small portrait photograph that Sally had given her. That marriage portrait showed an image of a dark-haired somber woman, seated alone and dressed in black.[33]

Sally died a so-called civilized death, in a bed inside a house. Her illness lasted just four days. The final breath came as morning light seeped into the small, dark room where she lay, yielding. Nearby mountains, sepulchral, silent, shone white under the cold sky as she left an earthly life of loss and exile. Death beckoned, and she followed. She expected to see the family she had long ago lost when captors took her north, when the surge of colonizing settlers brought killing epidemics, and the seizure and destruction of Ute lands brought violence. She expected to live with her family in a peaceful kingdom of glory, eternally at home.

When Adelia heard of Sally's death, she went to the house at Corn Creek and prepared the body for burial. Sally would not be interred in a wild place, a rock crevice in the mountains. Her body would not be wrapped in a blanket, and placed facing east, toward the rising sun, with her head toward the west and the setting sun. Instead, her body rested in a wooden coffin. It would join an orderly row of graves in the village cemetery, a place of human design and imposed order. In death, as in most of her adult life, she followed the ways of Clara's tribe, not the old ways of the People. She had tried to eliminate many of those from her life.[34]

Soon after the burial, Emily's father, George, wrote an obituary for a newspaper in the city. "Sally Kanosh died at 10 o'clock a.m. yesterday, December 9th, at the house recently put up at the Indian Farm," he reported. Many people had attended the funeral, he said. Some of the villagers brought wagons and teams to take the coffin and mourners to the cemetery. Three of the leading men in the village delivered addresses. "The faithful old chief, Kanosh, was deeply moved at the respect shown to his dead wife," George noted. The brief obituary ended with a few misguided words that he meant as high praise for Sally. "Beneath that tawny skin," he wrote, "was a faith, intelligence and virtue that would do honor to millions with a paler face."[35]

Sally's black hair and brown skin bespoke her good origins among the People. But George did not know that speaking of Sally, telling stories about her after she died—some fond, some sad—was not the Pahvant way. The other villagers and the readers of the city newspaper did not know that either. Neither did his daughter Emily, who soon married and moved to another remote settlement.

Recording the names of the dead, and naming their children after them, was the settlers' way. Praising the dead by name, especially ancestors and friends and prominent men, was their way. Emily talked about her friend Sally for the rest of her life, with deep respect, and always by her English name. After Emily's husband died, while she was pregnant, she faced the task of raising and supporting seven young children—reason enough to draw inspiration from her friend's example of strength in sorrow. She kept Sally's photograph in an old wooden chest with other treasured mementoes.[36]

If she or the other villagers ever knew Sally's later Ute name, Kah-peputz, they soon forgot it. Eliza always remembered her earlier name, Pidash, as she thought Sally said that name. Words stayed in a writer's mind. Years later, she praised Sally as "a good, virtuous woman," who "died beloved by all who knew her." Yet of all those people, only young Emily had measurably helped her in her final exile.[37]

Chief Kanosh lived quietly after Sally died, but the tumult of colonizing settlement went on unabated. Land-hungry settlers kept pouring into the territory, planning to acquire land and to stay. Most hoped to farm, but a few Texan ranchers had also come. They trailed thousands of longhorn cattle into land along the Sevier River and around A-vwa-pa, the long saltwater lake, to graze on the wild grasses and shrubs that remained. Ranchers from Texas had first brought cattle there twenty years earlier.[38]

Settler-colonists living on Pahvant lands already numbered in the thousands. They outnumbered Pahvants twenty-five to one, and their livestock outnumbered large wild game by multitudes. "We shall increase," the Leader had warned Ute chiefs some fifteen years earlier. A flood tide of colonizing settlers, along with the startling size of their families, fueled the population growth. They had given a prize one year to a woman with twenty-one children.[39]

There seemed to be no end to the colonizers, and no end to their ravening quest for wild arable land. They used that land for farming or raising livestock, which drove away wild game. Or they hunted out the wild game. Or they extracted things of value from the land, from water to wood, to use or to sell. Chief Kanosh had witnessed the sudden destruction of old hunting and gathering grounds. He had witnessed the death

of most of his people, including several wives and all of his children,
and the abrupt and bloody end of his cherished way of life, in just thirty
years, a generation. A city—with a multitude of shady, imported trees,
and imported, foreign people—stood on what was once the open land of
Tav'-o-kun. More than three hundred other settlements had taken root
north and south of Place of Sun. In earlier times and distant places, the
spread of farming and the destruction of wild lands had proceeded slowly,
over hundreds of years or more and many generations, not just one.[40]

The year after Sally died, White River Utes in western Colorado rose
up against an Indian agent who tried to force them to farm. Members of
Chief Douglas's band, Powell's old neighbors during the winter he spent
by the White River, killed the agent and some of his workers, and took
captives. Later, in the aftermath, colonizing settlers took their homeland,
which the White River Utes had been promised by treaty was theirs forever. They were forced west, to the Uintah Reservation, but Nicaagat
refused to go there. He went north, toward high mountains.[41]

The loss of Ute lands in western Colorado troubled any chief who
hoped to keep his people together on even a fragment of their homeland. Someone always wanted the land. One of the Ute leaders in Colorado—a man of imposing size named Colorow—had tried to keep colonizing settlers out. Some people later said he was Comanche by birth,
a captive who had been adopted into a band of Utes. They told a story of
how Colorow always confronted intruders when they entered Ute territory. Making a mark on the ground with his index finger, he told them,
"Ute's dirt. One sleep, you go!" Settlers rushed in to colonize Ute lands
as soon as he and his people were forced out.[42]

Chief Kanosh tried to keep peace with his neighbors who had taken
Pahvant land by the creek and elsewhere, and who took most of the creek's
water to irrigate their fields—but who might want more. Settler-colonists
always seemed to want more. They spoke of progress. That word, which
was foreign to the People, seemed to mean wanting more land, claiming
more land, and welcoming more colonizing settlers, who took still more
land. Progress seemed to mean transforming and taming, damaging or
destroying, much that was native or wild.

He knew about famous Indian chiefs who had tried to turn back
alarming waves of colonizing settlers and soldiers, in vain. Their names
still appeared in newspapers, years after their deaths in faraway places to
the east. Tecumseh, the Shawnee chief and charismatic leader of a tribal
confederation, was renowned for his many battles to stop American

colonization of Indian lands. Osceola had led the long and bloody struggle by Seminoles to keep Americans out of Florida. Metacomet, also called Metacom and King Philip, was a long-ago chief of a confederation of tribes that fought against settler-colonists in New England. The Sauk chief Ma-ka-tai-me-she-kia-kiak, also known as Black Hawk, had led warriors against colonizing settlers on the prairie. Even the American victors respected these men who had fought so bravely against foreign invaders who wanted their peoples' homelands.[43]

Chief Kanosh had lived through the violence of colonizing settlement, and seen the aftermath. What he had learned about the lives of these four leaders and others also led him to conclude that only a path of peace offered any hope for him and his few remaining people. He counseled his men against attacking settlers who lived on Pahvant lands. A villager, who heard him speaking loudly one night to his men, always believed that they were planning such an attack. But the villager did not speak Ute, and an attack never took place.[44]

Despite counseling his warriors to live peacefully with the intruders, Chief Kanosh had shown his respect for Tecumseh and the three other famous chiefs who fought to defend their liberty and protect their people and homelands. At his request, one of the settler-colonists' important rituals for ancestors was performed for each chief. In a striking parallel, a year later settlers followed Kanosh's precedent. They performed the same ritual for George Washington, Thomas Jefferson, and other revered leaders of the American Revolution.[45]

After Sally's death, Chief Kanosh still talked often to his people about their neighbors' ways. He spoke in a clear voice at a high pitch, and his words carried for a great distance. He exhorted Pahvants "to love God, and not to drink whiskey, or tea and coffee." They should love God, he explained, because He is good, and they should hate whiskey because it is bad. The settlers had doctrinal reasons for abstaining from tea and coffee, but Chief Kanosh advised his people to avoid both because they cost too much.[46]

Some of the villagers sold whiskey to Pahvant men, despite the chief's wishes and warnings. Liquor offered easy profit. Other villagers, including Emily's father, George, complained when men drank whiskey. He finally filed a newspaper report about it, but with little effect. If money talked, it spoke far more loudly than he or the chief.[47]

A few months later, in December, and nearly three years to the day after Sally's death, Chief Kanosh died. Many villagers had attended Sally's funeral, but more people turned out for his. Soon after the funeral, George again sent an obituary to the city newspaper. He had written a eulogy of the "respected old chief," as he called Kanosh, one far lengthier and more detailed than his account of Sally's life and death. He had known the chief for years.

Chief Kanosh, he told readers, died at sunset. He had been sick for weeks, and "had made up his mind" to die, George said. Receiving the best medical care in the county, ordered by the settlers' new leader, did not save him. He was sick and tired unto death. Sometime during those last weeks, Chief Kanosh asked the villagers to bury him next to Sally in their cemetery. Years earlier he had discovered, with indignation and disgust, that the graves of his brother and Chief Wákara had been looted and desecrated, and their bodies taken. Perhaps in the cemetery his remains would be left in peace.[48]

Villagers provided a well-made coffin for the chief's body, and they placed the coffin on a stand outside his house at Corn Creek. Pahvants and people from the village filed past the body, while a man named Azac eulogized the late chief, and spoke of his many virtues. Some prominent men from the village also spoke.

The villagers' choir sang several hymns. They ended with "O, stop and tell me, Red Man," a variation on the hymn "Come tell me, wandering sinner." The first verse posed a series of questions about wild wanderers:

> O, stop and tell me, Red Man,
> Who are ye? Why you roam?
> And how you get your living?
> Have you no God;—no home?

They could not have answered those questions about the man they were soon to bury, a man whose name meant Red Ute or Red (Ute) Person, not Willow Basket, as some later said. To Utes, red signified success. In the hymn, it signified race, the Indian race.[49]

The singers who addressed Red Man in their hymn asked if he had no home. Yet the chief named Red (Ute) Person had been born on his people's ancestral land, and had lived for many years near those singers and the other settler-colonists who arrived in unstoppable waves to occupy that land. But they still did not understand what his name meant, or exactly what he believed. They knew that he talked to his people about Chenob. Some people thought that must be the Ute name for God the Father, God the Creator. Chief Kanosh had learned about praying, and they thought that he told his people to pray to Chenob, God. But they did not know that the name they heard and recorded as Chenob or Shenob or Shin-nob, was Shin-au'-av, Wolf. Although he had created people, Wolf was not a supreme deity such as the one they worshipped.[50]

As the coffin was about to be closed, and the Pahvants took a last look at their chief, "there was one of the most genuine outbursts of grief," George wrote, "it has ever been our lot to witness." No amount of torture, he said, could have forced a sign of emotion from them, yet they cried sorrowfully over the body of their leader. The villagers still did not understand their concept of courage, in the face of death—or in daily, grinding hardship after settlement of their lands. And they did not understand Pahvant mourning practices.

A long procession of Pahvants and villagers walked four miles from the chief's house to the cemetery. George and another villager each spoke briefly about Chief Kanosh at the gravesite. By then it was sunset, and "Moshoquop, the war chief of the tribe, was invited to speak," George recorded. Moshhoquop, "this fearless man," as he called him, approached the edge of the grave and stared down into it. He stood there, silhouetted by an open sky shot with silver. Then Moshoquop began to speak calmly to his people in Ute, and it seemed that he praised Chief Kanosh, their leader for thirty years. But only Pahvants understood all of the war chief's words.[51]

What did Moshoquop say as he stood above the yawning hole in the earth? Did he talk about the journey of their chief through a dark underground passage? That dangerous passage, Tu-wĭp pu-ru'-kwa po, leads to the land of departed spirits. Each lone spirit must have courage to make a hard journey through the darkness to reach Na-gun'-tu-wĭp, a place of joy and light, the resting place of the brave.

Descending into the earth, Chief Kanosh would hear rumbling growls from the depths of the dark. He would see dimly, in the damp sand, the enormous tracks of monster animals. Shrieks would assault his ears, the cries of unseen monster birds flying heavily from rock to rock overhead. If he turned back in fear, he would wander the earth forever as a lonely, troubled spirit.

But Chief Kanosh would surely meet these ordeals with courage, and finally reach the perilous chasm called Pa'-kūp. A narrow bridge spans it. Only the brave dare try to cross, to confront and complete this last, hardest trial of the journey. On the other side of the bridge stand the radiant daughters of Wolf, beckoning and calling. Once Chief Kanosh crossed the bridge, they would greet him with cries of joy.

He would enter a rich and fertile valley abounding in fish and game, and perpetually yielding fruits and seeds. In that place of beauty, a land without want or pain or sorrow, people danced and feasted forever. There he would dwell in peace and in plenty, the last journey ended.

In his people's understanding, only his courage and effort could take him there—not special rites or prayers or help from Wolf.[52]

After the villagers buried Chief Kanosh, as a sign of respect they placed a painted headboard over the grave. The grave marker spoke his name in writing, but Pahvants did not hear the words because they did not read. The villagers recorded,

> In memory of Kanosh, chief of the Parvant Indians, who died December 4th, 1881, aged 67 years. Beloved by his tribe and respected by his white brethren.

He had suddenly looked much older in the last year of his life, but by his own telling he was not sixty-seven. By the chief's own claim, he had lived for fifty-seven winters. The settlers had never paid close attention to the details of his life. Where he traveled on his journeys, when and where he learned to speak Spanish fluently, exactly what he believed about Wolf, and much more about him remained opaque, matters of future speculation and misunderstanding. They showed far more interest in what they hoped he, and his people, would become: highly assimilated, like Sally.[53]

The simple grave marker made no mention of the chief's late wife. But in the city, readers of the newspaper learned from his obituary that he rested by Sally's side in the village cemetery. Decades later, descendants of the early settler-colonists erected a tall monument in Chief Kanosh's honor in a new cemetery. They inscribed his name and the dates of his birth and death. The year recorded for his death was mistaken. His grave, and Sally's, remained in the old cemetery, but no longer marked, the location finally forgotten.[54]

CHAPTER 12

The Telling

SIX YEARS AFTER SALLY DIED in exile, far from the Lion House, visitors from California stepped off a train in the city. They arrived in August, season of great heat and strong light, in a place far from the cool, fog-drenched coast that they had left. Hubert H. Bancroft, the wealthy owner of a publishing firm in San Francisco, planned to publish a book about how this wild and arid territory had been so quickly colonized by settlers and, he thought, transformed for the better.[1]

Bancroft had already published books about the native people of western North America, including Mexico and Central America. "Pah Vants" and other "Utaws" made an appearance in Volume One, under the title *Wild Tribes*. That first book launched an ambitious series meant to chart the history of what had become the Spanish and American West, or the progress from wild to civilized as he and his readers saw it. Now he had set to work on books about the settling and civilizing of western states and territories, from California to Colorado, lands once occupied solely by the so-called wild tribes.

A staff of researchers and writers read reports and pamphlets and books. They compiled notes and records, conducted and transcribed interviews, and produced text. One of his writers, an author of popular histories and dime novels about colonizing settlers on the frontier, had written more than four volumes for Bancroft's series. She never saw her name on the title page. Each volume appeared in print under his name.[2]

Bancroft and his wife checked into one of the city's best hotels. Despite the small size of the city, with a population far less than that of San Francisco, he found the expected amenities of civilization—some imported and others re-created in place, a standard practice of settler colonialism. There were libraries and theaters, clubs and saloons, and "all the modern comforts and conveniences," he said, including gaslights and new electric lights. Streets were illuminated at night. Streetcars conveyed passengers from place to place, and well-dressed citizens strolled along spacious sidewalks in the commercial district.

Bright and fragrant flowers crowded gardens next to houses. The orchards, in full flower just months earlier, had given the city "the appearance of Eden in bloom." Or so some people proudly told him. They wanted to "improve" wilderness, restoring the Earth to what they imagined as an Eden-like state. These were all signs of progress, Bancroft concluded, achieved in fewer than forty years.[3]

The wild land, in contrast, struck him as "forbidding," "inhospitable," and "barren." He saw the arid stretches mostly from the windows of the train, through eyes accustomed to fenced green fields and pastures in the eastern places where he had lived before going to California. Since so little of this western land was arable, the rest must be barren. So it seemed from his confined point of view, as an American man of his time gazing out a window and sizing up the prospects for farming and raising livestock. If he had spoken to the People, he would have learned that they saw beauty and sustenance where he saw only dry desolation.[4]

Bancroft's young wife, Matilda, often assisted him by conducting interviews and taking dictation. Lorenzo, the Leader's only surviving brother, was then in his late seventies, and he told her about the big valley when the first settlers arrived. She recorded his memories. But Matilda spent most of her time with women, asking questions and taking dictation as they spoke.

She met Clara, who at the age of fifty-six was the sole survivor among the first few women to reach the valley. Matilda recorded what she recalled about crossing the mountains and plains. If Clara mentioned Sally when she spoke about life at the old fort, Matilda did not include that in the finished manuscript.[5]

Eliza, unlike Clara, decided to give a written account of her life to Matilda's husband. She recorded memories of her early, eastern years, and said less about what she called the "wild mountain home" that she finally reached at the end of her journey west. She devoted two paragraphs to Sally, and her transformation—from a young girl who "crunched bones like a dog" and slept in a buffalo robe on the floor to an admirably civilized woman, "neat" and "delicate" and "tasteful." In a matter of months, Eliza sent her handwritten memoir to Bancroft, forty-nine pages telling of a long life of service and devotion. She was eighty-one years old.[6]

Five years later, Bancroft's book reached print. He praised the transformation of the territory, where wealth-producing land had replaced what he and others saw as wild and worthless waste. "As year followed year," he proclaimed, "the magic wand of progress touched life into these barren and sand-girt solitudes, and in their place sprang up a country teeming with the wealth of gardens and granaries, of mines and mills, of farms and factories."

Sally's story appeared in the book as a footnote about an unnamed captive. The footnote quoted the statement of a prominent settler-colonist: "Charles Decker bought one of the prisoners, a girl, who was afterward brought up in President Young's family. She married an Indian chief named Kanosh." Those words came from a man who was a thousand miles away when Sally reached the valley. He reduced her complex life to two sentences that named three men and left her anonymous and silenced.[7]

That footnote was a brief aside in a long wild/civilized narrative, telling how settlers had colonized and tamed this territory in the wild West. Bancroft's narrative, like most, praised cultivated land in highly romanticized terms as "Eden in bloom." Wild land was ignored or reviled as useless and barren. In his telling, the native wild tribes who lived on wild lands took part in troublesome, useless "outbreaks." Their resistance to seizure of their ancestral homelands, and control by colonizing settlers, impeded progress as he saw it. But still, civilization and progress had prevailed. The battle was won. Fields of wheat and flocks of sheep had replaced wild land and wolves. Settler-colonists greatly outnumbered Indians. All that was native seemed on the wane.[8]

This was a version of an old, familiar American story told by the evening hearth and in the pages of newspapers, magazines, and books. Tales of wild and tame, or wild and civilized, always found an appreciative audience. They sold well.

Some twenty years after the Bancrofts stepped off a train in the city, a short story about Sally appeared in print—yet another tale of the battle between wild and civilized. Susa, who had spent the first years of her life living next to Clara and Sally at the Lion House, wrote the story. She framed it as a romance, and filled it with stock elements of melodrama: suspense and danger, a dark villain, a brave young hero, the rescue of an innocent and beautiful young woman, and a happy ending. Susa's character Sally wears civilized clothing, but with her hair unbound and flowing she has what Susa calls a "wild comeliness." She attracts the attention of the wild and evil Wákara, who tries to take her captive. A young chief named Kanosh comes to her rescue and saves her from the villain's clutches. Sally then marries the courageous young chief because she has fallen deeply in love with him.

Five years earlier, Susa had fallen deeply into sorrow. She suffered a shattering breakdown. At the time, she was in her mid-forties, long married to her second husband, and the mother of five living children. She had endured nineteen pregnancies, including six painful miscarriages. Eight of the thirteen children she bore had already died, the last one at the age of four. Then came the collapse.[9]

By the time her story "The Courtship of Kanosh" appeared in print, Susa had recovered. Setting aside grief and doubt, she resumed work as a writer and editor. It filled her mind with half-formed sentences and narrative outlines and the steady march of deadlines. "Keep busy in the face of discouragement," she often advised. "Work! Blessed, saving toil! How many souls," she exclaimed, "you have redeemed from the throes of despair!" The books, pamphlets, articles, and stories that flowed forth conveyed a sense of certainty. They brimmed with confidence in the truths she had learned during a privileged and happy childhood at the Lion House, where each day she had benefited from Sally's labor.[10]

In Susa's telling, Sally's story became more than a footnote in a tale about the march of progress and civilization. For the first time, it was *the* story, told as a romance and melodrama. Still, it used the old master narrative structure of wild versus civilized, ending with the triumph of civilization over the wild. That was the happiest ending of all for many readers, eclipsing even love and marriage. But Susa did alter the usual telling by writing a kinder, gentler tale featuring women. She told about the taming of a native woman by a civilized Anglo-American woman, a story in which the battle with Sally was metaphorical and soon won.

Since Susa wanted to tell an engaging but morally uplifting tale about the virtues of civilization, she not only structured the narrative around women but also added allegorical elements. Although she used the names of real people and real places, the characters, events, and places in her story stood for abstract cultural values and spiritual meanings: good and evil, progress, redemption, a utopian future in which the native has been assimilated, and thereby eliminated. The character named Sally is not the

woman who worked hard each day for long years as an unpaid servant and
cook at the Lion House and later at the Beehive House. In Susa's telling,
Sally personifies the native and wild, made tame. Civilization has successfully, with effort and speed, brought her under control, and transformed
her into a useful and worthy young woman. Civilization has improved
her, and with a kind and loving hand.

As she wrote the story, Susa took liberties with the known facts of
Sally-the-servant's life to suit her narrative purpose. She made her character only twelve at the time of capture and sale, seven years younger than
Clara in fact judged. Susa's character is just fourteen, not nearly fifty, when
she marries Chief Kanosh. Her long years of servitude have vanished,
replaced by just two years spent under the tutelage of a motherly woman,
a benign symbol of settler-colonial society, civilization. Clara, christened
"Mrs. Mary" for the tale, is the mother of an infant. She also mothers
the Indian girl called Sally, one of those child-like wild people who must
be taught how to eat, how to dress, and how to live and work in the
correct way.

Mrs. Mary is not Clara as she was at the fort, years before Susa's birth.
When Sally first walked into the fort, Clara was nineteen, still slender
and childless. Mrs. Mary, who is short and ample, resembles Clara as Susa
knew her twenty years later—the loving mother of little Lulu, the cheerful
woman who lived in a nearby suite at the Lion House, the confidante of
young girls in love with young suitors. Mrs. Mary patiently teaches the
clumsy wild girl in her care the superior arts of civilized housekeeping.

Susa did not invent new names for three of her characters, Sally and
the two chiefs, Kanosh and Wákara. But she did alter the cultural origins
of Sally, who became Bannock, and Chief Kanosh, who became Shoshone. She identified only Chief Wákara, made the villain of her tale,
as Ute. Her readers had surely heard of him. They knew that Utes had
fiercely resisted the first colonizing settlers and their leader, Susa's father.
So too had Bannocks, who lived at a distance to the north. Like Utes,
they had attacked and killed men sent on a mission by the Leader. Like
Utes, Bannocks commanded respect, both admired and feared as expert
horsemen and warriors.

Susa decided that for Sally-of-the-story a new identity as Bannock was
more suitable than the identity she claimed, as Pahvant Ute. That identity
would simply not work because Ute men had sold Sally. Readers would
find it hard to understand why those men had forsaken her. And it was
questionable that Sally, who had been betrayed and mistreated by men

who spoke her language and shared ties of culture, would wish to marry one of them.

In reality, the Leader had ordered Sally, a middle-aged woman, to marry Chief Kanosh—as everyone knew at the time, including Susa. It was no secret that Sally had done so reluctantly and unhappily. But that was not romantic. Better to make her a young Bannock, and Chief Kanosh a friendly young Shoshone, for the sake of the story. Better to avoid puzzling the reader, and raising doubt about the Leader's judgment. Facts might interfere with the moral of the story.

In service of romance and her higher purpose, Susa also invented a new ending. Sally marries Chief Kanosh, and they seem set to live happily ever after among the settlers, enjoying the blessings of civilization. So too will the children they expect to raise. The tale ends with the young couple gazing westward toward the horizon at twilight. The scene suggests that the sun is setting on the wild West, that the dawning light of civilization will usher in a new and better era, a utopian era of progress and total assimilation. They are left wondering when they will become, as prophesied, "a white and delightsome people."[11]

When Susa's story reached print, her older cousin John, who in boyhood saw the captive girl sold to Clara's brother, was nearly seventy. He read Susa's story not as a mostly fictional romance but as a mostly factual story about Sally and her marriage to Chief Kanosh. Susa had told about purported events that took place years before her own birth. Since John was almost twenty years older and an eyewitness, he could add details to Susa's sketchy account about how the captive came to live at the fort. Sometime after reading Susa's story, John wrote what he recalled seeing as a little boy—mixed with what he remembered hearing or reading later, about who sold Sally and how she later died. He said nothing about her cultural origins. He had no reason to doubt Susa's claim that Sally was Bannock. Besides, her tribal identity mattered little in terms of the narrative aim of his memoir.

In John's telling, the man who traded Sally to Charley for a rifle was Chief Wanship, not Wákara or Baptiste. John said Wanship's warriors had fought Little Wolf's band, and that they had left with two girls who were being held captive by that band. They killed one, he said. But Sally was the sole captive on that cold December day when she was sold. The captors had reportedly killed a boy, not girl, sometime earlier when no one agreed to buy him. And Wanship's raid on an enemy chief's camp had yielded only horses, not human captives. It took place more than a year after Charley bought Sally. The raid had nothing to do with Sally, who was already living with Clara by then. John conflated different events some sixty years later, and he added to the confusion by mistakenly calling Little Chief by the name Little Wolf.[12]

When John finally wrote his account, Chief Wanship and his people metamorphosed from friendly hosts who had given food to the first colonizing settlers and allowed them to stay where they stopped in the big valley. They became, mistakenly, Sally's cruel captors, who were said to live somewhere in "the wilds," not nearby in the same valley, their homeland. So powerful was the narrative structure of wild against civilized that their peaceful, obliging neighbors were cast as merciless wild villains in the tale John later told of Sally's captivity. The structure made the story.

Likewise, the valley, once a place of high grass and generous creeks, had come to be misconstrued as barren waste, nearly without life at the time of settlement. One of the first settlers to glimpse that "vast rich fertile valley," as he called it, had seen a large herd of pronghorn antelope and flocks of mountain goats and mountain sheep in the foothills. Decades later, he recalled the valley as empty desert with only "a few black crickets, some coyote wolves, and a few poor wandering Indians." Yet the Leader, John's uncle, had told his followers just a few years earlier that hundreds of native people lived in the valley when the first colonizing settlers arrived. "At the Warm Springs, at this little grove where they would pitch their tents, we found perhaps three hundred Indians," he said in a public address.[13]

John's memories, shaped by a narrative structure of wild against civilized, and disordered by the passage of time and by hearsay, evolved into a story filled with errors of fact. He had in truth first seen the captive girl with unknown men, the Indian captors who sold her. He did not know their names, and Chief Wanship was not one of them. What he recalled years later were sounds and eyewitness images. He heard cries in the distance that he later assumed were her cries of pain, not the captors' cries of threat, or a ploy to attract the settlers' attention. He saw Barney arrive and speak to those men. He saw that the girl was covered in blood and ashes. He saw that her body bore cuts and burns, and that her hair had been hacked off. He saw Charley buy her. He saw her taken to the log house where he lived with his father, Lorenzo, and his stepmother, Harriet. The girl was washed and clothed at that house. Then Charley took her to the fort.

The eyewitness account ends there, and unacknowledged hearsay begins again. Sally lived happily with Clara and the family until she married Chief Kanosh, John said, although he knew nothing directly about those years because of his own wandering life. He lived far from the city, as far away as Mexico and Hawaii. Still later, he moved to a remote settlement near the border of Arizona Territory.[14]

Sometime during those years, he heard that Sally had married and then died. Someone from the village told him about the sad events of Sally's death, how one of the chief's other wives murdered her. John's acquaintance from the village had confused Sally with Mary. Or John misunderstood what he said. Or he confused Sally and Mary when he recorded what he heard, or thought he heard. That was one story of Sally's death, the one that ended in violence.[15]

John's story of Sally's life and death appeared as a few pages in his published memoir. Her life story, as he told it, fit well with his as he told it. John wrote about fighting the wild—from wild wolves and wild Indians to raging floods and other wild forces—in order to plant and grow a settler colony. It suited his narrative purpose to present Sally as once wild, but made civilized.

John was in his eighties when his memoir reached print. Horses and wagons had given way to motorcars and trucks, and narrow trails, to roads. Silent films on silver screens celebrated brave colonizing settlers and the conquest and taming of the American West. Films in theaters showed battles between wild and civilized, replacing the battles in Wild West shows once performed live in arenas.[16]

No one ever seemed to question John's account, or for that matter to read Susa's tale as something other than a mostly true story. To their readers, these wild/civilized narratives had the ring of truth. Some readers knew of Susa's short, largely factual articles about her father and the family, and the long book about his life that she completed near the end of hers. She mentioned Sally's murder in the book, repeating what John had earlier said in his memoir. It seemed credible to her, especially given the source. John was a first-generation colonist, the Leader's nephew, and an eyewitness who saw Charley buy Sally.[17]

No one questioned what John assumed about Sally's wounds—that her captors inflicted all of them. But other captives did not have the same sort of wounds. They were hungry and dirty, and some had burns on their bodies. Unlike Sally, they had not been cut with knives, and covered with ashes, and their hair had not been hacked off.

If Sally ever explained her wounds, no one seems to have listened closely and remembered. The code of courage and demeanor she had learned from growing up among the People may have rendered her nearly silent at first. But her illiteracy, stigmatized origins, race and gender, and invisibility as a servant in the busy house of an important family likely kept her unheard—silenced rather than silent. Only the villagers, to whom she was a personage, not a mere servant, seemed to recall anything that she said during the year she lived among them. Only they later recorded her words, and remembered her well.

They recalled that she spoke excellent English: "You are Miss Crane, the schoolteacher, are you not?" They believed that she felt homesick for the Lion House and the people she regarded as family. "I wonder," someone heard her muse sadly after a sentimental song ended. She had an earthy sense of humor, a legacy of her early life with the People: "Look at his teapot!" She showed intelligence. So said the man who wrote her obituary, an Englishman transplanted from metropolitan London to a remote village at the edge of a great desert in the American West. The village children thought her refined because she wore silk, spoke well, and had impeccable manners. She considered herself an adopted member of the Leader's family, and so did the villagers.

The Englishman, Emily's father, wrote that Sally had been "raised and educated" by the Leader. In truth, her birth family and the People had raised her to early womanhood. She had spent nineteen years in that native world, living freely and at home on wild lands. Later, as a captive, Clara and Lucy and other women had shown her how to live in a foreign world, brought west by colonizing settlers. They had subjected her to civilizing lessons each day. But she had learned most of their ways, and their language, through close study, by listening and watching carefully.

At the time she died, she had lived in their midst for two-thirds of her lifetime. The colonization of wild lands, the homelands of native people, continued in the territory, but the colonization of her labor and her identity was complete long before she died. She had arrived at the fort as a captive who identified herself as Pahvant Ute, and called herself Pidash, as Eliza heard it. Thirty years later, having mastered a new language along with housekeeping and culinary skills learned from Clara, Twiss, and Lucy, she introduced herself to Emily as Sally Kanosh, the new wife of the chief. She told Emily that she had lived for years with the Leader's family, after her rescue. The Leader, she said, had sent her on a mission to the Pahvants, to teach them how to live as she had learned to live. By then they inhabited another world, as colonized, dispossessed, and impoverished people. She lived with them briefly, unwillingly and unhappily.[18]

Sally's life in three worlds—the native and independent, the foreign and colonizing, the native and colonized—spanned fifty years. It spanned the time before, during, and after the first onslaught of colonization by settlers. Settler colonialism had soon prevailed. The construction of an imported way of life brought not only dispossession but also destruction to wild lands and to an indigenous way of life sustained by hunting and gathering on those lands. In her last twenty years, in death, and in stories later told about her, Sally embodied the elimination of the native.

To look closely at Sally's wounds is to ask who she was, not only when she appeared in the big valley with captors, and later, but also before. To examine her wounds is to ask whether the harm that men did to her explains her life.

The actions of her stepfather and of Baptiste and the other captors do explain her captivity, her deep hunger, the burns on her body—and her enduring effort to avoid those men at all costs. The trauma of captivity can explain what was later called her "'morbid' horror of Indians"—or rather, a shuddering fear of those who resembled her captors in any way. She carried a sense of trauma as a burden, an inert and heavy mass trapped in memory.

Narrative nourished it. Emotionally laden Indian stories, tales of cruelty and suffering, helped keep the trauma alive. Hearing the details of her own captivity and sale, told often as a family story and told to visitors such as Elizabeth Kane, no doubt triggered, and reinforced, myriad painful memories.

Hearing other Indian stories, mainly narratives of violence, likely did the same. She heard tales of wild and civilized in the parlor from the Leader. She heard them from women at the Lion House, recounting current or past events and family lore. Again and again she heard claims, many unfounded, that men such as her captors, and even some of Chief Kanosh's warriors, had killed William Hatton, Captain Gunnison, and more than a hundred overland travelers, including children. She heard how such men killed captive Indian children. Brutally. Truly, it seemed that the Leader and his people were her saviors.

For twenty-five years Sally managed to avoid direct contact with men who resembled her captors—except Chief Kanosh, who came to see her in the kitchen of the Beehive House despite her wishes. The family always wondered at her dislike of him and other Indians. Susa later said that her father, the Leader, never understood Sally's "bitterness towards her own race." He and his family may not have recognized that the captor who sold her to Charley was not just Ute but likely Pahvant Ute—good reason for such bitterness. And they seemed to see no connection between her persistent, or perhaps growing, aversion and the harrowing stories they told in her presence. Instead, some family members saw her aversion simply as evidence that, as one of Lucy's daughters put it, Sally had completely "converted to the ways of civilization."[19]

Still, the violence and betrayal she endured at the age of nineteen did not explain everything about her. She was already a young woman when she reached the valley, having spent her life until then with the People at the edge of mountains and desert that stretched north to the lake they called A-vwa-pa, Big Water. She showed quiet respect to other people, and affection and unusual kindness to children. She never struck a child for misbehavior, or spoke roughly to a child, although she saw others, and even the Leader, do so. That was not the People's way. She showed determination, and bore her loneliness in exile without open complaint.

Sally spoke of a mother and sisters, and a father who had died, a father she must have mourned deeply. It was customary for women in mourning to wail every day for a year, to cut their hair short, to cover their bodies with ashes, sometimes even to make cuts on their bodies. A woman whose husband died was supposed to mourn for a year before marrying again— or, some said, until her hair grew long. A woman whose father died should also mourn.[20]

Her mother remarried, which meant she had ended mourning. But Sally still bore the marks of mourning when Charley bought her: the ashes, short hair, and cuts on her body that may have been self-inflicted. The strangers at the fort, and later their descendants, regarded those as evidence of her captors' brutality, not as evidence of mourning. The burns and the starving hunger, torments suffered by many captives, were a different matter.

In any case, sometime after Sally's Pahvant Ute father died, her mother found a new husband. He may have been Southern Paiute. Pahvants and Southern Paiutes sometimes intermarried. They lived as near neighbors in Sho-av-ich, or Beaver Valley, Sally's homeland of record. Pahvant territory extended north of that valley, and Southern Paiute territory, south.

Sally called her stepfather cruel. If she said more about him, Eliza did not record it in her memoir, and no one else seems to have remembered it. Perhaps Sally's stepfather was cruel because she continued mourning, and it seemed a rebuke. Or perhaps he was Southern Paiute, and sold her under duress from well-armed men on horseback who rode into their camp one day and demanded human wares—as Utes commonly demanded of Southern Paiutes. Better to let them take this stubborn young woman, who could find her way home again, than to give up a young child. Perhaps.

Or, as likely, Baptiste or one of the other men wanted to take her away as his wife. She had reached the age to marry, as her community judged it. Perhaps she refused to marry this unwanted suitor, even after he gave a customary gift of value to a fellow Pahvant, her stepfather. (In Eliza's recollection, Sally said that her stepfather "sold" her—but the nature of the exchange remains unknown.) Perhaps she continued mourning in order to avoid leaving her mother and sisters, her family—just as she later tried to stay with the family she adopted. To remain in mourning may have been an act of resistance. Whatever the exact circumstances, armed men took away a young woman as a captive and slave. After Charley bought her, his mother Harriet washed away the ashes, which brought an end to mourning.[21]

No one ever suggested that Sally had been sexually assaulted by a captor. Susa, in fact, flatly, and delicately, denied that, saying "an Indian might kill, [but] he rarely dishonored a woman." To judge from ethnographic records, not simply Susa's words, such assaults were not customary. If Sally was assaulted, her code of courage or burden of fear and pain kept her silent—or if she spoke about it, this instance of sexual violence against an Indian woman went unrecorded, as was commonplace later.[22]

Chief Kanosh must have known exactly how Sally came to be sold. After his other wives died, he wanted to marry her, and take her south, near her old home. She steadfastly resisted him, not wanting to lose the safe home and the life she had made for herself at the Lion House—and then, for a few years and less happily, at the Beehive House, where no young children lived and where she cooked meals for the estate workmen instead of the family.

Over the course of many years she had transformed herself, taken on a new identity through effort made day by day, word by word, and dish by dish. That had come about during years of hard work and of deepening attachment to women and children she lived with behind walls at the Lion House. She did not want to leave the safety of a cherished home—again. She did not want to have contact with the chief or other men who had ever been allies of her violent captors. She did not regard Baptiste and his fellow warriors as resistance fighters who had shown courage and resolve, defending their homeland and way of life against a surge of foreign intruders. In a word, she did not want to go "home" with Chief Kanosh.

Years earlier, in Texas, the captive woman known as Naudah had been taken from her adopted Comanche family and returned forcibly to the Parker family, to life in civilization with settler-colonists. She was in her thirties, and took a young daughter with her. She had lived as Comanche for nearly twenty-five years when an attack by Texas Rangers and U.S. Army soldiers, which left many Comanche men, women, and children dead, resulted in her capture. The blue-eyed captive was soon identified.[23]

Cynthia Ann, as the Parkers still called her, repeatedly tried to run away, but never managed to escape. The twice-captured woman learned to speak English again, but preferred to speak Comanche. She remained an object of curiosity to her English-speaking neighbors, who brought deerskins to her for tanning. Her skill was unsurpassed.

Her young daughter died from influenza, a disease of civilization, four years after Cynthia Ann was "rescued," as it was always put. People said that the poor captive bore scars on her body, evidence of the Comanches' cruelty. But Naudah had made those marks by cutting herself, a mourning practice. She had mourned many deaths over the years in the usual manner of a Comanche woman.[24]

A few years later, she too died in exile, still grief stricken and profoundly alone. She had never again seen her son Quanah, who became the last great chief of the free Comanche. He and his people were finally forced away from their homeland and into exile on a reservation. Thousands of colonizing settlers crowded in to take and to transform the vacated wild lands, and government agents set about trying to transform what they called one of the wildest tribes of all.[25]

Almost a century later, a novelist and then a famous filmmaker told the story of Cynthia Ann's first and second capture. They had to change the facts to suit their narrative purpose, to fit the old and popular narrative structure of wild against civilized. Readers and viewers of *The Searchers* wanted Cynthia Ann to return gladly to civilization. The story was told as a heroic journey made by two American men, searching and battling the western wilds until at last they found her. The story ended with the rescue of a young and beautiful woman, not yet married and still childless—unlike the real Naudah, a middle-aged widow and mother sent into exile when she was taken "home" unhappily, by force. The story needed a happy ending, as the storytellers and their audience defined it.[26]

Fifty years earlier, Susa had refashioned the story of Sally in much the same way. She too replaced a middle-aged woman—a captive who was forced to return "home" and who died in exile there, profoundly alone—with a comely young character looking forward to a new and improved life in civilization.

Moshoquop, the once-feared war chief of the Pahvant Utes, lived quietly after Chief Kanosh died. Soon after the funeral, some of the settlers' leading men had visited the Pahvant camp and held a meeting. A few Pahvant men sat in chairs, like the visitors, but most followed the old way and squatted on their heels. Moshoquop was resolute as always, but he kept silent that day. Narrient, the man whose name meant strong, demanded a chance to speak.

Rumors had reached the People of yet another plan to displace them, to force them to move from their home to the distant Uintah Reservation. Their old chief, who had thwarted those plans for so many years, could no longer help them. They needed courage to keep resisting Washington's ceaseless efforts to control them, to force them into exile. They insisted that they would not "be driven from the land of their fathers." The People had resolved to stay. And so they did, on the small piece of ancestral land that they retained.[27]

Moshoquop stayed at Corn Creek for a time, but later moved fifty miles away, near the site of the old lake, A-vwa-pa or Pa-vwan, Sevier Lake. Settler colonization had transformed the land around the lakebed almost beyond recognition. He died there twelve years after the death of Chief Kanosh. When he set out on the journey to Na-gun´-tu-wīp, he was not yet sixty years old.[28]

By that time, A-vwa-pa had nearly died from thirst. Once twenty-five miles long and up to fifteen feet deep, the lake had first gone dry soon after Chief Kanosh died. It came back to life now and then, but never reached full size again. Long before Moshoquop's death, and the old chief's, settlers who colonized Ute lands had begun to draw more and more water from the bounteous river that fed the lake. They irrigated land that they plowed and sowed with seeds. They had tamed the river, they said proudly, but taking so much water for their fields finally killed the wild lake and surrounding marshlands. Only a ghostly lakebed remained, an apparition that shone bright white in strong sunlight. Buffeting winds raised choking clouds of noxious alkaline dust.[29]

The lake had nearly disappeared when some people began to speculate about the meaning of its Ute name. Powell had recorded it as A-vwa-pa and Pa-vwan, Big Water, but they knew nothing about that, or about his neglected manuscripts, languishing in storage thousands of miles away at the Smithsonian Institution. Years later, two young anthropologists would retrieve, edit, and publish Powell's manuscripts. But in the meantime, some settlers suggested that the name of the lake meant Bad Water, and the name of the surrounding valley, Water Gone.[30]

They could not agree about when the lake began to go dry, and when it revived, and then went dry again. They never resolved the question of the meaning of the lake's name, and they did not greatly mourn its death. No one suggested bringing the damaged, abandoned lake back to life. Water was too useful for irrigation. Taming the river that once fed the lake was a triumph, settlers agreed. The dry lakebed was just a curiosity of the wild from other times, long gone, like Sally and Chief Kanosh.

A thicket of conflicting details about Sally's life and death flourished and spread as the years passed, and stories were told about her. According to the narrators, she was Bannock—or Shoshone, some said. Others later claimed she was Paiute. Or was she Ute? Charley bought her for a rifle— or for a rifle and a horse—and gave her to his sister. Or he gave her to the Leader. Or his mother, Harriet, gave the captive girl to her daughter, Clara. She was adopted into the Leader's family, and Clara raised her. No, Lucy raised her. In any case, she was the Leader's foster child, they said.[31]

When descendants of the early settler-colonists told Sally's story, they borrowed heavily from Susa's and John's accounts. But often they added new details, and some of those details came from people who had known Sally in the village, or whose parents or grandparents said they had known her. In one later telling, Sally was an Indian princess, a latter-day Pocahontas. She was wearing silver foxtails—the sure sign of noble birth—when she was captured and then sold. And in most stories she had been taken captive as a little girl, at the age of seven, not nineteen. She was a small child, an empty vessel when colonizing settlers rescued her, soon after they entered an empty land. They filled her with superior values and habits and skills—just as they made a wasteland fruitful. That explained how she learned everything perfectly under Clara's, or Lucy's, loving care.

No, others said, she was thoroughly wild, "a genuine savage." She had wild ways that had to be eliminated, rooted out with great effort by Clara. Or was it Lucy? At first, some said, she stubbornly resisted being tamed, and learning to live in civilization—but finally she saw the light. No, she saw the greater virtue of civilized life from the start because of her noble birth (those silver foxtails again).[32]

It seemed fitting that the stolen daughter of a chief had grown up in the house of the greatest chief of all, the Leader, and that he and his family had raised and educated her. It made sense that a well-born child could grow so civilized, so refined. She had a "white soul," a village friend later remarked, words with a racist ring but meant as high praise. It seemed fitting, too, that Sally had married a chief—willingly, happily, as a young woman. No, others said, she married Chief Kanosh only as a matter of duty, and left the Lion House unhappily. Lucy's daughter admitted that privately, but later, in print, said that "romance finally took her back to her own people." Sally and Chief Kanosh lived together for ten years, some people said. Or less. Or more.[33]

And then she died violently, murdered by a jealous co-wife. Or she died from the rigors of native life at Corn Creek, having grown so sensitive and refined from living in civilization that she could not adapt to the hardships of "semi-savagery." In yet another rendition, she died from a broken heart, in unhappy exile from civilization, cast back into the wild. Or she died from loneliness.[34]

Chief Kanosh outlived her by three years. Or was it two? Or six? No, she outlived him by two years. Whatever happened, it made sense to many who heard her story that she came to a sad end, as so-called wild native people often do—even when, according to claim, civilized people try to help them. It seemed fated that the wild, the native, must go extinct, vanish. Even a lake had died when the river that fed it was "tamed."[35]

Details about Sally's life differed in nearly each version, and new conjectural stories emerged, including one that identified her as a secret plural wife of the Leader. Facts did not matter—or did not matter much. They could be bent, ignored, or guessed at because what mattered most to narrator and audience was the meaning of the story. The character called Sally, who in life served the Leader's family, in death served the wild/civilized narrative structure.[36]

That structure, like the circumstances of her life as a servant, did not give her voice or allow her visible agency. The tale of her life, like so many told about the American West—both the Wild West and the wild

West—was told in praise of colonizing settlement and progress, which meant the defeat and removal of the native, the taming of the wild. The daily realities, complexities, ambiguities, and mysteries of her life, before and after she was sold, vanished in that story. The narratives helped to eliminate the native.

In representing Sally as nearly empty, in need of filling with civilized habits and skills, those narratives presented her as acted upon, transformed, and improved—like open wild lands where she had once lived. But evidence of Sally's agency, and of her early and enduring enculturation as Pahvant, is undeniable. Again and again, she acted to achieve chosen ends that reflected Pahvant values, beliefs, and practices. That began at the fort and continued until the end of her life.

She refused to work at first because she did not want to be Clara's slave or live behind walls at the fort. No Pahvant would have wanted that. She wanted to go home. After Zina spoke in tongues, words that Sally understood as prophesy from a powerful medicine woman, she chose to work willingly while she waited for her mother and sisters. Zina's prophesy gave her hope that her exile among the strangers would someday end.

When Sally finally saw that she could not return to her family because they had died, she chose to stay with the settlers. She learned their language well, along with their way of life, in order to gain a sense of belonging and a home. She accepted certain religious ideas and practices, perhaps because she thought they offered protection from her captor and his powerful sorcery. They also promised eternal reunion, after death, with her family of birth.

She chose to work hard at the Lion House. It offered a place of safety, away from the violence of colonizing settlement. She spent long hours each day in the kitchen, which gave her the pleasure of feeding crowds of people, especially children. Early in life she had learned that honor came from preparing and sharing food. Choosing to ignore the family rule about mealtimes, she always gave food to hungry children or let them take it and tiptoe away. She quietly indulged them in other ways as well, as she had learned from the People.

When Chief Kanosh began to visit her in the kitchen of the Beehive House, she resisted his attention until the Leader ordered her to marry him. She did not consent to a ceremony meant to ensure that she would spend life after death with the chief. She did not consent to sit for a wedding portrait with him. In the photograph taken after the wedding, she sits alone, a fitting expression of her life as an Indian captive caught in civilization.

Months later, just after the Leader died, she enlisted Emily's help in contacting Clara. When she asked Clara specific questions in the first letter that Emily wrote for her, she indirectly and tactfully appealed to Clara to help her return to the Lion House or Beehive House. Clara's silence led her to enlist Emily's help again, because she wanted to move from Corn Creek to the village. Once there, she tried to re-create some semblance of her old life at the Lion House. She helped young mothers with their children. She fed hungry children when they visited her after school.

She disobeyed the Leader's final order, refusing to carry out the civilizing mission. But after spending just a year and a half in a second forced exile, she did not resist death. Her long and unnoticed quest, for a safe home and a family life, had ended. The only remaining hope was to reunite, after death, with the family that had never found her.

A few years after Sally died, and just months before the death of Chief Kanosh, Jim Bridger too died in exile. He died a famous man, celebrated in published stories as a heroic fur trapper and explorer. Along with Jefferson, Lewis and Clark, and many other American men, he had gained fame for promoting and enabling colonizing settlement on western wild lands.

Jim had spent the last years of his life with his daughter Virginia, the child borne by his Ute wife. His farm stood on land some miles south of a great bend in the Missouri River. The river was his only link to the western plains and mountains, but he could no longer see what came from creeks high in the Rocky Mountains. The water rushed past in spring in a roiling, muddy torrent, and slowed to a stately flow in summer.

The bright glare of light on rock and on snow had done its work, leaving him in deepening darkness. Virginia found a gentle old horse for her father, and he spent his days riding Ruff, as he called the horse, in company with an old dog named Sultan. Sometimes Ruff took a wrong turn into the woods, and wandered among the trees, lost. Then faithful Sultan ran home, and whined and barked until Virginia went to the woods with him to rescue her lost father—he who had always found his way back from exploring trips through western wilds, and who had famously held in memory all the western landscapes he saw. He had shared that valuable knowledge with military men and with settlers who planned to colonize western wild lands. Some hired him as a guide, and others bought essential goods at his trading-post fort. He had entertained them all with tall tales about wild Indians, Indian stories that warned and instructed even as they amused.

When she found her father in the woods, Virginia led Ruff slowly home, with Sultan trotting by her side. She later told one of Jim's old friends that he had mourned the loss of his eyesight because he longed to see the mountains again. He recalled unfettered peaks and forested slopes, herds of pronghorn antelope, a bare blue sky and sunlight on snow. He missed the wild lands where he had lived for so many years, but he did not seem to understand that he had helped to destroy much of what he valued about them.

He and other fur trappers had quickly killed out most of the beavers in the mountains, and wild bison on the plains had been nearly exterminated in a recent, final burst of slaughter. The transcontinental railroad, which followed a route he helped chart, carried commercial hunters in droves to the killing fields where they shot bison by the millions. An English traveler who crossed the plains a few years later by train remarked approvingly on the plowed, fenced fields that had replaced open grasslands once filled with free-roaming herds. He looked forward to a future when the entire world had been tamed, all wild beasts and so-called wild people transformed and brought under control—or gone extinct.[37]

By the time of that traveler's journey, houses, farm fields, and pastures covered broad valleys and sagebrush plains, places of sheltering solitude when Jim first crossed them. Some of the earliest colonizing settlers who had sought his advice or bought supplies from him had already died. But they had left multitudes of descendants in the valleys along the western edge of the mountains. Those descendants had filled empty wastelands, as they saw them. They proudly said that their fathers and mothers and grandparents had tamed the once-wild lands where they now lived. No one spoke of native lives and wild lands broken by the colonizing effort.

In the last years of his life, Jim saw the austere beauty of the mountains only in his mind's eye. He lived on, blindly, in the midst of fertile farmed flatlands. Sometimes, on a fine spring day, he walked with Sultan into a field of wheat. He knelt in the warm soil and felt the tender young shoots, using his hands to see how tall they had grown. He died at the age of seventy-seven, having spent the last seven years of life in darkness.[38]

Many years passed before there was a different telling of Sally's story—this one, about the life of a young native woman taken captive, and the so-called taming of the wild West. As soon as the writing began, the story chose a divergent narrative voice and a different angle of vision. It could not be told as a tale of heroic battles or struggles by men of civilization against hostile wild forces, which end in conquest and triumph or heroic survival against the odds. It could not be told as a tale that justified and celebrated violence against wild lands, or against people and other sentient beings who long made their homes on those lands.

Sally's life stands instead in this telling as the special case that illustrates a general process in American settler colonialism, the process of colonizing the wild. First, a young native woman was claimed and named. Then, caught among the foreign strangers, Sally was subjected to surveillance and control. The ensuing daily efforts to transform her, to tame or civilize her as it was put, slowly produced results. She finally accepted her new life, and learned to work as instructed. Her daily labor proved useful in settler-colonial society. Long years of subordination and service—or use—followed. In her life as a servant, she remained largely unseen, unheard, and misunderstood by most of those she served. When her usefulness to them declined, she was abandoned and sent into exile. She soon died.

The effort to transform Sally began inside a fort and continued later inside two grand houses. A similar effort took place outside, on wild lands, but with greater force. Years later, most of those who spoke about Sally showed indifference or contempt for her former way of life on wild lands. They showed the same indifference or contempt toward the land itself. The relentless effort to colonize wild lands entailed eliminating native wildlife, much of which remained unnamed and unknown, regarded as mere weeds and pests. There was a parallel effort to displace and dispossess, or otherwise eliminate, native peoples from those lands.

As elsewhere in the American West, the colonizing effort took place with frontier-style violence, or threats of violence. All must submit. Yet despite the odds, some number of the People survived. They told their own stories of struggle in their own way—and not as wild/civilized narratives.[39]

Narratives of wild against civilized served as the anthem of settler colonialism in the American wild West, justifying the seizure of Indian homelands. Implicitly or explicitly, these racist narratives legitimated the settler-colonists' permanent possession and transformation of those lands. The stories anticipated and celebrated the removal, the elimination, of the native—both the human and the nonhuman—in favor of the tame or civilized, the foreign and imported.

But colonizing settlers could not truly control, or permanently transform, or completely eradicate the wild. They could only do grievous damage to wild lands, and to people who lived freely on them—until they died from disease or hardship or violence, or were taken captive and sent into exile. As it happened, the people of American civilization lived in their own peculiar form of exile, with unease and a deep sense of separation from a world that is mostly wild. The stories that they told and heard and read, the narratives of wild against civilized, expressed and reinforced that sense of separation.

Children held Sally in memory. A boy named John Young first saw her on a cold December day, after snow had fallen. She wore a bark skirt. He never forgot the sight of her. Thirty years had passed when a village girl admired Sally's fine dresses of rustling, imported silk, and her refined, almost foreign manners. She too never forgot Sally. And multitudes of children, later grown, recalled the rich confections Sally made and gave to them. The sweetness lingered.

Acknowledgments

John Wesley Powell recorded much of the contextual evidence, linguistic and cultural, that I drew on to reconstruct an outline of Sally's early life. I thank anthropologists Don D. Fowler and Catherine S. Fowler for their contribution as editors of Powell's ethnographic and linguistic manuscripts, which they transcribed and published seventy years after his death. I thank them also for replying so promptly to questions that I sent their way. Linguist Tom Givón helped immeasurably by suggesting possible translations for old Ute names recorded by non-Ute speakers. The writings of Northern Ute elders Clifford Duncan and the late Fred Conetah offered much guidance about how Sally and her people lived before she was taken captive and before colonizing settlement of their lands. I am grateful to Forrest S. Cuch, then Director of the Utah Division of Indian Affairs, for telling a story of the past in Utah Territory that offered testimony to the lasting power of narrative.

Sally had no direct descendants; and because she also shifted her cultural identification, finding a descendant community is complicated. If she has living cousins of some remote degree, the linking ancestors are more than two hundred years in the past. A leader of their probable community preferred not to speak about her, and I respect that decision. This too is part of Sally's story, and of the community's own complex history and cultural identity.

Some descendants of Brigham Young, in contrast, now include Sally's name in the family genealogy. Increasingly, they identify her as Clara and Brigham Young's adopted or foster child, in keeping with the claim of a respected historian, made more than a century after Sally's death. This recent gesture is undoubtedly well meant. So far as I can tell, however,

. based on an enduring family memory. It is not supported by the
.entary and contextual evidence that provides the basis of this book.

Most of the documentary evidence that bears on Sally's later life comes
.n the following archives, whose staff members I thank for providing
generous assistance: Research Center for Utah State Archives and Utah
State History, Salt Lake City; Special Collections, Marriott Library, University of Utah, Salt Lake City; Family History Library, the Church of
Jesus Christ of Latter-day Saints, Salt Lake City; Church History Library,
the Church of Jesus Christ of Latter-day Saints, Salt Lake City; L. Tom
Perry Special Collections, Harold B. Lee Library, Brigham Young University, Provo, Utah; the Territorial Statehouse State Park Museum, Fillmore,
Utah; Iowa State Archives, Des Moines, Iowa; and Special Collections
Research Center, William & Mary Libraries, College of William & Mary,
Williamsburg, Virginia.

I also appreciate help given by staff and guides at the following sites
in Salt Lake City: the Lion House and the Beehive House at Temple
Square; and the Daughters of Utah Pioneers Museum. Staff at Red Butte
Garden in Salt Lake City and at the Utah Division of Wildlife provided
information and guidance about native flora and fauna, respectively.

A writing residency at the Mesa Refuge in Northern California
pointed me in the direction of this book while I worked there to complete
a previous one. It offered a place apart to think and read and write about
wild lands in the American West, before and after settlement. I am grateful
to the founder and other benefactors of the Mesa Refuge for supporting
writing at the edge.

Books are written to be read, and the initial readers of a manuscript
deserve special acknowledgment. I thank Mary Dickson not only for reading early drafts of chapters but also for sharing her insights about Utah,
past and present. Don D. Fowler, Catherine S. Fowler, Nancy J. Parezo,
Kelley Hays-Gilpin, and James F. O'Connell read the original, lengthy
manuscript. Don D. Fowler and Nancy J. Parezo offered useful suggestions
that helped me shorten that manuscript.

After consigning many pages to the cutting room floor, I asked a professional reader, Lynn Andrew Hanson, to read the shortened version for
narrative coherence. I appreciate her valuable guidance as I made repairs
to the manuscript, which included restoring, at her suggestion, a few of
the cast-off pages. I thank my husband, Ronald Hallett, the first and last
reader, for his perceptive comments and questions, and for steady encouragement over many years.

Reba Rauch, Acquisitions Editor for Anthropology and Archaeology at the University of Utah Press, has my gratitude for guiding the manuscript through the process of review and into production. I also appreciate the assistance of other members of the staff who helped turn a manuscript into this book. Ashly Bennett copyedited the final draft of the manuscript with patience and skill. I also appreciate the help of other members of the staff, including Managing Editor Patrick Hadley and Production Manager Jessica Booth, who helped turn a manuscript into this book.

Finally, I want to extend my thanks to the Family History Library in Salt Lake City for a highly personal reason. I spent many hours searching their collections for genealogical and other records of the people who appear in this book. Near the end of the project, when I had almost completed the manuscript, I took some time to search records and learn more about my ancestry. Unexpectedly, I found records of a forgotten ancestor: a woman called Ann who belonged to the Delaware (Lenape) Nation. I had not previously known of any Indian ancestors.

It came as no small irony, given the story I recount in this book, to learn that Ann left a Delaware longhouse to live in an Englishman's house. At a time when her people's numbers had plummeted, she married an English settler-colonist whose wealth rested on his claim of their homeland. As I came to realize, her descendants embody the elimination of the native, a loss she seems not to have foreseen. Some documentary evidence suggests that she actively sought to balance the Delaware and the English ways of life. Her efforts did not endure in the next generations.

This book is dedicated to Ann, with respect, and with regret for what was lost to her descendants.

Appendix: Sally and the House of Brigham Young

SALLY KNEW MOST of the people listed below, and dozens of others, as members of the Brigham Young extended family, which numbered in the hundreds. The people she knew best lived at the Lion House or Beehive House at some point between the 1850s and 1870s.

A few of the people listed below are Utes, including Pahvant Utes who lived at Corn Creek in the 1870s. Their homeland in the Great Basin had become part of the House of Brigham Young, metaphorically speaking, twenty years earlier, with colonization by settlers who regarded him as the Leader.

Genealogical and biographical details come from newspaper obituaries and articles, federal census records, cemetery headstones, death certificates, and genealogical records at the Family History Library, Salt Lake City, Utah. Bracketed surnames indicate plural marriages solemnized with religious ceremony but not recognized as legal under federal law.

Albert Jeddie: Albert Jeddie Young (1858–1864) was the second son of *Clara* with *Brigham*.

Amelia: Amelia Folsom [Young] (1838–1910), a plural wife of *Brigham*, moved to the Lion House after her marriage in 1863.

Baptiste: Baptiste (birth and death dates not known) was Ute, probably Pahvant Ute. According to court testimony of *Brigham* Young, he was the captor who sold Sally to *Charley*. He was a medicine man, or shaman, as well as a war chief. As a close ally of Chief *Wákara* and Chief Tintic he resisted settler colonization for at least a decade. He was the husband of a Shoshone woman called Peggy by settler-colonists.

Barney: Elijah Barney Ward (1813–1865), born in Virginia, became a
fur trapper, and later served as an explorer and Indian interpreter
for settler-colonists led by *Brigham* Young. He was the husband
of *Sally (Ward)*, the father of Polly and Louisa, and the stepfather
of Adelaide. He was present when *Baptiste* sold Sally to *Charley*.

Brigham or *Brother Brigham*: Brigham Young (1802–1877) was the
husband of *Clara, Lucy, Ellen, Eliza, Emeline, Lucy B., Margaret,
Zina*, and many others who lived at the Lion House. He was the
father of *Nettie, Nabbie, Jeddie, Albert Jeddie, Lulu, Eva, Mahonri,
Susa, Clarissa*, and dozens of others. As the president of the Church
of Jesus Christ of Latter-day Saints, and briefly as governor of Utah
Territory, he was the leader of most settler-colonists in that territory from their arrival in 1847 until his death in 1877.

Celestia: Zina Celestia Martin (1854–1891) lived with *Clara* and Sally
at the Lion House as Clara's foster child or ward, probably following the death of her mother (Sarah Ann Brown Martin [1812–
1864]) when she was ten. Her father had died earlier. Her marriage
to Elijah E. Cox (1853–1909) in 1876 was monogamous.

Charley: Charles Franklin Decker (1824–1901) was the brother of *Clara*
and *Lucy*, the son of *Harriet*, and the brother-in-law of *Brigham*.
When he married one of *Brigham*'s daughters, he became his son-
in-law as well. He bought Sally in December 1847, and gave her
to *Clara*.

Clara: Clarissa Caroline Decker [Young] (1828–1889), called Clara,
was the sister of *Charley* and *Lucy*, a daughter of *Harriet*, a stepdaughter of *Lorenzo*, and a plural wife of *Brigham*. She was the
birth mother of *Nettie, Nabbie, Lulu, Jeddie, and Albert Jeddie*, and
the foster mother of *Eva, Mahonry*, and *Celestia*. Sally lived with
Clara and her children for more than twenty years.

Clarissa: Clarissa Hamilton Young (1860–1939), the youngest daughter of *Lucy*, grew up at the Beehive House, where Sally worked in
the kitchen and lived for about five years. She married John D.
Spencer (1858–1947) in 1882, five years after her father's death. The
marriage was monogamous. Late in life she wrote a book about
her father and family life at the Lion House and Beehive House.

Dimick: Dimick B. Huntington (1808–1879) was the brother of
Zina and a brother-in-law of *Brigham*. He learned enough of the
Ute language to serve as an interpreter for Utes and his fellow
settler-colonists.

Eliza: Eliza Roxcy Snow [Smith Young](1804–1887), a plural wife and widow of Joseph Smith, and later a plural wife of *Brigham*, lived with Sally and *Clara* at the fort. She lived at the Lion House during the years when Sally lived there and worked in the kitchen. She was a published poet, and president of Relief Society for many years.

Ellen: Ellen Rockwood [Young] (1829–1866) was a plural wife of *Brigham*. She shared living quarters with Sally and *Margaret* after she moved from the fort and before they moved to the Lion House.

Emeline: Emeline Free [Young] (1826–1875) was a plural wife of *Brigham*, and lived at the Lion House with her children until he married *Amelia*.

Eva: Evaline or Evelyn Young (1850–1917) and her brother *Mahonri* were fostered by *Clara* after the death of their mother, a plural wife of *Brigham*. Eva's marriage to Milton H. Davis (1846–1890) in 1871 was monogamous.

Harriet: Harriet Wheeler Page Decker [Young] (1803–1871) was the mother of *Clara*, *Lucy*, and *Charley*, and other children, a plural wife of *Lorenzo*, and the stepmother of *John*.

Isaac: Isaac James (ca. 1820–1891) was born in New Jersey. Known to other settler-colonists as Black Isaac, he was a farmer, and worked for the Brigham Young family for many years as a coachman. His wife was *Jane* Manning James.

Jane: Jane Manning James (ca. 1819–1908) was born in Connecticut. She was known to other settler-colonists as Black Jane, and often called Aunt Jane. Her husband was *Isaac* James.

Jeannette: See *Nettie*.

Jeddie: Jedediah Grant Young (1855–1856), *Clara*'s first son with *Brigham*, died during a measles epidemic shortly before his first birthday.

John: John Ray Young (1837–1931) was the son of *Lorenzo* by his first wife, the stepson of *Harriet*, and a stepbrother of *Clara*, *Charley*, and *Lucy*.

Leader: See *Brigham*.

Lorenzo: Lorenzo Dow Young (1807–1895) was the husband of *Harriet*, younger brother of *Brigham*, father of *John*, and stepfather of *Clara*.

Kanosh: Chief Kanosh (ca. 1824–1881) was the leader of Pahvant Utes at Corn Creek from the early 1850s until his death. He was a strong ally of *Brigham*, and, briefly, Sally's husband.

Lucy: Lucy Decker Seeley [Young] (1822–1890) was *Clara*'s older sister, the mother of *Clarissa* and other children, and a plural wife of *Brigham*. She lived at the Lion House, and later at the Beehive House, where she surprised Sally in the kitchen.

Lucy B.: Lucy Bigelow [Young] (1830–1905) was a plural wife of *Brigham*, and lived at the Lion House until 1870, when she moved south to live in his winter house. She was the mother of *Susa* and other daughters with *Brigham*.

Lulu: Charlotte Talula Young (1861–1892) was the third daughter and youngest child of *Clara*. Her marriage to Augustus M. Wood (b. 1851) in 1891 was monogamous.

Mahonri: Mahonri M. Young (1852–1884) and his sister *Eva* were fostered by *Clara* after the death of their mother, a plural wife of *Brigham*. He married Agnes Mackintosh (1857–1943) in 1876. The marriage was monogamous.

Margaret: Margaret Pierce Whitesides [Young] (1823–1907) was a plural wife of *Brigham*. She briefly shared living quarters with Sally at the fort, and after they moved from the fort. She later lived at the Lion House.

Moshoquop: Moshoquop (ca. 1835–1893) was Pahvant Ute, a war chief, and a close associate of Chief *Kanosh*. He knew Sally at Corn Creek.

Nabbie: Nabbie Howe Young (1852–1894) was *Clara*'s second daughter with *Brigham*. Her marriage to Orson Spencer Clawson (1852–1916) in 1876 was monogamous.

Narrient: Narrient (b. ca. 1830) was Pahvant Ute, and knew Sally at Corn Creek. He was the husband of a Pahvant woman called Jane (b. ca. 1840) by settlers.

Nettie: Jeannette Richards Young (1849–1930), nicknamed Nettie and Nett, was *Clara*'s oldest child. Her marriage to Henry Snell (1845–1896) was monogamous, as was her marriage to Robert Easton (1858–1917).

Nimrod: Nimrod (birth and death dates not known) was Pahvant Ute. Settler-colonists called him Nimrod, a biblical name. He knew Sally at Corn Creek.

Sally (Ward): Sally Exervier (or Xavier) Ward (birth and death dates not known) was Eastern (Green River) Shoshone. She was the wife of *Barney*, and the mother of Adelaide, Polly, and Louisa.

Susa: Susan Amelia Young (1856–1933) was *Lucy B.*'s middle daughter. She lived at the Lion House, in a suite next to *Clara* and Sally, until the age of fourteen, when she moved away from the city with her mother. Her first marriage, to Alma B. Dunford (1850–1919), which ended in divorce, was monogamous, as was her second, lasting marriage to Jacob F. Gates (1854–1942). She wrote extensively about her father and family life at the Lion House.

Twiss: Naamah K. Carter Twiss [Young] (1821–1909) was a plural wife of *Brigham*. She lived at the Lion House and supervised Sally in the kitchen after *Lucy* moved to the Beehive House.

Wákara: Chief Wákara (d. 1855) was a Ute leader. He gained wealth through raiding and the slave trade, and briefly led Ute resistance to settler colonization of their homelands. *Baptiste* was one of his many allies.

Wanship: Chief Wanship (d. 1850), Ute by origin, became the leader of a band of Kumumpa, Shoshones whom the settler-colonists called the Cu-mum-bah. They were allies of Chief Goship and his band, and occupied Salt Lake Valley when the first colonizing settlers arrived in 1847. Chief Wanship died from measles, along with Chief Goship and members of the two bands, at Warm Springs in 1850.

Zina: Zina D. Huntington Jacobs [Smith Young] (1821–1901) was the sister of *Dimick*, a plural wife of Joseph Smith, and later a plural wife of *Brigham*. She was a well-known midwife and healer. She knew Sally at the fort, and then at the Lion House, where she lived for many years.

Notes

INTRODUCTION

1. The ethno-narrative style, as I call it here, is evidential, inductive, distinctively granular, and generally free of essentialist abstractions. This narrative style is rare in academic writing, especially in works about people and times long past. It places unique demands on the scholar-writer, particularly when evidence about the lives in question is scarce, elusive, or conflicting— as is true of the central figure in this book. This form of writing also offers scholars and their readers some unique benefits, including the potential for deeper learning through emotional engagement.

   The traditional form of writing in anthropology, like other academic fields, is expository, not narrative. But as Helena Wulff has recently suggested, different types of writing may better express and record "different aspects of social and cultural life" than traditional forms of writing in anthropology can do. See Wulff, "Introducing the Anthropologist," 15.

2. I suggest that wild/civilized or wild/tame are not universal paired oppositions in the tradition of French Structuralism, as developed in the twentieth century by Claude Lévi-Strauss. They are better thought of here as elements of a particular cultural model with deep roots. Cognitive anthropologists generally define the concept of a cultural model or schema as an interpretive framework: a shared set of assumptions and understandings— often unconscious, or tacit, and rooted in cultural knowledge learned from others as well as in personal experience. See, for example, Shore, *Culture in Mind*; and Garro, "Remembering What One Knows."

3. As Roberta Conner, whose ancestors lived by hunting and gathering until American settlers colonized their lands, states, "the concept of wilderness does not directly translate into our languages because it is a foreign construct." See Conner, "Our People Have Always," 96.

4. On Wild West shows, see, for example, Bridger, *Buffalo Bill and Sitting Bull*. On wild beast hunts as spectacle entertainments in ancient Rome, see

265

Auguet, *Cruelty and Civilization*, 81–106. Thousands of wild animals are said to have been massacred for a single event, the inauguration of the Colosseum. See Auguet, *Cruelty and Civilization*, 107.

5. The word control (meaning human control) figures prominently in recent discussions of genetic engineering, geo-engineering, and certain new, human-centered approaches to conservation. There are veiled or direct suggestions of a domesticated human body, and of domesticated nature or a domesticated planet. See, for example, Kareiva et al., "Domesticated Nature." These discussions share some of the language and also the utopian perspective that characterized much of the nineteenth-century discourse about taming wild lands in the American West. They employ an old binary perspective in the guise of new science.

6. Anthropologist Anne M. Smith recorded many stories in the 1930s that express this insight. They include several true stories of conflict and violence in the past. See A. Smith, *Ute Tales*.

7. This conception of wild land departs from the perspective of Kareiva et al., "Domesticated Nature," and also from social constructionist views of wilderness. On the latter views, see Crist, "Against the Social Construction of Nature."

8. For archaeological evidence of ancient farming peoples moving into lands occupied by hunter-gatherers in many parts of the world, see Mithen, *After the Ice*. Anthropologists have traditionally called the transition to farming the Neolithic Revolution.

9. This is my inference about beliefs concerning tame and wild animals, based on Genesis 1:24 (King James Version and New International Version, respectively). For archaeological evidence of the domestication of animals, see, for example, Mithen, *After the Ice*, 85, 414, on animals kept in herds, or penned. On stories of Wolf and Coyote, see Chapter Two and later chapters.

10. For a brief and cogent overview of the concept of civilization in anthropology, see Engelke, *How to Think Like an Anthropologist*, 56–82. For a classic critique by an anthropologist, see Diamond, *In Search of the Primitive*.

11. The word *civilization* entered the English language by the eighteenth century, and has been used in various ways since that time, as the *Oxford English Dictionary* documents. The term *complex society* came into common use in twentieth-century anthropology, and has a standard, textbook definition. I use the word civilization as synonymous with complex society throughout this book.

12. On settler colonialism as an event and a structure, see Wolfe, *Settler Colonialism*. For specific instances of settler colonialism, both ancient and recent, see Cavanaugh and Veracini, *Routledge Handbook*. While Wolfe used the term *settler colonization* interchangeably with *settler colonialism*, I use the former term in this book to refer primarily to the event:

the invasion of native peoples' lands by colonizing settlers from other places in the mid-nineteenth century. On settler colonialism as object of study or as framework for studying the past, see Limerick, "Comments on Settler Colonialism." On settler colonialism in the American West, see Jacobs, "Reproducing White Settlers"; and Lahti, "Introduction." Elise Boxer has written eloquently about settler colonialism and present-day representations of the past as expressed by a popular historic site. See Boxer, "Disrupting Mormon Settler Colonialism."

13. Wolfe uses this phrase in reference to native people. "Settler colonialism is inherently eliminatory," he observes, "but not inevitably genocidal." See Wolfe, "Settler Colonialism," 387.

14. Turner, *Brigham Young*, 164–68.

15. Most Mormons living today in the United States are regarded as comprising an American ethnic group. See May, "Mormons." On the reenactment of the "journey through wilderness," and Mormon ethnicity, see Shipps, *Mormonism*, 64, 187n23, 189.

16. Gates, *Life Story*.

17. On Brigham Young as colonizer, see Turner, *Brigham Young*, 3, 373.

18. Arrington made the claim of a foster relationship in his well-known biography of Brigham Young. See Arrington, *Brigham Young*, 171.

19. John Wesley Powell (1834–1902) recorded the vocabularies in the 1870s (see Chapter Nine). Don D. Fowler and Catherine S. Fowler transcribed dozens of his handwritten manuscripts, added important contextual material, and published the edited volume nearly a century after Powell's death. See Powell, *Anthropology of the Numa*. The Fowlers also brought attention to Powell as an early American anthropologist. See Fowler and Fowler, "John Wesley Powell."

20. For a classic study of "white Indians," see Axtell, "White Indians."

21. As Axtell notes, Indians taken into civilization nearly always left, a pattern that Benjamin Franklin, among others, early pointed out. See Axtell, "White Indians," 56–58; and Ebersole, *Captured by Texts*, 191.

22. On frightening "Indian stories," see, for example, E. Kane, *Twelve Mormon Homes*; and V. Murphy, "Across the Plains," 409. Some published works of the time—fiction and nonfiction, including some captivity narratives— also belong to the Indian story genre. I use the terms *story*, *tale*, and *narrative* interchangeably in this book for an oral or written recounting of characters and events (whether factual or imaginary, and sometimes both), told for the purpose of educating, instructing, memorializing or entertaining. On narrative knowledge, see Chapter One, note 63.

23. Ethnographic research is defined in part by the use of multiple methods in naturalistic settings, often including a research method known as participant observation. See Kerns, *Journeys West*, 301–9. Since this book is a work of historical anthropology, I necessarily made greater use of

observation (specifically, of landscapes and constructed sites) and written records (especially firsthand accounts of daily life). But I do indirectly draw on what I learned from participant observation and informal interviews carried out in conferences, classes, and workshops attended by descendants of early settler-colonists, among others. The Utah Genealogical Society and the Family History Library of the Church of Jesus Christ of Latter-day Saints, Salt Lake City, sponsored some of the events. What I learned in those settings helped shape my understanding of how the past is remembered and later told.

CHAPTER I

1. E. Snow, *Personal Writings*, 213, 214 (dated December 7, 14, 1847); J. Young, *Memoirs*, 62; M. Kimball, *Journal*, 37; Brigham Young Office Journal, entry dated September 28, 1860, Brigham Young Office Files, box 72, folder 5. The captive was sold to Charley in December 1847. Most of the other events in this chapter took place between the 1830s and 1848.
2. J. Young, *Memoirs*, 60–61; L. Young, "Diary."
3. L. Young, "Diary," 164 (dated Christmas 1847, recorded by Harriet). Harriet suffered from asthma, then known as phthisis, and her health was poor. See Little, "Biography of Lorenzo Dow Young," 104, 108.
4. John confused some names and events (see Chapter Twelve).
5. J. Young, *Memoirs*, 62; Sessions, *Mormon Midwife*, 104 (dated December 11, 1847).
6. Hafen, "Elijah Barney Ward," 344; "B. Young's Testimony, U.S. v. Pedro Leon," January 11, 1852, Papers Relating to Mexican Traders, 1851–1853, Brigham Young Office Files, box 47, folder 36. Various spellings of the name Utahs appear in articles, books, and letters written in English before 1850.
7. Jefferson, *Notes on the State of Virginia*, 186–87. Indian slavery remained legal in Virginia until 1705. See Everett, "Indian Slavery in Colonial Virginia," 68.
8. On the Utahs' involvement in the slave trade, see Blackhawk, *Violence over the Land*; Duncan, "Northern Utes of Utah," 181, 182–83; Malouf and Malouf, "Effects of Spanish Slavery." For more on the Southwestern slave trade, see J. F. Brooks, *Captives and Cousins*; and J. F. Brooks, "'We Betray Our Own Nation.'"
9. "Obituary Notes: Adelaide Brown," *Deseret News*, January 25, 1896; S. Jones, "'Redeeming' the Indian," 223; Hafen, "Elijah Barney Ward," 344.
10. "Obituary Notes: Adelaide Brown," *Deseret News*, January 25, 1896.
11. One such attempted escape to an island in the Mississippi River inspired Mark Twain's *Adventures of Huckleberry Finn*. See Powers, *Mark Twain*, 37.
12. Baptiste Exervier, or Xavier, was likely French Canadian. Frenchmen—a term that included French Canadians, French-speaking Creoles

from Louisiana, and natives of France—dominated the early fur trade in the Rocky Mountains. See Lecompte, "Introduction," 10, 12–14.

13. They reached the fort sometime between 1834, when the fort was built, and 1838, when Adelaide was born there. See "Obituary Notes: Adelaide Brown," *Deseret News*, January 25, 1896. The fort stood by the confluence of the North Platte and Laramie Rivers in what is present-day eastern Wyoming (personal observation at site, Fort Laramie, Wyoming, April 8, 2014).

14. Trahant, "Who's Your Daddy?" 55. The stories told for generations about Lewis, Clark, and Sacagawea constitute narrative knowledge (see note 63 below). To this day, some Mandan and Hidatsa say that Sacagawea's French-speaking husband was "very mean" to her. See Baker, "Mandan and Hidatsa," 135.

15. "Obituary Notes: Adelaide Brown," *Deseret News*, January 25, 1896.

16. Alter, *Jim Bridger*, 137, 219; Wishart, *Fur Trade*, 36. Most of the full-time trappers were Anglo-American and French-Canadian, but they also included Iroquois and Delaware Indians, among others.

17. Russell, *Journal*, 124. Many trappers left the mountains by the late 1830s. Information on the environmental effects of dam-building by beavers, and the historic loss of beavers, courtesy of the Utah Division of Wildlife Resources, Salt Lake City.

18. Bullock, *Pioneer Camp*, 220–21 (dated July 7, 1847). On the life of James Felix Bridger (1804–1881), see Dodge, *Biographical Sketch*. Dodge traveled with Bridger in the 1860s. See also Alter, *Jim Bridger*; and Ismert, "James Bridger."

19. Hafen, "Louis Vasquez," 333. The first-person, retrospective narrative by Virginia Reed Murphy (1833–1921), a member of the Donner party, contrasts with sensationalized accounts. See V. Murphy, "Across the Plains."

20. Dodge, *Biographical Sketch*, 7; Bullock, *Pioneer Camp*, 130; personal observation, Little Sandy Creek crossing site, Sweetwater County, Wyoming, August 27, 2014. The Red Desert is located in present-day south-central Wyoming. See Proulx, *Red Desert*. Most of the settlers whom Bridger met in June 1847 came originally from a single American cultural region, Yankeedom, which centers on New England, and extends west across upper New York State and beyond. See Woodard, *American Nations*, 5, 245. Genealogical records at the Family History Library in Salt Lake City show that many of the first settlers (members of what is now known as the Brigham Young vanguard company) had origins in New England and upper New York State. They were descendants, lineal or cultural or both, of Puritans. To Bridger, as a Virginian, anyone who came from a place north of Virginia qualified as a Yankee.

The three enslaved men were Oscar Crosby (ca. 1815–1870), possibly born in Virginia; Green Flake (ca. 1825–1903), born in North Carolina; and Hark Lay, also known as Hark Wales (ca. 1821–after 1880), born in

Mississippi (U.S. Census, 1850, Great Salt Lake County, Utah, and Utah County, Utah Territory; U.S. Census, 1880, Union, Salt Lake County, Utah Territory). See also Beller, "Negro Slaves in Utah," 122, 123; and Bullock, *Pioneer Camp*, 330, 334, 339.

21. Clayton, *Journal*, 273–78 (dated June 28, 1847); Bullock, *Pioneer Camp*, 209–13 (dated June 28, 1847); Alter, *Jim Bridger*, 84–85, 273; Dodge, *Biographical Sketch*, 26.

22. Dodge, *Biographical Sketch*, 24; Bullock, *Pioneer Camp*, 206–7.

23. Woodruff, *Journal*, 3:219–20 (dated June 28, 1847); Russell, *Journal*, 121; J. Smith, *Southwest Expedition*, 193 (dated June 27, 1827).

24. Dodge, *Biographical Sketch*, 5. William Henry Ashley (ca. 1778–1838) was born near Richmond, Virginia, and arrived in Missouri in the early 1800s. Bridger left St. Louis in 1822. See Ismert, "James Bridger," 86.

25. M. Peterson, *Visitors to Monticello,* 62, 67–68; personal observation, Monticello, Albemarle County, Virginia, March 3, 2008.

26. Stansbury, *Expedition*, 254.

27. The tall tale about the box canyon qualifies as one of the most enduring stories later told about Bridger as a storyteller.

28. Alter, *Jim Bridger*, 110; Dodge, *Biographical Sketch*, 19, 21. An affidavit dated April 23, 1853, bears the name Elijah B. Ward, along with an X labeled "his mark." See Papers Relating to Mexican Traders, 1851–1853, Brigham Young Office Files, box 47, folder 36.

29. Many trappers did not have the assistance of women. A sizable number never married. See Benemann, *Men in Eden*, 7–8. Of those who did marry, more than a third had Indian wives. Others married after they left the mountains.

30. Gray, "Journal," 56–57 (dated July 6, 1837).

31. Hafen, "Louis Vasquez," 321, 333; Bagley, *So Rugged and Mountainous*, 281–82; U.S. Census, 1850, Weber County, Utah Territory (census return for Vásquez). Pierre Louis Vásquez (1798–1868), who was the son of a Spanish father and a mother of French-Canadian ancestry, is often mistakenly identified as Mexican.

32. Crosby, *No Place*, 84 (dated September 29, 1848); Johnston, *Experiences of a Forty-Niner*, 163; Dodge, *Biographical Sketch*, 22.

33. Dodge, *Biographical Sketch*, 16–17; Johnston, *Experiences of a Forty-Niner*, 165; Hafen, "Louis Vasquez," 333.

34. Personal observation at site, Fort Bridger, Wyoming, March 20, 2012; Clayton, *Journal*, 285–86 (dated July 7, 1847); O. Pratt, "Interesting Items," 162–63 (dated July 7, 1847); Bullock, *Pioneer Camp,* 220–21 (dated July 7, 8, 1847); U.S. Census, 1850, Weber County, Utah Territory (see census return for Fort Bridger); Johnston, *Experiences of a Forty-Niner*, 145–46. On the historical archaeology of Fort Bridger, see Gardner, "Fort Bridger," 271–81.

35. Johnston, *Experiences of a Forty-Niner*, 163; Dodge, *Biographical Sketch*, 17; Stansbury, *Expedition*, 228; Clayton, *Journal*, 286 (dated July 7, 1847).
36. Green River Shoshones or "Snakes" were later commonly referred to as Eastern Shoshones. See Shimkin, "Eastern Shoshone," 334.
37. L. Young, "Diary," 163 (dated July 1, 2, 1847, recorded by Harriet); Bullock, *Pioneer Camp*, 217 (dated July 2, 1847); Woodruff, *Journal*, 3:226 (dated July 9, 10, 1847); Clayton, *Journal*, 299 (dated July 16, 1847).
38. Clayton, *Journal*, 301–12 (dated July 19–22, 1847).
39. Personal observation at sites, East Canyon and Emigration Canyon, Salt Lake County, Utah, July 24, 2011, and July 24, 2012; Clayton, *Latter-day Saints' Emigrants' Guide*, 19–20. The colonizing settlers descended some three thousand feet through "the large range of life zones" that characterize the Wasatch Range of the Rocky Mountains, bordering the eastern Great Basin. See Steward, *Basin-Plateau*, 14–17. Salt Lake Valley, the settlers' destination, stands at about 4,200 feet above sea level, and is much hotter and drier than nearby canyons in summer.
40. E. Snow, *Personal Writings*, 204 (dated October 2, 1847).
41. Woodruff, *Journal*, 3:234 (dated July 24, 1847); Clayton, *Journal*, 311–13 (dated July 22–23, 1847); O. Pratt, "Interesting Items," 178 (dated July 21, 1847); Bullock, *Pioneer Camp*, 232 (dated July 22, 1847).
42. E. Kane, *Twelve Mormon Homes*, 96–97; C. Young, "Woman's Experience," 175.
43. Barney and his wife and children may have reached the valley just three weeks after the first settlers. See Egan, *Diary*, 124 (dated August 19, 1847); and Bullock, *Pioneer Camp*, 261 (dated August 19, 1847).
44. Hafen, "Elijah Barney Ward," 345; Turner, *Brigham Young*, 144; Arrington, *Brigham Young*, 124. The report of explorer John C. Frémont (1813–1890) had been published two years earlier. He had seen Great Salt Lake as well as Utah Lake and Utah Valley. See Frémont, *Report*, 153–57, 273–74.
45. Clayton, *Journal*, 275, 277 (dated June 28, 1847); Bullock, *Pioneer Camp*, 210, 212 (dated June 28, 1847); Hafen, "Elijah Barney Ward," 344.
46. Clayton, *Journal*, 318, 329, 341–42 (dated July 26, 31, August 7, 1847); Bullock, *Pioneer Camp*, 237, 238, 246, 254 (dated July 24, 26, 31, August 10, 1847).
47. Woodruff, *Journal*, 3:239 (dated July 28, 1847). In 1858 Louis Vásquez recalled seeing herds of bison in the valley near Great Salt Lake in the early 1820s. See Alter, *Jim Bridger*, 274. An early explorer also reported seeing the bison. See Warner, "Peter Skene Ogden," 226.
48. Bullock, *Pioneer Camp*, 240 (dated July 27, 1847).
49. Densmore identified the eastern edge of Salt Lake Valley as part of the Utahs' territory, apparently on the basis of what she learned in 1915 from Ute elders, some presumably born before colonizing settlers arrived. See Densmore, *Northern Ute Music*, 23. Linguist Tom Givón suggests (personal

communication, November 7, 2019) that the name recorded by Powell in the 1870s as Tav′-o-kun means Place of Sun. See Powell, *Anthropology of the Numa*, 178.

50. Clayton, *Journal*, 324 (dated July 27, 1847); Bullock, *Pioneer Camp*, 240 (dated July 28, 1847); Woodruff, *Journal*, 3:238–39 (dated July 28, 1847).

51. On the ethnography and archaeology of native peoples of the Great Basin, see d'Azevedo, *Great Basin*; Simms, *Ancient Peoples*; and Parezo and Janetski, *Archaeology in the Great Basin*.

52. Osborne Russell (1814–1892) identified his destination as "the village" of Chief Wanship, which suggests a sizable and stable habitation site. The seasonal diversity and abundance of wildlife may have provided the occupants with a reliable food supply, allowing them to stay there for several seasons at a time. Russell left Salt Lake Valley in late March 1841. See Russell, *Journal*, 121–22.

53. Clayton, *Journal*, 323–24, 327–29 (dated July 27, 31, 1847); Bullock, *Pioneer Camp*, 240 (dated July 27, 1847); M. Snow, "From Nauvoo to Salt Lake," 410 (diary entry of Erastus Snow, dated July 28, 1847).

54. In 1855, eight years after settlement, George A. Smith (1817–1875) mentioned "Wanship, a hereditary chief of the Cum-um-buhs, who we found living on the site of G. S. L. [Great Salt Lake] City, in 1847." See "Correspondence: Provo-Pleasant Grove-Lehi," *Deseret News*, September 19, 1855. This public comment by Smith, a close associate of Brigham Young who reached Salt Lake Valley with the first settler-colonists in late July 1847, provides firsthand evidence that Chief Wanship and his people inhabited the valley. Likewise, Brigham Young later publicly mentioned the presence of hundreds of Indians in the valley, camped near Warm Springs. See B. Young, "Gathering the Saints," April 9, 1871, *Journal of Discourses*, 14:87. To the best of my knowledge, these recorded statements by Smith and Young have not previously been cited as firsthand, highly trustworthy evidence that Indians—and more specifically, Chief Wanship and his people—actively occupied the valley when the first settlers arrived.

     Although early settlers and Indian agents commonly heard and wrote their name as Cum-um-buh, one agent did record the name as "Cum-um-pahs." See Hurt, "Indians of Utah," 460. The name is better written as Kumumpa, following the practical orthography used for Great Basin languages, and Powell's spelling of the Ute word for water, *pa*. See d'Azevedo, *Great Basin*, x–xi; and Powell, *Anthropology of the Numa*, 164, 181. According to linguist Tom Givón (personal communication, June 8, 2018), the name Kumumpa incorporates the Ute "generic name for the Shoshone, meaning 'Strangers' or 'Others,'" along with the Ute word for water.

55. The first party of colonizing settlers to reach the valley included just three women—Harriet, her daughter Clara, and another woman—and two children, among more than a hundred and forty men. See C. Young, "Woman's

Experience," 174. The presence of so few women and children may well have led Chief Wanship to regard the visitors as temporary guests in the valley.

56. Pioneer Database, 1847–1868, http://history.churchofjesuschrist.org/overlandtravel (retrieved February 8, 2012); Bancroft, *History of Utah,* 267n38; E. Snow, *Personal Writings,* 185, 186, 188 (dated July 20 [19], 25, 31, 1847).

57. Woodruff, *Journal,* 3:236–38, 245 (dated July 26, 27, 28, 31, 1847). About a week after arriving in the valley, Brigham Young said, "The land belongs to our Father in heaven … and no man will have power to sell his inheritance [the land he cultivates]." See Clayton, *Journal,* 335 (dated August 1, 1847). In a short time, however, the settler-colonists did begin to buy and sell improved land, as they called it, such as farm fields. See, for example, "Notice to Proprietors of the Big Field," *Deseret News,* October 2, 1853. The Kumumpa undoubtedly did not want to "sell" the valley, to give up all rights to it permanently. Granting allies temporary use-rights of land was common among hunter-gatherers. Voluntary and permanent surrender of land in exchange for trade goods was not, because homelands were not commodities that could be "sold."

58. B. Young, "Gathering the Saints," *Journal of Discourses,* 14:87; Powell, *Anthropology of the Numa,* 253; Bullock, *Pioneer Camp,* 263 (dated August 22, 1847); Hafen, "Etienne Provost," 103. The mountain range that Shoshone speakers called O'-kar was known as the Oquirrh Mountains to settler-colonists. They called Pi'-o-wip the Jordan River, Sho-go'-gwun or U'-og the Weber River, and the large island, Antelope Island.

59. Arrington, *Brigham Young,* 147.

60. Bullock, *Pioneer Camp,* 339.

61. Sessions, *Mormon Midwife,* 270 (dated October 28, 1859); M. Kimball, *Journal,* 37; Spencer, *Brigham Young at Home,* 75. The source of her English name is my inference. The name Sally does not appear in genealogical records of Clara's or her husband's family of birth. There were a few women named Sally among the settlers who were present in 1847, but no evidence of a close connection between any of them and the Brigham Young family. See Pioneer Database, 1847–1868, http://history.churchofjesuschrist.org /overlandtravel (retrieved July 18, 2012). The former Indian captive Sally Ward was also present at the fort during that period. See Sessions, *Mormon Midwife,* 108 (dated February 14, 1848).

62. See Ebersole, *Captured by Texts,* on captivity narratives written from the seventeenth through the nineteenth centuries. James Fenimore Cooper, one of the most popular American authors in the nineteenth century, published the *Leatherstocking* series—historical romances of frontier life, which featured captivity as a theme—between 1823 and 1841. See also well-known stories by Nathaniel Hawthorne, such as "Roger Malvin's Burial" and "The Great Carbuncle," published in the 1830s.

63. To listeners and readers of such tales, they constituted what French philosopher Jean-Francois Lyotard has termed *narrative knowledge*. He writes, "Narration is the quintessential form of customary knowledge," and he contrasts such narrative knowledge with scientific knowledge. See Lyotard, *Postmodern Condition*, 18–19. Narrative knowledge is not restricted, however, to "primitive and traditional" societies. See Peregrine, "Science and Narrative," 645.

64. Schoolcraft, *Oneóta*, 17 [*sic*; the passage appears between pages 128 and 130]. Henry Rowe Schoolcraft (1793–1864) was a contemporary of Cooper and Hawthorne.

65. Plummer, *Narrative*. See also Exley, *Frontier Blood*.

66. Cynthia Ann's uncle continued the search for her until 1844, when he finally honored a promise to his family to stop searching. See Exley, *Frontier Blood*, 119, 122.

67. Exley, *Frontier Blood*, 133–35; Frankel, *Searchers*, 61–62. The Comanche name of Cynthia Ann Parker (ca. 1827–1870) is disputed. Naudah is the most common among several attributed to her.

68. V. Murphy, "Across the Plains," 409.

69. Joseph Smith was killed in 1844. See Turner, *Brigham Young*, 107–08. Many captivity narratives were in print in the 1840s. See, for example, Drake, *Tragedies of the Wilderness*. On captivity narratives and the Mormon migration west, see S. B. Kimball, "Captivity Narrative," 81–88.

70. Jefferson, *Notes on the State of Virginia*, 184–86. Georges-Louis LeClerc, Comte de Buffon (1707–1788), wrote about North America in his influential thirty-six-volume work, *Histoire naturelle*.

71. In 1830, Joseph Smith published the Book of Mormon: a "purported new work of scripture," "supplement to the Holy Bible," and revealed history of American Indians. See Arrington, *Brigham Young*, 19. Two centuries earlier, Rabbi Menasseh ben Israel, Thomas Thorowgood, and John Eliot, among others, had published works that similarly identified American Indians as descendants of ancient Hebrews. On genetic evidence about American Indian origins, see T. Murphy, "Lamanite Genesis, Genealogy, and Genetics"; and Southerton, *Losing a Lost Tribe*.

72. On the history and distinctive doctrines of Mormonism, see Arrington, *Brigham Young*; Shipps, *Mormonism*; and Turner, *Brigham Young*.

73. Woodruff, *Journal*, 3:245 (dated July 31, 1847); Marsh, *Lenape among the Quakers*, 161. Federal funds for civilizing missions to Indians were appropriated in 1819, as part of the Civilization Fund Act. The act authorized annual funds for introducing "the habits and arts of civilization" to Indians living near frontier settlements, in order to prevent their "further decline and final extinction." See Prucha, *Documents of United States Indian Policy*, 33.

74. A. Young, *Wife No. 19*, 486–87. Later estimates of the captive's age, given in a variety of popular accounts, varied from seven to seventeen, but she was

most commonly said to have been "a little girl." See, for example, Day and Ekins, *Milestones of Millard,* 346; and M. Dixon, *These Were the Utes,* 104.

75. In the 1850 federal census, taken three years after Sally arrived at the fort, her age was listed as twenty-two. In each subsequent census, her stated age consistently increased by about ten years. See U.S. Census, 1850, 1860, 1870, Salt Lake City, Salt Lake County, Utah Territory.

CHAPTER 2

1. Clayton, *Journal,* 331 (dated August 1, 1847), quoting Orson Pratt (1811–1881). Most of the events in this chapter took place in 1847 and 1848.

2. Clayton, *Journal,* 337 (dated August 1, 1847); Bullock, *Pioneer Camp,* 246 (dated August 1, 1847); M. Snow, "From Nauvoo to Salt Lake," 411 (diary entry by Erastus Snow dated August 1, 1847); B. Young, "Gathering the Saints," April 9, 1871, *Journal of Discourses,* 14:87.

3. Deuteronomy 32:10 (King James Version). One of the earliest settler-colonists, George Washington Brown (1827–1906) who arrived in July 1847, well remembered the gifts of food given to settlers. See Carter, *Our Pioneer Heritage,* 495–96 (letter from George W. Brown, dated December 29, 1896). Chief Goship and his people have sometimes been identified as "Cum-umbahs" (that is, Kumumpa) or alternatively, as Gosiutes (Steward, *Basin-Plateau,* 220–21).

4. Clayton, *Journal,* 345 (dated August 11, 1847); Dykman and Whitley, "Settling in Salt Lake City," 86. Three major types of forts were built in this western region during the nineteenth century. The first to be constructed were trading-post forts, such as Fort Bridger. Those that I term settlement forts, which were integral to this instance of settler colonization, came next (see Chapter Three). Military forts followed.

5. Powell, in *Anthropology of the Numa,* recorded thousands of words from several Numic languages, but the lists do not include words for wilderness or wild land. That concept presumably would not have held meaning before settler colonization led to the destruction of most of their hunting and gathering grounds.

6. Powell, *Anthropology of the Numa,* 171, 207. This and subsequent citations of Powell draw primarily on his observations and his interviews with Ute- and Shoshone-speaking men in Utah Territory in the 1870s (see Chapter Nine). Most of the settler-colonists were Anglo-American or British: generally fair skinned, often with light eyes, and with a range of hair color. On "dog face people," see Steward, *Basin-Plateau,* 149; and Kerns, *Journeys West,* 166.

7. Powell, *Anthropology of the Numa,* 167, 173, 174; Stewart, "Culture Element Distributions," 282. This and subsequent citations of anthropologist Omer C. Stewart (1908–1991) draw primarily on interviews with John Kanosh (b. 1881, U.S. Census, 1930, Kanosh, Millard County, Utah).

Stewart interviewed him for thirty hours at the Shivwits Reservation near Santa Clara, Utah, in 1937 or 1938. He identified John Kanosh, who was born near the site that became Kanosh, Utah, as the grandson of the famous Pahvant Ute leader known as Chief Kanosh. Other sources indicate that he was the adopted son of the chief, whose birth children did not survive to adulthood (see Chapters Nine and Eleven).

8. Powell, *Anthropology of the Numa*, 53; A. Smith, *Ethnography of the Northern Utes*, 65–66, 123–24. This and subsequent citations of anthropologist Anne M. Smith (1900–1981) draw on interviews with elders, women as well as men, that she carried out at the Uinta and Ouray Ute Reservation in Utah in the late 1930s. Some of the elders were born before the reservation was established in the 1860s.

9. A. Smith, *Ethnography of the Northern Utes*, 115–16.

10. Stewart, "Culture Element Distributions," 256–57.

11. Powell, *Anthropology of the Numa*, 164, 172, 189.

12. Brigham Young Office Journal, entry dated September 28, 1860, box 72, folder 5.

13. Powell, *Anthropology of the Numa*, 49, 173, 179; A. Smith, *Ethnography of the Northern Utes*, 60.

14. Powell, *Anthropology of the Numa,* 168; Horne, "Pioneer Reminiscences," 294. Wildcats, or lynxes and bobcats, are short tailed and larger than domestic cats.

15. Powell, *Anthropology of the Numa*, 172. The word for "wolf" is alternatively recorded as *sin-av* and *shin-av*, depending on dialect. Instances of settler-colonists eating wolf occurred, but rarely. See Whitney, *History of Utah*, 107; and J. Young, *Memoirs*, 64. See also Cheney, *Plain but Wholesome*, 81.

16. J. Young, *Memoirs*, 64; Bullock, *Pioneer Camp*, 265 (dated August 24, 1847).

17. Powell, *Anthropology of the Numa*, 47; A. Smith, *Ethnography of the Northern Utes*, 58.

18. Powell, *Anthropology of the Numa*, 69, 172. The term *animal-people* comes from Clifford Duncan, a Northern Ute elder. In the late nineteenth century, Powell called these beings "animal gods" as well as "ancient people" (who were not, however, human beings). See Duncan, "Northern Utes of Utah," 167; and Powell, *Anthropology of the Numa*, 69, 73. See also A. Smith, *Ute Tales*.

19. Conetah, *History of the Northern Ute*, 2; Givón, *Ute Texts*, 5–16. See Powell, *Anthropology of the Numa*, 77, for a version told in the early 1870s.

20. Callaway, Janetski, and Stewart, "Ute," 336.

21. Powell, *Anthropology of the Numa*, 170, 171. The name Kumunts or Kumuntsu referred to Shoshones, and specifically to the band of Green River Shoshones. On the life of Eliza Roxcy Snow, see E. Snow, *Personal Writings*, 6–45; E. Smith, "Sketch of My Life," 131–36, 313–14, 351;

De Pillis, "Eliza Roxcy Snow Smith," 307–9. On Eliza's appearance, see
B. Ferris, *Mormons at Home*, 158.

22. E. Snow, *Personal Writings*, 209 (dated October 20, 23, 1847).

23. Journal History of the Church, August 9, 1848; E. Snow, *Personal Writings*,
29–30; Horne, "Home Life," 182–83.

24. L. Young, "Diary," 165 (dated March 22, 1848, recorded by Lorenzo);
E. Snow, *Personal Writings*, 222 (dated March 23, 1848); Sessions, *Mormon
Midwife*, 110 (dated March 22, 1848). The man who spoke at the funeral
was Jedediah Morgan Grant (1816–1856).

25. Sessions, *Mormon Midwife*, 110 (dated March 22, 1848).

26. Charley bought Sally on Sunday, December 12, 1847. See E. Snow, *Personal
Writings*, 214 (dated December 14, 1847).

27. E. Snow, *Personal Writings*, 222 (dated March 28–30, 1848); Sessions,
Mormon Midwife, 110, 112, 139 (dated March 27–31, April 27, May 3, 1848;
November 28, 1849); Horne, "Home Life," 294.

28. E. Snow, *Personal Writings*, 30–31, 216, 222 (dated January 15, March 24–30,
1848); E. Smith, "Sketch of My Life"; Sessions, *Mormon Midwife*, 110–12
(dated between March 27 and May 4, 1848).

29. Clarissa ["Clara"] C. Decker Young to Brigham Young, October 3, 1847,
Brigham Young Office Files, box 44, folder 15; C. Young, "Woman's Expe-
rience," 176. On utensils, see Powell, *Anthropology of the Numa*, 42; and
Stewart, "Culture Element Distributions," 263.

30. Powell, *Anthropology of the Numa*, 48; Stewart, "Culture Element Distributions," 253, 263; E. Snow, *Personal Writings*, 31.

31. Powell, *Anthropology of the Numa*, 174, 185; A. Smith, *Ethnography of the
Northern Utes*, 87, 96.

32. The intricacy of cultural rules about food varies widely. See Douglas and
Gross, "Food and Culture." It seems likely that Sally entered a "higher
intricacy food system" when she began to live with Clara and Eliza. See also
Chapter Seven.

33. E. Snow, *Personal Writings*, 10, 207, 208, 210, 211, 223 (dated October 11, 17,
27, 28; November 6, 1847; April 1, 1848); Gates, "Brigham Young as I Knew
Him," 58, Susa Young Gates Papers, box 12. NB: The endnotes in this book
identify manuscripts in the Susa Young Gates Papers only by their box
numbers as of 2010. Many manuscripts were not in folders at that time; the
papers have since been reorganized.

34. Sessions, *Mormon Midwife*, 110 (dated March 31, 1848).

35. Brigham Young later told a visitor about Sally, "at first she slept outside."
See Brigham Young Office Journal, entry dated September 28, 1860,
Brigham Young Office Files, box 72, folder 5. Within four months after
first entering the fort, however, she was sleeping indoors on the floor.
See E. Snow, *Personal Writings*, 31. Some Americans who were taken cap-
tive, including Cynthia Ann Parker and Herbert Lehmann, came to prefer

sleeping on the ground outdoors; they later resisted sleeping on elevated beds indoors. See Frankel, *Searchers*, 83; and Lehmann, *Nine Years*, 207. Jim Bridger also shared that preference. See Alter, *Jim Bridger*, 187. So great was the cultural significance of sleeping practices to American settlers that such former captives, as well as fur trappers, were regarded as having fallen away from civilization if they preferred to "lie in the dirt."

36. E. Snow, *Personal Writings*, 7; Powell, *Anthropology of the Numa*, 63. George Washington Bean (1831–1897), an early settler, took a more positive view than most, writing that Utes "engaged in good sporting," including "horse-racing, trading, gambling, foot-racing, wrestling, etc." See Bean, *Autobiography*, 52.

37. Powell, "Sketch of the Mythology," 44.

38. Powell, *Anthropology of the Numa*, 39, 48; Conetah, *History of the Northern Ute*, 10–11; Stewart, "Culture Element Distributions," 274; Steward, *Basin-Plateau*, 227.

39. Powell, *Anthropology of the Numa*, 39, 42; Conetah, *History of the Northern Ute*, 10.

40. Powell, *Anthropology of the Numa*, 38, 39.

41. Powell, *Anthropology of the Numa*, 175; Conetah, *History of the Northern Ute*, 16; Duncan, "Northern Utes of Utah," 173.

42. Stewart, "Culture Element Distributions," 269, 298; A. Smith, *Ethnography of the Northern Utes*, 93–94.

43. Powell, *Anthropology of the Numa*, 173; Chamberlin, "Some Plant Names," 32, 35, 36, 38, 39; A. Smith, *Ethnography of the Northern Utes*, 91. See also Rhode, *Native Plants*, 73–80. For more on these native plants, see Moerman, *Native American Ethnobotany*.

44. Chamberlin, "Some Plant Names," 33, 34. Poison sego, also commonly known as death camas, is *Zigadenus nuttallii*. See Chamberlin, "Some Plant Names," 37, 39. A number of other species of toxic plants share the common name death camas, including *Zigadenus paniculatus* (see note 46 below). All species of *Zigadenus* are considered to be toxic, but *Zigadenus nuttallii* is the most toxic of all. See Burrows and Tyrl, *Toxic Plants*, 792.

45. Yampah, or wild carrot, *Perideridia gairdneri*, is a widely distributed plant valued for its edible root. See A. Smith, *Ethnography of the Northern Ute*, 47; and Chamberlin, "Ethno-Botany," 55, 99. Yampah and an edible wild parsnip, *Heracleum maximum*, belong to the same family as the deadly water hemlock. Identifying plants in this family requires skill, and confusing them can have fatal results. On the need for caution in eating wild plants in the Great Basin, see Rhode, *Native Plants*, 16. Water hemlock, *Cicuta douglasii*, is widely regarded as the deadliest plant native to North America. It contains a potent neurotoxin, which causes violent seizures. See Burrows and Tyrl, *Toxic Plants*, 62–63.

46. *Zigadenus paniculatus*, sometimes called foothill death camas, is considered the third most toxic species in a genus of poisonous plants. See Burrows

and Tyrl, *Toxic Plants*, 792. The edible blue camas lily, or common camas, *Camassia quamash*, was an important food in many parts of western North America, including lands that now lie within the states of California, Washington, Idaho, Montana, and Utah. See Moerman, *Native American Ethnobotany*, 134.

47. On "garden sauce," see, for example, L. Young, "Diary," 166 (dated May 19[?], 1848, recorded by Harriet), and Bullock, *Pioneer Camp*, 236. On edible wild plants, see also Horne, "Pioneer Reminiscences," 294; and J. Young, *Memoirs*, 64.

48. Chamberlin, "Some Plant Names," 35.

49. Chamberlin, "Some Plant Names," 33, 39; Chamberlin, "Ethno-Botany," 364; E. Snow, *Personal Writings*, 30. Shoshone-speaking Gosiutes as well as Utes used the name *si'go* for what the settlers came to call sego. A common name for this plant in California and other western states is mariposa lily or butterfly lily. The settlers saw their Kumumpa ("Cu-mum-buh") or Gosiute neighbors in the valley harvesting the bulbs for food. Newman Bulkley (1817–1893), an early settler, also recalled seeing Indian women carrying loads of thistle roots in fall 1847, and digging two bushels of the roots for himself. See "Extracts of Articles on Newman Bulkley," http://familysearch .org/photos/stories/1069203 (retrieved June 6, 2020). That sego lily, thistle roots, and other wild plants helped sustain the early colonizing settlers is well documented. Eliza Snow, for example, recorded making an eighteen-day camping trip to gather currants and serviceberries in canyons at some distance from the valley. See E. Snow, *Personal Writings*, 225 (dated August 5, 1848).

50. On the death and the funeral of Franklin Knox Shedd (1825–1848), see E. Snow, *Personal Writings*, 219 (dated February 22, 1848), 295n49; Sessions, *Mormon Midwife*, 108 (dated February 22, 23, 1848); and L. Young, "Diary," 165 (dated February 21, 22, 1848, recorded by Lorenzo).

51. E. Snow, *Personal Writings*, 220–21 (dated February 28, 1848), 239, 295n50.

52. Powell, *Anthropology of the Numa*, 38, 69; Powell, "Sketch of the Mythology," 44–45.

53. Burrows and Tyrl, *Toxic Plants*, 62–64; Chamberlin, "Some Plant Names," 33, 37, 39.

54. "Poison Roots," *Deseret News*, March 5, 1856; "A Sad Occurrence—Death by Poison," *Deseret News*, June 4, 1862. Charles Peter Hogan (1848–1850) died in April 1850. The cause of death was recorded as "poisoned by eating wild parsnip." See U.S. Census, 1850, Mortality Schedule, Davis County, Deseret [Utah Territory]. (According to the same mortality schedule, cholera, an infectious epidemic disease, caused many more child deaths.) As late as 1876, there was a report of "a hard Death" caused by eating poison sego. The decedent was eighteen years old. See Woodruff, *Journal*, 7:271–72 (dated April 20, 21, 1876).

55. Powell, *Anthropology of the Numa*, 141.

56. L. Young, "Diary," 165 (dated March 1, 1848, recorded by Lorenzo; May 19[?], 1848, recorded by Harriet); J. Young, *Memoirs*, 64; Journal History of the Church, August 10, 1848.

57. L. Young, "Diary," 166 (dated May 27–29, 1848, recorded by Harriet); Journal History of the Church, May 22, 1848. See also Hartley, "Mormons, Crickets, and Gulls," 230.

58. Journal History of the Church, May 6, June 4, 1848 (excerpt from the journal of Isaac C. Haight); L. Young, "Diary," 166 (dated May 19, 28, 29, 1848).

59. Journal History of the Church, March 6, 1848 (letter from High Council to Brigham Young). On the burning of grasslands, see O. Pratt, "Interesting Items" (dated May 4, 1847), 18. The so-called crickets, *Anabrus simplex*, belong to the katydid family. On their preference for forbs (herbage other than grasses and grass-like plants), see MacVean, "Mormon Crickets," 234–35.

60. Journal History of the Church, July 17, 1848 (quoting the journal of Isaac C. Haight); J. Young, *Memoirs*, 65; E. Snow, *Personal Writings*, 224 (dated May 28, June 10, 1848). See also Hartley, "Mormons, Crickets, and Gulls."

61. Journal History of the Church, August 10, 1848 (excerpt from the journal of Isaac C. Haight); Sessions, *Mormon Midwife*, 16, 117 (dated July 23, 29, August 9, 10, 1848); Crosby, *No Place*, 83 (dated September 9, 1848); P. Pratt, "To President Orson Pratt" (dated September 5, 1848), 22.

62. Journal History of the Church, April 21, June 9, 1848 (typescript of a letter dated February 13, 1869). Thousands of gulls migrate in spring to nest on islands in the saltwater lake. Gulls fly eastward toward the mountain valleys each day to find food, including crickets and grasshoppers, for their young. See Behle, *Bird Life*, 20–32, 64–68.

63. Powell, *Anthropology of the Numa*, 172, 173; La Rivers, "Mormon Cricket," 66, 68. The species of gull (*Larus californicus*) that ate the crickets is omnivorous, but favors insects. See Behle, *Bird Life*, 68. Information on feeding frenzies by trout, on burrowing owls, and on the historic range of prairie dogs, courtesy of the Utah Division of Wildlife Resources, Salt Lake City.

64. None qualified as food—despite a biblical verse that allows eating locusts and grasshoppers. See Leviticus 11:22 (King James Version): "Even these of them ye may eat; the locust after his kind, and the bald locust after his kind, and the beetle after his kind, and the grasshopper after his kind." In twentieth-century translations of Leviticus from Hebrew to English, the word *katydid* sometimes replaced *bald locust*. It seems that *Anabrus simplex*, the so-called cricket that is a katydid, qualifies as one "of them ye may eat." On their nutritional value, see Madsen and Madsen, "One Man's Meat," 52–67. See also Sutton, *Insects as Food,* on the practice of eating insects in the Great Basin.

65. Bullock, *Pioneer Camp*, 246, 255 (dated July 31, August 11, 1847); Clayton, *Journal*, 329 (dated July 31, 1847); Carter, *Our Pioneer Heritage*, 495–96 (George W. Brown, letter dated December 29, 1896).

66. Genesis 1:28 (King James Version).
67. Stansbury, *Expedition*, 126; E. Snow, *Personal Writings*, 213 (dated December 2, 1847).
68. Journal History of the Church, March 5, 1849; E. Snow, *Personal Writings*, 228 (dated April 22, 1849); C. Fowler, "Subsistence," 80–81, 85–87; Stout, *On the Mormon Frontier*, 338 (dated December 24, 1848), 351n21. A shorter report of the winter hunt, perhaps based on just portions of the two teams' lists, enumerated only about half the number of animals killed. See Kerns, *Journeys West*, 264. Some of the so-called wolves were undoubtedly coyotes, commonly called prairie wolves at the time. See Russell, *Journal*, 131. Some of the so-called ravens may have been non-migratory crows and blackbirds. Game animals that the settlers hunted to eat were not included in the tally of killed animals, with the exception of the two bears.
   There was precedent for collective hunts in the eastern United States in the eighteenth century. See Kerns, *Journeys West*, 264. Bounty systems were also established early in western territories. See Muir, *Steep Trails*, 313–14.
69. Isaiah 35:1 (King James Version). A British visitor saw a profusion of roses, along with geraniums, nasturtiums, tansy, and other domesticated flowers in the settlers' gardens when he visited the valley in fall 1860. See Burton, *City of the Saints*, 198.
70. Powell, *Anthropology of the Numa*, 46, 173. On wild rose, see Moerman, *Native American Ethnobotany*, 486.
71. Powell, *Anthropology of the Numa*, 42.
72. Information on wild grasses, balsamroot, sego lily, and other wild plants grazed by livestock, courtesy of Utah State University Cooperative Extension, Logan.
73. Stewart, "Culture Element Distributions," 261, 311; A. Smith, *Ethnography of the Northern Utes*, 129, 146–48; Chamberlin, "Some Plant Names," 40.
74. M. Kimball, *Journal*, 37.
75. Spencer, *Brigham Young at Home*, 122–23; E. Snow, *Personal Writings*, 210, 211, 212, 217 (dated October 27, 28, November 6, 14, 1847; January 21, 1848).
76. E. Kane, *Twelve Mormon Homes*, 32, quoting Mary Pitchforth in 1872; Morgan, "Letters by Forty-Niners," 100 (letter by John B. Hazlip, dated July 1849).
77. Powell, *Anthropology of the Numa*, 141, 142, 143; Chamberlin, "Some Plant Names," 35, 39; Brigham Young Office Journal, entry dated September 28, 1860, Brigham Young Office Files, box 72, folder 5.
78. Four years after Sally was sold to Charley, Brigham Young named Baptiste as the seller. See "B. Young's Testimony, U.S. v. Pedro Leon," January 11, 1852, Papers Relating to Mexican Traders, 1851–1853, Brigham Young Office Files, box 47, folder 36.
79. Powell, *Anthropology of the Numa*, 165, 208. The use of different terms for older and younger siblings appears to have been a universal feature of the

kinship systems of Numic peoples of the Great Basin. See Steward, *Basin-Plateau*, 288; and Shimkin, "Uto-Aztecan System," 223–45. This feature indicates what anthropologists call a seniority system in kinship terminology and kin relations. While such systems do vary cross-culturally, a usual practice is for juniors to show some degree of deference to their seniors.

CHAPTER 3

1. L. Young, "Diary," 166–67 (dated July 24, 26, 1848, recorded by Harriet); J. Young, "Reminiscences," 84. Most of the events in this chapter took place between 1848 and 1855.
2. L. Young, "Diary," 166–67 (dated July 31, August 1–5, 1848, recorded by Harriet); J. Young, "Reminiscences," 84.
3. More than 2,500 colonizing settlers arrived in 1848. See Pioneer Database, 1847–1868, http://history.churchofjesuschrist.org/overlandtravel (retrieved February 25, 2012).
4. Campbell, "Miles Morris Goodyear," 182, 185, 187. Miles Goodyear (1817–1849) built Fort Buenaventura in 1846, and sold it in late 1847.
5. For example, some 1,200 colonizing settlers who arrived as one group in 1848 brought about 3,500 animals, from horses and oxen to sheep and chickens to dogs and cats. See Arrington, *Brigham Young*, 157.
6. Crosby, *No Place*, 81 (dated August 18, 1848); Journal History of the Church, August 5, 1848 (excerpt from Thomas Bullock's journal); Heywood, *Not by Bread Alone*, 22 (dated September 5, 1850).
7. Crosby, *No Place*, 83 (dated September 12, 1848). Between 1847 and 1868, just two colonizing settlers among some 1,910 who died on the Mormon overland trail were said to have been "eaten by wolves." See Bashore and Tolley, "Mortality on the Mormon Trail," 115, 117, 122. Despite deep fears of Indian attack along the overland trail, only four deaths were attributed to Indians. According to the records, diseases and accidents led to most of the deaths for which a cause was recorded. More than half of those deaths were due to disease, such as cholera. See Bashore and Tolley, "Mortality on the Mormon Trail," 122.
8. Journal History of the Church, May 29, June 15, June 16, July 9, 1848. A census of livestock enumerated nearly 9,000 animals at the time of departure, but some died on the trek west. On measles, see Gates, "From Impulsive Girl," 274.
9. In 1850, just three years after settlement, more than 6,000 people lived in Salt Lake Valley, with another 5,000 to the north and south. See U.S. Census, 1850, Utah Territory. The number of livestock was evidently several times the number of people.
10. E. Snow, *Personal Writings*, 216–17 (dated January 21, 1848).
11. The titles Brother and Sister were customarily used in addressing and referring to fellow church members, including those unrelated by blood or

marriage. This practice does not fully qualify as fictive kinship. It does, however, give an appearance of a practice that was familiar to Sally: the use of
sibling terms for close cousins. See Stewart, "Culture Element Distributions,"
297; and Powell, *Anthropology of the Numa*, 129–30, 165. Sally had entered
a very different social world, despite flashes of familiarity now and then.
On faraway relatives, see A. Smith, *Ethnography of the Northern Utes*, 124.

   Finally, it is worth noting here that Utah (or Ute) chiefs commonly
called other chiefs, who were allies, their brothers. See, for example, Powell,
Anthropology of the Numa, 103. This was widely misunderstood at the time
by settler-colonists, and later by their descendants and many historians,
who assumed they were biological brothers or very close kinsmen. See, for
example, D. Huntington, *Vocabulary of the Utah*, 28. The chiefs were making strategic use of fictive kinship to forge alliances.

12. E. Snow, *Personal Writings*, 225 (dated September 20, 1848).
13. Carvalho, *Incidents of Travel*, 207; Powell, *Anthropology of the Numa*, 179;
    Callaway, Janetski, and Stewart, "Ute," 336.
14. Arrington, *Brigham Young*, 420–21; Waite, *Mormon Prophet*, 196.
15. On the nineteenth-century Mormon practice of plural marriage—specif-
    ically, the marriage of one man to two or more women, termed *polygamy*
    in most historical works—see Gordon, *Mormon Question*; and Ulrich,
    House Full of Females. Anthropologists use the term *polygyny* for this type
    of plural marriage, but I have followed historical usage in order to avoid
    confusion. Polygamy was briefly practiced in the Kingdom of Münster
    (1534–1535) until the kingdom fell, and its leader and some of his followers
    were executed. See Haude, *In the Shadow*.
16. Chandless, *Visit to Salt Lake*, 193; Stenhouse, *Exposé of Polygamy*, 77; Mor-
    gan, "Letters by Forty-Niners," 114 (letter by an anonymous traveler, dated
    October 1849).
17. Powell, *Anthropology of the Numa*, 51; A. Smith, *Ethnography of the North-
    ern Utes*, 131. Sororal polygyny, the marriage of two or more sisters to the
    same man, was a common practice among the Numic peoples of the Great
    Basin before American settlement. See Steward, *Basin-Plateau*, 242; and
    Kerns, *Journeys West*, 98.
18. Powell, *Anthropology of the Numa*, 50.
19. O. Huntington, "Journals," folder 5, 47; Z. Young, "'A Weary Traveler,'" 96
    (dated January 4, 1849).
20. Stout, *On the Mormon Frontier*, 344, 345 (dated February 28, March 2,
    1849); O. Huntington, "Journals," folder 5, 52–53; Wells, "Narrative," 7.
21. P. Pratt, "To President Orson Pratt," 21 (dated September 5, 1848). Dan-
    iel W. Jones (1830–1915), who worked as an interpreter and who knew
    Chief Wákara, recalled a bold and successful raid by the chief and his men
    in the early 1850s. "I have seen them in mimicry go through the whole

performance," he later wrote. See D. Jones, *Forty Years*, 41–42. See also Duncan, "Northern Utes of Utah," 184.

22. O. Huntington, "Journals," folder 5, 48–49, 53.

23. Journal History of the Church, March 6, 1848 (letter from the High Council of the City to Brigham Young).

24. O. Huntington, "Journals," folder 5, 53–55; Stout, *On the Mormon Frontier*, 346–47 (dated March 5, 1849). The attack at the creek took place in early March, 1849. See also Farmer, *On Zion's Mount*, 62; Turner, *Brigham Young*, 210–11.

25. O. Pratt, "Interesting Items," 179 (dated July 28, 1847); E. Snow, *Personal Writings*, 213 (dated December 2, 1847). Six months before the attack, a settler-colonist praised the lake and land, and implied that colonization was imminent. See P. Pratt, "To President Orson Pratt," 23–24. The letter made no mention of the Utahs who claimed and defended the valley as their homeland.

26. The colonizing settlers may first have heard the shorthand name, Ute, from Bridger, and then from Barney Ward and other trappers. See Bullock, *Pioneer Camp*, 248 (dated June 28, 1847). Warren Angus Ferris (1810–1873), who spent time with "Eutaws" in the early 1830s, also referred to them as "Ute," and to their language as "Eut." See W. Ferris, *Life in the Rocky Mountains*, 69, 219, 251. A settler-colonist recorded the name "Ute" in her diary as early as 1848. She used the word "Utah" for a place—Utah Valley, once the Valley of the Utahs—about two years later. See Sessions, *Mormon Midwife*, 112, 143 (dated May 16, 1848; February 4, 10, 27, 1850). For a perceptive account of "renaming the land," see Farmer, *On Zion's Mount*, 241–81.

27. Powell, *Anthropology of the Numa*, 178; Wells, "Narrative," 7. Wells identified the site as previously named Battle Creek, and "now called Pleasant Grove."

28. Journal History of the Church, May 7, 1849; U.S. Army Corps of Topographical Engineers, *Map of Great Salt Lake*; E. Kane, *Twelve Mormon Homes*, 36. On subsequent acts of lethal violence against Utahs in what came to be called Utah Valley, see Blackhawk, *Violence over the Land*, 233; Farmer, *On Zion's Mount*, 72–77; and Turner, *Brigham Young*, 212–13.

29. "B. Young's Testimony, U.S. v. Pedro Leon," January 11, 1852, Papers Relating to Mexican Traders, 1851–1853, Brigham Young Office Files, box 47, folder 36.

30. Journal History of the Church, May 31, 1850; Wells, "Narrative," 9. On the February 1850 massacre, see Farmer, *On Zion's Mount*, 74–77.

31. "B. Young's Testimony, U.S. v. Pedro Leon," January 11, 1852, Papers Relating to Mexican Traders, 1851–1853, Brigham Young Office Files, box 47, folder 36; E. Kane, *Twelve Mormon Homes*, 13–15.

32. Wells, "Narrative," 9; Blackhawk, *Violence over the Land*, 240–41; Knack, *Boundaries Between*, 56.

33. This practice was documented in eastern Pennsylvania, for example, at an earlier date. The Indian children came from New York, western Pennsylvania, and Ohio. See Marsh, *Lenape among the Quakers*, 161.

34. B. Young, H. C. Kimball, J. M. Grant, and E. T. Benson, "Times for All Things: Discourses [...] Delivered July 13, 1855, at a Conference Held at Provo City, Utah Territory," *Journal of Discourses*, 3:64. The two children Ezra T. Benson mentioned were no longer members of his household in 1860 (U.S. Census, 1860, Cache County, Utah Territory). Anthropologist Martha C. Knack argues that a pragmatic need for labor underlay the settlers' practice of taking Southern Paiute children into their homes. See Knack, *Boundaries Between*, 56–57.

35. Spencer, *Brigham Young at Home*, 122–23; Gates, "Courtship of Kanosh," 24; Powell, *Anthropology of the Numa*, 181. The story by Gates incorporates some plausible details about Sally's appearance and her demeanor: plausible because they can be attributed to her upbringing as Pahvant Ute, and to her situation as a lone captive. The storyline, however, is a romanticized invention (see Chapter Twelve). Gates was born years after Sally arrived at the fort, but she did spend the first fourteen years of her life in a suite at the Lion House next to Clara's, where Sally lived. Although the story Gates later wrote has often been treated as factual, great caution is required in using "Courtship of Kanosh" as a source of evidence about Sally's life.

36. Ezekiel 33:27 (King James Version).

37. Journal History of the Church, June 14, 1849; Hafen, "Elijah Barney Ward," 346; Stout, *On the Mormon Frontier*, 344–47 (dated March 1–5, 1849); T. Kane, *Mormons*, reproduced in Journal History of the Church, March 26, 1850. That Chief Wákara spoke English with some facility is clear from the accounts of Carvalho and others who recorded what he said. See, for example, Carvalho, *Incidents of Travel*, 193–94. Dimick Huntington moved to Utah Valley with the first colonists in late March 1849. See Z. Young, "'A Weary Traveler,'" 103 (undated, ca. March 31, 1849). To judge from the words he recorded, his knowledge of the Ute language may have been limited to some hundreds of words, mainly nouns and adjectives. See, for example, D. Huntington, *Vocabulary of the Utah*.

38. By June 1849 Sally had lived with the settler-colonists for eighteen months in a situation of near-total immersion, sufficient time to develop basic speaking ability and comprehension of English.

39. Journal History of the Church, June 14, 1849.

40. E. Snow, *Personal Writings*, 31; Powell, *Anthropology of the Numa*, 168, 208. The meaning of Pidash, as Eliza heard and recorded Sally's name, is uncertain. English-speakers often found it difficult to pronounce or transcribe Ute names. Linguist Tom Givón must resort to "plausible guesses" for some English written renderings of Ute names (Tom Givón, personal communication, June 7, 2018).

Pahvant Utes lived along the western flank of the Pahvant Mountains, along the lower Sevier River, in the adjacent desert, and as far south as Beaver Valley. A-vwa-pa was known to settler-colonists as Sevier Lake.

41. Steward recorded the name Pahvandüts and the English translation of the name given to him by Joseph Pikyavit (1892–1974) during an ethnographic interview at Kanosh Reservation in 1936. See Steward, *Basin-Plateau*, 227; and Kerns, *Journeys West*, 236. Stewart recorded that name and Pahvantinunts, given by his cultural informant John Kanosh (see Chapter Two, note 7). See Stewart, "Culture Element Distributions," 236. More than twenty varied spellings of the Pahvant Ute name appear in published and unpublished writings from 1850 to the 1870s.

42. Carvalho, *Incidents of Travel*, 205.

43. "B. Young's Testimony, U.S. v. Pedro Leon," January 11, 1852, Papers Relating to Mexican Traders, 1851–1853, Brigham Young Office Files, box 47, folder 36; Clayton, *Journals*, 409 (dated May 6, 1852). Brigham Young crossed the valley again in spring 1854. See Carvalho, *Incidents of Travel*, 205–06.

44. Based on ethnographic evidence, Kelly and Fowler suggest that Beaver Valley may have been a transitional zone, inhabited not only by Southern Paiutes but also by Pahvant Utes. See Kelly and Fowler, "Southern Paiute," 348. Documentary evidence, ranging from a French traveler's recorded observations in 1855 (see note 46 below) to Powell's encounter with a Pahvant chief in Beaver Valley in the 1870s (see Chapter Nine), also supports the view that Sho-av-ich (later, Beaver Valley) was part of Pahvant Ute territory.

45. Rémy, *Journey to Great-Salt-Lake City*, 2:354–56. Rémy traveled through Beaver Valley in late fall 1855.

46. Rémy, *Journey to Great-Salt-Lake City*, 2:356–57. Given their packhorse and their manner of dress, the women Rémy saw were clearly Pahvants. See Stewart, "Culture Element Distributions," 274, 280, 282. Southern Paiutes, who lived in Beaver Valley and farther south, traveled by foot and carried their burdens. See Kelly and Fowler, "Southern Paiute," 377.

47. Rémy, *Journey to Great-Salt-Lake City*, 2:355–57. Warren Ferris, who encountered "Utaws" about fifteen years earlier, noted that painting their faces red and black signified war. See W. Ferris, *Life in the Rocky Mountains*, 68. See also Powell, *Anthropology of the Numa*, 162; Carvalho, *Incidents of Travel*, 200; J. Young, *Memoirs*, 111.

48. The first colonizing settlers in Beaver Valley arrived from a nearby valley in 1856. See "Correspondence: Letter to the Editor from P. P. Pratt," *Deseret News*, July 16, 1856.

49. A. Kimball, "Memoirs," 7, 10–11; Hafen, "Elijah Barney Ward," 343.

50. "For the News: Indian Difficulties," *Deseret News*, October 1, 1853; A. Kimball, "Memoirs," 11.

51. A. Kimball, "Memoirs," 12.
52. For later stories of the Hatton murder, see, for example, Gibbs, *Lights and Shadows*, 202.
53. Powell, *Anthropology of the Numa*, 208. The settlement where the massacre took place was originally called Salt Creek, and then renamed Nephi. The massacre reportedly took place on October 2, 1853. See "Indian Difficulties," *Deseret News*, October 15, 1853, which reported, "On the 2nd inst., in a skirmish at Nephi, eight Indians were killed, and one squaw and two boys taken prisoner." Adelia's account of the murders, with no mention of any skirmish, appears in the undated memoir that she wrote near the end of her life. See A. Kimball, "Memoirs," 13. She may have learned of the victims' identities, as "Lake Indians" from the "Parvian Valley," years later, as a longtime resident of a village in that valley (see Chapter Eleven). The name Parvian was a common variant of Pahvant at the time. Sevier Lake, or A-vwa-pa, was located in Pahvant Valley, and part of the Pahvant Ute homeland.

    A few months after the killings another eyewitness recorded what she saw that day, and her brief account generally agrees with Adelia's. Martha Spence Heywood recalled that nine, not eight, Indians entered the fort and were immediately and "inhumanly" killed by order of a man from another settlement. This statement is part of a retrospective journal entry covering several months, and which identified the victims only as "Indians." See Heywood, *Not by Bread Alone*, 97 (dated January 1, 1854). The preponderance of evidence suggests that the "Lake Indians" who were murdered at the fort were Pahvant Utes from lands around Sevier Lake, and not Gosiutes. Pahvant Utes and Gosiutes occupied adjacent homelands, often regarded each other as allies, and sometimes intermarried (see Chapter Nine), but their languages and cultural identities differed.

    Recent archaeological research at Nephi revealed the skeletal remains of six Indian men and one boy, victims of the 1853 massacre. For a detailed and illuminating analysis of the site, and a list of victims by name, see Rood, "Archaeology of a Mass Grave."
54. Pahvant Utes are still generally regarded as solely responsible for killing Gunnison and his men, although there have always been doubters. See, for example, J. Brooks, *Mountain Meadows Massacre*, xiii; and Bagley, *Blood of the Prophets*, 44, 45; "Interesting from Utah," *New York Times*, May 18, 1855; and "The Mormon Outrages," *New York Times*, May 1, 1857.
55. J. Smith, *Southwest Expedition*, 193 (dated August 27, 1825).

CHAPTER 4

1. Most of the events in this chapter took place between 1849 and 1855. City planning began four days—and surveying the land, just nine days—after the first colonizing settlers arrived in the valley. See Bullock, *Pioneer Camp*,

241–43, 247 (dated July 28, August 2, 1847); Clayton, *Journal*, 326, 340 (dated July 28, August 2, 1847).

2. P. Pratt, "To President Orson Pratt," 22 (dated September 5, 1848); E. Snow, *Personal Writings*, 223 (dated May 17, 1848).

3. Stout, *On the Mormon Frontier*, 351 (dated April 19, 20, 28, 1849); E. Snow, *Personal Writings*, 223, 228 (dated May 17, 1848; April 28, 1849); Sessions, *Mormon Midwife*, 112–13 (dated May 16, 1848). On the city in 1849, see Morgan, "Letters by Forty-Niners," 103, 104 (letter by A. P. Josselyn, dated July 1849); and Stansbury, *Expedition*, 120, 122, 129–30. Stansbury was present from November 1849 until early April 1850.

4. Gates, "Lucy Bigelow Young," 30, Susa Young Gates Papers, box 14. Clara and Lucy moved from the fort to Log Row in March 1849. See E. Snow, *Personal Writings*, 227 (dated March 1, 1849). Clara later moved from Log Row to a house (U.S. Census, 1850, Great Salt Lake City, Great Salt Lake County, Utah Territory).

5. E. Snow, *Personal Writings*, 225, 229 (dated October 23, 1848; June 28, 1849); U.S. Census, 1850, Great Salt Lake City, Great Salt Lake County, Utah Territory.

6. Brigham Young moved into a house that he bought soon after he returned to the valley. See Z. Young, "'A Weary Traveler,'" 91 (dated September 24, 1848). His "large White house" was reportedly completed in 1849. See M. Young, "Journal." For descriptions of the house, see Cummings, "Trip across the Continent," 152 (dated July 6, 1852); and B. Ferris, *Mormons at Home*, 93, 112 (dated October 30, November 26, 1852).

7. Dykman and Whitley, "Settling in Salt Lake City," 92–93. Log Row housed some of Brigham Young's wives and children, but others shared small houses. See Z. Young, "'A Weary Traveler,'" 102 (dated March 17, 1849).

8. Clara gave birth to her first child in October 1849. The midwife recorded in her journal that she gave Clara a blessing and spoke in tongues in mid-June. See Z. Young, "'A Weary Traveler,'" 109–110 (dated June 16, 1849).

9. E. Snow, *Personal Writings*, 178, 179, 211 (dated June 14, 16, November 2, 1847), 280n44; Woodruff, *Journal*, 4:245 (dated February 3, 1854). Visitors to the city also reported the practice. See Gunnison, *Mormons*, 74; B. Ferris, *Mormons at Home*, 202–03 (dated April 5, 1853); Chandless, *Visit to Salt Lake*, 165–66; Burton, *City of the Saints*, 296. Linguistic anthropologists use the term *glossalalia* for the practice of speaking in tongues, which occurs during an altered state of consciousness. *Xenoglossy* (or *xenolalia*) refers to highly unusual—and highly contested—instances of speaking a foreign language without having learned it.

10. E. Snow, *Personal Writings*, 112. Speaking in tongues was rather common at this time. See E. Snow, *Personal Writings*, 211–13 (dated November 2–December 2, 1848); Sessions, *Mormon Midwife*, 92, 107 (dated July 19, 1847; January 30, 1848).

11. Z. Young, "'A Weary Traveler,'" 109–110 (dated June 16, 1849); Powell, *Anthropology of the Numa*, 165, 181, 208.

12. Powell, *Anthropology of the Numa*, 57, 179. In shamanic traditions, including that of Sally's people, shamans sometimes speak in a way that is not easily understood, even by other native speakers. Powell witnessed such a shamanic performance in the late 1860s while camped near Utes in northwestern Colorado Territory. I have witnessed such performances elsewhere in Native America, and this informs my interpretation. See also J. Miller, "Numic Religion," 337–54.

13. The five children were born between 1849 and 1855. The birth mother of Clara's stepchildren, Eva and Mahonri, was one of Brigham Young's other wives. See Spencer, *Brigham Young at Home*, 75; and Arrington, *Brigham Young*, 420.

14. Genesis 1:28 (King James Version); B. Ferris, *Mormons at Home*, 111 (dated November 26, 1852); E. Kane, *Twelve Mormon Homes*, 76, 86.

15. D. Huntington, *Vocabulary of the Utah*, 30; Powell, *Anthropology of the Numa*, 179; Conetah, *History of the Northern Ute*, 8; A. Smith, *Ethnography of the Northern Utes*, 87, 144.

16. Powell, *Anthropology of the Numa*, 60–62, 283n17.

17. Powell, *Anthropology of the Numa*, 179; A. Smith, *Ethnography of the Northern Utes*, 101–04, 144; Conetah, *History of the Northern Ute*, 14.

18. Z. Young, "'A Weary Traveler,'" 116 (dated December 24, 1849); Daybook, August–November 1854, Brigham Young Office Files, box 120, folder 1; Dykman and Whitley, "Settling in Salt Lake City," 93. On hearth cooking, cast iron pots, and the early introduction of cast-iron cook stoves, see Cheney, *Plain but Wholesome*, 15–18, 20–21.

19. On "times of great hunger" when wild foods were scarce, see A. Smith, *Ethnography of the Northern Utes*, 47.

20. Gates, "From Impulsive Girl," 276; Z. Young, "'A Weary Traveler,'" 92, 93, 94 (dated October 16, December 13, 19, 20, 22, 1848); Family information, ca. 1853–1858, Brigham Young Office Files, box 170, folder 26; Daybook, August–November 1854, Brigham Young Office Files, box 120, folder 1.

21. In 1850 Sally shared a room, probably in a small house, with two young women who did not have children: Ellen Rockwood, twenty-two years old; and Margaret Pierce Whitesides, twenty-seven years old. Sally's age was listed as twenty-two. See U.S. Census, 1850, Great Salt Lake City, Great Salt Lake County, Utah Territory.

22. A. Smith, *Ethnography of the Northern Utes*, 74; Sessions, *Mormon Midwife*, 72n158, 110, 114 (dated April 5, June 7, 1848).

23. Spencer, *Brigham Young at Home*, 122–23; Gates, "Courtship of Kanosh," 23.

24. A. Smith, *Ethnography of the Northern Utes*, 70–71, 90–94. On wild flax, see also Clayton, *Journal*, 277 (dated June 28, 1847).

25. Sessions, *Mormon Midwife*, 246n36; Daybook, August–November 1854, Brigham Young Office Files, box 120, folder 1.
26. Powell, *Anthropology of the Numa*, 172; Gates, "Courtship of Kanosh," 28. Margaret Pierce Whitesides recalled, "We had spun a lot of wool for the President [Brigham Young], and he told us to take time, and make some for ourselves." She recalled making forty-five yards. See M. Young, "Journal."
27. E. Snow, *Personal Writings*, 218 (dated February 4, 1848); Sessions, *Mormon Midwife*, 81, 108, 122 (dated May 13, 1847, February 4, 19, 1848).
28. A. Smith, *Ethnography of the Northern Utes*, 72–74, 100; Gates, "Courtship of Kanosh," 28.
29. Whitney, *History of Utah*, 585; Stewart, "Culture Element Distributions," 281; A. Smith, *Ethnography of the Northern Utes*, 70–71, 77.
30. Powell, *Anthropology of the Numa*, 207, 208.
31. Mary Isabella Horne, an early settler, recalled, "As soon as the children were large enough to assist in the work, boys and girls had to take an active part." See Whitney, *History of Utah*, 585. See also Dykman and Whitley, "Settling in Salt Lake City," 93. Clara's children, however, always had the privilege of living in households with servants. An undated document from this period lists Clara, Lucy, and other wives, along with their children and the "Help." Internal evidence suggests that the document dates from about 1853. "Susan," whose surname is illegible, and "Sally" appear beside Clara's name, as her servants or helpers. See "A List of President Brigham Young's Family Residing in the 18th Ward," family information, ca. 1853–1858, Brigham Young Office Files, box 170, folder 26.
32. Gates, "Courtship of Kanosh," 25.
33. D. Smart, introduction to *Mormon Midwife*, 14; Sessions, *Mormon Midwife*, 84 (dated June 5, 1847); E. Snow, *Personal Writings*, 152, 211, 212, 221 (dated January 15, November 6, 13, 1847; March 18, 1848).
34. Sessions, *Mormon Midwife*, 100, 101, 102, 104, 106, 111, 117, 118, 119, 129, 138, 140, 152, 160–61, 171 (dated between October 1847 and January 1852). Patty Sessions's diaries cover some forty years, and provide a remarkable record of women's work during the first decades of settlement.
35. Sessions, *Mormon Midwife*, 112, 115 (dated May 13, 14, July 1,3, 1848). Thousands of acres of land were surveyed and divided into five- and ten-acre plots. An early map of the valley (see U.S. Army Corps of Topographical Engineers, *Map of the Great Salt Lake*) shows a feature identified as the Big Field. Burton described the field as "a six-mile square" divided into five-acre plots. See Burton, *City of the Saints*, 21. Patty's husband and other settler-colonists grew grains such as wheat, buckwheat, oats, and corn in their irrigated fields. See Sessions, *Mormon Midwife*, 102 (dated October 27, 1847); E. Snow, *Personal Writings*, 223 (dated April 15, 1848); and Morgan, "Letters by Forty-Niners," 103 (letter by A. P. Josselyn, dated July 1849).
36. Sessions, *Mormon Midwife*, 111–12 (dated April 21, 1848). Patty was still living at the fort. She moved to a house on a city lot in 1850, shortly before

the city was incorporated. See Sessions, *Mormon Midwife*, 153 (dated December 3, 1850).

37. Sessions, *Mormon Midwife*, 111, 117, 131, 132, 134, 146, 147, 164, 176, 192 (dated between April 1848 and April 1853).

38. Sessions, *Mormon Midwife*, 112, 113, 114, 115, 117, 132, 134, 147, 148, 166, 177, 192 (dated between May 1848 and April 1853). Consumption was the name then used for tuberculosis.

39. Sessions, *Mormon Midwife*, 121, 138, 140, 142, 152, 170, 173 (dated between December 1848 and March 1852).

40. Sessions, *Mormon Midwife*, 112, 114, 130, 145, 149–50, 164, 176, 184, 206 (dated between May 1848 and July 1854).

41. Sessions, *Mormon Midwife,* 112, 115, 116, 119 (dated between May and October 1848). She also often recorded feeling ill and tired in the following years.

42. Sessions, *Mormon Midwife*, 104, 108, 150, 189–90, 194 (dated December 14, 1847; February 18, 22, 1848; August 5, 1850; February 9–12, June 13, 30, 1853). Despite the rigors of settlement, and the toll it took on her health, Patty outlived her two husbands by decades. She died in 1892, two months before her ninety-eighth birthday. See D. Smart, introduction to *Mormon Midwife*, 1.

43. By one estimate, Patty delivered nearly four thousand babies. See D. Smart, introduction to *Mormon Midwife*, 8.

44. Clayton, *Journal*, 326 (dated July 28, 1847); Greeley, *Overland Journey*, 236–37; Burton, *City of the Saints*, 218–21; Morgan, "Letters by Forty-Niners," 109 (letter by James E. Squire, July 1849). Estimates of the city's size between 1850 and 1860 ranged from about four to more than ten square miles. See Stansbury, *Expedition*, 128; Chandless, *Visit to Salt Lake*, 151; and Burton, *City of the Saints*, 219.

45. Powell, *Anthropology of the Numa*, 37–38, 39, 176. The streets were planned and named within three weeks of the settler-colonists' arrival in the valley, some three years before the city was formally incorporated. See Bullock, *Pioneer Camp*, 257–58 (dated August 16, 1847). In 1849, a fence surrounded the entire city. See Morgan, "Letters by Forty-Niners," 109, 110 (letters by J[ames] E. S[quire] and by an anonymous traveler, dated July 1849). Residents routinely built fences around their city lots. See, for example, Stout, *On the Mormon Frontier*, 350 (dated April 2, 1849); Sessions, *Mormon Midwife,* 146, 163, (dated May 6, 1850; March 27, 28, 1851).

46. Morgan, "Letters by Forty-Niners," 104, 109 (letters by A. P. Josselyn and by J[ames] E. S[quire], dated July 1849); B. Ferris, *Mormons at Home*, 111 (dated November 26, 1852). Cornelia (Mrs. B. G.) Ferris, who visited the city in 1852–1853, thought it a serious breach of etiquette when she was repeatedly "obliged to retreat back from these crossing places, and stand on one side for men to cross over." Male precedence was the accepted practice, as a visiting Englishman reported. See Burton, *City of the Saints*, 296.

47. Burton, *City of the Saints*, 219; Morgan, "Letters by Forty-Niners," 112 (letter by Beeson Townsend, dated August 1849).
48. "A Stranger in the Land of Gold," reprinted in the *Frontier Guardian*, January 9, 1850; reproduced in Journal History of the Church for the date July 8, 1849.
49. E. Snow, *Personal Writings,* 229 (dated June 19, 1848). The Mexican-American War (1846–1848) had ended a few months earlier.
50. Morgan, "Letters by Forty-Niners," 100, 101 (letters by John B. Hazlip and by C. H. M., dated July 1849).
51. E. Snow, *Personal Writings*, 229, 230 (dated June 19, August 16, 1848); Clayton, *Journal*, 342 (dated August 9, 1847); Bullock, *Pioneer Camp*, 254 (dated August 9, 1847); Burton, *City of the Saints*, 3.
52. Frémont, *Report*, 151; Alter, *Jim Bridger*, 59–60; Hafen, "Etienne Provost," 103. For a later exploring trip around the lake, see Stansbury, *Expedition*, 156–211 (dated April 3–20, 1850).
53. Morgan, "Letters by Forty-Niners," 100, 110–11 (letters by John B. Hazlip and an anonymous traveler, dated July 1849); Chandless, *Visit to Salt Lake*, 148–49.
54. Gunnison, *Mormons*, 20.
55. Morgan, "Letters by Forty-Niners," 100, 103, 109 (letters by John B. Hazlip, A. P. Josselyn, and J[ames] E. S[quire], dated July 1849).
56. Stansbury, *Expedition*, 128.
57. M. Snow, "From Nauvoo to Salt Lake," 554 (diary entry of Erastus Snow, dated August 26, 1847); Bullock, *Pioneer Camp*, 248 (dated August 4, 1847); Sessions, *Mormon Midwife*, 164 (dated April 11, 1851). See also Chandless, *Visit to Salt Lake*, 152.
58. B. Young, "Use and Abuse of Blessings," June 5, 1853, *Journal of Discourses,* 1:254.
59. B. Ferris, *Mormons at Home*, 94 (dated October 30, 1852). Elizabeth Cornelia Woodcock Ferris (1809–1903) and her husband Benjamin G. Ferris (1802–1891) arrived in October 1852, and left the city for California in May 1853.
60. B. Ferris, *Mormons at Home*, 113, 132 (dated November 26, and December 1852). On the importance of wild rabbits as food for early settler-colonists, see Cheney, *Plain but Wholesome*, 85.
61. B. Ferris, *Mormons at Home*, 191–93 (dated March 20, 1853). She encountered the hunter in City Creek Canyon.
62. E. Snow, *Personal Writings*, 31.
63. Gates, "Courtship of Kanosh," 23; Callaway, Janetski, and Stewart, "Ute," 346; Nickerson, "Some Data," 48; A. Smith, *Ethnography of the Northern Utes*, 82–83.
64. Powell, *Anthropology of the Numa*, 162, 175. Powell's comment about red signifying joy refers specifically to Southern Paiutes—who shared much

culturally and linguistically with neighboring Pahvant Utes—but the liking for red was widespread. On Puritan heritage and avoidance of the color red, see Arrington, *Brigham Young*, 335. On Eliza's clothing, see Gates, "Brigham Young as I Knew Him," 58, Susa Young Gates Papers, box 12; and Spencer, *Brigham Young at Home*, 82–83. See also a portrait photograph of Eliza: the frontispiece in E. Snow, *Personal Writings*.

65. Gates, "Courtship of Kanosh," 23, 28; "Funeral of a Lamanite," *Deseret News*, December 18, 1878; "A Rare Picture of the Old Days," *Millard County Chronicle*, November 6, 1930. See Stewart, "Culture Element Distributions," 278, on hairstyle. The phrase "a white and delightsome people" appears in the Book of Mormon (2 Nephi 30:6), first published in 1830. See also Chandless, *Visit to Salt Lake*, 165, who heard this phrase in 1855. The original wording was changed in the late twentieth century. In the 1981 edition of the Book of Mormon, the word "pure" was substituted for "white": "and many generations shall not pass away among them, save they shall be a pure and a delightsome people."

66. Spencer, *Brigham Young at Home*, 71; "Weight, size, etc. of Indians," August 2, 1852, Indians, 1852–1865, Brigham Young Office Files, box 74, folder 46. The man whom members of the Young family referred to as Black Isaac was Isaac James (1823–1891). Brigham Young employed him as a coachman for many years. See Spencer, *Brigham Young at Home*, 22; Turner, *Brigham Young*, 218, 228–29. The wife of Isaac James, Jane Manning James (1822–1908), commonly identified as Black Jane, was also called Aunt Jane. See Sessions, *Mormon Midwife*, 112 (dated May 8, 1848); and "Death of Jane Manning James," *Deseret News*, April 16, 1908. She and her husband were among the very few African-Americans who lived in Utah Territory in the nineteenth century.

67. Morgan, "Letters by Forty-Niners," 104 (letter by A. P. Josselyn, dated July 1849); "The 24th of July, 1850," *Deseret News*, July 27, 1850; "Continued," *Deseret News*, August 3, 1850.

68. "Celebrations, Continued: Fort Supply," *Deseret News*, August 13, 1856; Pulsipher, "Diaries," 56 (recorded between July 2 and August 3, 1856). The celebration that took place followed what had become a standard format. Pioneer Day, as it came to be known, remains an annual event and major state holiday in Utah.

69. "Celebration of the Twenty Fourth of July, 1856," *Deseret News*, July 30, 1856.

70. Adelia married Heber C. Kimball (1801–1868) and moved to the city in 1857, after the brief marriage to her second husband ended. See A. Kimball, "Memoirs," 14–17.

71. S. Kimball, "Our Pioneer Boys," 736–37; Powell, *Anthropology of the Numa*, 253. The 1910 federal census lists Dave Kimball as Dave Eagle, age 65. See U.S. Census, 1910, Iosepa, Skull Valley, Tooele County, Utah.

72. S. Kimball, "Our Pioneer Boys," 735–36; U.S. Census, 1860, Great Salt Lake City, Great Salt Lake County, Utah Territory (census returns for the Joseph Young and John Young households).

73. A. Kimball, "Memoirs," 23. In the 1860 census, Kate was listed as a member of the Heber C. Kimball household, and her age given as sixteen years old. See U.S. Census, 1860, Great Salt Lake City, Great Salt Lake County, Utah Territory.

74. "RAN AWAY," *Deseret News*, October 2, 1852.

75. Burton recorded *A Preamble and an Act for the Further Relief of Indian Slaves and Prisoners* (1852) in *City of the Saints*, 297–99. On Indian slavery and indenture, see Cannon and Kitchen, "Indenture and Adoption"; Cannon, "Adopted or Indentured"; and S. Jones, "'Redeeming' the Indian," 231, on slavery in the southwestern borderlands, where from 1700 to 1850 some three thousand captive Indians entered New Mexican society as slaves, "primarily through the artifice of 'ransom' by colonial purchasers."

76. According to staff members at the Research Center for the Utah State Archives and Utah State Historical Society, records of Indian indenture have never been found in the state archives. Whether the records are lost, were removed, or never existed, is unknown (personal communication, September 20, 2016).

77. E. Snow, *Personal Writings*, 31. Blackhawk tells the affecting story, recorded in the Spanish archives of New Mexico, of a Ute father who traced his captive daughter to Abiquiú, hundreds of miles south. After confronting many obstacles, he finally rescued her from domestic slavery and took her home. See Blackhawk, *Violence over the Land*, 113.

78. Emmitt, *Last War Trail*, 39–40; Wilkinson, *Fire on the Plateau*, 133, 145; Conetah, *History of the Northern Ute*, 67. Utah Territory included part of what is now western Colorado until 1861, when Colorado Territory was formed.

CHAPTER 5

1. Most of the events in this chapter took place between 1850 and 1856. On the early epidemics and mortality rates, see Stoffle, Jones, and Dobyns, "Direct European Immigrant Transmission."

2. On Walker's War, as settler-colonists called the 1853–1854 conflict, see Blackhawk, *Violence over the Land*, 244–46; Peterson, *Utah's Black Hawk War*, 63–69. A visitor saw the wall in spring 1854. See Carvalho, *Incidents of Travel*, 141–42; and also "City Wall," *Deseret News*, October 1, 1853.

3. In the early 1870s, Powell noted that some Utes attributed disease and deaths "to sorcery practiced by other Indians." See Powell, *Anthropology of the Numa*, 103. Linguistic evidence also suggests that individuals who used sorcery had the power to heal as well as to kill. See Powell, *Anthropology of the Numa*, 178. That is, they possessed "good medicine" as well as "bad

medicine." My interpretation of evidence about sorcery draws on an extensive body of research in anthropology, and on my own experience of ethnographic fieldwork elsewhere in Native America.

4. "Vision of Arapene on the night of the 4th of February 1855," Indians, 1850–1865, Brigham Young Office Files, box 74, folder 49. Chief Wákara died in late January 1855. See "Death of Indian Walker," *Deseret News*, February 8, 1855; and "Trip to Manti," *Deseret News*, February 22, 1855.

5. Sessions, *Mormon Midwife*, 107, 242 (dated January 30, 1848; February 15, 1857); E. Snow, *Personal Writings*, 212 (dated November 14, 1847); Journal History of the Church, February 15, 1857; Powell, *Anthropology of the Numa*, 51.

6. Rémy, *Journey to Great-Salt-Lake City*, 1:187, 192. This took place in 1855. The two guides, whom Rémy identified as Shoshone, had joined the travelers in what is present-day northern Nevada.

7. Hafen, "Louis Vasquez," 335; Alter, *Jim Bridger*, 264–65; Dodge, *Biographical Sketch*, 22. Vásquez opened the store in 1849, and apparently sold it in 1855. See Alter, *Jim Bridger*, 237, 264.

8. "Meeting of the Snakes and Utahs," *Deseret News*, September 12, 1855, September 19, 1855. Two chiefs, one known as "White Men's Son," and the other as "Ka-tat-o, Chief of the northern Snakes," led the Shoshones.

9. Rémy, *Journey to Great-Salt-Lake City*, 2:291. Rémy apparently heard Shoshones singing at their campsite near a hotel at Union Square, west of Temple Square. Some sixty Shoshones stayed in the city until they met with a second group of Utahs, thirty warriors led by Chief Arapeen, for a peace treaty ceremony. See "Meeting of the Snakes and Utahs," *Deseret News*, September 19, 1855.

10. A letter attributed to an unidentified wife of Brigham Young, and written in late December 1855, reported that "Mary Emily" and "Caroline" had "had the Measels but are better." See Unidentified wife to Brigham Young, December 28, 1855, Brigham Young Office Files, box 44, folder 23. A week or two later, Zina wrote to Emeline, who had accompanied their husband to the annual legislative assembly in Fillmore, the short-lived capital of Utah Territory. Zina told her that Sally and the children had had measles. See Zina D. Huntington [Young] to Emeline Free [Young], "Wednesday" [ca. January 9, 1856], Brigham Young Office Files, box 44, folder 17.

11. Gates, "Brigham Young as I Knew Him," 26, Susa Young Gates Papers, box 12; Gates, *Life Story*, 327; Bradley and Woodward, *Four Zinas*, 215; Spencer, *Brigham Young at Home*, 77. Asafetida is a gummy resin obtained from the roots of some plants of the genus *Ferula*. It was used in medicine in various ways, including as a carminative and antispasmodic. Children wore asafetida bags during epidemics of measles, mainly as a protective measure, but also because of presumed healing properties. See Gates, *Life Story*, 327. Zina said that she and Clara "upheld there hands continually." See Zina D.

Huntington [Young] to Emeline Free [Young], "Wednesday" [ca. January 9, 1856], Brigham Young Office Files, box 44, folder 17. On the new house, known as the Lion House, see Chapter Six.

12. On healing techniques and medicinal plants presumably known to Sally, see Chamberlin, "Some Plant Names"; Powell, *Anthropology of the Numa*, 57, 59, 179; and Conetah, *History of the Northern Ute*, 8. On Zina's skill as a healer and midwife, see Gates, *Life Story*, 327; Spencer, *Brigham Young at Home*, 77; and Bradley and Woodward, *Four Zinas*, 231–34. Zina reported in a letter, "it has been cold for awhile but we have all been comfortable." See Zina D. Huntington [Young] to Emeline Free [Young], "Wednesday" [ca. January 9, 1856], Brigham Young Office Files, box 44, folder 17.

13. Lucy Decker [Young] to Brigham Young, January 9, 1856, Brigham Young Office Files, box 44, folder 16; Zina D. Huntington [Young] to Emeline Free [Young], "Wednesday" [ca. January 9, 1856], Brigham Young Office Files, box 44, folder 17. The men were called in to administer to the sick by anointing them with oil, and praying for them.

14. Conetah, *History of the Northern Ute*, 8; Lucy Decker [Young] to Brigham Young, January 9, 1856, Brigham Young Office Files, box 44, folder 16. Among Numic-speaking Indians, shamans were as likely to be women as men. See Callaway, Janetski, and Stewart, "Ute," 354. In a letter Robert Campbell wrote to Brigham Young and associates (dated December 25, 1849), he mentioned an Indian guide who grew so sick that "he was compelled to stay with some lake Utes" whose medicine woman could cure him. See Smart and Smart, *Over the Rim*, 77.

15. Zina D. Huntington [Young] to Emeline Free [Young], "Wednesday" [ca. January 9, 1856], Brigham Young Office Files, box 44, folder 17; Lucy Decker [Young] to Brigham Young, January 9, 1856, Brigham Young Office Files, box 44, folder 16. Clara's baby son, Jedediah Grant Young, was buried in the Salt Lake City Cemetery. The headstone on his grave gives his date of death as January 11, 1856, just ten days before his first birthday.

16. Over the years, Sally was exposed to many of the settlers' diseases, from measles and whooping cough to chickenpox and mumps. See Gates, *Life Story*, 327. From a purely medical perspective, Sally's surviving a bout of measles could be attributed to individual resilience, and an immune system strengthened by exposure to new pathogens during the previous nine years; to Zina's attentive and skillful care as a nurse; to the advantages of recuperating in a warm, sheltered place; to a placebo effect; or to all of those. It is also possible that Sally had some European ancestry, and thus some inherited immunity to European diseases. According to Spanish explorers who in the late eighteenth century met some western Utes (presumed to be Pahvant Utes), they had Spanish facial features, and the men wore beards. See Steward, *Basin-Plateau*, 227.

17. Gates, *Life Story*, 327; Gates, "From Impulsive Girl," 274. On the many deaths from measles among Utes and other Numic Indians in 1849 through

spring 1850, see Stoffle, Jones, and Dobyns, "Direct European Immigrant Transmission," 183, 191, 192. They estimate that 25 percent of the Numic population died in that epidemic of measles, a mortality rate only eclipsed by an epidemic of mumps in 1854–1855. It does not appear that measles was recorded as an important cause of mortality among Mormons on the overland trail between 1847 and 1868. See Bashore and Tolley, "Mortality on the Mormon Trail," 122. In Salt Lake Valley in the first years of settlement, from 1847 through 1850, one death was attributed to measles. See "Valley Journal," *Deseret News*, March 8, 1851.

18. For Robert Campbell's journal entry (dated December 7, 1849) and "Pratt's Report to the Legislative Council" (dated February 5, 1850), see Smart and Smart, *Over the Rim*, 42, 175. See also Smart and Smart, *Over the Rim*, 40–45, for the journal entries of Parley P. Pratt's fellow explorers for that period.

19. Powell thought that the main curing techniques were healing ceremonies, such as the one he witnessed among White River Utes (see Chapter Nine), and "sweating and steaming," as he called it. See Powell, *Anthropology of the Numa*, 53, 57. He seems not to have recorded their deep knowledge of wild plants with medicinal qualities. See, for example, Chamberlin, "Some Plant Names."

20. "Pratt's Report to the Legislative Council" (dated February 5, 1850), in Smart and Smart, *Over the Rim*, 175. Dimick Huntington claimed that Arapeen had burned his wife and had killed a Paiute child whom the settler-colonists would not buy. See D. Huntington, *Vocabulary of the Utah*, 28–29. See also D. Jones, *Forty Years*, 53. These incidents, if true, may have occurred after the measles epidemic of 1849–1850, when settlers had greater contact with him.

21. Z. Young, "'A Weary Traveler,'" 118 (dated March 13, 1850).

22. Journal History of the Church, June 13, 1849 (summary of Brigham Young's meeting with "Walker, the Utah Chief, and twelve of his tribe").

23. Powell, *Anthropology of the Numa*, 103; Bullock, *Pioneer Camp*, 238 (dated July 26, 1847); E. Snow, *Personal Writings*, 206 (dated October 6, 1847); Sessions, *Mormon Midwife*, 99–100 (dated September 27, 1847).

24. Cyrena Dustin Merrill (1817–1907), "Autobiography"; U.S. Census, 1850, Great Salt Lake City, Great Salt Lake County, Utah Territory. Cyrena Merrill's baby son, born in mid-February 1850, was three weeks old when the family moved to the new house. The deaths at Warm Springs occurred soon after that, in mid-March 1850.

25. Nebeker, "Early Justice," 2; Kerns, *Journeys West*, 366–67n48. In 1999, historical markers were placed at the site, memorializing the deaths of the two chiefs and their people in March 1850 (personal observation at site, Warm Springs Park, Salt Lake City, Utah, August 1, 2008). The markers were later removed, without public explanation, while two markers commemorating early explorers and a historic trail remained in place. The small natural pool

was no longer in evidence, having been filled in (personal observation at site, Warm Springs Park, Salt Lake City, Utah, June 1l, 2016).

26. Spencer, *Brigham Young at Home*, 21–23; Turner, *Brigham Young*, 310. The Warm Springs Bath House was reported to be near completion in late September 1850. See "Greeting," *Deseret News*, September 28, 1850. It was dedicated in November 1850. See Gates, *Life Story*, 262. Cornelia Ferris reported bathing there a few years later, but evidently did not hear about deaths at the site. See B. Ferris, *Mormons at Home*, 118–20 (dated November 26, 1853). Likewise, others who visited Warm Springs after 1850 apparently heard nothing. The springs drew tourists and local visitors until the 1940s according to Farmer, *On Zion's Mount*, 106–7, 112–13.

27. Heywood, *Not by Bread Alone*, 90 (dated February 20, 1853); E. Kane, *Twelve Mormon Homes*, 37–38. The settlement near Salt Creek soon took the name Nephi. On Baptiste's renown as a medicine man, see E. Kane, *Twelve Mormon Homes*, 38–41. He had presumably been dead for years, or had otherwise disappeared, when Elizabeth Kane heard stories about him from settler-colonists in the city and elsewhere. He was often identified as a chief, not only as a medicine man. See, for example, Journal History of the Church, May 2, 1853, March 2, 1856; and Gottfredson, *Indian Depredations*, 21. See also W. Ferris, *Life in the Rocky Mountains*, 237. He observed a Ute war dance in the 1830s.

28. Journal History of the Church, May 11, May 12, 1854 (record of Brigham Young's meeting with Chief Wákara at his camp); Heywood, *Not by Bread Alone*, 102 (dated June 15, 1854). The two promised houses do not seem to have been built.

29. On the grasshoppers, drought, and famine, see Stout, *On the Mormon Frontier*, 555 (dated May 20, 1855). On herding grounds, see Stout, *On the Mormon Frontier*, 572 (dated December 17, 1855). Stout recorded many such petitions for herding grounds between 1855 and 1859. On winter conditions, see Woodruff, *Journal*, 4:398, 400 (dated February 2, 10, 1856).

30. The attack took place in Cedar Valley, west of Utah Lake. See "Disturbance with Indians," *Deseret News*, February 27, March 5, 1856; "The Indian Disturbance," *Deseret News*, March 12, 1856; "News," *Deseret News*, March 19, 1856; and Clark, "Auto-Biography." On Chief Tintic and the conflict that settlers came to call the Tintic War, see also Peterson, *Utah's Black Hawk War*, 72–74; and R. Walker, "Tintic War."

31. "Disturbance with Indians," *Deseret News*, March 5, 1856; Journal History of the Church, March 2, 1856 (letter from George A. Smith to the editor of *The Mormon*, a short-lived New York newspaper). The misspelled variants of Baptiste's name reflect the silent *p* in the French pronunciation.

32. "Disturbance with Indians," *Deseret News*, March 5, 1856; "Correspondence: Payson," *Deseret News*, April 16, 1856.

33. Between 1847 and 1856, untold numbers of Numic Indians died during epidemics of eight diseases in Utah Territory: measles, cholera, malaria,

tuberculosis, scarlet fever, whooping cough, typhoid, and mumps. Small-pox reached the city with travelers in 1856. See "Small Pox," *Deseret News*, August 13, 1856. Stoffle, Jones, and Dobyns estimate that in 1856 the surviving Numic population constituted less than 15 percent of that in 1845, before settlement. Simms mentions earlier epidemics in the Southwest. See Stoffle, Jones, and Dobyns, "Direct European Immigrant Transmission," 181; and Simms, *Ancient Peoples*, 268. In 1860, Brigham Young commented that "the Indians are declining in numbers," but without attributing this to epidemics. See Brigham Young Office Journal, entry dated October 5, 1860, Brigham Young Office Files, box 72, folder 5.

My inference, that Sally's mother and sisters had died or otherwise disappeared by 1856, is based on the weight of compelling circumstantial evidence: the severity of the epidemics and high mortality rate in the decade after settlement; Sally's apparent lack of interest by the mid-1850s in returning to her old home; and her possible contact in August 1856, and her known contact later, with a chief who had close knowledge of the people who had survived the epidemics and episodes of violence, or had not. See D. B. Huntington to Brigham Young, August 21, 1856, Brigham Young Office Files, box 24, folder 22. At some point, the chief presumably told Sally, or Brigham Young, about the fate of her family. On the number of epidemics, see Stoffle, Jones, and Dobyns, "Direct European Immigrant Transmission," 192.

34. Woodruff, *Journal*, 4:425 (dated June 28, 1856). Arapeen told Brigham Young that Baptiste wanted peace in a letter dictated in April 1856, some two months after Baptiste was shot. See R. Walker, "Tintic War," 66–67.

CHAPTER 6

1. J. Young, *Memoirs*, 61. Most of the events in this chapter took place between the mid-1850s and mid-1860s. The Lion House, according to later accounts, was completed in 1856. See Gates, *Life Story*, 322; and Arrington, *Brigham Young*, 170. But a visitor who saw the house in late 1855 implied that it was occupied at that time. See Chandless, *Visit to Salt Lake*, 152.

2. I draw on six books written by five women as primary sources on daily life at the Lion House. Each has certain drawbacks and each offers a somewhat different perspective, but they agree on many of the factual details about the house and the daily routine. Four of the books, written by an outsider and by two dissidents, contain negative commentary on polygamy. Some of that commentary qualifies as anti-Mormon discourse, focusing on the practice of polygamy to the near exclusion of other cultural practices, and questioning moral character on the basis of that single practice. The first book was written by Catharine V. Waite, who lived in Salt Lake City for a few years in the early 1860s. By necessity, she resorted to the firsthand observations of unnamed sources, which were privately reported to her. Two women, Fanny Stenhouse and Ann Eliza Webb [Young], who spent time in

the house and knew the wives well, but who grew disaffected with polygamy, also published books. Finally, two daughters of Brigham Young later wrote affectionate and retrospective insider accounts. Susa Young Gates wrote extensively about growing up in the Lion House in the late 1850s and 1860s. She moved away from the house and the city in 1870 when she was fourteen (see note 54 below). Her writings include published articles, a book, and unpublished manuscripts, with generally positive commentary on polygamy in the Brigham Young family. Her paternal half-sister Clarissa Young Spencer recalled life next door at the Beehive House in the 1860s and 1870s.

The Lion House and the Beehive House still stand; and my observations at the two houses, which I visited between 2010 and 2017, also inform this chapter. The stone lion is still in place at the Lion House; and today, as in the past, the meaning remains somewhat contested. A visitor to the city in 1860 noted that Brigham Young was deemed a prophet and "Lion of the Lord" by his followers. Indeed, references to "Brigham Young, Lion of the Lord" appeared in the local newspaper. See Burton, *City of the Saints,* 291, 295; and "Valley Journal," *Deseret News,* March 8, 1851. Another visitor saw the statuary as a warning that the Lion House had a "resting, but watchful," guard. See Waite, *Mormon Prophet,* 180. Young's daughter Susa thought that the stone lion stood for "the Lion of the Tribe of Judah." See Gates, *Life Story,* 325.

3. On Brigham Young's physical appearance and his forceful way of speaking, see Gates, "How Brigham Young," 31; and Arrington, *Brigham Young,* 406.

4. Powell, *Anthropology of the Numa,* 172; A. Smith, *Ethnography of the Northern Utes,* 59; Arrington, "Taming the Turbulent Sevier," 396. Burton listed mountain lions, or cougars, in first place among the "principal carnivores" of the region. See Burton, *City of the Saints,* 339.

5. Waite, *Mormon Prophet,* 180–86; Gates, "Brigham Young and His Wives," Susa Young Gates Papers, box 12; Gates, *Life Story,* 326; Bradley and Woodward, *Four Zinas,* 202. Emeline's name is usually spelled Emmeline in twentieth-century works. I have retained the original spelling, which appears on the headstone of her grave, in family records of the time (in Brigham Young Office Files), and in most nineteenth-century published works.

6. Burton, *City of the Saints,* 296; Greeley, *Overland Journey,* 205. Burton estimated Brigham Young's worth at about $250,000: an enormous sum for that time and place, and equivalent to nearly $7 million today. A year earlier, Brigham Young had estimated his worth at $300,000 dollars. See Woodruff, *Journal,* 5:364 (dated July 13, 1859).

7. Waite, *Mormon Prophet,* 177; Greeley, *Overland Journey,* 206. A standard city lot was one and a quarter acres in size. See Bullock, *Pioneer Camp,* 242 (dated July 28, 1847); and Burton, *City of the Saints,* 266.

Among hunter-gatherers, as anthropologists have documented, leaders have generally acted as first among equals, leading by example and persuasion. They are not authoritarian rulers who can compel others to do as they wish.

Brigham Young served as territorial governor until 1858. Thereafter, until his death in 1877, he still wielded enormous influence and power as president of a church that claimed most of the Utah settlers, and some beyond its borders, as loyal and obedient members. See Arrington, *Brigham Young*; and Turner, *Brigham Young*.

8. A list of family members, as well as census data for the Brigham Young family, corroborate retrospective estimates of about fifty residents in the Lion House during the late 1850s and the 1860s. See Arrington, *Brigham Young*, 420–21; census return for the Brigham Young household, U.S. Census, 1860, Great Salt Lake City, Great Salt Lake County, Utah Territory; Gates, "Brigham Young as I Knew Him," 44, Susa Young Gates Papers, box 12; and Gates, *Life Story*, 329.

9. "B. Young's Testimony, U.S. v. Pedro Leon," January 11, 1852, Papers Relating to Mexican Traders, 1851–1853, Brigham Young Office Files, box 47, folder 36; Gates, "Brigham Young as I Knew Him," 26, Susa Young Gates Papers, box 12; Spencer, *Brigham Young at Home*, 75. Lucy's youngest daughter Clarissa, who was Clara's niece and namesake, said that, among others, Clara "had under her protection at the Lion House . . . [the] Indian girl whom they called Sally." See Spencer, *Brigham Young at Home*, 75. Clara did not construe her relationship with Sally as sisterly (see Chapter Ten).

10. Greeley saw the estate wall in July 1859. It was apparently constructed from cobblestones set in clay mortar, and was a costly construction at "sixty dollars a rod." A rod is about sixteen feet in length. A visitor did not report seeing the wall four years earlier, in late 1855, but a portion had been constructed by September 1856. See Greeley, *Overland Journey*, 237; Chandless, *Visit to Salt Lake*; and Woodruff, *Journal*, 4:448 (dated September 13, 1856). In 1860, guards reportedly stood at the gate to protect Brigham Young in those volatile, sometimes violent times. See Burton, *City of the Saints*, 276.

11. E. Kane, *Twelve Mormon Homes*, 44; Spencer, *Brigham Young at Home*, 75, 122. Brigham Young reportedly had more than fifty children, most of them born after 1847, the year when Sally arrived in the valley as a captive. See Arrington, *Brigham Young*, 420–21. Those children spent many, and in some cases all, of their childhood years at the Lion House while Sally lived there.

12. On guests, see Gates, "Brigham Young as I Knew Him," 38–39, Susa Young Gates Papers, box 12; Gates, *Life Story*, 331; Waite, *Mormon Prophet*, 181. As documented by anthropologists, bands of hunter-gatherers typically number from thirty people to as many as a hundred. They often disperse in

small family groups in some seasons, and coalesce in other seasons, depending on food availability.

13. William Chandless (1829–1896) arrived in the city in early November
    1855, and departed two months later, in early January 1856. He was a highly
    educated man, and quotations in Greek, French, and Italian are sprinkled
    in the text of his book. Having worked as a teamster on his trip west,
    he identified himself as a working man to people he met at his destination.
    See Chandless, *Visit to Salt Lake*, iv, 130, 266. He later explored rivers of the
    Amazon Basin and wrote *Ascent of the River Purus*, published by the Royal
    Geographical Society of London in 1866.

14. The late 1850s, when the estate wall was built, was a time of escalating con-
    flict with the federal government. See Arrington, *Brigham Young*, 250–81;
    and Turner, *Brigham Young*, 265–300. The stated reason for building the
    wall, as explained seventy years later by a daughter who had not yet been
    born when the wall went up, was primarily protection from other threats:
    namely, floods and Indians. See Spencer, *Brigham Young at Home*, 61.
    No Indian attacks on the Lion House, Beehive House, or others dwellings
    in the city seem to have been recorded.

15. Visitors and settler-colonists reported hearing of acts of violence, some
    attributed to Indians. See, among others, Burton, *City of the Saints*, 411;
    Chandless, *Visit to Salt Lake*, 195, 240; Greeley, *Overland Journey*, 224–28;
    Waite, *Mormon Prophet*, 24–25, 37, Stenhouse, *"Tell It All,"* 169, 319;
    A. Young, *Wife No. 19*, 160–61, 196–98, 229–60, 268–79. See also Farmer,
    On Zion's Mount, 84–85. Sally no doubt heard about all of the acts of vio-
    lence attributed, and misattributed, to Indians during this period.

16. At least one visitor expressed some doubt about "sham Indians." See
    Chandless, *Visit to Salt Lake*, 240. But he visited the city two years
    before the most notorious instance in which some settlers donned Indian
    clothing: the 1857 massacre of overland travelers at Mountain Meadows.
    Throughout the late nineteenth and much of the twentieth century,
    it was commonplace to read that "Indians" were the sole or main perpe-
    trators of the massacre, which was allegedly carried out in revenge for acts
    against Pahvant Utes committed by overland travelers. See, for example,
    Arrington, *Brigham Young*, 258–59; and Gates, *Life Story*, 142–45. In 1859,
    the federally appointed Indian agent reported that he had found no
    evidence that any Pahvant Utes were present at the massacre, which an
    eyewitness also confirmed years later. See Bagley, *Blood of the Prophets*, 129.
    For recent historical scholarship on the massacre, including the question
    of Southern Paiute participation, see Bagley, *Blood of the Prophets*; Den-
    ton, *American Massacre*; and Walker, Turley Jr., and Leonard, *Massacre at
    Mountain Meadows*. Shannon A. Novak, a forensic anthropologist who has
    examined the bones of people who died at Mountain Meadows, did not
    find evidence of Southern Paiute involvement in the massacre. This was

based on the pattern of skeletal trauma and other factors. See Novak, *House of Mourning*, 159–74. Martha C. Knack, a cultural anthropologist, presents ethnographic evidence that "sole and autonomous Paiute responsibility" for the massacre is "unlikely." See Knack, *Boundaries Between*, 79–80. For Southern Paiute oral tradition, which denies direct involvement, see Tom and Holt, "Paiute Tribe of Utah," 131–39; and Martineau, *Southern Paiutes*, 62. Lila Carter, a member of the Las Vegas tribe of Southern Paiutes has said, "I never heard any stories about Paiute warriors. Only how the whites would kill their own people and blame the Indians for it. . . . They'd dress up like the Indians with the feather up and all that. We didn't really wear those feathers." See Hebner, *Southern Paiutes,* 153.

17. This particular version of the Mountain Meadows massacre comes from a letter written by George A. Smith, one of Brigham Young's closest associates. See Journal History of the Church, April 13, 1859; and J. Brooks, *Mountain Meadows Massacre*, 248–51.

18. On violence in the city attributed to (sham) "Indians," see, for example, a diary entry of Hosea Stout, a settler-colonist who practiced law and knew local officials well. He recorded a chilling instance in just one sentence, and in language that suggests close knowledge: "This evening several persons disguised as Indians entered Henry Jones' house and dragged him out of bed with a whore and castrated him by a square & close amputation." See Stout, *On the Mormon Frontier*, 653 (dated February 27, 1858). Stout recorded many murders and other violent acts in his diary in the 1850s, some of which were evidently not prosecuted. Census records of the time list more than one man named Henry Jones, making it difficult to identify him further. On acts of violence in the city, see Moorman, *Camp Floyd*, 231–46. On the "culture of violence," see Quinn, *Mormon Hierarchy*, 241–61.

19. Peter Gottfredson (1846–1934) compiled many such narratives, mostly about events that took place between the late 1840s and the early 1870s. See Gottfredson, *Indian Depredations*. His book includes fewer accounts of attacks on Indians. Many of the stories about attacks by so-called wild Indians on colonizing settlers qualify as wild/civilized narratives, in which the civilized triumphs over the wild, sooner or later.

20. Whitney, among others, recounts this tale. See Whitney, *History of Utah*, 66. The event apparently took place sometime in 1858 or 1859, and perhaps on a Sunday evening. Church services were held on Sunday morning, afternoon, and evening during that time, and Clara did not attend church. See Chandless, *Visit to Salt Lake*, 205–09; and Gates, "Brigham Young as I Knew Him," 26, Susa Young Gates Papers, box 12. Details of the story suggest that the intruder was a disaffected settler.

21. Powell, *Anthropology of the Numa*, 49; A. Smith, *Ethnography of the Northern Utes*, 47. The severe famine of 1855–1856 led to food rationing for settler-colonists, including those of means. In spring 1856, even Brigham

Young is said to have rationed bread for his family. See Rémy, *Journey to Great-Salt-Lake City*, 1:467. On the flour taken from a bakery, see Woodruff, *Journal*, 4:410 (dated April 13, 1856).

22. U.S. Army Corps of Topographical Engineers, *Map of the Great Salt Lake*; Powell, *Anthropology of the Numa*, 253. The territorial legislature granted Brigham Young the canyon in 1850 for a fee of five hundred dollars. See Stout, *On the Mormon Frontier*, 384 (dated December 3, 1850).

23. Gates, *Life Story*, 323–25; Spencer, *Brigham Young at Home*, 23–29; Arrington, *Brigham Young*, 333. Accounts for the family store show that Sally and other women servants obtained some goods there. Bergamot oil and Epsom salts had medicinal purposes. Unusually, Sally once received eleven yards of woolen fabric, presumably for a dress. See Family store daybook, July 1862–July 1863, entry dated July 16, 1862, Brigham Young Office Files, box 120, folder 4; Family store daybook, July 1863, entry dated July 11, 1863, Brigham Young Office Files, box 120, folder 5; and Family store ledger, October 1865–September 1966, Brigham Young Office Files, box 122, folder 1. Each wife had a separate account, and some wives drew heavily on the stock of goods.

24. "Journal of the travels of President Brigham Young and company from Great Salt Lake City, Utah Territory to Fort Limhi in Oregon Territory," dated April 27–May 26, 1857, Brigham Young Office Files, box 73, folder 13; "Excursion to Fort Limhi," *Deseret News*, June 10, 1857. On the fort and mission, see also Bigler, *Fort Limhi*, 135–54, 318–19, 331–33; and Gottfredson, *Indian Depredations*, 89–100. The fort stood in present-day Idaho, near a tributary of the Salmon River. John W. Powell (1836–1879), not to be confused with John Wesley Powell (Chapter Nine), was reportedly born in Loudon County, Virginia. I have not found evidence that the Indian wives of men at Fort Limhi remained with them after the raid.

25. Chandless, *Visit to Salt Lake*, 152.

26. Burton, *City of the Saints*, 325; U.S. Census, 1860, Great Salt Lake City, Great Salt Lake County, Utah Territory; Arrington, *Brigham Young*, 420–21. Susan, or Susannah, Sniveley (1815–1892) was the Virginian. A later census taker did use the term "Domestic Servant" for Sally and her fellow workers. See census return for the Brigham Young household in U.S. Census, 1870, Salt Lake City, Salt Lake County, Utah Territory.

27. Richard F. Burton (1821–1890) posed as a physician from India and a Muslim in order to gain entry to forbidden places. See Brodie, introduction to *City of the Saints*, xiii. The census taker recorded the names of the occupants of the Lion House in mid-October 1860. Burton arrived in the city in late August 1860. See Burton, *City of the Saints*, 235, 244. On his translation of the Arabian Nights tales, see Brodie, introduction to *City of the Saints*, xxxiii–xxxiv; Burton, translator's foreword to *Book of a Thousand Nights and a Night*, vii–xxi.

28. Burton, *City of the Saints*, 25, 137–40, 247, 391–92, 536.
29. Burton, *City of the Saints*, 247, 394. Burton lodged at the Salt Lake House on Main Street, which also served briefly as a Pony Express Station.
30. Burton, *City of the Saints*, 402, 420.
31. Burton, *City of the Saints*, 370, 402; Powell, *Anthropology of the Numa*, 173; U.S. Army Corps of Topographical Engineers, *Map of the Great Salt Lake*. Utes called the creek in Big Cottonwood Canyon by the name We-en-de-quint, or so the name was recorded on an early map. See U.S. Army Corps of Topographical Engineers, *Map of the Great Salt Lake*. Cottonwood trees were *so'-wip*. The word recorded as de-quint was likely *nu-kwint,* the Ute word for creek. Some of the new English names were recorded within a month of the arrival of the first colonizing settlers. See Bullock, *Pioneer Camp*, 263–64 (dated August 22, 1847).
32. Burton, *City of the Saints*, 420.
33. Burton, *City of the Saints*, 297–99. Burton's 1860 visit came just months before the Civil War began, and five years before passage of the Thirteenth Amendment to the U.S. Constitution, which made slavery illegal throughout the United States. The 1860 census lists Indian children living with prominent families by the name of Kimball, Pratt, Woodruff, and Young, among others. See U.S. Census, 1860, Great Salt Lake City, Great Salt Lake County, Utah Territory. Parley P. Pratt was no longer alive, but the little girl he had named Abish and given to one of his plural wives still lived with her at the time of the 1860 federal census. Her name was recorded as Abiah, and her age as eight. On Abish, see Givens and Grow, *Parley P. Pratt*, 343–44.
34. Burton, *City of the Saints*, 267–68; Chandless, *Visit to Salt Lake*, 12.
35. Burton, *City of the Saints*, 296, 301; Brigham Young Office Journal, entry dated August 31, 1860, Brigham Young Office Files, box 72, folder 5; Woodruff, *Journal,* 5:488–89 (dated August 31, 1860).
36. Brodie, introduction to *City of the Saints*, xii.
37. Burton, *City of the Saints*, 327–28. By 1856, homemade wine was already being produced in the territory. On the beehives and the various workshops on the estate, see Arrington, *Brigham Young*, 333.
38. Burton, *City of the Saints*, 254n28, 272, 278, 302, 508; Chandless, *Visit to Salt Lake*, 192, 241, 260; Z. Young, "'A Weary Traveler,'" 95 (dated December 26, 1848). See also Bradley and Woodward, *Four Zinas*, 182. Burton did meet wives of federal officials, but unlike Fanny Stenhouse they were outsiders. Chandless recorded hearing men "argue the physical and mental inferiority of the female sex" in the presence of women.
39. Rémy, *Journey to Great-Salt-Lake City*, 2:290.
40. Woodruff, *Journal,* 5:359 (dated July 13, 1859). Horace Greeley (1811–1872) visited the city in July 1859, a year before Burton arrived. The interview, published in the *New York Tribune*, appeared in a slightly abridged form in

his book. See Greeley, *Overland Journey*, 209–216. Woodruff was present for the interview, and recorded questions and answers that in some cases contrast with Greeley's. See Woodruff, *Journal*, 5:359–67 (dated July 13, 1859).

41. Woodruff, *Journal*, 5:217–18.

42. Twain, *Roughing It*, 97. The meeting of "Mr. Clements," or Orion Clemens, and his brother Samuel Clemens (1835–1910), with Brigham Young and his associates took place in August 1861. See Brigham Young Office Journal, 1858–1862, 1863, entry dated August 7, 1861, Brigham Young Office Files, box 72, folder 5.

43. Twain, "Memoranda," 112–13. On family stories of Indian attacks told by Twain's mother, and on his manner of speaking and appearance, see Powers, *Mark Twain*, 23–24, 127, 147, 169. The villainous character Injun Joe appeared in two of Twain's most famous novels, *Adventures of Tom Sawyer* and *Adventures of Huckleberry Finn*. Twain expressed his views satirically, and venomously, in the short essay, "The Noble Red Man," which mocked the characterizations in James Fenimore Cooper's very successful novels.

44. Waite, *Mormon Prophet*, 187; Stenhouse, *Exposé of Polygamy*, 195; Gates, *Life Story*, 348; Spencer, *Brigham Young at Home*, 65. In 1860, Burton was told that "not even the wives of the Prophet" (Brigham Young) were "allowed to live in idleness." See Burton, *City of the Saints*, 302. They did, however, have the benefit of help from servants.

45. Gates, "Brigham Young as I Knew Him," 44, Susa Young Gates Papers, box 12; Gates, *Life Story*, 343; Spencer, *Brigham Young at Home*, 80.

46. Gates, "Brigham Young as I Knew Him," 42, Susa Young Gates Papers, box 12; Spencer, *Brigham Young at Home*, 27. The number of Clara's and Emeline's young children, as of about 1862 when Waite lived in the city, comes from a list of Brigham Young family members. See Arrington, *Brigham Young*, 420–21. Waite's floor plan of the house shows a room marked "E's servant's room" across the hall from the room for Emeline's children. See Waite, *Mormon Prophet*, 181. Clara likely always had assistance with laundering, whether from Sally or someone else. According to records of the family store, even when most her children were grown and she no longer lived at the Lion House, she still had assistance, and reimbursed the laundress with provisions.

47. Waite, *Mormon Prophet*, 181, 186, 207; Spencer, *Brigham Young at Home*, 28.

48. Waite, *Mormon Prophet*, 181. Fanny, who visited the Lion House, knew all of the wives, including Eliza. See Stenhouse, *"Tell It All,"* 275, 430–31.

49. Waite, *Mormon Prophet*, 180–81; Gates, *Life Story*, 324; Spencer, *Brigham Young at Home*, 24, 26. Details about the occupants of rooms on the second floor vary because of changes over the years. Waite's floor plan shows servants' quarters upstairs.

50. Waite, *Mormon Prophet*, 185–86, 198, 203; A. Young, *Wife No. 19*, 502, 513; Gates, "From Impulsive Girl," 274.
51. Waite, *Mormon Prophet*, 181.
52. This account of the Lion House is confined to the years from 1856 to the mid-1860s. Seven of the wives lived in suites on the main floor, and others lived in bedrooms upstairs. See Waite, *Mormon Prophet*, 181. Clara, Lucy, and Emeline had more than the usual space, but also more than the usual number of young children in their care. Gates, recalling the house later in the 1860s, gave a slightly different account because some of the women had moved into other houses by that time. See Gates, "Brigham Young as I Knew Him," 14, Susa Young Gates Papers, box 12; Gates, *Life Story*, 350–52; and Spencer, *Brigham Young at Home*, 24.
53. Waite, *Mormon Prophet*, 182.
54. Waite, *Mormon Prophet*, 182–83. Lucy B.'s youngest daughter, Mabel, told Alice Morrey Bailey, probably in the 1930s, that Sally lived with Clara. See Bailey, "What Is the Truth," 6, Alice Morrey Bailey Papers, box 33, folder 1. Mabel, who was born in 1863, recalled the mid-to-late 1860s at the Lion House, when she lived in a suite next to Clara's, and some period of the 1870s when she returned as a visitor. In 1870, when she was seven years old, she moved away from the city with her mother and her fourteen-year-old sister Susa. See Gates, *Life Story*, 352. Mabel returned briefly in 1872 when she was nine. See E. Kane, *Twelve Mormon Homes*, 6.

    The oil portrait of Clara's husband may have been one of two that the artist Solomon N. Carvalho (1815–1897) reportedly painted in 1854. See Carvalho, *Incidents of Travel*, 181.
55. Waite, *Mormon Prophet*, 182–83; Gates, "Brigham Young and His Wives," 7, Susa Young Gates Papers, box 12; Gates, "My Recollections," [fragment], 1, Susa Young Gates Papers, box 12; Arrington, *Brigham Young*, 397. According to May, "the early church disapproved of novels." See May, "Mormons," 58. On Brigham Young's "steadfast opposition" to novel reading, see Cracroft, "'Cows to Milk.'" The highly popular novels of Charles Dickens drew his explicit disapproval. Other well-known people of that time also recommended against allowing children to read fiction—including even Harriet Beecher Stowe, whose novel *Uncle Tom's Cabin* reputedly outsold any other book in the nineteenth century except the Bible. See Beecher and Stowe, *American Woman's Home*, 294.
56. Spencer, *Brigham Young at Home*, 50, 123; Gates, *Life Story*, 326.
57. Spencer, *Brigham Young at Home*, 50. Anthropologist Mary Douglas argues that "dirt is essentially disorder": in cleaning and organizing, "we ... are positively re-ordering our environment, making it conform to an idea." See Douglas, *Purity and Danger*, 2. I want to suggest that, in the context of American civilization, past and present, for soil ("dirt") from outdoors, or for a wild (and "dirty") living thing, to enter a house is especially

disturbing. Cleaning the domesticated space of a house requires ridding it of anything wild. Nearly anything from the wild outside, which remains untransformed by purposeful human action, is seen as out of place in civilized, controlled indoor space.

58. On sitting "in the dirt," see, for example, B. Young, "Gathering the Saints," April 9, 1871, *Journal of Discourses*, 14:87.

CHAPTER 7

1. Most of the events in this chapter took place between 1856 and 1876.
2. Gates, *Life Story*, 329.
3. Powell, *Anthropology of the Numa*, 173; Gates, "Brigham Young as I Knew Him," 65, Susa Young Gates Papers, box 12; Gates, *Life Story*, 329, 346.
4. Gates, *Life Story*, 330, 331. On Emeline's appearance and her status as a favorite, see Gates, "Brigham Young as I Knew Him," 28, Susa Young Gates Papers, box 12; Waite, *Mormon Prophet*, 201; Stenhouse, *"Tell It All,"* 281, 350. Clara and Lucy were commonly named as other longtime favorites. See, for example, Stenhouse, *"Tell It All,"* 278; Waite, *Mormon Prophet*, 181, 196. On seating arrangements at supper, which changed over the years, see Gates, "Brigham Young as I Knew Him," 58, and "Brigham Young and His Wives," 39, Susa Young Gates Papers, box 12; Gates, *Life Story*, 330–31; Waite, *Mormon Prophet*, 185. Lucy was in charge of the kitchen at the Lion House from 1856 to 1860. See Spencer, *Brigham Young at Home*, 28; Waite, *Mormon Prophet*, 180, 191–92.
5. Gates, *Life Story*, 331; Spencer, *Brigham Young at Home*, 183.
6. Conetah, *History of the Northern Ute*, 8.
7. Spencer, *Brigham Young at Home*, 28, 69.
8. Gates, "Brigham Young as I Knew Him," 65, Susa Young Gates Papers, box 12; Spencer, *Brigham Young at Home*, 28.
9. On the division of labor in the kitchen, see Gates, "Brigham Young as I Knew Him," 41, Susa Young Gates Papers, box 12.
10. For particular dishes served at the Lion House and the Beehive House, see Gates, "Brigham Young as I Knew Him," 65, Susa Young Gates Papers, box 12: Gates, *Life Story*, 329; Spencer, *Brigham Young at Home*, 17, 58–59.
11. The recipe for a far smaller number of doughnuts than Sally prepared calls for 5 to 6 cups of flour, 2 1/2 cups of sugar, 4 eggs, 6 tablespoons of butter, 1 teaspoon of baking soda, 1/2 teaspoon of baking powder, 1 teaspoon of salt, 3 teaspoons of nutmeg, a quart of buttermilk (or less, as needed), and lard or vegetable oil heated to 375 degrees. (Historic recipe courtesy of the Lion House.)
12. Gates, *Life Story*, 329–30.
13. Powell, *Anthropology of the Numa*, 49, 168.
14. Spencer, *Brigham Young at Home*, 28. Twiss married Brigham Young as a plural wife.

15. Spencer, *Brigham Young at Home*, 39, 71, 209.

16. Spencer, *Brigham Young at Home* 39, 182; Bailey, "What Is the Truth," 6, Alice Morrey Bailey Papers, box 33, folder 1.

17. Gates, "Brigham Young as I Knew Him," 76, Susa Young Gates Papers, box 12; Spencer, *Brigham Young at Home*, 21. Mary Ann "Rollings" (Rawlins), Emma Hanson, and Sophia "Swinson" (Swenson) were among the several domestic servants who received goods in 1866 from the family store (Family store ledger, October 1865–September 1866, Brigham Young Office Files, box 122, folder 1). Their names appear with Sally's in the same section of the ledger.

18. Spencer, *Brigham Young at Home*, 21.

19. Spencer, *Brigham Young at Home*, 21, 123. Among the settler-colonists, as Burton reported, women often married in their teens. See Burton, *City of the Saints*, 518. The weight of evidence suggests that Sally did not want to leave the Lion House. There appears to be no evidence that she was ever prevented from leaving. On her suitor, see Chapter Ten.

20. Burton, reporting on the high cost of labor in Utah Territory, stated that servants earned from $30 to $40 a month, wages far higher than servants earned in England at the time. See Burton, *City of the Saints*, 388–89. These were evidently the wages of male servants and workers.

21. These desserts, which were served at a banquet hosted by Brigham Young and others, were among the many known to settlers at the time. See Stout, *On the Mormon Frontier*, 538 (dated January 1, 1855).

22. Bailey, "What Is the Truth," 6, Alice Morrey Bailey Papers, box 33, folder 1, quoting Mabel Young Sanborn, youngest daughter of Lucy B.; Gates, *Life Story*, 329–30; Gates, "How Brigham Young," 29, and Gates, "Brigham Young as I Knew Him," 39–40, Susa Young Gates Papers, box 12.

23. See Bailey, "What Is the Truth," 6, Alice Morrey Bailey Papers, box 33, folder 1, quoting Susa Young Gates and Clarissa Young Spencer, respectively. Gates named "fried cakes" as one of the desserts. She perhaps meant crullers, made with flour, sugar, eggs, cream, and spices, and fried in deep fat.

24. Gates, "Brigham Young as I Knew Him," 41, Susa Young Gates Papers, box 12; Spencer, *Brigham Young at Home*, 71.

25. See Bailey, "What Is the Truth," 6, 12, Alice Morrey Bailey Papers, box 33, folder 1, quoting Lucy's daughter, Clarissa, probably in the 1930s. See also Gates, "Brigham Young and His Wives," 4, Susa Young Gates Papers, box 12; and Powell, *Anthropology of the Numa*, 180. Lucy "was sometimes very sharp tongued," Susa wrote, a candid comment that remained unpublished. See Gates, "My Recollections," 5, Susa Young Gates Papers, box 12.

26. Whitney, *History of Utah*, 67.

27. Gates, "Courtship of Kanosh," 24.

28. Powell, *Anthropology of the Numa*, 51; A. Smith, *Ethnography of the Northern Utes*, 145.

29. Powell, *Anthropology of the Numa*, 180; Spencer, *Brigham Young at Home*, 33; Gates, *Life Story*, 333–34.

30. Stewart, "Culture Element Distributions," 313; A. Smith, *Ethnography of the Northern Utes*, 151; W. Ferris, *Life in the Rocky Mountains*, 238.

31. Arrington, *Brigham Young*, 418, 420; A. Smith, *Ethnography of the Northern Utes*, 143, 151. Brigham Young's sister and mother died when he was young: first his sister, Nabby; then, eight years later when he was fourteen, his mother, Nabby. See Turner, *Brigham Young*, 9, 13. Clara's first son, Jedediah Grant Young, called Jeddie, was named after his father's close associate Jedediah Morgan Grant (Chapter Two, note 24). See Gates, "My Recollections," 2, Susa Young Gates Papers, box 12. Her second son, Albert Jeddie Young, bore his brother's, and Grant's, nickname as a middle name.

32. Gates, *Life Story*, 334; Spencer, *Brigham Young at Home*, 33. On daily talks by chiefs, see Powell, *Anthropology of the Numa*, 51; and A. Smith, *Ethnography of the Northern Utes*, 125–26. Sally's participation in the family's evening prayers was not unusual. One visitor to Utah Territory observed in 1872 that as a general practice servants joined in prayers with family members after the evening meal: "No one was excused; wives, daughters, hired men and women, all shuffled in." See E. Kane, *Twelve Mormon Homes*, 18.

33. Gates, *Life Story*, 27, 294–95, 334; E. Snow, *Personal Writings*, 109–10. On Eliza and the Mother in Heaven, see Wilcox, "Mormon Concept," 79.

34. On the ritual of proxy baptism, or baptisms for the dead, see Chapters Ten and Eleven.

35. Powell, *Anthropology of the Numa*, 69, 179; D. Huntington, *Few Words in the Utah and Shosho-ne Dialects*; D. Huntington, *Vocabulary of the Utah*, 7; Brigham Young Office Journal, entry dated May 7, 1860, Brigham Young Office Files, box 72, folder 5. The stories that settlers told about ancient ancestors came from the Book of Mormon. See, for example, Enos 1:20, on Indian ancestors who "became wild, and ferocious . . . dwelling in tents and wandering about in the wilderness with a short skin girdle about their loins."

36. Spencer, *Brigham Young at Home*, 128. Ute warriors attacked and killed several missionaries in September 1855. See "Massacre Near Elk Mountains," *Deseret News*, October 10, 1855. The survivors left, marking the end of the Elk Mountain Mission. Conetah notes that three Elk Mountain Utes as well as three settlers died in the conflict. See Conetah, *History of the Northern Ute*, 88–89.

37. Powell, who heard many stories told by elders, pointed out that each one had "a moral point," and they comprised an "unwritten bible." See Powell, *Anthropology of the Numa*, 43. See A. Smith, *Ute Tales*, 27–28, 79, for specific tales she recorded in the 1930s: "Coyote Learns to Fly," narrated by Lulu Chepoose; and "Coyote's Adventures," narrated by Archup. The narrators were elders who were alive during the last years of Sally's life, and

who heard these stories as children. "Coyote Learns to Fly," in particular, was widely told throughout the Great Basin. See A. Smith, *Shoshone Tales*, 129–32, 159–62.

38. Sessions, *Mormon Midwife*, 270 (dated October 28, 1859). Sessions provides what may be the only recorded sighting of Sally outside the house during these years. Gates later wrote that Sally "could scarcely be persuaded to leave the house, except in company with some white man or woman." See Gates, "Courtship of Kanosh," 27. Sally's companion was Phebe Jones Works, the wife of James Works, a member of the Brigham Young extended family who was employed to help with heavy work at the Lion House. See "Married," *Deseret News*, April 14, 1858; Gates, *Life Story*, 323; U.S. Census, 1860, Great Salt Lake City, Great Salt Lake County, Utah Territory. Phebe lived at least briefly at the Lion House with a young daughter, where Sally knew them as a family members. See Family information, ca. 1853–1858, Brigham Young Office Files, box 170, folder 26. The other Sally was Sarah Ann Barker, who worked for many years as a kitchen servant at the Lion House. See U.S. Census, 1870, Salt Lake City, Salt Lake County, Utah Territory; and Gates, "Brigham Young as I Knew Him," 41, Susa Young Gates Papers, box 12.

CHAPTER 8

1. J. Peterson, *Utah's Black Hawk War*, 135, 137–38. Most of the events in this chapter took place between 1865 and 1875.

2. J. Peterson, *Utah's Black Hawk War*, 140–41; Gottfredson, *Indian Depredations*, 130–40. Barney Ward died in April 1865, in Salina Canyon, Utah Territory. He was one of the first to die in the armed resistance by Utes that settler-colonists called the Black Hawk War. Polly and Louisa's mother, Sally Exervier (or Xavier) Ward, may have died earlier, before their father's death in 1865. See Hafen, "Elijah Barney Ward," 350. Polly worked at the Lion House as a domestic servant and lived there for at least five years. See U.S. Census, 1870, Salt Lake City, Salt Lake County, Utah Territory. She received room and board as well as goods from the family store. See Family store ledger, October 1865–September 1866, Brigham Young Office Files, box 122, folder 1.

3. Lyman, "Chief Kanosh," 177–79; J. Peterson, *Utah's Black Hawk War*, 230–41. Sanpitch and his men were taken prisoner in mid-March 1866. They were killed a month later by members of the county militia.

4. On the settler-colonists' war with Black Hawk, see J. Peterson, *Utah's Black Hawk War*. See also Lyman, "Chief Kanosh," on the chief's actions during the war with Black Hawk.

5. "Letter from Mr. Wallace, in Utah: Great Salt Lake City, October 1, 1858," *Daily Alta California* (San Francisco), October 21, 1858; "Editor of the Valley Tan," *Valley Tan*, November 12, 1858. Tintic's death was reported in spring 1859. See "Letter from Manti," *Deseret News*, April 6, 1859.

6. Chief Arapeen died in early December 1860, reportedly from natural causes. See "Death of Arapeen," *Deseret News*, December 19, 1860.

7. See Chapter Five, note 33, for circumstantial evidence of the deaths of Sally's mother and sisters years earlier.

8. The treaty talks at Spanish Fork took place in 1865, but the treaty was not ratified. See Indian treaty, June 8, 1865, Brigham Young Office Files, box 29, folder 26; O'Neil, "History of the Ute," 60–67; and J. Peterson, *Utah's Black Hawk War*, 148–155. Between 1860 and 1870, the number of settler-colonists grew from about 40,000 to more than 86,000, and the size of the Indian population in Utah Territory fell to a fraction of its former estimated size. See U.S. Census, 1860, 1870, Utah Territory. Powell enumerated fewer than 1,500 Indians in the early 1870s. See Powell, *Anthropology of the Numa*, 104.

9. About 556 Utes lived on the reservation in the early 1870s. See Powell, *Anthropology of the Numa*, 104. For Ute perspectives on the reservation, see Conetah, *History of the Northern Ute*, 41, 89–92; and Duncan, "Northern Utes of Utah," 193–94. For accounts by historians, see O'Neil, "History of the Ute"; and Lewis, *Neither Wolf nor Dog*, 38–70. Ute elder Clifford Duncan has remarked that reservation life was difficult for Utes, who felt "caged in." See Duncan, "Northern Utes of Utah," 197. A surveying party saw no value in what became reservation land. See "Uinta Not What Was Represented," *Deseret News*, September 25, 1861. In contrast, in the early 1870s Powell praised that land as good range for livestock and suitable for some crops. Winters, however, are unusually cold. See Powell, *Anthropology of the Numa*, 100; and Janetski, *Ute of Utah Lake*, 20.

10. B. Young, "Our Indian Relations—How to Deal with Them," July 28, 1866, *Journal of Discourses*, 11:264. On the deep attachment to homelands, see Powell, *Anthropology of the Numa*, 38.

11. Eugene Traugher, "The Prophet's Courtship," *Salt Lake Tribune*, March 11, 1894. The marriage took place in late January 1863. In early February 1863, Emeline gave birth to Daniel Wells Young. See Arrington, *Brigham Young*, 420. Her son died soon after birth.

12. Gates, "Brigham Young as I Knew Him," 28, Susa Young Gates Papers, box 12; Waite, *Mormon Prophet*, 201, 211; Arrington, *Brigham Young*, 420, 421. Lucy's daughter Clarissa thought she recalled that Emeline lived at the Lion House with nine children. See Spencer, *Brigham Young at Home*, 24. Clarissa, born in 1860, would have been only three or four at the time. Emeline's tenth and last child, her ninth surviving child, was born in 1864. She apparently moved from the Lion House before that birth. Artist Solomon Carvalho had seen Emeline ten years earlier, in 1854. Rémy saw her a year later. See Carvalho, *Incidents of Travel*, 188; and Rémy, *Journey to Great-Salt-Lake City*, 1:261.

It is common to read that Amelia was not a favorite, and moreover, that there were no favorite wives. See, for example, Spencer, *Brigham*

Young at Home, 80–81. The weight of evidence strongly suggests otherwise. Many insiders and outsiders, friendly and unfriendly, expressed the view that Clara, Lucy, and Emeline were the earlier, longtime favorites. See, for example, Gates, "My Recollections," [fragment], 3, Susa Young Gates Papers, box 12; and Waite, *Mormon Prophet,* 181. Although Amelia denied her status as a favorite in a newspaper interview, she is regarded as the last and final favorite. See Trauber, "The Prophet's Courtship," *Salt Lake Tribune,* March 11, 1894; and Arrington, *Brigham Young,* 371.

13. Brigham Young family store ledger, January 1874–December 1875, Brigham Young Office Files, box 123, folder 2; Gates, "My Recollections," 1, Susa Young Gates Papers, box 12. (This is a third document by Gates with the title "My Recollections.") Gates mentioned Emeline's addiction to morphine in an unpublished reminiscence but not in print. Emeline was not at all unique in her addiction. In the nineteenth century, women often took opiates, unwittingly, in proprietary medicines used to treat a range of problems, from anxiety and insomnia to asthma, rheumatism, and physical pain. Some became addicted to undisclosed ingredients in the medicines, which could include alcohol as well as opiates. Harriet Beecher Stowe's daughter, Georgiana, the wife of an Episcopalian rector, was one of the casualties. She grew addicted to morphine and died prematurely. See Goodwin, *Pure Food,* 47. Drug abuse by women, most often based on medical use, became so widespread that women's groups, including the Women's Christian Temperance Union, launched a campaign for pure food, drink, and drugs, in the late nineteenth century (Goodwin, *Pure Food,* 47). That campaign began in 1879, four years after Emeline's death.

14. Stenhouse described Clara in her forties as "short and stout," adding, "She was once quite a favorite" of the Leader. See Stenhouse, *"Tell It All,"* 278. Records of the family store show that "Clara D," "Emeline F," and some other wives obtained brandy, wine, and whiskey, as well as coffee, tea, and sugar—all of which were rather expensive and qualified as luxury goods. See, for example, Brigham Young family store ledgers, October 1865–September 1866, Brigham Young Office Files, box 122, folder 1; and January 1876–September 1877, Brigham Young Office Files, box 123, folder 2. A church teaching known as the Word of Wisdom discouraged the use of all of these items except for sugar. They may have been stocked by the family store for reasons of lower cost and discretion. Susa Gates recalled "the awful indictment [her] father issued against his family" for breaking the Word of Wisdom and for other actions, a memory that she did not put into print. See Gates, "My Recollections," 2, Susa Young Gates Papers, box 12. The family store ledgers contain accounts for the Beehive House and the Lion House, and for "Pres. B. Young," which also show charges for some of the discouraged items. See, for example, Family store daybook, July 1863, Brigham Young Office Files, box 120, folder 5; Brigham Young family

store ledger, January 1876–September 1877, Brigham Young Office Files, box 123, folder 2.

15. Clara's first son, Jeddie, died in early January 1856 (Chapter Five, note 15). Her second son, Albert Jeddie, died on December 16, 1864, according to the headstone on his grave in the Salt Lake City Cemetery. A variety of documentary evidence suggests that deaths disproportionately occurred in winter. When Jeddie died in January 1856, Brigham Young was in Fillmore, then the territorial capitol, for the Fifth Utah Territorial Legislative Assembly, which began in early December 1855, and ended in mid-January, 1856. See "Doings at the Capitol," *Deseret News*, December 13, 1855; and "Legislative Proceedings," *Deseret News,* January 30, 1856. As was usual, Emeline accompanied him while the other wives remained at the Lion House. See Lucy Decker [Young] to Brigham Young, January 9, 1856, Brigham Young Office Files, box 44, folder 16.

16. Spencer, *Brigham Young at Home*, 75.

17. Gates, "Lucy Bigelow Young," 70, Susa Young Gates Papers, box 14.

18. Gates, "Brigham Young as I Knew Him," 26, Susa Young Gates Papers, box 12; A. Young, *Wife No. 19*, 487.

19. Gates, "Brigham Young as I Knew Him," 27, Susa Young Gates Papers, box 12.

20. Gates, "My Recollections," [fragment], 1, Susa Young Gates Papers, box 12. Although Susa said she had borrowed every one of Clara's books, this is the only one she mentioned by title, and she still remembered it later in life. Richard F. Burton's translation of these stories from Arabic to English appeared in print about fifteen years later.

21. On the schools for Brigham Young's children, see Gates, "Brigham Young as I Knew Him," 43, Susa Young Gates Papers, box 12; Gates, *Life Story*, 284–85; Spencer, *Brigham Young at Home*, 136, 140–43; Bradley and Woodward, *Four Zinas*, 185.

22. Powell, *Anthropology of the Numa*, 176. Susa ended a short story with a scene of Sally looking at the marks in her copy of the Book of Mormon. See Gates, "Courtship of Kanosh," 38; see also Chapter Twelve. Sally, like other converts, was undoubtedly given a copy of the Book of Mormon.

23. A year earlier, in 1862, Emerson's son, Edward, had made an overland trip from Massachusetts to California. He not only crossed the "vast desert" but also stopped in Salt Lake City where he had some contact with Brigham Young. See Emerson, *Journals*, 256, 499n19. The famous phrase about wilderness and "wild men" comes from William Bradford's *Of Plimouth Plantation*, written in the seventeenth century.

24. Emerson, *Journals*, 379 (dated 1863).

25. E. Snow, *Personal Writings*, 31.

26. Gates, "Brigham Young as I Knew Him," 77, Susa Young Gates Papers, box 12; Gates, "My Recollections," 1, Susa Young Gates Papers, box 12; Gates, "From Impulsive Girl," 279.

27. Gates, "My Recollections," 1, Susa Young Gates Papers, box 12; Gates, "Lucy Bigelow Young," 70, Susa Young Gates Papers, box 14.

28. Gates, "Brigham Young as I Knew Him," 27–28, Susa Young Gates Papers, box 12. This was apparently Julia Young Burton (1853–1889). She was raised by Susan, or Susannah, Snively, and married Charles Samuel Burton in 1878. Arrington does not list Julia as a member of Brigham Young's family, but she does appear as Susannah's adopted daughter in some other sources. See Arrington, *Brigham Young*, 420–21.

29. "B. Young's Testimony, U.S. v. Pedro Leon," January 11, 1852, Papers Relating to Mexican Traders, 1851–1853, Brigham Young Office Files, box 47, folder 36; Gates, "Brigham Young as I Knew Him," 76, Susa Young Gates Papers, box 12; Muhlestein, "Utah Indians," 191. Federal census takers in 1850, 1860, and 1870—recording information provided to them, likely by Brigham Young as family head—never recorded the surname Young along with Sally's given name.

30. Spencer, *Brigham Young at Home*, 75, 123; Bailey, "What Is the Truth," 6, 12, Alice Morrey Bailey Papers, box 33, folder 1. Sally is uniformly identified in census records and in family records as "Sally," a "domestic servant" or "help," and "Indian." See, for example, Family information, Brigham Young Office Files, box 170, folder 126.

31. Spencer, *Brigham Young at Home*, 75. In 1870, Maria Decker, Clara's half-sister, and her foster daughter Celestia Martin were listed after Clara's name (misrecorded as Clara Sniveley), along with five other children. See U.S. Census, 1870, Salt Lake City, Salt Lake County, Utah Territory. Polly Ward, like Sally, was identified to the 1870 census taker as Indian (although only one parent was Indian) and as a domestic servant. See U.S. Census, 1870, Salt Lake City, Salt Lake County, Utah Territory. Louisa Ward worked as a servant for another family. See U.S. Census, Ogden, Weber County, Utah Territory. On Mary Jane Farnham, see B. Ferris, *Mormons at Home*, 104; and Rémy, *Journey to Great-Salt-Lake City*, 2:287–88. Exactly when and how long Mary Jane Farnham and her son lived with Clara in the 1860s, as well as the circumstances of their stay, are unclear. By 1870, they had left Utah Territory for St. Louis, Missouri, where they still resided in 1880. See U.S. Census, 1870, 1880, St. Louis, St. Louis County, Missouri.

32. Clara was born in late July 1828, and married in early May 1844. She was fifteen when she married Brigham Young, who was twenty-six years older. Bradley and Woodward remark about him, "As community leader, he was virtually free to do as he chose." They add, "He had enormous power over his wives and children and acted toward them from a mixture of motives—possessiveness, at least some affection, and a pragmatic sense of what would work best, not necessarily from a consistent moral and ethical base." See Bradley and Woodward, *Four Zinas*, 200.

According to census data and other records at the Family History
Library in Salt Lake City, Utah, twenty of Brigham Young's daughters were
born in the ten years between 1847 and 1857. (Nineteen were his offspring;
one was adopted.) Five of the older ten daughters, born between 1847 and
1850 and known as the "Ten Big Girls," made monogamous marriages with
young men who were about their age; the other five entered polygamous
marriages. Each of the younger ten daughters entered a monogamous
marriage with a man who was close in age. (One daughter later divorced
her husband, who eventually had three other wives. She married again,
monogamously.) All but one of the marriages took place during the heyday
of polygamy, and during their father's lifetime, yet only five of the twenty
daughters married men who were polygamists and associates of their father.
This seems a surprising figure given the strength of their father's advocacy
of polygamy, and given his own practice of marrying much younger women
as plural wives.

33. Gates, "Lucy Bigelow Young," 71–72, Susa Young Gates Papers, box 14.
    Susa's frank words about Dora's elopement appeared only in her unpub-
    lished recollections about her mother, not in her later book about her
    father. On Nabbie's attempted elopement, see "Utah: A Daughter of
    Brigham Young Attempts to Elope, and Fails," *Chicago Tribune*, Septem-
    ber 15, 1869; and "A Mormon Romance," *New York Times*, September 19,
    1869. The third, unnamed daughter was intercepted by General Gren-
    ville M. Dodge, who cautioned her father not to force her to marry the
    man in question. See Dodge, "Autobiography," 826–27.

34. Spencer, *Brigham Young at Home*, 75; Gates, "Brigham Young and His
    Wives," 7, Susa Young Gates Papers, box 12.

35. Clarissa ["Clara"] C. Decker Young to Brigham Young, October 3, 1847,
    Brigham Young Office Files, box 44, folder 15.

36. Letter from Brigham Young to Clarissa ["Clary"] Decker Young, Septem-
    ber 8, 1847, MS 4825, Church History Library, Church of Jesus Christ of
    Latter-day Saints.

37. Gates, "Brigham Young and His Wives," 7, Susa Young Gates Papers, box
    12; A. Young, *Wife No. 19*, 487. That Clara came to discourage, very qui-
    etly, marriages of young women to polygamous older men is my inference,
    based on a wide range of evidence. She may constitute the unique case in
    this regard among Brigham Young's wives who remained married to him.
    Other women in Utah Territory, including many of his wives, seem to have
    accepted and adapted to polygamy in the early years of settlement. See
    Ulrich, *House Full of Females*.

38. "Departed This Life," *Deseret News*, July 21, 1875; Stenhouse, *"Tell It All,"*
    282. Susa learned of her father's remarks at Emeline's funeral from the man
    who gave the eulogy. See Gates, "My Recollections," 3, Susa Young Gates
    Papers, box 12.

39. Arrington, *Brigham Young*, 371; Turner, *Brigham Young*, 384; A. Young, *Wife No. 19*, 516.

40. By the 1860s, their homeland was so "thickly settled" that they had to ask settlers who lived there for food, to supplement low yields from hunting and fishing. See U.S. Office of Indian Affairs, *Annual Report* (1865), 114; U.S. Office of Indian Affairs, *Annual Report* (1869), 230.

41. Spencer, *Brigham Young at Home*, 117–18; Arrington, *Brigham Young*, 312–13, 483n30. On Utes' "beautiful, even-set teeth," see W. Ferris, *Life in the Rocky Mountains*, 233; and D. Huntington, *Vocabulary of the Utah*, 30.

CHAPTER 9

1. Most of the events in this chapter took place between 1872 and 1874. The transcontinental railroad had been completed in 1869. On traveling by train across the American West, see Codman, *Mormon Country*, 1.

2. Thayer, *Western Journey* 5, 33–36. Emerson made the cross-country trip in spring 1871.

3. Codman, *Mormon Country*, 2.

4. Wolfe notes, with regard to settler colonialism, the "incessant flow of knowledge" about native people by "a comprehensive range of authorities." See Wolfe, *Settler Colonialism*, 3. In the present case, not only officials such as Powell, but also travelers, including the Kanes and John Codman (see below), wore the mantle of authority.

5. On Thomas Kane (1822–1883) and Elizabeth Wood Kane (1836–1909), see Grow, *"Liberty to the Downtrodden,"* 217–18, 221–22.

6. Grow, *"Liberty to the Downtrodden,"* 237–38, 262; "The Original Tom Thumb and Wife," *Deseret News*, July 14, 1869; Spencer, *Brigham Young at Home*, 209–19.

7. Grow, *"Liberty to the Downtrodden,"* 128–32; E. Kane, *Twelve Mormon Homes*, 21, 149. See also Bushman, "Mormon Domestic Life," 91–118.

8. E. Kane, *Twelve Mormon Homes*, 44.

9. E. Kane, *Twelve Mormon Homes*, 42–43. Elizabeth used a pseudonym for the Pitchforth family. Lehi was listed in the federal census as twenty-nine years old, Indian, and an adopted son. To judge from later censuses, he never married, and he lived with one of the birth sons of the family later in his life. He was listed in the 1910 census as the adopted brother of the household head, and as "white," not Indian. See census return for the Pitchforth household, U.S. Census, 1880, 1910, Nephi, Juab County, Utah.

10. E. Kane, *Twelve Mormon Homes*, 42–43, 44; Ebersole, *Captured by Texts*, 10; Stratton, *Captivity*, 283. The captivity narrative of Mary Jemison (1743–1833), or Deh-he-wä-mis, was first published in 1824 under the title *A Narrative of the Life of Mrs. Mary Jemison*. A best seller, it was regularly reprinted in the nineteenth century. Olive Oatman's narrative reached print in 1857, initially under a different title.

11. E. Kane, *Twelve Mormon Homes*, 71–72. The Kanes met Chief Kanosh and other Pahvants in Fillmore, the county seat of Millard County, which encompassed Pahvant lands.

12. B. Ferris, *Mormons at Home*, 193.

13. E. Kane, *Twelve Mormon Homes*, 72; Conetah, *History of the Northern Ute*, 83.

14. E. Kane, *Twelve Mormon Homes*, 72; E. Kane, Notes of Kanosh's interview.

15. Chief Kanosh's ability to speak Spanish was so common among Utes of his generation that it does not provide good evidence that he was born far from the region in Utah Territory that he called home. As an American fur trapper, who lived in the Rocky Mountains in the 1830s, reported, Utes often visited Taos and California: "consequently, many speak, and nearly all understand, the Spanish language." See W. Ferris, *Life in the Rocky Mountains*, 251. Historians and descendants of early settlers have offered varying versions of the chief's origins and ancestry, but have often suggested a distant location as his place of birth. See, for example, Lyman, "Chief Kanosh," 161, 166; Lewis, "Kanosh and Ute Identity," 332–33; Reay, *Lambs in the Meadow*, 95. A federal census taker, however, recorded Chief Kanosh's birthplace as Utah [Territory], presumably based on information that the chief provided. See U.S. Census, 1870, Corn Creek, Millard County, Utah Territory.
   It is telling that settlers recalled and recorded Chief Kanosh's enforcement of good table manners when dining with them. It provides more evidence of the symbolic importance of such manners in their understanding of "civilized behavior," and the chief's acute grasp of their practices. See Merkeley, *Monuments of Courage*, 25; and Melville, *Interview Histories*, 32 (from an interview with James Day [1849–1934]).

16. Conetah, *History of the Northern Ute*, 82–85; Kerns, *Journeys West*, 227. On attempts to persuade or force Pahvants to leave their homeland and move to the Uintah Reservation, see Lyman, "Chief Kanosh," 174–76, 190.

17. E. Kane, *Twelve Mormon Homes*, 73–75; E. Kane, Notes of Kanosh's interview. For details about the life of Chief Kanosh, see also Lyman, "Chief Kanosh." On suspicions about sorcery as the source of killing disease, see Powell, *Anthropology of the Numa*, 103.

18. U.S. Census, 1870, Corn Creek, Millard County, Utah Territory. The name Corn Creek was applied to both a creek and to the nearby Pahvant community (see Chapters Ten and Eleven). By one estimate, Pahvant Valley alone encompasses some two thousand square miles. See Gibbs, "Gunnison Massacre," 68. Other estimates of the valley size vary. The Pahvant homeland also included some part of Beaver Valley in the mid-nineteenth century.

19. E. Kane, *Twelve Mormon Homes*, 79; Spencer, *Brigham Young at Home*, 123–24; Bailey, "What Is the Truth," 9, Alice Morrey Bailey Papers, box 33,

folder 1. Tom Givón (personal communication, November 9, 2019) has suggested that the Ute name recorded as Tanequickeup may mean Root Gatherer. Betsy Hancock Shurtliff (1851–1933) recalled Mary, or Tanequickeup, in a recorded reminiscence. See Daughters of Utah Pioneers Lesson Committee, *Chronicles of Courage*, 56. The 1860 federal census did not list Mary with the family of George W. Hancock (1826–1901) in Payson. See U.S. Census, 1860, Payson, Utah County, Utah Territory. Several lines of evidence suggest that she lived with the family in the early and mid-1860s, and that she was the same Mary who later became a wife of Chief Kanosh.

20. E. Kane, *Twelve Mormon Homes*, 79; Daughters of Utah Pioneers Lesson Committee, *Chronicles of Courage*, 56.

21. E. Kane, *Twelve Mormon Homes*, 79; Spencer, *Brigham Young at Home*, 124. The murder of Mary reportedly took place in June or July 1869, a few miles from Corn Creek. See "Correspondence—Fillmore City, July 25, 1869," *Deseret News*, August 11, 1869. Another wife was identified as the murderer. Her name was variously recorded at the time as Bretsken and Patsey-kin. See U.S. Census, 1870, Corn Creek, Millard County, Utah Territory; and Baptisms for the dead, May 3, 1876, George W. Hill Papers. The name was later usually recalled and written as Betsykin.

22. E. Kane, *Twelve Mormon Homes*, 79–81. Elizabeth heard this story about Mary, probably from Brigham Young, in December 1872, three years after Mary was murdered. The alleged murderer was still alive a year after Mary died. See U.S. Census, 1870, Corn Creek, Millard County, Utah Territory.

23. E. Kane, *Twelve Mormon Homes*, 78, 81–83, 89. Cove Fort is located some thirty miles south of Fillmore, and at an elevation of nearly six thousand feet—or about two thousand feet higher than Salt Lake City.

24. Pratt, "Correspondence: Letter to the Editor from P. P. Pratt," *Deseret News*, July 16, 1856. "The Indians were generally peaceful," Pratt remarked, "and some of them hard at work at cultivating the earth." Whether they worked on their own account or as hired labor is not clear. For Ute words for the color white, and the Pahvant name for Mount Baldy, see Powell, *Anthropology of the Numa*, 167, 175, 208. On Mount Baldy, which stands in the Tushar Mountains east of Beaver Valley, see Cott, *Utah Place Names*, 260, 376.

25. E. Kane, *Twelve Mormon Homes*, 90, 102, 103–04. See also Bradley, *History of Beaver County*, 25, 50–51.

26. See Grow, *"Liberty to the Downtrodden,"* on Thomas Kane's code of honor and chivalry, and his Virginia relatives. In the 1880 federal census, General T. L. Kane's occupation was recorded as "Gentleman." See U.S. Census, 1880, McKean County, Pennsylvania.

27. E. Kane, *Twelve Mormon Homes*, 103–104; Bennion and Carter, "Touring Polygamous Utah," 171, 172, 173.

28. E. Kane, *Twelve Mormon Homes*, 104; Tanner, *John Riggs Murdock*.

29. E. Kane, *Twelve Mormon Homes*, 105–06.

30. In 1870, some two thousand settler-colonists lived in Beaver County, mainly in Beaver Valley. See U.S. Census, 1870, Beaver County, Utah Territory.

31. On the estimated acreage farmed in 1872, see E. Kane, *Twelve Mormon Homes*, 102. On the settlement of Beaver after 1856, see Bradley, *History of Beaver County*, 50–63.

32. The Kanes' host, John Riggs Murdock (1826–1913), was a bishop, and he evidently dispensed the hay from the church tithing house. The president of his church, the Leader, was the man the Pahvants wanted to see. Elizabeth used a pseudonym for the Murdock family. See Tanner, *John Riggs Murdock*; and E. Kane, *Twelve Mormon Homes*, 103.

33. E. Kane, *Twelve Mormon Homes*, 108–09.

34. E. Kane, *Twelve Mormon Homes*, 107, 129; "Utah Indians: Attack on Herders—The Savages Routed," *New York Times*, August 14, 1872; "The Indians: The Outbreak in Utah Serious," *New York Times*, August 15, 1872; "Utah: The Indians in Council," *New York Times*, August 24, 1872; "The Hostile Savages," *New York Times*, September 10, 1872; "Telegraphic News," *New York Times*, September 17, 1872.

35. Turner, *Brigham Young*, 366–71; "Troops to Be Employed against the Indians," *New York Times*, August 17, 1872; "Utah: Serious Troubles in the Territory," *New York Times*, August 18, 1872; Duncan, "Northern Utes of Utah," 193–94, 199, 220; J. Peterson, *Utah's Black Hawk War*, 362n53. The Ghost Dance was held in Sanpete Valley in May 1872. See S. Jones, *Being and Becoming Ute*, 175. The Ghost Dance was a new religious movement that promised the return of ancestors and their way of life, and the removal of settler-colonists and other invaders from Indian land.

36. Grow, *"Liberty to the Downtrodden,"* 264. The Kanes reached the town of St. George just before Christmas 1872, and stayed until mid-February 1873. See E. Kane, *Twelve Mormon Homes*, 158; and E. Kane, *Gentile Account*, 174n146.

37. E. Kane, *Twelve Mormon Homes*, 5; E. Kane, *Gentile Account*, 96–108, 178–79; Grow, *"Liberty to the Downtrodden,"* 267.

38. E. Kane, *Twelve Mormon Homes*, 15–16.

39. B. Young, "Gathering the Saints," April 9, 1871, *Journal of Discourses*, 14:86; E. Kane, *Gentile Account*, 177.

40. Powell, *Anthropology of the Numa*, 98, 208; Worster, *River Running West*, 301; Fowler and Fowler, "John Wesley Powell."

41. Worster, *River Running West*, 155–202, 218–33; personal observation at site, August 26, 2014, Green River, Wyoming. Powell made the first Colorado River expedition in 1869, and the second in 1871.

42. Worster, *River Running West*, 156; Conetah, *History of the Northern Ute*, 2.

43. Powell, *Anthropology of the Numa*, 57, 178. Powell camped near Chief Douglas and his band in winter 1868–1869. See Worster, *River Running West*, 148.

44. See Emmitt, *Last War Trail*, 13–15, 39–40, 326. Emmitt carried out extensive interviews with Ute elders in the 1940s.
45. Worster, *River Running West*, 114–17, 135, 147–48, 150.
46. Powell, *Anthropology of the Numa*, 57, 164; Worster, *River Running West*, 143.
47. Powell, *Anthropology of the Numa*, 53–59. The ceremony Powell described was based on an understanding of disease as caused by the intrusion of something malignant and supernatural into the human body. The shaman cured by removing the source of disease. As anthropologists have documented, this is a widespread understanding in shamanic healing traditions.
48. Powell met Chief Kanosh in 1873. See Powell, *Anthropology of the Numa*, 103.
49. The Utes' name for Powell was translated as "stump of arm" or "no right arm." See Powell, *Anthropology of the Numa*, 164, 191; Worster, *River Running West*, 99–100.
50. Powell, *Anthropology of the Numa*, 53.
51. U.S. Office of Indian Affairs, *Annual Report* (1868), iii, 5.
52. E. Kane, *Twelve Mormon Homes*, 74.
53. Powell's fellow emissary, George W. Ingalls (1838–1921), was a United States Indian agent who, with Powell, was appointed Special Indian Commissioner in 1873. For their report, see Powell, *Anthropology of the Numa*, 97–119.
54. Powell, *Anthropology of the Numa*, 16, 170; Lincoln University, *Catalogue*, 22, 23. Lincoln University, was founded in the 1850s by a Presbyterian minister.
55. Powell, *Anthropology of the Numa*, 103, 111, 207, 258; "History of East Millard County: Chief Kanosh and Kanosh Town, by E. [Edward] L. Black, dated November 12, 1930," *Millard County (Utah) Progress*, June 19, 1936; "Indian Chief Kanosh," *Millard County (Utah) Chronicle*, June 12, 1930. The two chiefs, as close allies, treated each other as fictive kin, as "brothers."
56. Powell, *Anthropology of the Numa*, 111, 207–09. On Numic languages see W. Miller, "Numic Languages," 98–106. On the prehistory of Numic peoples, see Simms, *Ancient Peoples*, 248–63.
57. Powell, *Anthropology of the Numa*, 106, 111.
58. Powell, *Anthropology of the Numa*, 116, 117–18. The words *civilized* and *civilizing* in the report by Powell and Ingalls refer to the process that came to be called assimilation. The goal, which the earlier usage makes more apparent, is the incorporation into settler-colonial society, or civilization, of people who have lived in other sorts of social and political formations, such as bands and tribes. This incorporation includes the appropriation and control of their lands and their labor for the benefit of the colonizers.
59. John Codman, "Through Utah," 790–91.
60. Codman, *Mormon Country*, 56; Codman, "Through Utah," 793, 794. John and Anna Codman visited the area in fall 1874. Codman reversed the names of the village and the Pahvant community in his article.

61. Extinction discourse (which might also be called elimination discourse in the context of settler colonialism) is a common feature of many of these nineteenth-century narratives. Brantlinger uses this term in his illuminating study of the many nineteenth- and early twentieth-century works written in English that predict or lament the disappearance of dark-skinned "primitive races." See Brantlinger, *Dark Vanishings*.

CHAPTER 10

1. Most of the events in this chapter took place between 1870 and 1877. Chief Kanosh had asked to talk to Sally as early as 1856. See D. B. Huntington to Brigham Young, August 21, 1856, Brigham Young Office Files, box 24, folder 22. Whether he spoke to her then is unknown. A prevailing assumption is that he already wanted to marry her. See, for example, Turner, *Brigham Young*, 348. Alternatively, he may have wanted to tell her whether any members of her family survived, or not; or about Baptiste who had survived the gunshot; or about other matters. When the one-way courtship began is not known, but it probably dates to 1873 or so, after Sally moved to the Beehive House (see below, notes 20 and 21). Elizabeth Kane, who met the chief and Sally separately in late 1872, some five years before they married, did not report hearing of any quest to marry Sally. See E. Kane, *Twelve Mormon Homes*. Stories of their supposed romance and courtship, sometimes told with belittling humor, reached print decades later. See, for example, Gates, "Courtship of Kanosh"; and Spencer, *Brigham Young at Home*, 123.
2. "Massacre near Elk Mountains," *Deseret News*, October 10, 1855.
3. Polly Ward was listed with the Brigham Young household in the 1870 federal census. See U.S. Census, 1870, Salt Lake City, Salt Lake County, Utah Territory.
4. E. Kane, *Twelve Mormon Homes*, 44.
5. Powell, *Anthropology of the Numa*, 165, 208. On the distinction between older and younger siblings in Numic kinship terminologies, see Shimkin, "Uto-Aztecan System," 226.
6. Members of the Brigham Young family most commonly referred to Sally in terms of racial identity, as Indian; or by occupation, as a maid or servant. In contrast, a few families of settlers did explicitly identify Indian children to census takers as adopted family members who shared their surname: for example, Lehi Pitchforth (see Chapter Nine).
7. Powell, *Anthropology of the Numa*, 172.
8. Bailey, "What Is the Truth," 11, Alice Morrey Bailey Papers, box 33, folder 1; Whitney, *History of Utah*, 67.
9. To the best of my knowledge, this unusual marriage pattern (of strictly monogamous marriages to spouses close in age) by Clara's three daughters and three foster children has not been previously and explicitly noted.

It may long ago have provoked Tullidge's elliptical comment that Clara had an "interesting family." The brevity of his remark gains meaning when compared to his lengthy comments about other wives who clearly supported the practice of polygamy. See Tullidge, *Women of Mormondom*, 443.

10. Woodruff, *Journals*, 6:470–71 (dated May 5, 1869).

11. According to only Whitney, Sally married Chief Kanosh as a plural wife. See Whitney, *History of Utah*, 67. It is likely, however, that he confused Sally with Mary, as others did (see Chapter Twelve). The chief's 1870 census record lists the names of two women: one, Mary's accused murderer, who died soon after the census was taken; and another who then was thirty-five years old. See U.S. Census, 1870, Corn Creek, Millard County, Utah Territory. According to Clarissa, the latter wife died in childbirth at a young age (presumably before Sally's marriage). See Spencer, *Brigham Young at Home*, 123.

12. Turner, *Brigham Young*, 210. According to the 1870 federal census, an elderly woman was the sole unmarried woman at Corn Creek. See U.S. Census, 1870, Corn Creek, Millard County, Utah Territory.

13. "More Mormon Troubles—Escape of the Murderers of Captain Gunnison," *New York Daily Times*, May 18, 1855.

14. Dodge, "Autobiography," 826–27. According to General Dodge, who did not disclose the daughter's name, the attempted escape took place in October 1868.

15. Bullock, *Pioneer Camp*, 243 (dated July 28, 1847), summarizing a discourse of Brigham Young; Chandless, *Visit to Salt Lake*, 254; B. Young, "The Gifts of God," April 7, 1861, *Journal of Discourses*, 9:37.

16. Turner, *Brigham Young*, 386; U.S. Census, 1870, Corn Creek, Millard County, Utah Territory.

17. B. Young, "Gathering the Saints," April 9, 1871, *Journal of Discourses*, 14:86; Powell, *Anthropology of the Numa*, 104; U.S. Census, 1870, Corn Creek, Millard County, Utah Territory.

18. Spencer, *Brigham Young at Home*, 123. Neither the Church History Library of the Church of Jesus Christ of Latter-day Saints, with its extensive collections of papers relating to Brigham Young and his family, nor the Utah State Archives (see Chapter Four, note 76) appear to have a legal document of indenture for Sally.

19. Codman, *Mormon Country*, 10; Spencer, *Brigham Young at Home*, 220.

20. Arrington, *Brigham Young*, 329. Sometime after the federal census was taken in 1870 and before 1877, Sally moved to the Beehive House and lived "downstairs with the other maids," as Lucy's daughter Clarissa put it. See Bailey, "What Is the Truth," 6, Alice Morrey Bailey Papers, box 33, folder 1.

21. Gates, *Life Story*, 351. Clara lived at the Lion House until at least 1870. See census return for Brigham Young household, U.S. Census, 1870, Salt Lake City, Salt Lake County, Utah Territory. She later moved, apparently in

the early 1870s, to a cottage on State Street, a block from the Lion House. On the Social Hall, see Spencer, *Brigham Young at Home*, 171–74.

22. By 1877, only three of the children were under the age of fifteen, and they did not live at the Lion House or the Beehive House. See Arrington, *Brigham Young*, 420. Zina had moved to her own house, deeded to her by her husband, in 1870. See Bradley and Woodward, *Four Zinas*, 215.

23. Grow, *"Liberty to the Downtrodden,"* 270–72; Arrington, *Brigham Young*, 422–30 (Appendix D).

24. B. Young, "Gathering the Saints," April 9, 1871, *Journal of Discourses*, 14:87; Bennion, "Indian Reminiscences," 44. Young's remarks qualify as extinction discourse but also accurately reflect the Native population collapse in the first decade after settlement. See Brantlinger, *Dark Vanishings*; and Stoffle, Jones, and Dobyns, "Direct European Immigrant Transmission."

25. Baptisms for the dead, May 3, 1876, George W. Hill Papers. The three wives were Mary, Patsey-kin, and Ea-wids. Chief Kanosh and Sally served as proxies in baptisms for twelve Pahvant males and eight Pahvant females (Pah-vants baptized, May 3, 1876, George W. Hill Papers). Eight of the deceased males were identified as Chief Kanosh's father, uncle, and six sons. The deceased females, and several of the deceased males were identified by name, but not by specific kin relationship to Chief Kanosh or Sally. It is likely that Sally took part in the ritual of proxy baptism in order to have her deceased close relatives baptized. This was a standard practice, based on established church doctrine; see Turner, *Brigham Young*, 83–84, 403–04.

26. B. Young, "Gathering the Saints," April 9, 1871, *Journal of Discourses*, 14:87.

27. Lyman, "Chief Kanosh," 190–91. Chief Kanosh was baptized in 1858 according to church records. See Bailey, "What Is the Truth," 18, Alice Morrey Bailey Papers, box 33, folder 1.

28. Powell, *Anthropology of the Numa*, 98. Chief Kanosh was ordained an elder three years before his marriage to Sally. See Journal History of the Church, May 11, 1874.

29. Woodruff, *Journals*, 6:470 (dated May 5, 1869).

30. The record of her marriage lists Sally's age as fifty, and Kanosh's age as fifty-three. See Marriage certificate of "Kanosh (Indian) to Kahpeputz or Sally, also an Indian," June 8, 1877, Historian's Office Marriage Certificates, 1876–1888, Salt Lake County, 1876–1879, CR 100 424, Church History Library, Church of Jesus Christ of Latter-day Saints. According to the ages given in federal census records, she was slightly younger, between forty-seven and forty-nine years old.

31. E. Kane, *Twelve Mormon Homes*, 44; Bailey, "What Is the Truth," 11, Alice Morrey Bailey Papers, box 33, folder 1, quoting Clarissa Young Spencer on her father's decision about Sally as "a wise move for everybody concerned." According to church records available to church members, Sally was never sealed to the Brigham Young family. See Muhlestein, "Utah Indians," 91.

Years later, Jane Manning James (see Chapter Four, note 66), who was African American, petitioned to be sealed to the important family she had worked for as a domestic servant in Nauvoo, Illinois: the Joseph Smith family. She was told that she could be sealed to that family only as an eternal servant. See Turner, *Brigham Young*, 229.

32. Marriage certificate of "Kanosh (Indian) to Kahpeputz or Sally, also an Indian," June 8, 1877, Historian's Office Marriage Certificates, 1876–1888, Salt Lake County, 1876–1879, CR 100 424, Church History Library, Church of Jesus Christ of Latter-day Saints. Linguist Tom Givón suggests that the name heard and spelled as Kahpeputz may be aka-papu-ch(i). The /u/ in this word is pronounced without lip rounding, and does not exist in English. The name may mean "red drum (or red bucket)" (Tom Givón, personal communication, June 7, 2018). The name Red Drum seems likely, given Sally's mission: communicating successfully about how to live properly in civilization.

33. The marriage certificate does not support the common claim that Sally's marriage ceremony was performed by Brigham Young at the Endowment House. See, for example, Reay, *Lambs in the Meadow*, 53, among many others. By holding the marriage ceremony at Clara's cottage, Sally and Chief Kanosh married only "for time" (their mortal lives), not for eternity. Bailey, who examined church documents available to church members, also confirms that Sally was not sealed to her husband when they married. See Bailey, "What Is the Truth," 19, Alice Morrey Bailey Papers, box 33, folder 1. An array of evidence indicates that Sally did not want to marry Chief Kanosh, and certainly not for eternity.

34. Brigham Young family store ledger, January 1876–September 1877, Brigham Young Office Files, box 123, folder 2. See account of "Clara D.," and notations "for Sally," dated June 7, 8, 9, 1877.

35. Gates, "Brigham Young and His Wives," 7, Susa Young Gates Papers, box 12; photograph of Clara Decker Young, Bathsheba Bigler Smith Photograph Collection, 1865–1900, PH 8004, Church History Library, Church of Jesus Christ of Latter-day Saints. Lucy's daughter Clarissa, as an old woman, denied that Sally could have worn a silk dress. When told of the wedding portrait, she insisted that the dress must have been handed down by Clara or one of the other wives. See Bailey, "What Is the Truth," 13, Alice Morrey Bailey Papers, box 33, folder 1. On Sally's photograph, see Chapter Eleven, note 33.

36. Burton, *City of the Saints*, 370; Muir, *Steep Trails*, 106–09 (dated May 15, 1877); Codman, *Mormon Country*, 92; E. Kane, *Twelve Mormon Homes*, 99; U.S. Census, 1870, 1880, Salt Lake County, Utah Territory.

37. In Susa's creative telling, the stated reason for Sally's earlier trip south differed. See Gates, "Courtship of Kanosh," 29. On the evacuation of the city in spring 1858, see Turner, *Brigham Young*, 293–98. See also Grow, *"Liberty to the Downtrodden,"* 149–206, and Moorman, *Camp Floyd*, on events of 1857–1858.

38. Kanosh to Dimick Huntington, June 13, 1877, Brigham Young Papers, box 46, folder 13; Thomas Callister to Brigham Young, June 13, 1877, Brigham Young Papers, box 46, folder 12. A public stagecoach was later represented, in error, as "a carriage pulled by two fine horses." See Reay, *Lambs in the Meadow*, 105. The implication was that Chief Kanosh and Sally had traveled in the same style as members of the Brigham Young family.

39. "Mrs. Maud Crane Melville Writes Interestingly of Past," *Millard County (Utah) Chronicle*, October 30, 1930.

40. Powell, *Anthropology of the Numa*, 208; Steward, *Basin-Plateau*, 224; Lyman and Newell, *History of Millard County*, 115; Christensen, *Birth of Kanosh*, 15–16. Chief Kanosh told Powell the name of the creek: red (*un-kar*), stone (*tump*), creek (*nu-kwint*), or Red Stone Creek. See Powell, *Anthropology of the Numa*, 168, 175, 181.

41. Beeton, "'Teach Them to Till,'" 305; Steward, *Aboriginal and Historical Groups*, 53, 54, 55; Kelly and Fowler, "Southern Paiute," 368. In 1870, 83 people lived in 32 dwellings, mostly lodges and tents, at Corn Creek. See U.S. Census, 1870, Corn Creek, Millard County, Utah Territory. Three years later, in 1873, Powell met with Chief Kanosh, and calculated a total of 134 Pahvants, all living at Corn Creek. See Powell, *Anthropology of the Numa*, 104, 111. The number enumerated in 1873 may have included Pahvants who had moved to the Uintah Reservation before 1870, and stayed. See Lyman, "Chief Kanosh," 190. Chief Kanosh's complaint in 1872, about being "poked off with guns," (Chapter Nine), offers evidence that he and his people had been forced to move to the reservation, although many of them soon returned home.

42. The first gaslights appeared in the city in 1873, four years before Sally left. See Bancroft, *History of Utah*, 695n8.

43. E. Snow, *Personal Writings*, frontispiece; Spencer, *Brigham Young at Home*, 82.

44. Powell, *Anthropology of the Numa*, 208; U.S. Census, 1870, Corn Creek, Millard County, Utah Territory; Gibbs, "Moshoquop," 7. See also Knack, *Boundaries Between*, 75–76, 329n14.

45. Gibbs, *Lights and Shadows*, 109.

46. Gibbs, *Lights and Shadows*, 12–13; Gibbs, "Moshoquop," 5–7. The farmhouse and acreage, called Forest Farm, was one of Brigham Young's many properties. See Spencer, *Brigham Young at Home*, 79–80.

47. Powell, *Anthropology of the Numa*, 180, 208; D. Huntington, *Vocabulary of the Utah*, 3; Genesis 10:9 (King James Version).

48. Gibbs, "Moshoquop," 5–6; Codman, "Through Utah," 793; Ott, "Sally Kanosh." These events took place in July 1871.

49. Gibbs, "Moshoquop," 6–8. Josiah F. Gibbs (1845–1932) published this retrospective account when he was in his eighties.

50. Gibbs, "Moshoquop," 6.

51. E. Kane, *Twelve Mormon Homes*, 79. Chief Kanosh allegedly "told her that God had seen her do it; and bade her die."

52. U.S. Census, 1870, Corn Creek, Millard County, Utah Territory.

53. Mary Ann George Chesley (1859–1930), a longtime village resident who was eighteen when Sally married Chief Kanosh, recalled that the Pahvant women never accepted Sally. See Robison, "Sketch of the Life," 3.

54. E. Kane, *Twelve Mormon Homes*, 80; Ott, "Sally Kanosh"; Melville, *Interview Histories*, 32.

55. Powell, *Anthropology of the Numa*, 193; Ott, "Sally Kanosh."

56. "Death of President Brigham Young," and "Funeral of President Brigham Young," *Deseret News*, September 5, 1877; "Brigham Young's Funeral," *New York Times*, September 3, 1877; Woodruff, *Journal*, 7:371 (dated September 2, 1877).

57. Woodruff, *Journal*, 7:372 (dated September 3, 1877); W. Dixon, "Beehive and Lion Houses," 130; Arrington, *Brigham Young*, 422–30 (Appendix D); Gates, "My Recollections," [fragment], 4, Susa Young Gates Papers, box 12.

58. McGregor and Watson Jr., *Lorenzo Dow Watson*, 72–78; Ott, "Sally Kanosh."

59. Gates, *Life Story*, 284–85; Spencer, *Brigham Young at Home*, 141–42; Melville, *Interview Histories*, 286 (from an interview in 1938 with Clara Kimball Christensen [1866–1939], Adelia Hatton Kimball's granddaughter, who knew Sally in the last year of her life).

60. Crane, "Autobiography," 1; Ott, "Sally Kanosh"; McGregor and Watson Jr., *Lorenzo Dow Watson*, 72–75. Sally probably arrived at Corn Creek in mid-June 1877. Several lines of evidence suggest that she went to see Emily in September or early October, soon after Brigham Young's funeral in early September 1877. The biographical sketch by Ott apparently quotes (Alice) Nevada Watson Driggs (1891–1976), and focuses on the last year of Sally's life. Although secondhand and retrospective, it appears to be a generally reliable account of events that Driggs heard about from her mother, Emily Crane Watson (1855–1933), the daughter of George Crane (1832–1919).

61. Ott, "Sally Kanosh"

62. Thomas Kane noted in fall 1877 that the Lion House had grown "shabbier" and "dingier" since his last visit in 1872. See Grow and Walker, *Prophet and the Reformer*, 510.

63. Ott, "Sally Kanosh." The letters that Sally dictated and received do not appear to be extant.

64. Sally appears to have moved from the Lion House to the Beehive House in the early 1870s, when Clara vacated her suite and moved into a cottage. In the five years after Sally's departure from the Lion House, it grew visibly "dingier," although fewer people lived there (see note 62 above). The Leader's will was still not settled in spring 1878, months after Sally's first letter to Clara in fall 1877. See Woodruff, *Journal*, 7:411 (dated April 19, 1878).

65. Villagers understood that Sally was "called and set apart by Brigham Young" for a civilizing mission to "her people," one meant to "uplift" them "morally and spiritually." See, for example, "A Rare Picture of the Old

Days," *Millard County (Utah) Progress*, November 6, 1930; and Bailey, "Strange Mission," 18–19, 39–42.

CHAPTER 11

1. Most of the events in this chapter took place between 1877 and 1881. Records of the Brigham Young family, like federal census records, list Sally without a surname. On Sally and the dishcloth, see B. Young, "Gathering the Saints," April 9, 1871, *Journal of Discourses*, 14:89; and "Riches," May 26, 1872, *Journal of Discourses*, 15:37.

2. Christensen, *Birth of Kanosh*, 162. Mary Jane Abraham Ross (1856–1942), who was about twenty at the time, recalled the black suit, as did others, including several people who had known Sally and Chief Kanosh when they were children. See Bailey, "What Is the Truth," 13, Alice Morrey Bailey Papers, box 33, folder 1. Alice Morrey Bailey (1903–1997) questioned a number of them in the late 1920s or 1930s. Her unpublished manuscript "What Is the Truth about Sally Kanosh?" summarizes some of the many conflicting and erroneous details recalled or recorded about Sally. Some of these errors appear in her later published articles. See Bailey, "Last Wife"; and Bailey, "Strange Mission." The few excerpts from her conversations with five people who knew Sally appear to be trustworthy. I draw mainly on the comments of Clarissa Young Spencer, Susa Young Gates, Mabel Young Sanborn, Clara Kimball Christensen (see Chapter Ten, note 59), and her husband, Christian Franklin Christensen (1864–1940). The last two knew Sally in the final year of her life when she lived in their village.

3. "Obituary Notes: Adelia A. Kimball," *Deseret News*, November 14, 1896.

4. Spencer, *Brigham Young at Home*, 33.

5. E. Snow, *Personal Writings*, 35–36, 266n53.

6. The song was popular during the Civil War and for decades after the war ended, an era with high rates of migration.

7. Bailey, "What Is the Truth," 14, Alice Morrey Bailey Papers, box 33, folder 1; "A Rare Picture of the Old Days," *Millard County (Utah) Progress*, November 6, 1930. Maude Crane Melville (1875–1968) was the source for the story about Sally at the Relief Society meeting. Since Melville was only two or three years old at the time, she evidently repeated a story she later heard about Sally, perhaps from Emily, her half-sister, or from her parents.

8. Black, "Autobiography," 70; Robison, "Sketch of the Life," 3. Ted was eleven years younger than his sister, Alice Grow Black Rappleye (1857–1941). Alice gave birth to her first child in February 1877, at age nineteen, a few months before Sally arrived in the village.

9. Black, "Autobiography," 51; Melville, *Interview Histories*, 105 (from an interview with Clara Kimball Christensen in 1938).

10. Melville, *Interview Histories*, 105; Bailey, "What Is the Truth," 13, Alice Morrey Bailey Papers, box 33, folder 1.

11. When Sally arrived in the village, there were fewer than five hundred residents, and some 90 percent were younger than Sally. See U.S. Census, 1870, 1880, Kanosh, Millard County, Utah Territory.

12. A. Kimball, "Memoirs," 13; Powell, *Anthropology of the Numa*, 66.

13. Ott, "Sally Kanosh."

14. Gates, "Courtship of Kanosh," 37; Spencer, *Brigham Young at Home*, 123; "A Rare Picture of the Old Days," *Millard County (Utah) Chronicle*, November 6, 1930.

15. Christensen, *Birth of Kanosh*, 6; Black, "Autobiography," 41. This form of food collecting was maligned and called begging by most settler-colonists and by many other Americans, including Powell in a report to the federal government. See Powell, *Anthropology of the Numa*, 108.

16. Christensen, *Birth of Kanosh*, 3–4, 23; Melville, *Interview Histories*, 21. Melville's source is a 1930 interview with Harriet Ellen ("Nell") George Bird (1858–1945), a resident of Kanosh who was about nineteen when Sally moved there.

17. Melville, *Interview Histories*, 7. Melville's source is an interview with Josiah F. Gibbs in 1928. On Jane and Narrient, see U.S. Census, 1870, Corn Creek, Millard County, Utah Territory. On tattooing, see Stewart, "Culture Element Distributions," 276; and A. Smith, *Ethnography of the Northern Utes*, 79.

18. Christensen, *Birth of Kanosh*, 4.

19. Powell, *Report*, 75, 135, 142, 146–48; Arrington, "Taming the Turbulent Sevier," 405–06.

20. According to Christian F. Christensen, Sally did not ride horses. He was about fourteen years old when Sally lived in the village (see note 2 above). See Bailey, "What Is the Truth," 10, Alice Morrey Bailey Papers, box 33, folder 1.

21. Powell, *Anthropology of the Numa*, 111.

22. See, for example, "Indian Chief Kanosh," *Millard County (Utah) Chronicle*, June 12, 1930, which drew on the firsthand memories of Ellen George Bird (see note 16 above). She was in her twenties when Chief Kanosh died.

23. On the hand game, see Powell, *Anthropology of the Numa*, 62, 63.

24. Melville, *Interview Histories*, 179. The source is an interview with George Alma George (1854–1939) in 1937.

25. Clara's oldest daughter, Jeannette or Nettie, married Henry Snell, who was a few years older, sometime in the early 1870s. See A. Young, *Wife No. 19*, 487. Nettie was listed as Nett Snell in the 1880 census. See U.S. Census, 1880, Salt Lake City, Salt Lake County, Utah Territory. Nabbie married Spencer Clawson, who was her age, in February 1876. See "Local and Other Matters," *Deseret News*, February 23, 1876. Also in the 1870s, the three foster children—Celestia, Eva, and Mahonri—each married a spouse who was slightly older or younger. According to diverse genealogical records I

consulted at the Family History Library in Salt Lake City, Utah, these marriages remained monogamous. Lulu entered a monogamous marriage years later. See Appendix.

26. "Correspondence," *Deseret News*, April 11, 1877; Gates, "Courtship of Kanosh," 37.

27. Susa married in 1872, divorced in 1877, and married again in 1880. See Person, "Susa Young Gates," 201.

28. Spencer, *Brigham Young at Home*, 187.

29. Emily appears to have remained in the village until July 1878. She spent the next school year teaching in Fillmore. See "Local and Other Matters: Affairs in Kanosh," *Deseret News*, July 24, 1878; and "Correspondence: Fillmore," *Deseret News*, June 11, 1879. The solar eclipse occurred on July 29, 1878. See "The Eclipse," *Salt Lake Herald*, July 30, 1878.

30. "Funeral of a Lamanite," *Deseret News*, December 18, 1878.

31. Gates, "Brigham Young as I Knew Him," 10, Susa Young Gates Papers, box 12.

32. Powell, *Anthropology of the Numa*, 53, 57; Chamberlin, "Some Plant Names."

33. "Funeral of a Lamanite," *Deseret News*, December 18, 1878; Callaway, Janetski, and Stewart, "Ute," 352; Ott, "Sally Kanosh." Sally apparently gave the photograph to Emily sometime during the months when Emily wrote letters for her. Emily reportedly later gave the original copy to a museum in Fillmore, Utah. See "A Rare Picture of the Old Days," *Millard County (Utah) Chronicle*, November 6, 1930.

34. Stewart, "Culture Element Distributions," 313; A. Smith, *Ethnography of the Northern Utes*, 150; "Funeral of a Lamanite," *Deseret News*, December 18, 1878; Melville, *Interview Histories*, 105 (from an interview in 1938 with Clara Kimball Christensen, who went with her grandmother, Adelia, to prepare Sally's body for burial).

35. "Funeral of a Lamanite," *Deseret News*, December 18, 1878.

36. Emmitt, *Last War Trail*, 324; Callaway, Janetski, and Stewart, "Ute," 352; "Last Rites Held for E. Crane Watson," *Parowan (Utah) Times*, March 17, 1933; McGregor and Watson Jr., *Lorenzo Dow Watson*, 152–53; Ott, "Sally Kanosh."

37. E. Snow, *Personal Writings*, 31.

38. Lyman and Newell, *History of Millard County*, 136. The first ranchers from Texas settled at a site along the Sevier River in 1859. See the reminiscence of Jacob Croft (1808–1900), in Carter, *Our Pioneer Heritage*, 204.

39. Indian treaty, June 8, 1865, Brigham Young Office Files, box 29, folder 26; Woodruff, *Journal*, 7:418 (dated June 11, 1878); E. Kane, *Twelve Mormon Homes*, 76.

40. In the thirty years between Brigham Young's entry into the Great Basin, in 1847, and his death, in 1877, he reportedly established some 360 settlements in Utah Territory and adjacent areas. See Turner, *Brigham Young*, 373.

41. Conetah, *History of the Northern Ute*, 96–102; Emmitt, *Last War Trail*, 320.

42. Conetah, *History of the Northern Ute*, 101–02.

43. The names of three of these famous chiefs appeared in newspaper articles in the early 1870s. See, for example, "The Red Man," *Deseret News*, June 11, 1873; and "Eastern Notes," *Deseret News*, July 2, 1873. Chief Kanosh could not read, but he was attentive to news from non-Indian as well as Indian sources.

44. "History of East Millard County: Chief Kanosh and Kanosh Town, by E. [Edward] L. Black, November 12, 1930," *Millard County (Utah) Progress*, June 19, 1936. On Chief Kanosh's efforts to keep peace, see Lyman, "Chief Kanosh."

45. Baptisms for Pahvant dead, May 3, 1876, George W. Hill Papers. Chief Kanosh and Sally served as proxies in baptisms for the chief's deceased family members and three of his wives, as well as for the four Indian leaders. To the best of my knowledge, it has not been recognized or reported in print that Wilford Woodruff, a prominent church official, began a similar practice of proxy baptisms (for famous American leaders and eminent European men) a year after Chief Kanosh requested and took part in proxy baptisms for the four famous Indian leaders. See Woodruff, *Journal*, 7:367–69 (dated August 19, 21, 1877); and Woodruff, "Not Ashamed of the Gospel," September 16, 1877, *Journal of Discourses*, 19:229. On Wilford Woodruff (1807–1898), see Alexander, *Things in Heaven*.

46. Codman, "Through Utah," 794; "History of Millard County: Chief Kanosh and Kanosh Town, by E. [Edward] L. Black, November 12, 1930," *Millard County (Utah) Progress*, June 19, 1936.

47. "Correspondence: Kanosh, Millard County, August 11, 1881," *Deseret News*, August 24, 1881.

48. "Correspondence: Death of Kanosh," *Deseret News*, December 28, 1881; R. A. McBride to D. B. Huntington, August 18, 1874, Brigham Young Office Files, box 35, folder 9. Sally and Chief Kanosh were buried in the village cemetery. Around the turn of the twentieth century, a new cemetery was established. Reportedly, few bodies were moved from the old cemetery, but grave markers were taken to the new site. The bodies of Chief Kanosh and Sally may remain in unmarked graves in the first cemetery. See Christensen, *Birth of Kanosh*, 160, 161. If so, a monument erected years after Chief Kanosh's death, and still standing in that second cemetery, does not stand at his gravesite (personal observation at site, Kanosh Cemetery, Kanosh, Utah, December 20, 2013).

49. Christensen, *Birth of Kanosh*, 157; Bailey, "Wives of Chief Kanosh," 1–2, Alice Morrey Bailey Papers, box 33, folder 1. Linguist Tom Givón suggests that the name that English speakers wrote as Kanosh was likely aka-nuuch(i), meaning Red Ute or Red (Ute) Person. In the twentieth century, another Ute leader—a Southern Ute Sun Dance chief—also bore this name (Tom Givón, personal communication, June 7, 2018).

50. "They have no conception of a supreme being," Powell wrote. He recorded the name for Wolf as Shin-au′-av and Sin-au′-av. See Powell, *Anthropology of the Numa*, 69, 72, 172. Forty years later, Frances Densmore recorded a Northern Ute word that she transcribed as So′nawav, which she was told meant "God." See Densmore, *Northern Ute Music*, 19. See also Conetah, *History of the Northern Ute*, 2; Duncan, "Northern Utes of Utah," 167; and Hebner, *Southern Paiute*, 66, quoting McKay Pikyavit (1930–2004). Dimick Huntington, in contrast and evidently for theological reasons, consistently translated Shin-nob as "Devil," as did other settlers. See D. Huntington, *Few Words in the Utah Dialect*, 6; D. Huntington, *Few Words in the Utah and Sho-sho-nee Dialects*, 7; D. Huntington, *Vocabulary of the Utah*, 7; and Gottfredson, *Indian Depredations*, 322.

51. "Correspondence: Death of Kanosh," *Deseret News*, December 28, 1881. Levi Christensen draws on Edward (Ted) L. Black's memories or written account of the funeral, which took place when he was thirteen years old. See Christensen, *Birth of Kanosh*, 160.

52. Powell, *Anthropology of the Numa*, 66, 69. Powell recorded this Ute account of the journey after death, probably in the early or mid-1870s with the close assistance of Ai-po-up (Richard Komas). Many Pahvant Utes at Corn Creek had been baptized but apparently did not have a deep understanding of church doctrines. In contrast, the particular understanding of Chief Kanosh about death and afterlife presumably did incorporate some features of church doctrine.

53. In 1872, Chief Kanosh said that he was forty-eight years old. See E. Kane, Notes of Kanosh's interview. Five years later, when he married Sally, he gave his age as fifty-three. See Marriage certificate of "Kanosh (Indian) to Kahpeputz or Sally, also an Indian," June 8, 1877, Historian's Office Marriage Certificates 1876–1888, Salt Lake County, 1876–1879, CR 100 424, Church History Library, Church of Jesus Christ of Latter-day Saints. Chief Kanosh was presumably about fifty-seven at the time of his death in 1881.

54. "Correspondence: Death of Kanosh," *Deseret News*, December 28, 1881; "History of East Millard County: Chief Kanosh and Kanosh Town, by E. [Edward] L. Black, November 12, 1930," *Millard County (Utah) Progress*, June 19, 1936; Christensen, *Birth of Kanosh*, 160, 161. The monument that was erected in his honor in the twentieth century mistakenly gives his date of death as 1884 (personal observation at site, December 20, 2013, Kanosh Cemetery, Kanosh, Utah).

CHAPTER 12

1. Most of the events in this chapter took place between 1884 and 1920. The Bancrofts visited the city in 1884. See "A Great Work by a Great Historian," *Deseret News*, August 27, 1884.

2. Bancroft, *Native Races,* 422, 463–68; Bancroft, *Literary Industries.* See also C. Peterson, "Hubert Howe Bancroft"; and Ellsworth, "Hubert Howe Bancroft."

   On Frances Auretta Fuller Victor (1826–1902), one of Bancroft's writers who single-handedly wrote several volumes on the Northwestern states, see Johannsen, *House of Beadle and Adams,* 2:29–30; and F. Walker, "Frances Auretta Fuller Victor," 519.

3. Bancroft, *History of Utah,* 695–98; Bancroft, *Literary Industries,* 407–09. On restoring the Earth to what settler-colonists imagined as an Eden-like state, see Kay and Brown, "Mormon Beliefs about Land," 253.

4. Bancroft, *History of Utah,* 691–92. In 1870, Utah Territory reportedly counted only 119,000 "improved farm acres" among more than fifty million acres of land within its borders. See Worster, *River Running West,* 352.

5. Bancroft, *Literary Industries,* 409; C. Young, "Woman's Experience" (recorded by Matilda Bancroft in 1884). See Bancroft, *History of Utah,* 283n24, 331; and Ellsworth, "Guide to the Manuscripts," 231. Clara was one of only three women to reach the valley with the first party of settlers in July 1847.

6. E. Smith, "Sketch of My Life," 135, 314, 351; Ellsworth, "Guide to the Manuscripts," 213–14. Eliza's manuscript was dated April 13, 1885. She had written an earlier version, portions of which appeared in print in 1877, with no mention of Sally. See Tullidge, *Women of Mormondom.*

7. Bancroft, *History of Utah,* 278n12, 692. The footnote about Sally came from the "Narrative of Daniel H. Wells," recorded in 1884. See Ellsworth, "Guide to the Manuscripts," 229. Wells reached the valley in 1848, nearly a year after the trade for Sally.

8. Bancroft, *History of Utah,* 472, 473, 696.

9. Susa's young son, Brigham Young Gates (1896–1900), died in April 1900. In a census taken later that year, she was listed as the mother of thirteen children, five still living. See U.S. Census, 1900, Provo, Utah County, Utah. Her "nervous breakdown," as she called it, also occurred sometime in 1900. (According to her later written statement, the breakdown came eleven years after she founded a magazine for young women, in 1889). She did not mention that the eighth death of a child occurred in the same year as her breakdown. See Person, "Susa Young Gates," 217; and Jenson, "Susa Young Gates," 137.

10. Gates, "Lucy Bigelow Young," 69, Susa Young Gates Papers, box 14. On the literary and other professional activities of Susa Young Gates, see Person, "Susa Young Gates."

11. Gates, "Courtship of Kanosh," 38. Susa wrote this story as a faith-promoting, morally uplifting tale, and published it in a church-sponsored magazine. On early Mormonism as a utopian movement deeply imbued with notions of progress, see Leone, *Roots of Modern Mormonism.*

12. Chief Wanship's raid took place in April 1849. See Stout, *On the Mormon Frontier*, 351 (dated April 20, 28, 1849). On the captive boy and the sale of Sally, see E. Snow, *Personal Writings*, 31, 214 (dated December 14, 1847).

13. Woodruff, *Journal*, 3:234, 239 (dated July 24, 28, 1847); B. Young, "Gathering the Saints," April 9, 1871, *Journal of Discourses*, 14:87. Thirty years after settlement, Woodruff, like many others, recalled the valley as a "barren desert." See Woodruff, "Not Ashamed of the Gospel," September 16, 1877, *Journal of Discourses*, 19:224.

14. J. Young, Memoirs, 63.

15. J. Young, Memoirs, 63.

16. Internal evidence in John R. Young's memoir, published in 1920, suggests that he began to write it sometime around 1906, a year after Susa's story "The Courtship of Kanosh" reached print. On Buffalo Bill and the rise and demise of Wild West shows, see Bridger, *Buffalo Bill and Sitting Bull*.

17. Gates, *Life Story*, 136.

18. "Correspondence: Funeral of a Lamanite," *Deseret News*, December 18, 1878; Ott, "Sally Kanosh."

19. Gates, "Courtship of Kanosh," 29; Spencer, *Brigham Young at Home*, 123. What the family in 1872 represented to Elizabeth Kane as Sally's "'morbid' horror" would today most likely be called post-traumatic stress disorder. The violence of the Indian stories she heard presumably triggered memories of the trauma she experienced as a captive.

    My inference that Baptiste may have been Pahvant Ute is based on a variety of circumstantial evidence, including his long and well-documented association with Chief Tintic. According to Northern Ute elder Clifford Duncan ("Northern Utes," 192), Tintic was Pahvant Ute.

20. Gates, *Life Story*, 355; A. Smith, *Ethnography of the Northern Utes*, 151; Stewart, "Culture Element Distributions," 313–14. In the 1830s, during Sally's early life, Warren A. Ferris observed mourning practices of the "Eutaws" and other "Rocky Mountain tribes." Some mourners cut off a finger at the joint; they cut their hair, and remained in mourning until it grew back; they blackened their faces; and all wailed in "a piercing, wild, monotonous lamentation." See W. Ferris, *Life in the Rocky Mountains*, 238. A century later, in the 1930s, Ute informants denied that mourners gashed shoulders and legs or cut off part of a finger. See Stewart, "Culture Element Distributions," 314, 333. It may be that such practices had ended years earlier, and were forgotten; or that death and the dead remained highly sensitive topics, not to be discussed in detail with outsiders.

21. It has not previously been suggested by those who have written about Sally—from Eliza Snow and John R. Young to later writers and historians—that she was in mourning when Charley bought her. Eliza's account (E. Smith, "Sketch of My Life"), which reports Sally's self-identification as Pahvant and her statement that her father had died, was overlooked. So too

were ethnographic sources about death and mourning, and the physical appearance of mourners.

On Ute raids for slaves, see Kelly and Fowler, "Southern Paiute," 369. According to Anne M. Smith (*Ethnography of the Northern Utes*, 25), "Though the Utes raided the Southern Paiutes and took slaves, there is no record of such incidents among the various bands of Utes." If Sally was living with Pahvant Utes at the time of capture, as seems likely, the circumstances leading to her captivity were complicated and unusual.

A twenty-first-century American might well conjecture or conclude that sexual orientation explains Sally's avoidance of marriage. So far as I can tell, that possibility is not supported by documentary or ethnographic evidence.

22. Gates, "Courtship of Kanosh," 25. See also Gates, "Brigham Young and the Indians," 12, Susan Young Gates Papers, box 12. Cross-cultural research by anthropologists shows that rape is not a universal practice, and the incidence of rape varies greatly, with some societies qualifying as rape-free and others as rape-prone. See Sanday, "Rape-Free versus Rape-Prone," 337–61. I have found only two reported instances of rapes by Indian men in the era soon after Anglo-American settlement. Alcohol, newly introduced, was implicated as a cause of the violence. On a case from Colorado—the rape of a Ute woman by a Ute man, as reported years later to Anne M. Smith by a Ute informant in the 1930s—see A. Smith, *Ute Tales*, 162. In contrast, the second case, from Utah Territory, was reported soon after the alleged event, but in a newspaper article written by a transient visitor to the city ("Letter from Mr. Wallace in Utah," *Daily Alta California* [San Francisco], October 21, 1858). The visitor heard that Ute men raped a Danish woman and her daughter. See also Moorman, *Camp Floyd*, 197–98. Sondra Jones cites an eighteenth-century report of a Spanish friar in New Mexico that mentions the public rape of a young Indian woman by her Indian captors. See S. Jones, "'Redeeming' the Indian," 223n8. (But Spanish men seem to have raped, and impregnated, far more captive Indian women. See, for example, J. F. Brooks, *Captives and Cousins*, 51, 56.)

23. Exley, *Frontier Blood*, 153–61. Naudah was captured in 1860.

24. Exley, *Frontier Blood*, 173–74, 177, 179; Frankel, *Searchers*, 67–72, 78, 91–92. Naudah died in 1870.

25. Exley, *Frontier Blood*, 179; Frankel, *Searchers*, 120–24; U.S. Office of Indian Affairs, *Annual Report* (1874), 3–4. Comanches were counted as one of "the wildest of the tribes."

26. The 1954 novel by Alan Le May and the 1956 film directed by John Ford, *The Searchers*, took great liberties with the facts of Cynthia Ann Parker's life. See Frankel, *Searchers*.

27. "Correspondence: Death of [Chief] Kanosh," *Deseret News*, December 28, 1881.

28. Moshoquop reportedly died in 1893. See Gibbs, "Gunnsion Massacre," 71. Twenty-three years earlier, a census taker recorded Moshoquop's age as thirty-five, which suggests that he was about fifty-eight years old when he died. See U.S. Census, 1870, Corn Creek, Millard County, Utah Territory.

29. Personal observation at site, Sevier (Dry) Lake, Millard County, Utah, September 19, 2017; Arrington, "Taming the Turbulent Sevier." Some years after Sevier Lake, on the eastern edge of the Great Basin, died of thirst, Owens Lake, on the western edge, also succumbed. Most of the Owens River's water was diverted not to irrigate crops but to support the growth of a distant city, Los Angeles. The dry lake became the largest source of dust pollution in the United States. See Kerns, *Scenes,* 8, 91, 177–78.

30. Lyman and King, *History of Millard County*, 52; Gibbs, "Gunnison Massacre," 69. Catherine S. Fowler recovered the manuscripts from storage in 1963 (Don D. Fowler, personal communication, June 21, 2018; Catherine S. Fowler, personal communication, June 23, 2108).

31. In 1985, when the respected historian Leonard J. Arrington explicitly identified Sally as the foster child of Brigham Young, he may have borrowed silently from Alice M. Bailey's language in an article about Sally, published in 1980. See Arrington, *Brigham Young*, 171; and Bailey, "Last Wife," 20. I was one of many who later repeated this claim in print. See Kerns, *Journeys West*, 228.

32. Whitney, *History of Utah*, 67. The different claims about Sally's cultural origins, the nature of the trade for her, when she died, and other aspects of her story, occur in a wide range of sources: from newspaper and magazine articles to general-audience books to scholarly works published in the twentieth and early twenty-first centuries. I have cited only a few representative examples of the many in print.

33. "A Rare Picture of the Old Days," *Millard County (Utah) Chronicle*, November 6, 1930; Bailey, "What Is the Truth," 11, Alice Morrey Bailey Papers, box 33, folder 1; Spencer, *Brigham Young at Home*, 122.

34. "Mrs. Ellen Bird Corrects Early Kanosh History about Betsykin," *Millard County (Utah) Chronicle*, September 3, 1936; "The Accepted History of Sally, Kanosh's Wife," *Millard County (Utah) Chronicle*, April 3, 1941; Bailey, "Wives of Chief Kanosh," 18, Alice Morrey Bailey Papers, box 33, folder 1; Whitney, *History of Utah*, 67. George Crane gave no cause of death in the obituary he wrote soon after Sally's death. See "Funeral of a Lamanite," *Deseret News*, December 18, 1878. Emily Crane thought that Sally had grown "too sensitive and cultured to endure the test of living as did her native people." See "A Rare Picture of the Old Days," *Millard County (Utah) Progress*, November 6, 1930; and "Just History," *Salt Lake Telegram*, September 4, 1924. Mary Jane Abraham Ross (see Chapter Eleven, note 2), a longtime resident of the village who was in her early twenties when Sally died, later said, "She died of a broken heart." See M. Dixon, *These Were the*

Utes, 107. A growing body of medical and psychological research now links social isolation and loneliness to premature mortality. Socially isolated adults are more likely to succumb to disease than those who are strongly embedded in families and communities. See Holt-Lunstad et al., "Loneliness and Social Isolation."

35. Arrington, "Taming the Turbulent Sevier." According to some sources Sally died before her husband (as is documented by her published obituary); and according to others, she died after him. See, for example, "History of East Millard County: Chief Kanosh and Kanosh Town, by E. [Edward] L. Black, November 12, 1930," *Millard County (Utah) Progress*, June 19, 1936; "Pageant Depicting the Life of Chief Kanosh," *Millard County (Utah) Chronicle*, June 21, 1934; Gates, *Life Story*, 136; M. Dixon, *These Were the Utes*, 108.

36. A photograph of Brigham Young and an unidentified woman (unidentified because she is defaced) gave rise in recent years to stories in Salt Lake City media that Sally was his secret plural wife. The woman in the photograph wears what have been described as "Indian bracelets." That photograph, dated between 1850 and 1854, was earlier the subject of an article by two scholars who offered suggestions about the identity of the woman, but who did *not* identify her as Sally. Lucy was one of the three women they named. See Holzapfel and Schwartz, "Mysterious Image," 49–58.

I suggest, given the following evidence, that the defaced woman in the photograph is Zina. The woman wears a dress that appears to be the same dress that Zina wore in an 1856 photograph with her daughter, who was born in 1850. I base that judgment on various design details of the dress (the fabric, white cuffs, collar, and what appears to be a smocked waist). Zina also wears a bracelet, although a different one, in the 1856 photograph (which is reproduced in Bradley and Woodward, *Four Zinas*, between pages 274 and 275). She may have obtained Indian bracelets shown in the earlier photograph during her month-long visit in August and September 1849 to the Valley of the Utahs (Utah Valley), where her brother Dimick had recently moved. See Z. Young, "'A Weary Traveler,'" 114 (dated August 14, September 10, 1849). The earlier photograph, with her husband, Brigham Young, probably dates from fall 1849, before Zina was visibly pregnant; or perhaps from sometime in 1850, after she gave birth to her daughter.

37. Dodge, *Biographical Sketch*, 21, 23, 25, 26; White, *Railroaded*, 462–66; Froude, *Oceana*, 257–58, 373. James Anthony Froude (1818–1894) crossed the United States by train in about 1885.

38. Dodge, *Biographical Sketch*, 23–24. Bridger's death was widely reported. See, for example, "Death of a Famous Ranger," *New York Times*, July 20, 1881.

39. See, for example, McKay Pikyavit and Lila Carter, in Hebner, *Southern Paiute*, 64–68, 153. See also Conetah, *History of the Northern Ute*; and Duncan, "Northern Utes."

Bibliography

ARCHIVAL AND PRINT PRIMARY SOURCES

Bailey, Alice Morrey. Alice Morrey Bailey Papers. Accn 1676. Marriott Library Special Collections, University of Utah, Salt Lake City.

Baker, Gerard A. "Mandan and Hidatsa of the Upper Missouri." In *Lewis and Clark through Indian Eyes*, edited by Alvin M. Josephy Jr., with Marc Jaffe, 123–36. New York: Alfred A. Knopf, 2006.

Bancroft, Hubert Howe. *Literary Industries: A Memoir.* New York: Harper and Brothers, 1891.

Bean, George Washington. *Autobiography of George Washington Bean.* Edited by Flora Diana Bean Horne. Salt Lake City: Utah Publishing Company, 1945.

Beecher, Catharine, and Harriet Beecher Stowe. *The American Woman's Home.* New York: J. B. Ford, 1869.

Bennion, Israel. "Indian Reminiscences." *Utah Historical Quarterly* 2, no. 2 (1930): 43–46.

Black, Edward L. "Autobiography." 1946. MSS A 47. Research Center for Utah State Archives and Utah State History, Salt Lake City.

Bullock, Thomas. *The Pioneer Camp of the Saints: The 1847 and 1848 Trail Journals of Thomas Bullock.* Edited by Will Bagley. Spokane, WA: A. H. Clark, 1997.

Burton, Richard F. *The City of the Saints, and across the Rocky Mountains to California.* London: Longman, Green, Longman, and Roberts, 1861.

———. Translator's Foreword to *The Book of a Thousand Nights and a Night: A Plain and Literal Translation of the Arabian Nights' Entertainments*, vol. 1, vii–xxi. Translated by Richard F. Burton. [London?]: privately printed by the Burton Club, 1885.

Carvalho, S. N. *Incidents of Travel and Adventure in the Far West; with Col. Fremont's Last Expedition.* New York: Derby and Jackson, 1857.

Chamberlin, Ralph V. "Some Plant Names of the Ute Indians." *American Anthropologist* 11, no. 1 (1909): 27–40.

———. "The Ethno-Botany of the Gosiute Indians of Utah." *American Anthropological Association Memoirs* 2, pt. 5 (1911): 331–53.

Chandless, William. *A Visit to Salt Lake; Being a Journey across the Plains and a Residence in the Mormon Settlements at Utah.* London: Smith, Elder, 1857.

Clark, John. "Auto-Biography." Microfilm US/CAN 1036356, item 27. Family History Library, The Church of Jesus Christ of Latter-day Saints, Salt Lake City, UT.

Clayton, William. *An Intimate Chronicle: The Journals of William Clayton.* Edited by George D. Smith. Salt Lake City, UT: Signature Books, 1995.

———. *The Latter-day Saints' Emigrants' Guide.* St. Louis: Missouri Republican Steam Power Press–Chambers and Knapp, 1848.

———. *William Clayton's Journal.* Salt Lake City, UT: Deseret News, for the Clayton Family Association, 1921.

Codman, John. *The Mormon Country: A Summer with the "Latter-day Saints."* New York: United States Publishing Company, 1874.

———. "Through Utah." *The Galaxy* 20, no. 6 (1875): 790–99.

Conetah, Fred A. *A History of the Northern Ute People.* Edited by Kathryn L. MacKay and Floyd A. O'Neil. Salt Lake City, UT: Uintah-Ouray Ute Tribe, 1982.

Conner, Roberta. "Our People Have Always Been Here." In *Lewis and Clark through Indian Eyes*, edited by Alfred M. Josephy Jr., with Marc Jaffe, 85–119. New York: Alfred A. Knopf, 2006.

Cooke, Lucy Rutledge. "Letters on the Way to California." In *Covered Wagon Women: Diaries and Letters from the Western Trails, 1852*, compiled and edited by Kenneth L. Holmes, vol. 4, 209–95. Lincoln: University of Nebraska Press, 1985.

Crane, George. "George Crane Autobiography, 1832–1879." 1913. MS 75. Marriot Library Special Collections, University of Utah, Salt Lake City.

Crosby, Caroline Barnes. *No Place to Call Home: The 1807–1857 Life Writings of Caroline Barnes Crosby, Chronicler of Outlying Mormon Communities.* Edited by Edward Leo Lyman, Susan Ward Payne, and S. George Ellsworth. Logan: Utah State University Press, 2005.

Cummings, Mariett Foster. "A Trip across the Continent." In *Covered Wagon Women: Diaries and Letters from the Western Trails, 1852*, vol. 4, 117–68. Compiled and edited by Kenneth L. Holmes. Lincoln: University of Nebraska Press, 1985.

Daughters of Utah Pioneers Lesson Committee, comp. *Chronicles of Courage.* Vol. 1. Salt Lake City: Daughters of Utah Pioneers, 1990.

Dodge, Grenville M. "Autobiography." Personal Biography, Vol. 3, Grenville Mellon Dodge Papers, 1850–1916. MS 98. Special Collections, State Historical Society of Iowa, Des Moines.

———. *Biographical Sketch of James Bridger: Mountaineer, Trapper and Guide.* New York: Unz and Company, 1905.

Drake, Samuel G. *Tragedies of the Wilderness; or, True and Authentic Narratives of Captives.* Boston: Antiquarian Bookstore and Institute, 1841.

Duncan, Clifford. "The Northern Utes of Utah." In *A History of Utah's American Indians*, edited by Forrest S. Cuch, 167–224. Salt Lake City: Utah State Division of Indian Affairs/Utah State Division of History, 2000.

Egan, Howard. *Pioneering the West, 1846 to 1878: Major Howard Egan's Diary.* Richmond, UT: H. R. Egan Estate, 1917.

Emerson, Ralph Waldo. *The Journals and Miscellaneous Notebooks of Ralph Waldo Emerson.* Vol. 15, 1860–1866, edited by Linda Allardt, David W. Hill, and Ruth H. Bennett. Cambridge, MA: Belknap Press of Harvard University Press, 1982.

Farnham, Thomas J. *Travels in the Great Western Prairies, the Anahuac and Rocky Mountains, and in the Oregon Territory.* New York: Wiley and Putnam, 1843.

Ferguson, Charles D. *Experiences of a Forty-Niner during Thirty Years' Residence in California and Australia.* Edited by Frederick T. Wallace. Cleveland, OH: Williams, 1888.

Ferris, Mrs. B. G. [Elizabeth Cornelia]. *The Mormons at Home; with Some Incidents of Travel from Missouri to California, 1852–53.* New York: Dix and Edwards, 1856.

Ferris, Warren Angus. *Life in the Rocky Mountains, 1830–1835.* Salt Lake City, UT: Rocky Mountain Book Shop, 1940.

Frémont, John C. *Report of the Exploring Expedition to the Rocky Mountains in the Year 1842, and to Oregon and North California in the Years 1843–44.* Washington, D.C.: Gales and Seaton, Printers, 1845.

Froude, James Anthony. *Oceana; or, England and Her Colonies.* London: Longmans, Green, 1886.

Gates, Susa Young. "The Courtship of Kanosh: A Pioneer Indian Love Story." *Improvement Era* 9, no. 9 (1905): 21–38.

———. "From Impulsive Girl to Patient Wife: Lucy Bigelow Young." Edited by Miriam Murphy. *Utah Historical Quarterly* 45, no. 3 (1977): 270–88.

———. "How Brigham Young Brought Up His Fifty-Six Children." *Physical Culture* (February 1925): 29–31, 138–44.

———. *The Life Story of Brigham Young.* With Leah D. Widtsoe. New York: Macmillan, 1930.

———. Susa Young Gates Papers. MSS B 95. Research Center for Utah State Archives and Utah State History, Salt Lake City.

Gibbs, Josiah F. "Gunnsion Massacre, 1853, Millard County, Utah—Indian Mareer's Version of the Tragedy—1894." *Utah Historical Quarterly* 1, no. 3 (1928): 67–75.

———. *Lights and Shadows of Mormonism.* Salt Lake City, UT: Salt Lake Tribune, 1909.

———. "Moshoquop: The Avenger and Loyal Friend." *Utah Historical Quarterly* 2, no. 1 (1929): 3–8.

Givón, T., comp. and ed. *Ute Texts*. Vol. 7, *Culture and Language Use*. Amsterdam and Philadelphia: John Benjamins, 2013.

Gottfredson, Peter, comp. *Indian Depredations in Utah*. Salt Lake City, UT: Skelton, 1919.

Gray, William H. "The Unpublished Journal of William H. Gray, from December, 1836 to October, 1837." *Whitman College Quarterly* 16, no. 2 (1913).

Greeley, Horace. *An Overland Journey from New York to San Francisco*. New York: C. M. Saxton, Barker, 1860.

Gunnison, John W. *The Mormons; or, Latter-day Saints in the Valley of the Great Salt Lake*. Philadelphia: Lippincott, Grambo, 1852.

Heywood, Martha Spence. *Not by Bread Alone: The Journal of Martha Spence Heywood, 1850–56*. Edited by Juanita Brooks. Salt Lake City: Utah State Historical Society, 1978.

Hill, George W. George W. Hill Papers, 1842–1883. MS 8172. Church History Library, The Church of Jesus Christ of Latter-day Saints, Salt Lake City, UT.

Horne, M. Isabella. "Home Life in the Pioneer Fort." *Juvenile Instructor* 29, no. 6 (1894): 181–85.

———. "Pioneer Reminiscences." *Young Woman's Journal* 13, no. 7 (1902): 292–95.

Huntington, Dimick B. *A Few Words in the Utah and Sho-sho-nee Dialects, Alphabetically Arranged*. 2nd ed., rev. and enlarged. Great Salt Lake City, Utah Territory: W. Richards, 1854. Copy at Marriott Library Special Collections, University of Utah, Salt Lake City.

———. *A Few Words in the Utah Dialect, Alphabetically Arranged*. [Fragment, 1853?] Copy at Church History Library, The Church of Jesus Christ of Latter-day Saints, Salt Lake City, UT.

———. *Vocabulary of the Utah and Sho-sho-ne or Snake Dialects*. 3rd ed. Salt Lake City, UT: Salt Lake Herald Office, 1872. Copy at Church History Library, The Church of Jesus Christ of Latter-day Saints, Salt Lake City, UT.

Huntington, Oliver Boardman. "Oliver Boardman Huntington Journals, 1842–1900." MSS A 858-1. Research Center for Utah State Archives and Utah State History, Salt Lake City.

Hurt, Garland. "Appendix O: Indians of Utah." In *Report of Explorations across the Great Basin of the Territory of Utah*, by J. H. Simpson, 459–64. Washington, D.C.: Government Printing Office, 1876.

Jefferson, Thomas. *Notes on the State of Virginia*. 1787. Reprinted in *Writings*, 123–325. Edited by Merrill D. Peterson. New York: Literary Classics of the United States, distributed by Penguin Putnam, 1984.

Jenson, Harold H. "Susa Young Gates." *Juvenile Instructor* 64, no. 3 (1929): 135–37.

Johnston, William Graham. *Experiences of a Forty-Niner*. Pittsburgh, 1892.

Jones, Daniel W. *Forty Years among the Indians*. Salt Lake City, UT: Juvenile Instructor Office, 1890.

Journal History of the Church, 1830–1973. Microfilm US/CAN 1259729-1259975. Family History Library, The Church of Jesus Christ of Latter-day Saints, Salt Lake City, UT.

Journal of Discourses, by Brigham Young, His Two Counsellors, the Twelve Apostles, and Others. Recorded by G. D. Watt et al. 26 vols. Liverpool and London, 1854–1886.

Kane, Elizabeth Wood. *A Gentile Account of Life in Utah's Dixie, 1872–73: Elizabeth Kane's St. George Journal*. With a preface and notes by Norman R. Bowen. Salt Lake City: University of Utah Library, 1995.

———. Notes of Kanosh's interview with K, taken at Fillmore, [Utah Territory,] December 1872. MSS 792. Harold B. Lee Library, L. Tom Perry Special Collections, Brigham Young University, Provo, Utah.

———. *Twelve Mormon Homes Visited in Succession on a Journey through Utah to Arizona*. Philadelphia: printed for private circulation, 1874.

Kane, Thomas. *The Mormons: A Discourse Delivered before the Historical Society of Pennsylvania, March 26, 1850*. Philadelphia: King and Baird, 1850.

Kimball, Adelia Wilcox Hatton. "Memoirs of Adelia Almira Wilcox, One of the Plural Wives of Heber C. Kimball." Edited by Stanley H. B. Kimball. Adelia Almira Wilcox Hatton Woods Kimball Papers. Accn 2234, folder 1. Marriott Library Special Collections, University of Utah, Salt Lake City.

Kimball, Mary Ellen. *Journal of Mary Ellen Kimball*. Salt Lake City, UT: Pioneer Press, 1994.

Kimball, Solomon. "Our Pioneer Boys." *Improvement Era* 11, no. 10 (1908): 734–42.

Lehmann, Herman. *Nine Years among the Indians, 1870–1879*. Austin, TX: Von Boeckmann-Jones, ca. 1927. Reprint. Edited by J. Marvin Hunter. Albuquerque: University of New Mexico Press, 1993. Page references are to the 1993 edition.

Lincoln University. *Catalogue of the Officers and Students of Lincoln University, 1872–'73*. Pennsylvania: Lincoln University, 1872–1873.

Melville, Maude Crane. *Interview Histories of Pioneers from East Millard County and Other Areas of Utah: Interviews and Writings by Maude Crane Melville, 1920–1949*. Edited by Randall J. Staples. Centerville, UT: R. J. Staples, 2009. Copy at Family History Library, The Church of Jesus Christ of Latter-day Saints. Salt Lake City, UT.

Merrill, Cyrena Dustin. "Autobiography." MSS SC 2180. Harold B. Lee Library, L. Tom Perry Special Collections, Brigham Young University, Provo, UT.

Morgan, Dale L., comp. and ed. "Letters by Forty-Niners." *Western Humanities Review* 3, no. 2 (1949): 98–116.

Muir, John. *Our National Parks*. Boston: Houghton, Mifflin, 1901.

———. *Steep Trails: California, Utah, Nevada, Washington, Oregon, the Grand Cañon*. Boston: Houghton, Mifflin, 1918.

Murphy, Virginia Reed. "Across the Plains in the Donner Party (1846): A Personal Narrative of the Overland Trip to California, 1846–47." *Century Illustrated Monthly Magazine* 42, no. 35 (1891): 409–26.

Nebeker, John. "Early Justice." [Recorded in 1884.] MSS A 766. Research Center for Utah State Archives and Utah State History, Salt Lake City.

Ott, Layton J. "Sally Kanosh." Works Progress Administration (Utah Section), Biographical Sketches, ca. 1930–1940, MS B 289, Research Center for Utah State Archives and Utah State History, Salt Lake City.

Plummer, Rachel. *Rachel Plummer's Narrative of Twenty One Months Servitude as a Prisoner among the Commanchee.* Houston, TX: Telegraph Power Press, 1838.

Powell, John Wesley. *Anthropology of the Numa: John Wesley Powell's Manuscripts on the Numic Peoples of Western North America, 1868–1880.* Edited by Don D. Fowler and Catherine S. Fowler. Washington, D.C.: Smithsonian Institution Press, 1971.

———. *Report on the Lands of the Arid Region of the United States, with a More Detailed Account of the Lands of Utah.* 2nd ed. Washington, D.C.: Government Printing Office, 1879.

———. "Sketch of the Mythology of the North American Indians." In *First Annual Report of the Bureau of Ethnology for the Years 1879–1880*, 19–56. Washington, D.C.: Government Printing Office, 1881.

Pratt, Orson. "Interesting Items [...] (Extracted from the Private Journal of Orson Pratt)." *Millenial Star*, 12, no. 2 (1850): 17–19; no. 11 (1850): 161–66; no. 12 (1850): 177–80.

Pratt, Parley P., "To President Orson Pratt and the Saints in Great Britain (dated September 5, 1848)," *Millennial Star* 11, no. 2 (1849): 21–24.

Prucha, Francis Paul, ed. *Documents of United States Indian Policy.* 3rd ed. Westport, CT: Praeger, 2000.

Pulsipher, John. "John Pulsipher Diaries." MS 92. Marriott Library Special Collections, University of Utah, Salt Lake City.

Rémy, Jules. *A Journey to Great-Salt-Lake City.* 2 vols. London: W. Jeffs, 1861.

Russell, Osborne. *Journal of a Trapper; or, Nine Years in the Rocky Mountains, 1834–1843.* Boise, ID: Syms-York, 1921.

Schoolcraft, Henry R. *Oneóta; or, Characteristics of the Red Race of America: From Original Notes and Manuscripts.* New York and London: Wiley and Putnam, 1845.

Sessions, Patty Bartlett. *Mormon Midwife: The 1846–1888 Diaries of Patty Bartlett Sessions.* Edited by Donna Toland Smart. Logan: Utah State University Press, 1997.

Smart, William B., and Donna T. Smart, eds. *Over the Rim: The Parley P. Pratt Exploring Expedition to Southern Utah, 1849–1850.* Logan: Utah State University Press, 1999.

Smith, Anne M., comp. *Shoshone Tales.* With the assistance of Alden Hayes. With a foreword by Catherine S. Fowler and an afterword by Beverly Crum. Salt Lake City: University of Utah Press, 1993.

———. *Ute Tales.* With the assistance of Alden Hayes. With a foreword by Joseph Jorgenson. Salt Lake City: University of Utah Press, 1992.

Smith, Eliza R. Snow. "Sketch of My Life." *Relief Society Magazine* 31, no. 3 (1944): 131–36; 31, no. 6 (1944): 313–14, 351.

Smith, Jedediah S. *The Southwest Expedition of Jedediah S. Smith: His Personal Account of the Journey to California, 1826–1827.* Edited by George H. Brooks. Lincoln: University of Nebraska Press, 1989.

Snow, Eliza R. *The Personal Writings of Eliza Roxcy Snow.* Edited by Maureen Ursenbach Beecher. Salt Lake City: University of Utah Press, 1995.

Snow, Moroni, ed. "From Nauvoo to Salt Lake in the Van of the Pioneers: The Original Diary of Erastus Snow." *Improvement Era* 15, no. 5 (1912): 407–11; 15, no. 6 (1912): 551–54.

Spencer, Clarissa Young. *Brigham Young at Home.* With Mabel Harmer. Salt Lake City, UT: Deseret Book, 1940.

Stansbury, Howard. *An Expedition to the Valley of the Great Salt Lake in Utah.* Philadelphia: Lippincott, Grambo, 1855.

Stenhouse, Mrs. T. B. H. [Fanny]. *Exposé of Polygamy in Utah.* New York: American News, 1872.

———. *"Tell It All": The Story of a Life's Experience in Mormonism.* Hartford, CT: A. D. Worthington, 1875.

Stewart, Omer C. "Culture Element Distributions: XVIII, Ute-Southern Paiute." *Anthropological Records* 6, no. 4 (1942): 231–356.

Stout, Hosea. *On the Mormon Frontier: The Diary of Hosea Stout.* Vol. 2, 1848–1861, edited by Juanita Brooks. Salt Lake City: University of Utah Press, 1964.

Stratton, R. B. *Captivity of the Oatman Girls: Being an Interesting Narrative of Life among the Apache and Mohave Indians.* New York: published for the author by Carlton and Porter, 1858.

Thayer, James Bradley. *A Western Journey with Mr. Emerson.* Boston: Little, Brown, 1884.

Trahant, Mark N. "Who's Your Daddy?" In *Lewis and Clark through Indian Eyes,* edited by Alfred M. Josephy Jr., with Marc Jaffe, 49–68. New York: Alfred A. Knopf, 2006.

Tullidge, Edward W. *The Women of Mormondom.* New York: Tullidge and Crandall, 1877.

Twain, Mark. "Memoranda: The Noble Red Man." *Galaxy* 10, no. 3 (1870): 426–29.

———. *Roughing It.* Vol. 1. Hartford, CT: American Publishing Company, 1872. Reprint. New York: Harper and Brothers, 1913. Page references are to the 1913 edition.

United States Army Corps of Topographical Engineers. *Map of the Great Salt Lake and Adjacent Country in the Territory of Utah.* Philadelphia: Lippincott, Grambo, 1852.

United States Bureau of the Census. 1850, 1860, 1870, Utah Territory.

United States Office of Indian Affairs. *Annual Report of the Commissioner of Indian Affairs.* Washington, D.C.: Government Printing Office, 1856–1905.

Waite, Mrs. C. V. *The Mormon Prophet and His Harem; or, An Authentic History of Brigham Young, His Numerous Wives and Children.* Cambridge, MA: Riverside Press, 1867.

Wells, Daniel H. "Narrative of Daniel H. Wells." 1884. MSS A 687. Research
    Center for Utah State Archives and Utah State History, Salt Lake City.
Woodruff, Wilford. *Wilford Woodruff's Journal, 1833–1898: Typescript.* 9 vols.
    Edited by Scott G. Kenney. Midvale, UT: Signature Books, 1983.
Young, Ann Eliza. *Wife No. 19; or, the Story of a Life in Bondage.* Hartford, CT:
    Dustin, Gilman, 1876.
Young, Brigham. Brigham Young Office Files. Church History Library,
    The Church of Jesus Christ of Latter-day Saints, Salt Lake City, UT.
———. Brigham Young Papers. Church History Library, The Church of Jesus
    Christ of Latter-day Saints, Salt Lake City, UT.
Young, Clara Decker. "A Woman's Experience with the Pioneer Band."
    [Recorded in 1884.] *Utah Historical Quarterly* 14, no. 1–4 (1946): 173–76.
Young, John R. *Memoirs of John R. Young: Utah Pioneer, 1847.* Salt Lake City,
    UT: Deseret News, 1920.
———. "Reminiscences of John R. Young." *Utah Historical Quarterly* 3, no. 3
    (1930): 83–86.
Young, Margaret Pierce Whitesides. "Journal of Margaret Pierce Whitesides
    Young." MSS SC 68. Harold B. Lee Library, L. Tom Perry Special Collec-
    tions, Brigham Young University, Provo, Utah.
Young, Lorenzo Dow. "Diary of Lorenzo Dow Young." *Utah Historical Quarterly*
    14, no. 1–4 (1946): 133–70.
Young, Zina D. H. "'A Weary Traveler': The 1848–50 Diary of Zina D. H.
    Young." Edited by Marilyn Higbee. *Journal of Mormon History* 19, no. 2
    (1993): 86–125.

OTHER SOURCES
Alexander, Thomas G. *Things in Heaven and Earth: The Life and Times of Wil-
    ford Woodruff, a Mormon Prophet.* Salt Lake City, UT: Signature Books,
    1991.
Alter, J. Cecil. *Jim Bridger.* Norman: University of Oklahoma Press, 1962.
Arrington, Leonard J. *Brigham Young: American Moses.* New York: Alfred A.
    Knopf, 1985.
———. "Taming the Turbulent Sevier: The Mormon Conquest of the Desert."
    Western Humanities Review 5, no. 4 (1951): 393–406.
Auguet, Roland. *Cruelty and Civilization: The Roman Games.* London: George
    Allen and Unwin, 1972.
Axtell, James. "The White Indians of Colonial America." *William and Mary
    Quarterly* 32, no. 1 (1975): 55–88.
Bagley, Will. *Blood of the Prophets: Brigham Young and the Massacre at Mountain
    Meadows.* Norman: University of Oklahoma Press, 2002.
———. *So Rugged and Mountainous: Blazing the Trail to Oregon and California,
    1812–1848.* Norman: University of Oklahoma Press, 2010.
Bailey, Alice Morrey. "Last Wife of Chief Kanosh." *Frontier Times* 54, no. 2
    (1980): 16–22, 50–51.

———. "The Strange Mission of Sally Kanosh." *Utah Magazine* 11 (January 1947): 18–19, 39–42.

Bancroft, Hubert Howe. *History of Utah, 1540–1886*. San Francisco: History Company, 1889.

———. *The Native Races of the Pacific States of North America*. Vol. 1, *Wild Tribes*. New York: D. Appleton, 1875.

Bar-On, Yinon, Rob Phillips, and Ron Milo. "The Biomass Distribution on Earth." *Proceedings of the National Academy of Sciences* (2018). pnas.org /content/115/25/6506.

Bashore, Melvin L., and H. Dennis Tolley. "Mortality on the Mormon Trail: 1847–1868." *BYU Studies Quarterly* 53, no. 4 (2014): 109–23.

Beeton, Beverly. "'Teach Them to Till the Soil': An Experiment with Indian Farms, 1850–1862." *American Indian Quarterly* 3, no. 4 (1977): 299–320.

Behle, William H. *The Bird Life of Great Salt Lake*. Salt Lake City: University of Utah Press, 1958.

Beller, Jack. "Negro Slaves in Utah." *Utah Historical Quarterly* 2, no. 3 (1929): 122–26.

Benemann, William. *Men in Eden: William Drummond Stewart and Same-Sex Desire in the Rocky Mountain Fur Trade*. Lincoln: University of Nebraska Press, 2012.

Bennion, Lowell C., and Thomas R. Carter. "Touring Polygamous Utah with Elizabeth W. Kane, Winter 1872–1873." *BYU Studies Quarterly* 48, no. 4 (2009): 159–92.

Bigler, David L. *Forgotten Kingdom: The Mormon Theocracy in the American West, 1847–1896*. Spokane, WA: Arthur H. Clark, 1998.

———. *Fort Limhi: The Mormon Adventure in Oregon Territory, 1855–1858*. Spokane, WA: Arthur H. Clark, 2003.

Blackhawk, Ned. *Violence over the Land: Indians and Empires in the Early American West*. Cambridge, MA: Harvard University Press, 2006.

Boxer, Elise. "'This is the Place!': Disrupting Mormon Settler Colonialism." In *Decolonizing Mormonism: Approaching a Postcolonial Zion*, edited by Gina Colvin and Joanna Brooks, 77–99. Salt Lake City: University of Utah Press, 2018.

Bradley, Martha Sonntag. *A History of Beaver County*. Salt Lake City: Utah State Historical Society/Beaver County Commission, 1999.

Bradley, Martha Sonntag, and Mary Brown Firmage Woodward. *Four Zinas: A Story of Mothers and Daughters on the Mormon Frontier*. Salt Lake City, UT: Signature Books, 2000.

Brantlinger, Patrick. *Dark Vanishings: Discourse on the Extinction of Primitive Races, 1800–1930*. Ithaca, NY: Cornell University Press, 2003.

Bridger, Bobby. *Buffalo Bill and Sitting Bull: Inventing the Wild West*. Austin: University of Texas Press, 2002.

Brodie, Fawn M. Introduction to *The City of the Saints,* by Richard Burton, vii–xxxvi. New York: Alfred A. Knopf, 1963.

Brooks, James F. *Captives and Cousins: Slavery, Kinship, and Community in the Southwest Borderlands*. Chapel Hill: published for the Omohundro Institute of Early American History and Culture, Williamsburg, Virginia, by the University of North Carolina Press, 2002.

———. "'We Betray Our Own Nation': Indian Slavery and Multi-ethnic Communities in the Southwest Borderlands." In *Indian Slavery in Colonial America*, edited by Alan Gallay, 319–51. Lincoln: University of Nebraska Press, 2009.

Brooks, Juanita. *The Mountain Meadows Massacre*. Norman: University of Oklahoma Press, 1991.

Burrows, George E., and Ronald J. Tyrl. *Toxic Plants of North America*. 2nd ed. Hoboken, NJ: Wiley-Blackwell, 2013.

Bushman, Claudia. "Mormon Domestic Life in the 1870s: Pandemonium or Arcadia?" In *The Collected Leonard J. Arrington Mormon History Lectures*, 91–118. Logan: Special Collections and Archives, Utah State University Libraries, 2005.

Callaway, Donald G., Joel C. Janetski, and Omer C. Stewart. "Ute." In *Handbook of North American Indians*. Vol. 11, *Great Basin*, edited by Warren L. d'Azevedo, 336–67. Washington, D.C.: Smithsonian Institution, 1986.

Campbell, Eugene E. "Miles Morris Goodyear." In Hafen, *Mountain Men and the Fur Trade*, vol. 2 (1965), 179–88.

Cannon, Brian Q. "Adopted or Indentured, 1850–1870: Native Children in Mormon Households." In *Nearly Everything Imaginable: The Everyday Life of Utah's Mormon Pioneers*, edited by Ronald W. Walker and Doris R. Dant, 341–57. Provo, UT: Brigham Young University Press, 1999.

Cannon, Brian Q., and Richard D. Kitchen. "Indenture and Adoption of Native American Children by Mormons on the Utah Frontier, 1850–1870." In *Common Frontiers: Proceedings of the 1996 Conference and Annual Meeting*, 131–44. Bloomfield, OH: Association for Living History Farms and Agricultural Museums, 1997.

Carter, Kate B., comp. *Our Pioneer Heritage*. Vol. 2. Salt Lake City: Daughters of Utah Pioneers, 1959.

Cavanaugh, Edward, and Lorenzo Veracini, eds. *The Routledge Handbook of the History of Settler Colonialism*. New York: Routledge, 2017.

Cheney, Brock. *Plain but Wholesome: Foodways of the Mormon Pioneers*. Salt Lake City: University of Utah Press, 2012.

Christensen, Leavitt. *Birth of Kanosh*. N.p., 1995. Copy at Research Center for Utah State Archives and Utah State History.

Cracroft, Richard H. "'Cows to Milk Instead of Novels to Read': Brigham Young, Novel Reading, and Kingdom Building." *BYU Studies* 40, no. 2 (2001): 102–31.

Crist, Eileen. "Against the Social Construction of Nature and Wilderness." *Environmental Ethics* 26, no. 1 (2004): 5–24.

Cronon, William. "The Trouble with Wilderness, or, Getting Back to the Wrong Nature." *Environmental History* 1, no. 1 (1996): 7–28.

Day, Stella Huntsman, and Sebrina C. Ekins, comps. *Milestones of Millard: 100 Years of History of Millard County, 1851–1951.* [Springville, UT]: Art City, 1951.

d'Azevedo, Warren L. Introduction to *Handbook of North American Indians.* Vol. 11, *Great Basin*, edited by Warren L. d'Azevedo, 1–14. Washington, D.C.: Smithsonian Institution, 1986.

———, ed. *Great Basin.* Vol. 11 of *Handbook of North American Indians*, edited by William C. Sturtevant. Washington, D.C.: Smithsonian Institution, 1986.

Densmore, Frances. *Northern Ute Music.* Bureau of American Ethnology Bulletin, no. 75. Washington, D.C.: Government Printing Office, 1922.

Denton, Sally. *American Massacre: The Tragedy at Mountain Meadows, September 11, 1857.* New York: Alfred A. Knopf, 2003.

De Pillis, Mario S. "Eliza Roxcy Snow Smith." In *Notable American Women.* Vol. 3, edited by Edward T. James, 307–09. Cambridge, MA: Belknap Press of Harvard University Press, 1971.

Derr, Jill Mulvay. "'I Have Eaten Almost Everything Imaginable': Pioneer Diet." In *Nearly Everything Imaginable: The Everyday Life of Utah's Mormon Pioneers*, edited by Ronald W. Walker and Doris R. Dant, 223–48. Provo, UT: Brigham Young University Press, 1999.

DeSimone, Linda Wilcox. Introduction to *Exposé of Polygamy: A Lady's Life Among the Mormons,* by Fanny Stenhouse, 1–21. Edited by Linda Wilcox DeSimone. Logan: Utah State University Press, 2008.

Diamond, Stanley. *In Search of the Primitive: A Critique of Civilization.* New Brunswick, NJ: Transaction, 1974.

Dixon, Madoline Cloward. *These Were the Utes: Their Lifestyles, Wars, and Legends.* Provo, UT: Press Publishing Limited, 1983.

Dixon, W. Randall. "The Beehive and Lion Houses." In *Brigham Young's Homes*, edited by Colleen Whitley, 124–146. Logan: Utah State University Press, 2002.

Douglas, Mary. *Purity and Danger: An Analysis of the Concepts of Pollution and Taboo.* London and New York: Routledge and Kegan Paul, 1984. First published 1966.

Douglas, Mary, and Jonathan Gross. "Food and Culture: Measuring the Intricacy of Rule Systems." *Social Science Information* 20, no. 1 (1981): 1–35.

Dykman, Judy, and Colleen Whitley. "Settling in Salt Lake City." In *Brigham Young's Homes*, edited by Colleen Whitley, 82–123. Logan: Utah State University Press, 2002.

Ebersole, Gary L. *Captured by Texts: Puritan to Post-Modern Images of Indian Captivity.* Charlottesville: University Press of Virginia, 1995.

Ellsworth, George. "A Guide to the Manuscripts in the Bancroft Library Relating to the History of Utah." *Utah Historical Quarterly* 22, no. 3 (1954): 197–247.

———. "Hubert Howe Bancroft and the History of Utah." *Utah Historical Quarterly* 22, no. 2 (1954): 99–124.

Emmitt, Robert. *The Last War Trail: The Utes and the Settlement of Colorado.* Norman: University of Oklahoma Press, 1954.

Engelke, Matthew. *How to Think Like an Anthropologist.* Princeton, NJ: Princeton University Press, 2018.

Everett, C. S. "'They Shalbe Slaves for Their Lives': Indian Slavery in Colonial Virginia." In *Indian Slavery in Colonial America*, edited by Alan Gallay, 67–108. Lincoln: University of Nebraska Press, 2009.

Exley, Jo Ella Powell. *Frontier Blood: The Saga of the Parker Family.* College Station: Texas A&M University Press, 2001.

Farmer, Jared. *On Zion's Mount: Mormons, Indians, and the American Landscape.* Cambridge, MA: Harvard University Press, 2008.

Foley, William E. "Slave Freedom Suits before Dred Scott: The Case of Marie Jean Scypion's Descendants." *Missouri Historical Review* 79, no. 1 (1984): 1–23.

Fowler, Catherine S. "Subsistence." In *Handbook of North American Indians.* Vol. 11, *Great Basin*, edited by Warren L. d'Azevedo, 64–97. Washington, D.C.: Smithsonian Institution, 1986.

Fowler, Don D., and Catherine S. Fowler. Introduction to *Anthropology of the Numa: John Wesley Powell's Manuscripts on the Numic Peoples of Western North America, 1868–1880*, edited by Don D. Fowler and Catherine S. Fowler, 1–34. Washington, D.C.: Smithsonian Institution Press, 1971.

———. "John Wesley Powell, Anthropologist." *Utah Historical Quarterly* 37, no. 2 (1969): 153–72.

Fowler, Don. D., ed. *Cleaving an Unknown World: The Powell Expedition and the Scientific Exploration of the Colorado Plateau.* Salt Lake City: University of Utah Press, 2012.

Frankel, Glenn. *The Searchers: The Making of an American Legend.* New York: Bloomsbury, 2013.

Gardner, Dudley. "Fort Bridger and Camps Stambaugh and Pilot Butte." In *Red Desert: History of a Place*, edited by Annie Proulx, 271–81. Austin: University of Texas Press, 2008.

Garro, Linda C. "Remembering What One Knows and the Construction of the Past: A Comparison of Cultural Consensus Theory and Cultural Schema Theory." *Ethos* 28, no. 3 (2000): 275–319.

Givens, Terryl L., and Matthew J. Grow. *Parley P. Pratt: The Apostle Paul of Mormonism.* New York: Oxford University Press, 2011.

Goodwin, Lorine Swainston. *The Pure Food, Drink, and Drug Crusaders, 1879–1914.* Jefferson, NC: McFarland, 1999.

Gordon, Sarah Barringer. *The Mormon Question: Polygamy and Constitutional Conflict in Nineteenth-Century America.* Chapel Hill: University of North Carolina Press, 2002.

Grow, Matthew J. *"Liberty to the Downtrodden": Thomas L. Kane, Romantic Reformer*. New York: Oxford University Press, 2009.

Grow, Matthew J., and Ronald W. Walker, eds. *The Prophet and the Reformer: The Letters of Brigham Young and Thomas L. Kane*. New York: Oxford University Press, 2015.

Hafen, LeRoy R. "Elijah Barney Ward." In Hafen, *Mountain Men and the Fur Trade*, vol. 7 (1969), 343–51.

———. "Etienne Provost, Mountain Man and Utah Pioneer." *Utah Historical Quarterly* 36, no. 2 (1968): 99–112.

———. "Louis Vasquez." In Hafen, *Mountain Men and the Fur Trade*, vol. 2 (1965), 321–38.

———, ed. *The Mountain Men and the Fur Trade in the Far West*. 10 vols. Glendale, CA: Arthur H. Clark, 1965–1972.

Hartley, William. "Mormons, Crickets, and Gulls: A New Look at an Old Story." *Utah Historical Quarterly* 38, no. 3 (1970): 224–39.

Haude, Sigrud. *In the Shadow of "Savage Wolves": Anabaptist Münster and the German Reformation during the 1530s*. New York: Humanities Press, 2000.

Hays, Samuel P. "Comment: The Trouble with Bill Cronon's Wilderness." *Environmental History* 1, no. 1 (1996): 29–32.

Hebner, William Logan. *Southern Paiute: A Portrait*. Logan: Utah State University Press, 2010.

Helprin, Mark. Introduction to *The Arabian Nights: Their Best-Known Tales*, edited by Kate Douglas Wiggin and Nora A. Smith, vii–xiii. New York: Quality Paperback Book Club, 1996.

Holt-Lunstad, Julianne, Timothy B. Smith, Mark Baker, Tyler Harris, and David Stephenson. "Loneliness and Social Isolation as Risk Factors for Mortality: A Meta-analytic Review." *Perspectives on Psychological Science* 10, no. 2 (2015): 227–37.

Holzapfel, Richard Neitzel, and Robert F. Schwartz. "A Mysterious Image: Brigham Young with an Unknown Wife." *BYU Studies Quarterly* 41, no. 3 (2002): 49–58.

Hultkrantz, Ake. "Mythology and Religious Concepts." In *Handbook of North American Indians*. Vol. 11, *Great Basin*, edited by Warren L. d'Azevedo, 630–40. Washington, D.C.: Smithsonian Institution, 1986.

Ismert, Cornelius M. "James Bridger." In Hafen, *Mountain Men and the Fur Trade*, vol. 6 (1968), 85–104.

Jackson, Donald. *Thomas Jefferson and the Rocky Mountains: Exploring the West from Monticello*. Norman: University of Oklahoma Press, 2002.

Jacobs, Margaret D. "Reproducing White Settlers and Eliminating Natives: Settler Colonialism, Gender, and Family History in the American West." *Journal of the West* 56, no. 4 (2017): 13–24.

Janetski, Joel C. *The Ute of Utah Lake*. University of Utah Anthropological Papers No. 116. Salt Lake City: University of Utah Press, 1991.

Johannsen, Albert. *The House of Beadle and Adams and Its Dime and Nickel Novels: The Story of a Vanished Literature*. 2 vols. Norman: University of Oklahoma Press, 1950.

Jones, Sondra G. *Being and Becoming Ute: The Story of an American Indian People*. Salt Lake City: University of Utah Press, 2019.

———. "'Redeeming' the Indian: The Enslavement of Indian Children." *Utah Historical Quarterly* 67, no. 3 (1999): 220–41.

Kareiva, Peter, Sean Watts, Robert McDonald, and Tim Boucher. "Domesticated Nature: Shaping Landscapes and Ecosystems for Human Welfare." *Science* 316, no. 5833 (2007): 1866–69.

Kay, Jeanne, and Craig J. Brown. "Mormon Beliefs about Land and Natural Resources, 1847–1877." *Journal of Historical Geography* 11, no. 3 (1985): 253–67.

Kelly, Isabel, and Catherine S. Fowler. "Southern Paiute." In *Handbook of North American Indians*. Vol. 11, *Great Basin*, edited by Warren L. d'Azevedo, 368–97. Washington, D.C.: Smithsonian Institution, 1986.

Kerns, Virginia. *Journeys West: Jane and Julian Steward and Their Guides*. Lincoln: University of Nebraska Press, 2010.

———. *Scenes from the High Desert: Julian Steward's Life and Theory*. Urbana: University of Illinois Press, 2003.

Kimball, Stanley B. "The Captivity Narrative on Mormon Trails, 1846–65." *Dialogue: A Journal of Mormon Thought* 18, no. 4 (1985): 81–88.

King, Volney. "Millard County, 1851–1875" [Part I]. *Utah Humanities Review* 1 (1947): 18–37.

Knack, Martha C. *Boundaries Between: The Southern Paiutes, 1775–1995*. Lincoln: University of Nebraska Press, 2001.

Lahti, Janne. "Introduction: What Is Settler Colonialism and What It Has to Do with the American West?" *Journal of the West* 56, no. 4 (2017): 8–12.

La Rivers, Ira. "The Mormon Cricket as Food for Birds." *Condor* 43, no. 1 (1941): 65–69.

Lecompte, Janet. "Introduction: Voyageurs and Other Frenchmen in the American Fur Trade." In *French Fur Traders and Voyageurs in the American West*, edited by LeRoy R. Hafen, 9–26. Lincoln: University of Nebraska Press, 1997.

Leone, Mark P. *Roots of Modern Mormonism*. Cambridge, MA: Harvard University Press, 1979.

Lewis, David Rich. *Neither Wolf nor Dog: American Indians, Environment, and Agrarian Change*. New York: Oxford University Press, 1994.

Lewis, Hyrum S. "Kanosh and Ute Identity in Territorial Utah." *Utah Historical Quarterly* 71, no. 4 (2003): 332–47.

Limerick, Patricia. "Comments on Settler Colonialism and the American West." *Journal of the West* 56, no. 4 (2017): 90–96.

Little, James Amasa. "Biography of Lorenzo Dow Young." *Utah Historical Quarterly* 14, no. 1–4 (1946): 25–132.

Lyman, Edward Leo. "Chief Kanosh: Champion of Peace and Forbearance." *Journal of Mormon History* 35, no. 1 (2009): 157–207.

Lyman, Edward Leo, and Linda King Newell. *A History of Millard County*. Salt Lake City: Utah State Historical Society and Millard County Commission, 1999.

Lyotard, Jean-François. *The Postmodern Condition: A Report on Knowledge*. Translated by Geoff Bennington and Brian Massumi. Minneapolis: University of Minnesota Press, 1984.

Mack, Robert L. Introduction to *Arabian Nights' Entertainments*, edited by Robert L. Mack, ix–xxiii. New York: Oxford University Press, 1998.

MacVean, Charles. "Mormon Crickets: A Brighter Side." *Rangelands* 12, no. 4 (1990): 234–35.

Madsen, David B., and Brigham D. Madsen. "One Man's Meat Is Another Man's Poison: A Revisionist View of the Seagull 'Miracle.'" In *A World We Thought We Knew: Readings in Utah History*, edited by John S. McCormick and John R. Sillito, 52–67. Salt Lake City: University of Utah Press, 1995.

Malouf, Carling, and A. Arline Malouf. "The Effects of Spanish Slavery on the Indians of the Intermountain West." *Southwestern Journal of Anthropology* 1, no. 3 (1945): 378–91.

Marsh, Dawn M. *A Lenape among the Quakers: The Life of Hannah Freeman*. Lincoln: University of Nebraska Press, 2014.

Martineau, LaVan, comp. *Southern Paiutes: Legends, Lore, Language and Lineage*. Las Vegas: KC Publications, 1992.

———. *Southern Paiute Genealogy*. 2nd rev. ed. Globe, AZ: Martineau Publications, 1996.

May, Dean L. "Mormons." In *Mormons and Mormonism: An Introduction to an American World Religion*, edited by Eric A. Eliason, 47–75. Urbana: University of Illinois Press, 2001.

McGregor, Alma Gertrude Watson, and Daniel Clark Watson Jr. *Lorenzo Dow Watson*. Provo, UT: J. Grant Stevensen, 1970.

McPherson, Robert S., and Mary Jane Yazzie. "White Mesa Utes." In *A History of Utah's American Indians*, edited by Forrest S. Cuch, 225–63. Salt Lake City: Utah State Division of Indian Affairs/Utah State Division of History, 2000.

Merkely, Aird G., ed. *Monuments to Courage: A History of Beaver County*. Beaver: Daughters of Utah Pioneers of Beaver County, Utah, 1948.

Miller, Jay. "Numic Religion: An Overview of Power in the Great Basin of Native North America." *Anthropos* 9, no. 3 (1983): 337–54.

Miller, Wick. "Numic Languages." In *Handbook of North American Indians*. Vol. 11, *Great Basin*, edited by Warren L. d'Azevedo, 98–106. Washington, D.C.: Smithsonian Institution, 1986.

Mithen, Steven. *After the Ice: A Global Human History, 20,000–5,000 B.C.* Cambridge, MA: Harvard University Press, 2006.

Moerman, Daniel E. *Native American Ethnobotany*. Portland, OR: Timber Press, 1998.

Moorman, Donald R. *Camp Floyd and the Mormons: The Utah War.* With
    Gene A. Sessions. Salt Lake City: University of Utah Press, 1992.
Muhlestein, Robert M. "Utah Indians and the Indian Slave Trade: The Mormon
    Adoption Project and Its Effect on the Indian Slaves." Master's thesis,
    Brigham Young University, 1991.
Murphy, Thomas W. "Lamanite Genesis, Genealogy, and Genetics." In *American
    Apocrypha: Essays on the Book of Mormon,* edited by Dan Vogel and Brent
    Lee Metcalfe, 47–77. Salt Lake City, UT: Signature Books, 2002.
Nickerson, Gifford S. "Some Data on Plains and Great Basin Indian Uses of Cer-
    tain Native Plants." *Tebiwa* 9, no. 1 (1966): 45–51.
Novak, Shannon A. *House of Mourning: A Biocultural History of the Mountain
    Meadows Massacre.* Salt Lake City: University of Utah Press, 2008.
O'Neil, Floyd A. "A History of the Ute Indians of Utah until 1890." PhD disser-
    tation, University of Utah, 1973.
Parezo, Nancy J., and Joel C. Janetski, eds. *Archaeology in the Great Basin and
    Southwest: Papers in Honor of Don. D. Fowler.* Salt Lake City: University of
    Utah Press, 2013.
Peregrine, Peter Meal. "Science and Narrative in the Postmodern World." *Ameri-
    can Anthropologist* 115, no. 4 (2013): 645.
Person, Carolyn W. D. "Susa Young Gates." In *Mormon Sisters: Women in Early
    Utah,* edited by Claudia L. Bushman, 198–223. Logan: Utah State University
    Press, 1997.
Peterson, Charles S. "Hubert Howe Bancroft: First Western Regionalist."
    In *Writing Western History: Essays on Major Western Historians,* edited by
    Richard W. Eulain, 43–70. Reno: University of Nevada Press, 1991.
Peterson, John Alton. *Utah's Black Hawk War.* Salt Lake City: University of
    Utah Press, 1998.
Peterson, Merrill D., ed. *Visitors to Monticello.* Charlottesville: University Press of
    Virginia, 1989.
Pioneer Database, 1847–1868, The Church of Jesus Christ of Latter-day Saints,
    Salt Lake City, UT. http://history.churchofjesuschrist.org/overlandtravel.
Powers, Ron. *Mark Twain: A Life.* New York: Free Press, 2005.
Proulx, Annie, ed. *Red Desert: History of a Place.* Austin: University of Texas
    Press, 2008.
Quinn, D. Michael. *The Mormon Hierarchy: Extensions of Power.* Salt Lake City,
    UT: Signature Books, 1997.
Reay, Lee. *Lambs in the Meadow.* Provo, UT: Meadow Lane, 1979.
Rhode, David. *Native Plants of Southern Nevada: An Ethnobotany.* Salt Lake
    City: University of Utah Press, 2002.
Rood, Ronald J. "The Archaeology of a Mass Grave from Nephi, Utah, and One
    Event of the Walker War, Utah Territory: Excavations at 42JB1470, Nephi,
    Utah." In *The Materiality of Troubled Pasts: Archaeologies of Conflicts and
    Wars,* edited by Anna Zalewska, John M. Scott, and Grzegorz Kiarszys,

137–61. Warsaw and Szczecin, Poland: Department of Archaeology, University of Szczecin, and Roadside History Lessons Foundation, 2017.

Robison, Dean Chesley. "Sketch of the Life of Chief Kanosh." Territorial Statehouse State Park Museum, Fillmore, UT, n.d.

Sanday, Peggy. "Rape-Free versus Rape-Prone: How Culture Makes a Difference." In *Evolution, Gender, and Rape*, edited by Cheryl Brown Travis, 337–61. Cambridge, MA: MIT Press, 2003.

Shimkin, D. B. "Eastern Shoshone." In *Handbook of North American Indians*. Vol. 11, *Great Basin*, edited by Warren L. d'Azevedo, 308–35. Washington, D.C.: Smithsonian Institution, 1986.

———. "The Uto-Aztecan System of Kinship Terminology." *American Anthropologist* 43, no. 2, part 1 (1941): 223–45.

Shipps, Jan. *Mormonism: The Story of a New Religious Tradition*. Urbana: University of Illinois Press, 1985.

Shore, Bradd. *Culture in Mind: Cognition, Culture and the Problem of Meaning*. New York: Oxford University Press, 1996.

Simms, Steven R. *Ancient Peoples of the Great Basin and Colorado Plateau*. Walnut Creek, CA: Left Coast Press, 2008.

Smart, Donna Toland. Introduction to *Mormon Midwife: The 1846–1888 Diaries of Patty Bartlett Sessions*, edited by Donna Toland Smart, 1–29. Logan: Utah State University Press, 1997.

Smith, Anne M. *Ethnography of the Northern Utes*. Papers in Anthropology, No. 17. Santa Fe: Museum of New Mexico Press, 1974.

Southerton, Simon G. *Losing a Lost Tribe: Native Americans, DNA, and the Mormon Church*. Salt Lake City, UT: Signature Books, 2004.

Steward, Julian H. *Aboriginal and Historical Groups of the Ute Indians of Utah: An Analysis with Supplement*. Ute Indians, I. New York: Garland, 1974.

———. *Basin-Plateau Aboriginal Socio-political Groups*. Bureau of American Ethnology Bulletin 120. Washington, D.C.: Government Printing Office, 1938.

Stoffle, Richard W., Kristine L. Jones, and Henry F. Dobyns. "Direct European Immigrant Transmission of Old World Pathogens to Numic Indians during the Nineteenth Century." *American Indian Quarterly* 19, no. 2 (1995): 181–203.

Sutton, Mark Q. *Insects as Food: Aboriginal Entomophagy in the Great Basin*. Menlo Park, CA: Ballena Press, 1988.

Tanner, John C. *A Biographical Sketch of John Riggs Murdock*. Salt Lake City, UT: Deseret News, 1909.

Thomas, Dorothy. "Catharine Van Valkenburg Waite." In *Notable American Women*. Vol. 3, edited by Edward T. James, 523–25. Cambridge, MA: Belknap Press of Harvard University Press, 1971.

Tom, Gary, and Ronald Holt. "The Paiute Tribe of Utah." In *A History of Utah's American Indians*, edited by Forrest S. Cuch, 123–65. Salt Lake City: Utah State Division of Indian Affairs/Utah State Division of History, 2000.

Turner, John G. *Brigham Young: Pioneer Prophet*. Cambridge, MA: Harvard University Press, 2012.

Ulrich, Laurel Thatcher. *A House Full of Females: Plural Marriage and Women's Rights in Early Mormonism, 1835–1870*. New York: Alfred A. Knopf, 2017.

Unruh, John D., Jr. *The Plains Across: The Overland Emigrants and the Trans-Mississippi West, 1840–60*. Urbana: University of Illinois Press, 1979.

Van Cott, John W. *Utah Place Names*. Salt Lake City: University of Utah Press, 1990.

Walker, Franklin. "Frances Auretta Fuller Victor." In *Notable American Women*. Vol. 3, edited by Edward T. James, 518–19. Cambridge, MA: Belknap Press of Harvard University Press, 1971.

Walker, Ronald W. "The Tintic War of 1856: A Study of Several Conflicts." *Journal of Mormon History* 42, no. 3 (2016): 35–68.

Walker, Ronald W., Richard E. Turley Jr., and Glen M. Leonard. *Massacre at Mountain Meadows: An American Tragedy*. New York: Oxford University Press, 2008.

Warner, Ted J. "Peter Skene Ogden." In Hafen, *Mountain Men and the Fur Trade*, vol. 3 (1966), 213–38.

Weber, David J. *The Taos Trappers: The Fur Trade in the Far Southwest, 1540–1846*. Norman: University of Oklahoma Press, 1971.

White, Richard. *Railroaded: The Transcontinentals and the Making of Modern America*. New York: W. W. Norton, 2011.

Whitney, Orson F. *History of Utah*. Vol. 4. Salt Lake City, UT: George Q. Cannon and Sons, 1904.

Wilcox, Linda. "The Mormon Concept of a Mother in Heaven." *Sunstone* 5, no. 5 (1980): 78–87.

Wilkinson, Charles. *Fire on the Plateau: Conflict and Endurance in the American Southwest*. Washington, D.C.: Island Press, 1999.

Wishart, David J. *The Fur Trade of the American West, 1807–1840: A Geographical Synthesis*. Lincoln: University of Nebraska Press, 1979.

Wolfe, Patrick. "Settler Colonialism and the Elimination of the Native." *Journal of Genocide Research* 8, no. 4 (2006): 387–409.

———. *Settler Colonialism and the Transformation of Anthropology*. New York and London: Cassell, 1999.

Woodard, Colin. *American Nations: A History of the Eleven Regional Cultures of North America*. New York: Viking, 2011.

Worster, Donald. "Encountering Mormon Country: John Wesley Powell, John Muir, and the Nature of Utah." In *The Collected Leonard J. Arrington Mormon History Lectures*, 185–203. Logan: Special Collections and Archives, Utah State University Libraries, 2005.

———. "The Kingdom, the Power, and the Water." In *Great Basin Kingdom Revisited: Contemporary Perspectives*, edited by Thomas G. Alexander, 21–38. Logan: Utah State University Press, 1991.

———. *A River Running West: The Life of John Wesley Powell.* New York: Oxford University Press, 2001.

Wulff, Helena. "Introducing the Anthropologist as Writer across and within Genres." In *The Anthropologist as Writer: Genres and Contexts in the Twenty-First Century*, edited by Helena Wulff, 1–18. New York: Bergahn, 2016.

Index

beavers, 66; decline of, 23, 78, 177, 251; in fur trade, 21

beef, 48, 66, 140, 142,184

Beehive House, 133, 144, 153, 163, 168, 201, 207, 211, 214, 216–17, 223, 225, 237, 242, 249–50, 322n1;

construction of, 120; current status of, 300n2; dining room, 132; Emeline, funeral at, 166; estate wall, 122–23, 125–26; family store at, 127, 158, 196, 201, 225; Indian attacks, lack of, 302n14; kitchen, Lucy in charge of, 144; kitchen, Sally works in, 144–45, 167, 24; Lucy, deeded to, 197; moving to, 327n64; photograph of house and estate wall, 165; residents of, 128–29, 137, 144–46, 153; Sally, lives at, 163–64, 167, 196–98, 323n20; visitors to, 169

Betsykin. *See* Patsey-kin

Bible, 6, 40, 43, 63, 76, 121, 162

Big Field, 95, 290n35

Bigelow [Young], Lucy, 88–89, 114, 121, 136, 158, 163–64, 170, 222, 225, 262

birds: chickens and other domesticated (introduced), 34, 48–49, 70, 92; wild (native), 48, 62, 64, 100, 140. *See also* gulls

bison, 23, 26, 31, 41, 251, 271n47

Black Hawk, Chief (Sauk and Fox, or Meskwaki, Indian), 229

Blackhawk, Chief (Ute), 154–56, 173, 196, 204, 207, 209

Blue-shirt (Timpanogos Ute), 73–74, 77

Bradford, William, 314n23

Bridger, James Felix (Jim), 28, 30, 68, 74, 87, 100; and Ashley's Hundred, 25–27; assisting colonizing settlers, 23–24, 250; death of, 250–51; early life of, 23–24; as explorer and fur trapper, 23–24, 250; and horse racing, 221–22; illiteracy of, 27; Indian

wives of, 27, 110–11, 250; as story-teller, 24–25. *See also* Fort Bridger

Bridger, Virginia, 250–51

Brown, Adelaide Exervier (Xavier), 21–23, 30, 36, 72, 260, 262

Buffon, Comte de (George-Louis Le Clerc), 40–41

Burton, Richard F., 129–33, 135, 304n27, 305n29, 305n38

Captain Jack. *See* Nicaagat

captives. *See* Indian captives

captivity narratives. *See* Indian captivity narratives

cats (domestic), 34, 49, 51, 90, 282n5

Chandless, William, 302n13

chiefs, Ute (or Utah). *See* Arapeen, Baptiste, Black Hawk, Colorow, Kanosh, Little Chief, Moshoquop, Pe-teet-neet, Tintic, Wákara

Christensen, Clara Kimball, 327n59, 328n2

civilization (complex society): defined, 8, 266n11; and inequality, 8. *See also* settler colonialism; wild/civilized narratives

civilizing missions, 42, 127–28, 151, 191, 194, 195, 198–99, 200, 201, 215, 224, 250; federal funds for, 274n74, 327n65

Clara. *See* Decker [Young], Clara

Clark, William, 22, 26

Clemens, Samuel Langhorne. *See* Twain, Mark

cloth, 93–94, 110, 135, 151, 178

colonialism. *See* settler colonialism

Colorado (Territory), 108, 182–84, 187, 228, 233, 289n12, 294n78

Colorado River, 182, 187

Colorow (Ute chief), 228

Comanche (Indians), 20, 37–38, 228, 245, 274n67, 335n25

complex society. *See* civilization

Corn Creek (Pahvant Ute community), 175, 176, 187, 196, 205–7,
209–12, 248, 250, 259, 261–62; distance from city, 205; distance from
Kanosh (village), 219, 224; distance
from Sho-av-ich, 205; and horse
racing in, 221–22; house of
Chief Kanosh in, 176, 187, 205, 223;
men of, 206, 210; Moshoquop lives
in, 246; names, in English, 205,
223, 226, 318n18; population of,
175, 196, 205, 210; Sally, lives in,
213–14, 215, 223–24; women of,
210.
Corn Creek (watercourse), 205,
318n18
Coyote, stories about, 6, 49–50, 150,
152, 161
coyotes (wildlife), 31, 49, 51, 62, 64,
102, 281n68
Crane, Emily, 212–15, 217–20, 222–27,
229, 241, 250, 327n60, 328n8,
330n29, 330n33, 336n34
Crane, George, 229–31, 327n60,
336n34
crickets, 61; and birds, 62, 64, 280n63;
as food, 61–64, 219; and desert
fruitcake, 220; devouring crops,61,
68; killing of, 220; katydid family,
280n59, 280n64
Crosby, Oscar (enslaved), 269n20
cultural model, 3, 265n2
Cum-um-buh, 33, 272n54. *See*
Kumumpa

Decker, Charley, 19–20, 35–36,
42–44, 46, 52, 68, 71, 75, 94, 120,
123, 151, 155, 204, 238–40, 243–
44,247, 260, 277n26
Decker [Young], Clara, 18, 20, 25,
29–30, 34, 37, 42; birthplace of,
129; books and reading by, 40–41,
137, 160–61, 314n20; Brigham

Young daughters, relations with,
159–66, 193–97, 249; Brigham
Young, letter to, 165; Brigham
Young, travels with, 18, 25, 127–28,
165, 260; children, gives birth to,
90, 150; church, nonattendance of,
159; daughters, monogamous marriages of, 194; and family store
account, 127, 158, 201, 306n46,
313n14; as favored wife, 137, 308n4,
313n14; first son (Jeddie), death of,
113, 150, 158, 314n15; fosters children, 90, 137, 159; ill, with mountain fever, 29; influence with husband, 159; letter from Sally to, 213;
Lion House, moves to, 120; Lion
House, suite of rooms at, 136, 137;
lives with Eliza and Sally at fort,
50; moves from fort, 88; moves
from Lion House to cottage, 197;
moves from Log Row, 97; physical
appearance of, 71, 202, 313n14; and
polygamy, 71, 164, 194–95, 316n37;
public appearances with husband,
avoids, 159; Sally, relations with, 19,
36, 40, 42, 91, 103–4, 120, 122–25,
128, 201; reminiscence of, 234; second son (Albert Jeddie), death of,
158, 314n15; story about, 125–26;
servants, personal, 91, 92, 94, 135,
137, 290n31; work, teaches Sally to,
65, 94, 194, 214–15
Decker [Young], Harriet Wheeler
Page, 59, 101, 113, 202, 261; and
cricket plague, 60–61; death of
son, 51; ill health of, 18–19 68,
268n3; overland trip by, 18, 25,
29–30; washes and clothes captive
(Sally), 19
Decker Seeley [Young], Lucy, 68, 113,
123, 127, 136, 139, 143, 196, 205–6,
216, 241, 247–48, 262; Beehive
House deeded to, 197; Beehive